The Future of Multi-Ethnic Britain

Report of the Commission on the Future of Multi-Ethnic Britain
Chair: Bhikhu Parekh
The Commission was established by The Runnymede Trust

PROFILE BOOKS

First published in Great Britain in 2000 by
Profile Books Ltd
58A Hatton Garden
London EC1N 8LX
www.profilebooks.co.uk

Reprinted with corrections, 2000 and 2002

10 9 8 7 6 5 4 3

Photocredits: Anthony Lam/Autograph, The Association of Black
Photographers, pp. 70 and 275; all other photographs were supplied by
FORMAT photographers. The artists were Jacky Chapman, pp. 45 and
228; Melanie Friend, p. 98; Judy Harrison, p. 121; Roshini Kempadoo,
p. 244; Maggie Murray, p. 30; Joanne O'Brien, pp. 195 and 287;
Ulrike Preuss, pp. 155, 186 and 209; Brenda Prince, p. 17;
Karen Robinson, pp. 9, 134 and 259; Paula Solloway, p. 83; Mo Wilson,
p. 104; Lisa Woollett, p. 173.

Typeset in Stone by MacGuru
info@macguru.org.uk

Designed by Geoff Green
Printed and bound in Great Britain by Biddles Ltd, *www.biddles.co.uk*

A CIP catalogue record for this book is available from the
British Library.

ISBN 1 86197 227 X

The Runnymede Trust
Commission on the Future of Multi-Ethnic Britain

University of Wolverhampton

The Commission on the Future of Multi-Ethnic Britain

Commission on the Future of Multi-Ethnic Britain
133 Aldersgate Street
London EC1A 4JA
Website: www.runnymedetrust.org.uk

Contents

Preface

The Commission on the Future of Multi-Ethnic Britain was set up in January 1998 by the Runnymede Trust, an independent think-tank devoted to the cause of promoting racial justice in Britain. The Commission's remit was to analyse the current state of multi-ethnic Britain and to propose ways of countering racial discrimination and disadvantage and making Britain a confident and vibrant multicultural society at ease with its rich diversity. It was made up of 23 distinguished individuals drawn from many community backgrounds and different walks of life, and with a long record of active academic and practical engagement with race-related issues in Britain and elsewhere. They brought to their task different views and sensibilities and, after a good deal of discussion, reached a consensus. The report is the product of their two years of deliberation.

Given the fluidity of social and political affairs, and the constant emergence of new ideas and insights, no report can claim to be the last word on its subject, and this one certainly advances no such claim. However, as a carefully researched and thought-out document, hammered out in searching discussions conducted in a spirit of intellectual and moral responsibility, it represents, we hope, a major contribution to the national debate. In view of the violence inspired by racist doctrines, race is too important and sensitive an issue to be turned into a political football or approached in terms of narrow electoral calculations. We hope that our report will form the basis of, or at least pave the way for, a much-needed national consensus.

It is informed by several fundamental beliefs that in our view are, or deserve to be, shared by most people in Britain.

First, all individuals have equal worth irrespective of their colour, gender, ethnicity, religion, age or sexual orientation, and have equal claims to the opportunities they need to realise their potential and contribute to collective wellbeing. The principle of equal moral worth cannot take root and flourish within a structure of deep economic or social inequalities.

Second, citizens are not only individuals but also members of particular religious, ethnic, cultural and regional communities, which are comparatively stable as well as open and fluid. Britain is both a community of citizens and a community of communities, both a liberal and a multicultural society, and needs to reconcile their sometimes conflicting requirements.

Third, since citizens have differing needs, equal treatment requires full account to be taken of their differences. When equality ignores relevant differences and insists on uniformity of treatment, it leads to injustice and inequality; when differences ignore the demands of equality, they result in discrimination. Equality must be defined in a culturally sensitive way and applied in a discriminating but not discriminatory manner.

Fourth, every society needs to be cohesive as well as respectful of diversity, and must find ways of nurturing diversity while fostering a common sense of belonging and a shared identity among its members.

Fifth, although every society needs a broadly shared body of values, of which human rights are an important part, there is a risk of defining the values so narrowly that their further development is ruled out or legitimate ways of life are suppressed. While affirming such essential procedural values as tolerance, mutual respect, dialogue and peaceful resolution of differences, and such basic ethical norms as respect for human dignity, equal worth of all, equal opportunity for self-development and equal life chances, society must also respect deep moral differences and find ways of resolving inescapable conflicts. Human rights principles provide a valuable framework for handling differences, but they are never by themselves enough.

Lastly, racism, understood either as division of humankind into fixed, closed and unalterable groups or as systematic domination of some groups by others, is an empirically false, logically incoherent and morally unacceptable doctrine. Racism is a subtle and complex phenomenon. It may be based on colour and physical features or on culture, nationality and way of life; it may affirm equality of human worth but implicitly deny this by insisting on the absolute superiority of a particular culture; it may admit equality up to a point but impose a glass ceiling higher up. Whatever its subtle disguises and forms, it is deeply divisive, intolerant of differences, a source of much human suffering and inimical to the common sense of belonging lying at the basis of every stable political community. It can have no place in a decent society.

We approach the current state of multi-ethnic Britain against the background of these and related beliefs. We believe that it is both possible and vitally necessary to create a society in which all citizens and communities feel valued, enjoy equal opportunities to develop their respective talents, lead fulfilling lives, accept their fair share of collective responsibility and help create a communal life in which the spirit of civic friendship, shared identity and common sense of belonging goes hand in hand with love of diversity. Having sketched our vision of a relaxed and self-confident multicultural Britain with which all its citizens can identify, we analyse the obstacles standing in its way and propose policies most likely to overcome them. The obstacles include racial discrimination, racial disadvantage, a racially oriented moral and political culture, an inadequate philosophy of government, a lack of carefully thought-out and properly integrated administrative structures at various levels of government, and a lack of political will. The policies we propose address each of these. They require not only appropriate legislative, administrative and other measures, but also a radical shift in the manner in which British identity and the relations between different groups of citizens are generally defined. Further, important changes are also needed within Asian and black communities themselves if they are to overcome the obstacles which they face and take full advantage of the opportunities offered by wider society. But since the nature and extent of such changes vary from community to community, and are best identified and undertaken by each community separately, discussion of them clearly falls outside the scope of this report.

The very language used to describe and define race relations in Britain is a source of considerable conceptual and political muddle. Such terms as 'minority' and 'majority' signify fixed blocs and obscure the fluidity and heterogeneity of real life. The term 'ethnic group' traps the group concerned into its ethnicity, and suppresses both its multiple identity and its freedom of self-determination. The term 'integration' is even more misleading, as it implies a one-way process in which 'minorities' are to be absorbed into the non-existent homogeneous cultural structure of the 'majority'. We are fully aware of these and other limitations of the dominant language of debate. Inventing a wholly new vocabulary does not help, for such a language would be too abstract, artificial and unrelated to the idioms of everyday life to be intelligible, let alone provide a vehicle for meaningful dialogue. We have therefore thought it best to avoid parts of the current vocabulary when we could conveniently do so, and to make suitable qualifications and warnings when we could not.

A word about our mode of working is pertinent. We visited many regions, consulted a wide range of organisations, conducted interviews, organised focus group discussions and received several hundred written submissions. We also held several day-long seminars where well-known activists and experts in the field debated relevant issues in great detail; some of the participants later commented at length on the written reports of these seminars. The seminars were particularly helpful in relation to Part 1 of the report, which deals with issues of considerable theoretical and practical significance. For Part 2 we commissioned papers from experts in the relevant areas, invited comments on them from other experts, and discussed these in full Commission meetings. Broadly the same procedure was followed for Part 3.

We were frequently struck by the absence or inadequacy of research data in significant areas of public policy. We hope very much, therefore, that the Economic and Social Research Council will earmark funding for policy-related research on race and diversity issues, and similarly that other funding bodies will give high priority to research on the topics and concerns covered in this report.

For my part, it has been a great privilege to chair this Commission of distinguished and talented individuals over a period of two years. It was a delight to see them debate complex issues. I was also deeply moved by their enormous generosity and patience. In meeting after meeting they dissected drafts of the chapters, revising and even rethinking them in the light of their colleagues' searching comments. They gave most magnanimously of their time and energy without any hope of reward, and sometimes wrote and rewrote whole chapters out of loyalty to their colleagues and commitment to the cause of a better Britain. Working with such wonderful colleagues has been both a humbling and an uplifting experience. The report is entirely their creation, and I only hope that the understandable but regrettable tendency to identify a report with a commission's chair will be studiously resisted.

The Commission owes a deep debt of gratitude to a large number of individuals and organisations. They are all named in the acknowledgements in Appendices A and B. The report would not have been possible without the continuing support of the Runnymede Trust and the generosity of the Joseph Rowntree Charitable Trust, the Nuffield Foundation and the Paul Hamlyn Foundation, our three funders. I should like to express my own and the Commission's profound indebtedness to Robin Richardson for his marvellous skill in turning discussions and thoughts into a cogent text. I also thank my predecessor and good friend John Burgh, and Kate Gavron and the Commission's staff for their support over the last two years.

The report was inspired by and intended to rethink the seminal report *Colour and Citizenship* by Jim Rose and his colleagues, published in 1969. As a founder and trustee of the Runnymede Trust, Jim took a keen interest in our work and was most anxious to see its publication. Sadly, he died last year. We salute his memory with pride, remember with sorrow those who died victims of or in the course of struggle against racial injustice, and express our deepest gratitude to those countless white, black and Asian people in Britain who are continuing the struggle in small and large ways. Every generation owes its successors a duty to bequeath them a better country than it inherited. This report offers one way of discharging that great historical obligation.

Bhikhu Parekh
July 2000

Executive Summary

Overall summary

1   England, Scotland and Wales are at a turning point in their history. They could become narrow and inward-looking, with rifts between themselves and among their regions and communities, or they could develop as a community of citizens and communities. Britain as a whole could be such a community, and so could each part or region, and each city, town and neighbourhood. Building and sustaining a community of citizens and communities will involve:
   - rethinking the national story and national identity;
   - understanding that all identities are in a process of transition;
   - developing a balance between cohesion, equality and difference;
   - addressing and eliminating all forms of racism;
   - reducing material inequalities;
   - building a pluralistic human rights culture.

2   Part 1 of this report discusses each of these six themes. Part 2 considers what the tasks involve in various areas of social policy. Part 3 is concerned with strategies for change at national, regional, local and institutional levels.

3   Part 2 starts with a discussion of police and policing. This is where, for many citizens and communities, the abstract concepts of equality, rights, difference and belonging are most clearly and concretely seen – or not seen. But the police service is only one part of the wider criminal justice system. The report looks next at this wider structure. It continues by considering the education systems of England, Scotland and Wales, then cultural policy, health and welfare, and employment. How a state sees and controls the borders between itself and others is of paramount importance. Thus the report looks also at immigration and asylum policy. This is currently a topic of great political sensitivity, and the report considers the responsibilities of politicians in leading public

opinion. The discussion of politics also embraces issues of representation on elected and unelected bodies. Part 2 closes with a consideration of religious motivations and affiliations, and of relations between religious bodies and the state in a multi-faith society.

4   Part 3 begins with a discussion of the role of government in providing direction and resources, driving through change and leading by example. The report then argues that legislation on equality needs reforming and strengthening, and discusses how this might be achieved. Lastly, there is consideration of what every organisation or institution needs to do if Britain is to develop as a community of citizens and communities.

Summary by chapter

1 *The Turning Point*
The futures facing Britain may be summarised as static/dynamic; intolerant/cosmopolitan; fearful/generous; insular/internationalist; authoritarian/democratic; introspective/outward-looking; punitive/inclusive; myopic/far-sighted. It is the second term in each of these pairings that evokes the kind of Britain proposed in this report. Many customary images of Britain are England-centred – and, indeed, southern England-centred – and leave many millions of people out of the picture. Increasingly, in Scotland and Wales people have a sense of multiple identity. Englishness is also in the process of being redefined. People in Britain have many differences, but they inhabit the same space and share the same future. All have a role in the collective project of fashioning Britain as an outward-looking, generous, inclusive society.

2 *Rethinking the National Story*
A state is not only a territorial and political entity, but also an 'imagined community'. What is Britain's understanding of itself? How are the histories of England, Scotland and Wales understood by their people? Of what may citizens be justly proud? How has the imagined nation stood the test of time? What should be preserved, what jettisoned, what revised or reworked? How can everyone have a recognised place within the larger picture? These are questions about Britain as an imagined community, and about how a genuinely multicultural Britain urgently needs to reimagine itself. Among other things, such reimagining must

take account of the inescapable changes of the last 30 years – not only postwar migration but also devolution, globalisation, the end of empire, Britain's long-term decline as a world power, moral and cultural pluralism, and closer integration with Europe.

3 *Identities in Transition*

All communities are changing and all are complex, with internal diversity and disagreements, linked to differences of gender, generation, religion and language, and to different stances in relation to wider society. There are also many overlaps, borrowings and two-way influences – no community is or can be insulated from all others. Increasingly, people have the capacity to manoeuvre between distinct areas of life and to be 'cross-cultural navigators'. Hybrid cultural forms have emerged, especially in music and the arts. In this context, does 'Britishness' have a future? Or have devolution, globalisation and the new cultural diversity undermined it irretrievably?

4 *Cohesion, Equality and Difference*

The government has stated that it is committed 'to creating One Nation', a country where 'every colour is a good colour ... every member of every part of society is able to fulfil their potential ... racism is unacceptable and counteracted ... everyone is treated according to their needs and rights ... everyone recognises their responsibilities ... racial diversity is celebrated'. The statement invites several searching questions. What values and loyalties must be shared by communities and individuals in One Nation? How should disputes and incompatible values between different communities be handled? How is a balance to be struck between the need to treat people equally, the need to treat people differently, and the need to maintain shared values and social cohesion? Most theoretical debates on such questions in Britain have been between what may be called nationalist and liberal theories of society. However, this chapter argues that the need now is for debates between liberal and pluralist theories. Britain should develop both as a community of citizens (the liberal view) and as a community of communities (the pluralist view).

5 *Dealing with Racisms*

In other European Union countries it is customary to use the phrase 'racism, xenophobia and antisemitism' as a way of summarising the issues to be addressed. The term is cumbersome and is unlikely to become widespread in Britain. It is, however, helpful, for it stresses that hostility that uses skin colour and physical appearance as markers of supposed difference does not represent the whole picture. There is also hostility using markers connected with culture, language and religion. The plural term 'racisms' is sometimes used to highlight such complexity. A distinction needs also to be drawn between overt racism and institutional racism. This chapter discusses the history and development of racism and reviews and expands on the definition of institutional racism in the Stephen Lawrence Inquiry report. Tabulation of the interacting components of institutional racism is provided.

6 *Reducing Inequalities*

Three main approaches to combating social exclusion must be combined: (a) improving physical infrastructure; (b) using welfare-based measures; and (c) pursuing labour market strategies to improve underlying economic potential and performance. A single-pronged attack will not work. Within this framework key tasks include securing long-term financial and political support for projects in specific local areas; achieving and sustaining inter-agency working; empowering local communities; maintaining local commitment and avoiding activist burn-out; redirecting main programmes and resources; providing access to credit; striking the right balance between area-based projects and conurbation-level measures; striking the right balance between central government initiative and local responsibility; and engaging the private sector. Further, and essentially, measures should not be colour- or culture-blind.

7 *Building a Pluralistic Human Rights Culture*

Negotiations over contested issues – for example, the content of the national curriculum, sensitivity to cultural diversity in the health service, the wearing of religious clothing at work, equality for women in the home – cannot take place in an ethical vacuum. They require ground rules that provide a minimum guarantee of protection for individuals and a framework for handling conflicts of interest. The argument in this chapter is that such ground rules are provided in part by international human rights standards, for example those enshrined in the European Convention on Human Rights (ECHR) and the UN Convention on the Rights of the Child. The Home Secretary has said of the new Human

Rights Act, which brings the ECHR into domestic law, that it is 'an ethical language we can all recognise and sign up to, a ... language which doesn't belong to any particular group or creed but to all of us. One that is based on principles of common humanity.'

8 *Summary of the Vision*

Chapter 8 summarises the key points made in the report so far. The fundamental need, both practical and theoretical, is to treat people equally and with due respect for difference; to treasure the rights and freedoms of individuals and to cherish belonging, cohesion and solidarity. Neither equality nor respect for difference is a sufficient value in itself. The two must be held together, mutually challenging and supportive. Similarly, neither personal liberty nor social cohesion is sufficient on its own. They too must be held together, qualifying and challenging each other, yet also mutually informing and enriching.

9 *Police and Policing*

The values of community, citizenship, social inclusion and human rights, and the balance between cohesion and difference and between equality and diversity, discussed in Chapters 2–7, can all be either sustained or undermined by the way in which a country arranges and runs its criminal justice system. In the context of this report, the system comes under the microscope in two particularly sensitive ways. On the one hand, it must deal with racist crime with the utmost vigour; on the other, it must engage in its own processes with the utmost professionalism and fairness, and with the minimum of damage to wider relationships and public trust. This chapter discusses the impact of the Stephen Lawrence Inquiry on the police service. It notes criticisms of many forces made by Her Majesty's Inspectorate of Constabulary, and makes practical recommendations about the use of discretionary powers, the need for a better complaints system and better training, and the need to reduce deaths in custody.

10 *The Wider Criminal Justice System*

There is a growing body of data (albeit collected almost exclusively in England and Wales – the *British Crime Survey*, despite its name, does not cover Scotland) showing that black and Irish people are treated differentially at all stages of the criminal justice process, and that they are disproportionately likely to be imprisoned. This chapter discusses the response of the criminal justice system to racist crime and considers the role and responsibilities of the prison service and the Crown Prosecution Service. It notes that certain American approaches to penal policy currently being adopted in Britain are likely to have harmful effects, and discusses the likely impact, from the point of view of race equality and cultural diversity, of a range of new government measures and initiatives.

11 *Education*

A country's education system is a gateway to employment and to participation in political, social and cultural affairs. It also equips children and young people – or fails to equip them – with the essential understandings, skills and values they need to play a substantial role in the building and maintenance of Britain as a community of citizens and a community of communities. England, Scotland and Wales have different educational systems and curricula, but in each there are individuals and institutions engaged in fine work in relation to race equality and cultural diversity. However, there is also a lack of commitment and leadership on these issues from the respective government authorities. Monitoring by ethnicity is inadequate or non-existent; there are substantial inequalities affecting in particular pupils and students from African-Caribbean, Bangladeshi and Pakistani communities; there is insufficient official guidance on the content of the curriculum; teacher training – both initial and in-service – needs to be improved; and the inspection systems are insufficiently rigorous and authoritative.

12 *Arts, Media and Sport*

The cultural fabric of a society expresses ideas of who 'we' are. To the extent that it is inclusive, it gives all people a sense of belonging and makes a strong stand against racism. Cultural fabric has many strands, but of particular importance are the performing, visual and literary arts, the print and electronic media, and a wide range of representative and recreational sport. This chapter discusses issues of programming, staffing, bias and representation in the arts and media, and in sport at all levels. It cites specific examples of good practice, including an exhibit at the National Maritime Museum at Greenwich, the play *The Colour of Justice*, a book of oral history, a number of anti-racism projects in professional football, and the constructive way in which one newspaper responded to a complaint about bias. But the overall message of the chapter, in the words of a specialist who gave evidence to the Commission, is that 'the arts and media sectors do not see any implications for themselves in the Macpherson report', for they do not recognise that institutional racism needs urgently to be addressed within their own domains.

13 *Health and Welfare*

A recurring theme throughout the report is that public bodies should treat people both equally and differently. The need for both equal and different treatment is seen particularly clearly in services providing health and social care. This chapter reviews the twin roles of the NHS as (a) a provider of services and (b) an employer. The roles are linked in a striking paradox. The NHS depends, and for several decades has depended, on the contributions of Asian, black and Irish doctors, nurses, managers and ancillary staff. At the same time, patterns of mortality and morbidity are more serious in Asian, black and Irish communities than in the population as a whole, and there is much insensitivity in the NHS to the distinctive experiences, situations and requirements of these communities.

14 *Employment*

Broadly, in the context of this report, there are two large tasks to be undertaken: (a) to reduce unemployment and underemployment for all those who are affected; (b) to eliminate glass ceilings. The tasks have practical implications for the government at national, regional and local levels; for employers in the public, private and voluntary sectors; for unions and professional associations; and for those who provide financial and advisory support to new business enterprises. This chapter discusses practical implications, focusing in particular on the role of government, and stresses that there is substantial diversity among and within different communities, and that the labour market itself has changed substantially over the last 20 years.

15 *Immigration and Asylum*

Postwar British history is littered with legislation and regulations passed swiftly, and by both major political parties, to counter perceived 'floods' of immigrants and, latterly, asylum-seekers. There are two problems with this approach. First, the sense of panic the issue instils and the subjectivity with which it is discussed lead to bad law that does not work even in its own terms, giving rise to challenges both in UK courts and among international human rights bodies. Second, and even more seriously from the point of view of this report, it undermines Britain's development as a community of communities. This chapter reviews and criticises immigration and asylum policy over the years and makes several recommendations for short- and longer-term action.

16 *Politics and Representation*

If Britain is to flourish as a community of citizens and communities (Chapter 4), its political leaders should shape, not pander to, public opinion on issues relating to race and diversity. Their legitimate desires to maximise their own electoral support and to diminish the attractions of their opponents should never involve playing the race card, either openly or covertly. Further, black and Asian people should be more fully involved than at present in the party political system at local and national levels, both as elected representatives and as party activists, as well as fully involved in nominated bodies. Such bodies should be representative in the sense of exhibiting a spectrum of perspective and experience. Both elected and nominated bodies should be strenuously and explicitly concerned with the themes discussed in this report.

17 *Religion and Belief*

Article 13 of the Treaty of Amsterdam provides the European Union with a legal basis for action against discrimination based on, among other grounds, racial or ethnic origin and religion or belief. In Britain many public bodies have declared formally that, in addition to their obligations under the Race Relations Act 1976, they will not discriminate on grounds of religion. At present, however, such discrimination is not unlawful. This chapter considers the importance of religious identities and organisations in modern society; the practical and theoretical problems of introducing laws against discrimination on grounds of religion or belief; whether the Church of England should be disestablished; whether a range of religions and beliefs should be represented in public life; how to balance action against discrimination with the need for beliefs of all kinds to be challenged and interrogated; and ground rules for handling profound differences and disagreements between and within communities.

18 *Government Leadership*

Government has four principal functions: to provide political leadership; to allocate resources; to manage its own departments in ways that are both efficient and exemplary; and to formulate and implement legislation, with support, regulation and enforcement as necessary. During 1999 the government began to drop its colour- and culture-blind approaches to social policy and to modernisation, and by early summer 2000 it was able to itemise several specific and significant developments. It needs, however, to give a more explicit lead, to ensure greater consistency and co-ordination between its separate departments, to accord race equality and cultural diversity a higher profile, and to ensure that it hears and attends to a wider range of views and perceptions.

19 *Legislation and Enforcement*

The Race Relations Act 1976 has had a positive effect – it has helped to curb the worst kinds of discrimination in employment and the provision of services, and has had an invaluable impact on the general climate of opinion. The amendments made in 2000 will make it applicable to the functions of nearly all public bodies, and introduce a positive duty on public authorities to promote equality of opportunity. These changes are most certainly to be welcomed. In the longer term, however, amendments are not enough. A new Equality Act is required, together with a new Equality Commission. Furthermore, there needs to be a Human Rights Commission to promote a human rights culture, and the United Kingdom should formally declare itself to be a multicultural society.

20 *Organisational Change*

This chapter discusses issues that need to considered and acted on in every authority or organisation, including government departments. It follows on naturally from the previous chapter on legislation, since a recurring emphasis there was that one aim of legislation should be to promote and support self-generated organisational change. It is not necessary to wait for new legislation, however, before considering change at local or institutional levels. The chapter discusses leadership, documentation, management and mainstreaming, monitoring, training and the concept of 'a listening organisation'.

21 *Checklist of Recommendations*

This chapter summarises the recommendations made in Chapters 9–20. In most instances, it is up to a government department or agency at Cardiff, Holyrood or Westminster to take the first initiative. However, it is frequently not necessary or even desirable for other bodies to wait for government action. All individuals and organisations can be involved in advocating and lobbying for the implementation of the recommendations made in this report, and can set up pilot projects and feasibility studies at local and institutional levels.

Note on Terminology

Britain
The term 'Britain' is used in this report to refer to Great Britain, that is, to England, Scotland and Wales. General statements that are true of one part of Britain are not necessarily true of other parts, for there are three education systems and two justice systems, and additional constitutional differences of major importance have been introduced by the Scotland Act and the Government of Wales Act. Recommendations in the report are directed as appropriate to the administrations in Cardiff, Holyrood and Westminster.

Minority/majority
The term 'minority' has connotations of 'less important' or 'marginal'. In many settings it is not only insulting but also mathematically misleading or inaccurate. Furthermore, its use perpetuates the myth of white homogeneity – the notion that everyone who does not belong to a minority is by that token a member of a majority in which there are no significant differences or tensions. The terms 'minority' and 'majority' are not used in this report except in quotations from others.

Ethnic
There is a gulf between specialist and non-specialist usage of the term 'ethnic'. For specialists, an ethnic group is one whose members have common origins, a shared sense of history, a shared culture and a sense of collective identity. All human beings belong to an ethnic group in this sense. In popular usage, however, the term 'ethnic' implies not-Western (as in 'ethnic food'), not-classical ('ethnic music'), not-white ('ethnic communities') or not-British (as in the late 1990s dispute about insignia on British Airways aircraft). To avoid misunderstanding, the term ethnic is seldom used in this report; it is never used as a synonym for not-white or not-Western.

Race
The term 'race' is of essential importance, since it refers to the reality of racism. It is unhelpful, however, to the extent that it reflects and perpetuates the belief that the human species consists of separate races. A further disadvantage is that overuse can deflect attention from cultural and religious aspects of racism as distinct from those that are concerned with physical appearance. It needs often, therefore, to be complemented with other terms.

This report uses the phrase 'race equality and cultural diversity', sometimes shortened to 'race and diversity', to refer to its overall area of concern. The phrase stresses that addressing racism requires not only the creation of equality but also the recognition of difference.

The words 'race' and 'racial' are not used in the report in ways that might imply the view that the human species consists of separate races.

The term 'racist violence' is preferred to 'racial violence', as recommended by the Stephen Lawrence Inquiry report. It alludes to the causes of such violence and to how perpetrators justify it.

Asian, black and Irish
The report often uses the term 'black, Asian and Irish', or else 'black and Asian' or 'Asian and black', as appropriate. The word 'black' in this formulation refers to people with origins in Africa or the Caribbean. The word 'Asian' refers to all Asian countries and regions, not to Bangladesh, India and Pakistan only.

The report uses the term African-Caribbean in preference to Afro-Caribbean or Black Caribbean, and the term South Asian in preference to Asian if the reference is to Bangladesh, India and Pakistan.

Introduction

Chapter 1

The Turning Point

The future of multi-ethnic Britain, as also the future of multi-ethnic Europe, depends on many factors outside the specific struggle against racism: economic factors, the policies taken as a whole of different political parties, the adverse effect of harsh asylum policies, the prospects for real religious toleration, and much more. But despite the great difficulties to be faced, there is room for optimism at the beginning of the new century.

From a presentation to the Commission, autumn 1999

1.1 Britain is at a turning point, a crossroads. But was it not always so? Yes and no. Yes, there have frequently been times in the past when people in England, Scotland and Wales have believed themselves to be living at a propitious, historic moment. They were facing, they thought, a real parting of the ways. And yes, there have often been – in retrospect – unreal choices, illusory distinctions and false dawns. But no, it is not often that disparate but interacting forces come together so powerfully and so momentously as they do at present. It is a coincidence but symbolically apt that the current confluence occurs simultaneously with the start of a new millennium.

1.2 The interacting forces and trends of the present include devolution, and consequent questions about English, Scottish and Welsh identities; globalisation in a wide range of spheres, including economic, political and cultural; changes in Britain's sense of itself as a world power; cultural and moral pluralism, especially in views of gender relations, sexuality and the structures of families and households; and – the principal subject matter of this report – the recognition that England, Scotland and Wales are multi-ethnic, multi-faith, multicultural, multi-community societies.

1.3 Each of these changes involves dislocations in the way people see themselves, and in how they see the territorial, political and cultural space – 'Britain' – where they meet, and where they seek to build a common life. What will emerge? Possibly, and deplorably, a Britain where people are divided and fragmented among the three separate countries and among regions, cities and boroughs, and where there is hostility, suspicion and wasteful competition – the politics of resentment. The prevailing mood could turn out to be one of aloofness and apathy towards other European countries, and disinclination to be involved on the world stage – for example, in action to protect the global environment or international human rights. There could be profound divisions by culture, religion and history, with no joint deliberation among people of different religious or philosophical beliefs, or among people with different perceptions and collective memories of the past. There could be a punitive and impatient attitude towards the poor. There could be widespread intolerance of numerical minorities of many kinds, including communities with roots in Africa, Bangladesh, the Caribbean, Cyprus, Hong Kong, India, Ireland and Pakistan, and of Gypsies, travellers and asylum-seekers. A Little Englander mentality, and its equivalents in Wales and Scotland, could hold sway.

1.4   Alternatively, Britain could develop as what this report calls a community of communities. It would be at ease with its place within world society and with its own internal differences. In such a Britain there would be:

- mutually beneficial interaction between and within Scotland, Wales and England, and between regions, cities and boroughs;
- determination to develop each separate region, city or borough as a community of interacting and overlapping communities, proud of and learning from its own internal diversity;
- much engagement with the rest of Europe, with politics in the wider world and international law, particularly human rights law and standards;
- a readiness to share and to attend to conflicting perceptions of British and world history;
- resolution and action to remove racism and xenophobia in their various forms – colour/cultural; individual/institutional; behavioural/attitudinal; overt/subtle;
- dynamic contributions to world culture in a wide range of the arts, in science, medicine and technology, and in philosophical, political and moral theory.

1.5   The alternatives at the crossroads may be summarised as static/dynamic; intolerant/cosmopolitan; fearful/generous; insular/internationalist; authoritarian/democratic; introspective/outward-looking; punitive/inclusive; myopic/far-sighted. It is the second term in each of these pairs that evokes the kind of Britain we propose in this report. The forging and nurturing of such a society involves, at the outset, reinterpreting the past. Re-evaluating the past, said a Reith lecturer in the 1990s, is a basic civic duty:

> Arguing with the past, like paying taxes, like observing the law, like queuing, like not playing music full blast when others will be disturbed, has suddenly become a vital part of being a member of society, an ordinary but important act of citizenship, a factor in establishing the idea of a home as a place you would like to belong, and might be allowed to stay.[1]

1.6   Notions of Britishness originated in the 18th century, were developed in the 19th century, and were cemented through much of the 20th century. Nevertheless, in the words of the editors of *Political Quarterly*, in the journal's first issue of the new millennium:

> The British have long been distinguished by having no clear idea about who they are, where they are, or what they are. Most of them have routinely described England as Britain. Only business people talk about a place called the United Kingdom ... It is all a terrible muddle.[2]

1.7   If arguing with the past is one simple duty of citizenship, then arguing with the present, it follows, is another. 'Suddenly, in the space of a moment,' writes Bill Bryson in his bestselling *Notes from a Small Island*, 'I realised what it was that I loved about Britain.' In a way this travel book about England, Scotland and Wales introduced the inhabitants of these places to themselves. It depicted Britain as an endearingly eccentric place some of the time, and as essentially welcoming, friendly and calm most of the time. The author offered up a handful of criticisms – urban planners insufficiently respectful of tradition, a bossy landlady who interfered with his freedom, a waitress who did not understand him, an inflexible official, someone with a passionate interest he did not himself share – but basically he found Britain wholly lovable. No wonder the book was a bestseller. This is how he summed it up:

> Suddenly, in the space of a moment, I realised what it was that I loved about Britain – which is to say, all of it. Every last bit of it, good and bad – Marmite, village fetes, country lanes, people saying 'mustn't grumble'

and 'I'm terribly sorry but', people apologising to me when I conk them with a careless elbow, milk in bottles, beans on toast, haymaking in June, stinging nettles, seaside piers, Ordnance Survey maps, crumpets, hot-water bottles as a necessity, drizzly Sundays – every bit of it ... What other nation in the world could have given us William Shakespeare, pork pies, Christopher Wren, Windsor Great Park, the Open University, *Gardeners' Question Time*, and the chocolate digestive biscuit? None, of course.[3]

1.8 It is a beguiling but also remarkably limited and excluding list. Consider who and what it leaves out. For a start, it omits Scotland and Wales – the author claims to be writing about Britain (the 'small island' of his title), but much of this list, as indeed most of the book itself, is limited to England. Further, the list is limited in effect to the rural southern counties. It leaves out the English regions, with their distinctive identities and needs, and the urban and institutional life that is the daily experience of the vast majority of British people. It also leaves out the third of the population who are, by the government's own figures, classified as living in poverty. Most are unlikely to think of *Gardeners' Question Time* and Ordnance Survey maps as epitomising their country. Equally, it leaves out all or most people in Britain who have close family or community links with Africa, Bangladesh, the Caribbean, China, Cyprus, India, Ireland or Pakistan. There is barely anything in the list that resonates with their experience and perception of the land where they live. The references to Windsor Great Park and Christopher Wren evoke a national story that excludes them, or relegates them to subservient and marginal walk-on roles. Other than mentioning stinging nettles and careless elbows, the list leaves out all conflicts, difficulties and tensions, both in the present and in the past – it is both apolitical and ahistorical.

1.9 Significantly, the list gives no sense of the changes that have taken place in the very world it celebrates – the world of village fetes, country lanes and haymaking. Here, as elsewhere, there are conflicting loyalties and complex identities; profound disagreements about gender equality, sexuality, the upbringing of children, the nature and role of families; concerns about social class, status, life-chances and employment; disputes about the truth or otherwise of religion and the basis of morality; and unsettling anxieties about the cultural and economic dislocations brought on by modernisation and globalisation.

Box 1.2 **Voices: being black in Britain**

I wouldn't say I'm British, I'd say I'm Welsh. I always say Welsh.

Yeah. My children would say they feel Welsh because they were born in Wales.

No matter what colour you are, if you're not white, you're not British.

She's going to say a black man mugged me, she's not going to say a black British man mugged me. She's going to say a black man. So I don't feel British.

I don't think of myself as black, I think of myself as a black woman in a certain age group.

I saw a black chief inspector at a Swansea football match the other day. I was thinking how is this, a black chief inspector at Swansea, I was puzzling in my brain. I didn't feel any disrespect for the man. If you can make chief inspector, you're there ... you must have had a hard time getting there.

Music is breaking the boundaries. When I was younger only black people listened to reggae. Now, it's the thing to listen to.

One of the things I would like is to have that word tolerance abolished and have it replaced by acceptance. I don't want people to put up with me because I'm black, I want to be accepted.

You hope you'll get treated with equality, but you know it's not going to come.

Source: Focus group research in Cardiff, autumn 1999. All participants were African or African-Caribbean, and were aged 25–35.

In the current climate ... any failure to identify a positive multicultural English identity ... will be an historic opportunity missed. More cheap shots about the conflation of England and Britain simply will not do as a means of avoiding the question of a separate civic identity for people living in England. I hope the Commission's report has something to say on this issue. The key issue is not fundamentally one of British identity. It is one of English identity and how previous conceptions of English identity have excluded so many people who live in and richly contribute to English society.

1.14   A multicultural English civic identity depends to an extent, it is some-

times argued, on the creation and evolution of devolved elected government in the English regions analogous to developments in Wales and Scotland – an assembly for the North of England, for example. This will almost certainly be encouraged by the emergence of mayoral governance in other cities besides London. Our report does not discuss such constitutional matters directly. Throughout, however, it stresses that the development of Britain as a community of communities is not about 'multi-ethnic Britain' alone; it is for the benefit of all people, not just so-called minorities, and is dependent on much more than just race-specific policies.

1.15   Britain is a land of many different groups, interests and identities, from Home Counties English to Gaels, Geordies and Mancunians to Liverpudlians, Irish to Pakistanis, African-Caribbeans to Indians. Some of these identity groups are large, powerful and long-settled. Others are small, new and comparatively powerless. Some are limited to Britain but others have international links; some of the boundaries are clear, some are fuzzy. Many communities overlap; all affect and are affected by others. More and more people have multiple identities – they are Welsh Europeans, Pakistani Yorkshirewomen, Glaswegian Muslims, English Jews and black British. Most enjoy this complexity but also experience conflicting loyalties. The term 'communities' can give the impression of stable, coherent, historic groups with tidy boundaries. But situations and relationships are changing. It is simply wrong to think that there are easily measured groups of people – working-class Scots, black Londoners, Jews, Irish, 'middle' England – who all think alike and are not changed by those around them. For everyone life is more interesting than that.

1.16   The diversity of its population gives Britain important opportunities in the global markets that now shape the world economy. Britain's potential to become a community of communities is not something to shy away from – its people should celebrate it. In the world developing now, it is perhaps the country's biggest single national advantage.

1.17   Yet the opportunity is in danger of being squandered. It is endangered by the many varieties of racism and exclusion that disfigure modern Britain and that have been woven into the fabric of British history for many centuries. Racism and exclusion spoil millions of lives and waste the optimism and energy of people who could, and should, be building the country's prosperous future. Aggressive hostility to Islam is expressed in ways unthinkable in relation to other beliefs. Among the best-educated and more prosperous new British, there is a trend for re-emigration to the United States and Canada, countries seen as more open and equal. The state's attitude to asylum-seekers sends a shiver down many spines. Stories of murders, injustices and outrages – the Deptford fire, Quddus Ali, Michael Menson, Ricky Reel, Imran Khan, the Birmingham Six and the Guildford Four, arson attacks on Asian shops, graffiti on mosques – haunt many people's memories. The inquiry into Stephen Lawrence's murder and its aftermath confirmed that racist attitudes and assumptions are embedded in the routine working practices and in the occupational cultures of most or all public institutions.[5]

1.18 The essential task, we argue, is to move from 'multicultural drift' to a purposeful process of change. Along the way there are profound issues to be resolved. How to decide between the right of a religious community not to be offended by blasphemy or abuse and the right of freethinkers and secularists to express their views. How to reconcile the right of a newspaper to free speech with the right of groups it attacks to fight back. These are not abstract questions – they crop up all over the country all the time, creating hurt and confusion and mutual suspicion.

1.19 The compilation of this report has involved much consideration of tone, attitude and terminology. How can it give voice to the impatience and anger that many people feel? How can it avoid being merely deferential towards the government of the day, and at the same time being dismissed as out of touch with practical politics? What should the level of its language be, given that one person's specialist term is another's jargon, one's plain speech another's oversimplification? How should it use – if indeed it should use at all – contested terms such as 'ethnic', 'minority', 'race relations' and 'racial'? In its successive drafts this report has gone back and forth among a range of possible choices. It is now up to the reader to decide how close we have come to getting the various balances right.

1.20 Most of our recommendations are directed at the administrations at Cardiff, Holyrood and Westminster, for obvious reasons. But we do not believe that all social change comes pre-packaged in legislative paper, and we also address business, local government, health bodies, police authorities and community organisations. Not least we address the general reader, the individual citizen.

1.21 The report has not been compiled on behalf of any one community, or any one group of communities. We offer it as a resource for everyone who is interested in helping build a robust, successful and decent Britain for the century ahead. The opportunities and the dangers are common to everyone, whatever their 'race', community background, political outlook, gender, occupation, religion or class, and wherever they live. This land and its problems are shared. So is the future.

Chapter 2

Rethinking the National Story

The future of Britain lies in the hands of ... descendants of slave owners and slaves, of indentured labourers, of feudal landlords and serfs, of industrialists and factory workers, of lairds and crofters, of refugees and asylum-seekers.
From a response to the Commission

2.1   The movement towards a multi-ethnic, multicultural Britain has been decisive. However, it has not been the result of a concerted decision. Nor is it yet an accomplished fact. It has evolved as an unplanned, incremental process – a matter of multicultural drift, not of conscious policy. Much of the country, including many significant power-centres, remains untouched by it.

2.2   Attitudes towards multicultural drift vary widely. There are people who warmly welcome, to quote the resonant phrase used in the title of recent and influential documentation about it, 'the irresistible rise of multi-racial Britain'.[1] The new Britain was vividly seen in the *Windrush* celebrations of 1998, commemorating the arrival of Britain's Caribbean and Asian communities 50 years earlier. In those celebrations Britain was affirmed as a place where people of different cultural, religious and ethnic backgrounds live together on a permanent basis, and strive to build a common life. However, there are those who accept multicultural drift grudgingly as a fact of life, regretting the passing of the good old days when, they believe, Britain was a much more unified, predictable sort of place. There are also those who militantly resist and oppose it. The *Windrush* celebrations represented the good side of multiculturalism. The Stephen Lawrence Inquiry report, with its disturbing finding of institutional racism in the police service – and by extension in all public bodies and institutions – was a sombre reminder of the challenges that must be faced.

2.3   As noted in Chapter 1, Britain confronts a historic choice as to its future direction. Will it try to turn the clock back, digging in, defending old values and ancient hierarchies, relying on a narrow English-dominated, backward-looking definition of the nation? Or will it seize the opportunity to create a more flexible, inclusive, cosmopolitan image of itself? Britain is at a turning point. But it has not yet turned the corner. It is time to make the move.

Imagined communities

2.4   Constitutionally, it was only after the Union with Scotland (1707) that England, Scotland and Wales became known as Great Britain. From 1801 to 1922 Ireland was joined to Great Britain and the state's name changed to the United Kingdom. After Partition (1922) the state's name changed again. It was now the United Kingdom of Great Britain and Northern Ireland.[2]

2.5   A state is not only a territorial and political entity, but also, it has been said, an imagined community. Many reforms are needed to convert multicultural drift into a concerted drive towards a Britain with a broad framework of common belonging – one in which all citizens are treated with rigorous and uncompromising equality and social justice, but in which cultural diversity is cherished and celebrated. One critical prerequisite is to examine Britain's understanding of itself. How are the histories of England, Scotland and Wales understood by their people? What do the separate countries stand for, and what does Britain stand for? Of what may citizens be justly proud? How has the imagined nation stood the test of time? What should be preserved, what jettisoned, what revised or reworked? How can everyone have a recognised place within the larger picture? These are questions about Britain as an imagined community, and about how a genuinely multicultural Britain urgently needs to reimagine itself.

2.6   To call Britain a community is to speak metaphorically. Its members are not literally bound together in tight-knit, face-to-face relationships, as in a village. Inevitably, most citizens are strangers to one another: each has met only a minute proportion of fellow citizens. But large numbers of people share an idea of the nation and what it stands for. (It was Enoch Powell who once remarked that 'the life of nations, like that of men [sic], is lived largely in the imagination'.) They share a mental

2.11   The fourth theme is that the British are an island race, their mentality shaped by a long and sturdy independence, free from foreign contamination.[5] The national sense of humour is notably self-deprecating, but it is underpinned by a deep conviction that the British are a special and superior sort of people. A columnist recently cited lines by William Cowper: 'England, with all thy faults, I love thee still, My country!' She added, 'people everywhere love their own country, just as [they] love family, home, garden or local landscape. Life without deep affection for the familiar for its own sake is almost unthinkable.' The English, Scottish and Welsh do indeed have much to be proud of in their island story. However, 'these strong national sentiments turn into absurd and potentially dangerous nationalism when elevated into a general theory of the superiority of your own kind, your own people, your own language, just because it is yours'.[6] The dangers of nationalism are particularly great when there is ambiguity about who exactly the terms 'you' and 'yours' refer to. The so-called 'united' kingdom contains not one nation but four (five, if the two communities in Northern Ireland are counted separately), each with its own specific history and culture. The danger is further compounded in the case of an imperial or post-imperial nation like Britain, where the differences between 'us' and 'them' are imagined to be racial, rooted in unalterable nature.

2.12   A historian, commenting on the anglocentric tilt in the British national story, observes that 'wherever one looks at the map of Europe … one sees layer upon layer of settlement, statehood and occupation'. Most Europeans, when pressed, he argues, are aware that 'their present territory was once ruled by foreign powers, dominated by different cultures or inhabited by alien peoples'. They have varied historical origins and their culture is the product of a long process of reciprocal influence. The British, however, are foremost among present-day nations 'which have a strong inclination to believe that they and their forebears have "possessed" their present territory since time immemorial'.[7] This invocation of the ancestral heritage sustains the fantasy of multiple, unbroken connections between past and present and excludes or marginalises elements that do not fit or are considered politically inconvenient. For example, the story is typically told as if Scotland, Ireland and Wales are mere appendages of England, and as if 'England' and the 'United Kingdom' are alternative ways of describing the same country.[8]

2.13   Great Britain is the product largely of the 18th, 19th and 20th centuries. For most of prehistory, the geographical feature now known as the British Isles, or the British and Irish Isles, formed a promontory of the continental landmass. Separation occurred only 8,000 years ago. Culturally, the islands remained intimately related to Catholic continental Europe until the Reformation – the break that made English nationalism possible, powerfully fuelled by anti-Catholicism and anti-French sentiment.[9] For centuries before then England was dominated by France. English kings were vassals of French kings and not, as myth has it, the reverse. They and the ruling and professional classes commonly spoke French. The parliamentary tradition is an achievement of which the British are justly proud. However, the idea that parliament was a uniquely British institution, with exclusive Anglo-Saxon roots, is not supported by the known historical facts. Parliaments, diets and assemblies were thick on the ground throughout late medieval and early modern Europe. The primacy of parliament in Britain was achieved at the expense of civil war, a king's head, the persecution of Catholics and the crushing of revolt in Ireland. It did, however, help Britain escape the absolutism that dominated the rest of Europe in the 17th and 18th centuries.

2.14   The pact that underpinned the British constitutional settlement was based on civic principles, notably the rule of law, sovereignty of parliament, formal equality and procedural legality. The British take pride in the civic and secular character of their liberal constitutionalism and their record of religious toleration. In classic liberal doctrine, citizens maintain distinct religious and cultural traditions in private life; state institutions are neutral towards these, and free from specific cultural and religious trappings. This is said to distinguish British civic nationalism from the ethnic nationalisms found elsewhere.[10] However, the real story is not quite so straightforward. Civic nationalisms are always embedded in particular cultural values and traditions. They involve not only a rational allegiance to the state, but also an intuitive, emotional, 'ethnic' allegiance to the nation. It is these deeper cultural meanings that make a nation-state an imagined community, as outlined earlier.

2.15   Cultural meanings appeal to people's imaginations but are difficult to pin down. They are embedded not in formal rules and laws but in all the informal aspects of cultural life that are taken for granted: customs, habits, daily rituals, unwritten social codes, the way masculinity and femininity are expressed, speech, idiom and body language, feelings for the landscape, and collective memories of national glories – especially those associated with war. Shakespeare's 'sceptered isle ... this other Eden, demi-Paradise'; Stanley Baldwin's sights and sounds of the countryside ('the tinkle of the hammer on the anvil in the country smithy, the corncrake on a dewy morning ... the sight of a plough team coming over the brow of a hill'); John Major's warm beer and elderly ladies cycling to communion through the early-morning village mist; the passage in *Notes from a Small Island* quoted in the previous chapter – all these examples make it clear that image, metaphor and shared symbols play a crucial role in constructing and maintaining the idea of England as an imagined community. They not only express solidarity but also construct a solidarity that was not there before.

2.16   The grounding of British civic nationalism in a particular set of cultural meanings and traditions is best exemplified by religion. Henry VIII's break with Rome (1530s), the union of English and Scottish crowns (1603), the 'Glorious Revolution' (1688), the Hanoverian succession and the union of the English and Scottish parliaments (1707) secured a Protestant ascendancy over and against the Catholic ambitions of France and Spain. At the same time a solid connection was forged between Protestantism and the British way of life. Worship and scriptures in everyday language became instruments in the construction of a national uniformity. Church and state were drawn into close conjunction. Monarchs became, and remain, governors of the Church and Defenders of the Faith. For centuries local government and welfare services were inseparable from the parish system of church governance.

2.17   The settlement was never, however, universal or unproblematic. The Act of Settlement (1701), which debarred Catholics from 'inheriting, possessing or enjoying the Crown and Government of the Realm', remains unrepealed. The Act of Union (1801), which attempted to broker Ireland into the bargain, was continually contested. Between 1801 and Partition, the state proved incapable of incorporating Ireland into Great Britain, or Irishness into Britishness, or Irish Catholics into British society. Despite Catholic Emancipation (1829), Irish immigrants, though formally citizens, were never regarded as part of the national community: the British remained deeply ambivalent about the

Irish presence, despite its contribution to industrialisation. During the 19th century, the Irish were increasingly seen as a race apart. Anti-Irish and anti-Catholic sentiment remained critical to the notions of otherness that underpinned British national identity. At first sight this is a paradox, for the immigration legislation of the 1960s, modelled on the Aliens Act of 1905 (which was principally directed at Jewish immigrants), defined the Irish as insiders. It was the New Commonwealth immigrants who were the aliens. Race was not explicitly referred to, but the subtext was that the Irish were insiders because they were white. However, this belated attempt to include them did not substantially change the position of the Irish in Britain. They remain Britain's 'insider-outsiders'.

2.18 The unity of the United Kingdom that emerged from this long process was therefore always more complex than the conventional national story suggests. There are real, substantive differences of culture, history, tradition, power and resources between the different parts of the UK. Nevertheless, Englishness gradually acquired a dominant position within Britishness, as England did within the United Kingdom. England has often been surreptitiously extended, by the English themselves, to stand for the whole of the UK. It sometimes appears, indeed, that the UK is thought of as an essentially English nation-state, which happens for odd historical reasons to have Celtic fringes and (more recently) small pockets of non-English settlement. All this is changing now, with migration and devolution. The rising tides of nationalist sentiment in Scotland and Wales, however, have clearly been driven by historical resentments of long-standing relations of privilege and dependency.

2.19 Empire Britain's colonial and imperial role – did much to forge a common identity across internal differences. It welded England, Scotland and Wales together as one people and gave the British a powerful sense of natural superiority over others. Nineteenth-century politicians such as Disraeli and Chamberlain were acutely attuned to the role of empire in consolidating cross-national and cross-class solidarities. At its zenith the British Empire, incorporating more than a quarter of the world's population, was of primary importance in consolidating British national identity. Empire, it is important to recall, was a genuinely British, not just an English, enterprise: 'The Scots primarily', it has been pointed out, 'but also the Welsh and the Irish responded to the new opportunities with enthusiasm. They saw it as an imperial partner-ship.'[11] Also, 'Support for empire was one of the few issues that com-manded a general consensus in Scottish intellectual and political circles. The Scots regarded themselves as a "mother nation" of empire ...They rejoiced in their self-proclaimed status as "a race of empire builders".'

2.20   Despite this, there has never been a single 'British way of life'. The idea that Britishness is universally diffused across society is seriously mis-leading. For there have always been many, often contested, ways of being British. Outside the heartland (earlier 'the Home Counties'; more re-cently 'middle England'), Britishness always existed alongside, and was strongly challenged by, the Irish, Scots and Welsh, and also by a range of local and regional loyalties. Identification with Yorkshire, the North-East, Manchester, Lancashire, the West Midlands, East Anglia and the West Country has co-existed with, and sometimes seems to override, na-tional identity – there have been alternative versions of national identity not only within Britain but also within England itself. The achievements now said to characterise Englishness were staunchly resisted by some English people while being vigorously championed by others. For example, constitutional monarchy, religious toleration, parliamentary democracy, the rule of law, trial by jury, freedom of the press – now con-sidered the cornerstones of the political system – were achieved only through protracted struggle. English people experienced English liber-ties in significantly different ways. The majority were disenfranchised until the early 20th century; the poor have always been socially ex-cluded. The right to free assembly, to vote, the destruction of the old Poor Law, the outlawing of child labour, limiting working hours and im-proving working conditions, the National Health Service, the welfare state itself, are now all represented as great national achievements. Yet each was at one time the cause of bitter struggle between vested interests and sections of the British people – that is, between one sort of British person and another. Only after the dust had settled were such changes retrospectively incorporated into an all-embracing, essential British-ness.

2.21   Deep differences in social and political outlook and opinion continue to exist, even in today's less politicised climate, and reflect different, often dramatically opposed, versions of national identity. A young columnist remarked: 'It could be argued that a universal sense of "Englishness" is impossible when our class system provides so many different "Englands". Depending on whether you're black, white, old, young, privileged, disadvantaged, healthy, sick, living in the provinces or the cities, England means a million different things to a million different people. Everyone is still staring out of the same window and seeing entirely different views.'[12] Exactly the same would be true of Britishness as a whole, as seen from Scotland, Wales or Northern Ireland, or by people of different genders, regions and generations. The roll-call of traditional British virtues – tolerance, moderation, readiness to compromise, fair play, individualism, love of freedom, eccentricity, ironic detachment, emotional reticence – is understood in different ways by men and women, and by different generations. All classes were involved in and benefited from empire, but men and women related to it in different ways.[13]

The unsettling of Britain: seven recent trends

2.22   Our argument, then, is that British national identity has always been more diverse than it is normally imagined to be. In recent decades it has become more complex than ever before.[14] We summarise below seven main sources of social and cultural change. Both separately and in interaction with each other, these have eroded the patterns of gender, class and regional and generational differences that stabilised Britain in the past as an imagined community. They have shaken the unified conception of Britishness hitherto taken for granted and have injected a sense of fluidity and uncertainty into what was formerly experienced by many as a settled culture.

Globalisation
The growing interdependence of the world's major regions results from the rapid movement of global capital and investment, deregulation of financial and other markets, the rise of multinational corporations, the spread of new information and communication technologies, the new cultural industries and global consumption patterns.[15] One effect has been to weaken, though not yet fatally undermine, aspects of national sovereignty, the nation-state as an exclusive political focus, national economies and the idea of nation as the guarantor of citizenship. There has been a corresponding growth in local and regional attachments ('glocalisation').

The long-term decline in Britain's position as a world power

Militarily, Britain is dependent on alliances for effective influence. It is no longer the centre of a worldwide empire, and no longer plays a pre-eminent role in technological advance. Overall, Britain has slipped to a position as a middle-ranking power. This has undermined its long-standing sense of the inevitability of British 'greatness'. There is widespread concern that Britain has lost its historical vocation, and the country is tempted to look back, nostalgically, to past glories.

Britain in Europe

This is part of an inevitable trend towards larger regional associations. However, the idea of an island people with an island destiny has been central to British national identity. Indeed, Britishness has been most effectively described negatively, in terms of what it is not – especially not 'European'. Euroscepticism is not so much a considered policy as gut nationalism, a refusal to accept the full implications of Britain's increasingly close ties with other European countries.

Devolution

Many factors have conspired to stimulate pressure to devolve power from England to Scotland, Wales and Northern Ireland. The process is said to represent a loosening of ties, not a breaking of ancient bonds. However, as the new parliaments and assemblies flex their muscles, significant divergences between Westminster and how things are done elsewhere will develop. These will inevitably weaken the centralised idea of a united kingdom. What symbolic glue can hold these increasingly autonomous entities together? The Union Jack is losing its significance and the emblems of the individual countries, like the St George Cross, are now preferred. The English regions feel that power is being devolved to everybody but themselves. At some point, this English democratic deficit could become the focus of a new kind of little Englandism, especially if there is mileage in it for certain political parties.

The end of empire

This is often described as the shedding of a burden whose time has passed. However, expunging the traces of an imperial mentality from the national culture, particularly those that involved seeing the white British as a superior race, is a much more difficult task. This mentality penetrated everyday life, popular culture and consciousness. It remains active in projected fantasies and fears about difference, and in racialised stereotypes of otherness. The unstated assumption remains that Britishness and whiteness go together, like roast beef and Yorkshire pudding. There has been no collective working through of this imperial experience. The absence from the national curriculum of a rewritten history of Britain as an imperial force, involving dominance in Ireland as well as in Africa, the Caribbean and Asia, is proving from this perspective to be an unmitigated disaster.

The rapid advance of social pluralism

Some trends here are economic – for example, the shift from an industrial to a post-industrial and service economy; the decline of traditional skills; the rise of new technological elites; the eroding expectations of steady employment; the expansion of consumer choice; the feminisation and casualisation of the workforce; the increase in corporate management. Many are social – for example, the breakdown in older class hierarchies; the break-up of the older occupational communities; the decline in male manual working-class culture; the revolution in the position of women; the comparative decline of marriage and the nuclear family and new attitudes to parenting and sexuality. Many are cultural – the decline of a public-service ethos and diminished respect for traditional sources of authority; generational differences within an ageing population; shifting gender and sexual norms; the erosion of the established cultural canon; the pervasive influence of the media; the new individualism. Some are moral, including the decline of organised religion; the rise of New Age spirituality; growing moral relativism; more personalised ethics; the competitive entrepreneurial ethos; and the new hedonism.

2.23 The consequence of the six trends summarised above is that the world has become an unpredictable place, one in which attitudes and values diverge significantly from one neighbourhood or community to another. People have competing attachments to nation, group, subculture, region, city, town, neighbourhood and the wider world. They belong to a range of different but overlapping communities, real and symbolic, divided on all the critical issues of the day, from private medicine and abortion to the environment and the welfare state. Identities, in consequence, are more situational. This makes Britain, contrary to the stereotype, more open. It has also made the British less certain

about who they are, for the pace of change has created anxiety and uncertainty. Increasingly, Britain is a place without boundaries, lacking
not only signposts to future directions but also standards against which
conduct can be measured. In this shifting scenario there is a seventh
factor of change.

Postwar migration

Migration is a worldwide phenomenon. It affects every metropolitan
Western country, for all have needed influxes of labour from outside. It
is also driven by globalisation, poverty, underdevelopment, natural dis-
asters, famines and civil wars. Migration to Britain from the Caribbean,
the South Asian subcontinent, China and Africa has raised many questions, discussed throughout this report, about British identity and
British institutions.

2.24   How are the new communities to be viewed in relation to the nation?
One customary approach, which co-exists with the dominant version of
the national story outlined above, is to see them as bounded, homogeneous groupings, each fixedly attached to its ethnicity and traditions.
The 'majority', by the same token, is imagined to be fixed, unified,
settled. This attitude underlies most public policy – for example, school
curricula, many aspects of the criminal justice system and the health
service, official policy on asylum and immigration, and the way the government addresses social exclusion. We consider these topics in later
chapters. There are two things wrong with this mental picture of a large
homogeneous majority and various equally homogeneous minorities.
First, Britain is not and never has been the unified, conflict-free land of
popular imagination. There is no single white majority. Second, the 'minority' communities do not live in separate, self-sufficient enclaves, and
they do display substantial internal differences. They too must be
reimagined. What this involves is the subject of the next chapter.

Chapter 3

Identities in Transition

> *The young participants, school and college pupils, stated that they were proud to be Scottish. 'I want to be Scots not English. I want to be Scottish and British, but not if people assume that being British means being English. Too often people talk about England when they mean Britain and they forget Scotland.' But they also asked a number of pointed questions. Why should it be a problem to be Scottish, born in England, of French nationality and part Indian? Or to be from the north-east of England, although born in Scotland ... How late it is, how late to be asking these questions.*
>
> From an article about the Commission, December 1998[1]

3.1   'Community' is a tricky term. To speak of 'the black community', 'the Irish community', 'the Bangladeshi community', and so forth, is to refer accurately to a strong sense of group solidarity. But it may also imply a homogeneous set, with fixed internal ties and strongly defined boundaries, and this is a hopelessly misleading picture of a complex, shifting multicultural reality. Post-migration communities are distinct cultural formations, but they are not cut off from the rest of British society. It is true that maintaining tradition is critical to their self-identities, but their sense of community owes as much to how they are treated as to where they came from.

3.2   These communities are not, and have never aspired to be, separate enclaves. They are not permanently locked into unchanging traditions, but interact at every level with mainstream social life, constantly adapting and diversifying their inherited beliefs and values in the light of the migration experience. 'Minority cultures in Britain', concluded a substantial research project in the 1990s, 'are ... constantly changing and rewriting themselves through fusing their traditions of origin [which in any case were not monolithic] with elements of the majority culture. The process of mixing and hybridisation will increasingly be the norm where rapid change and globalisation have made all identities potentially unstable.'[2]

3.3   A fixed idea of community understates the degree of differentiation within the new communities. Disadvantage continues, but there is considerable variation in socio-economic positions. Many remain at the bottom of the ladder. Overall, unemployment rates for black and Asian people of working age are double those for the white population, and even higher for the 16–24 age group. (See Chapters 6 and 14.) There is, however, substantial divergence, and the earnings and educational achievements of some groups compare favourably with the national average. For example, Indians and Chinese are proportionally better qualified than the rest of the population. Nearly 20 per cent of hospital doctors and 12 per cent of pharmacists are South Asian, mainly Indian. But a few 'Asian millionaires' cannot disguise the fact that many Pakistanis and Bangladeshis experience serious household poverty. Also, young African-Caribbean men are notably disadvantaged in employment and education. Among African-Caribbean women, however, earnings and social mobility are growing at a faster rate than among white women. There is no uniform story of blanket disadvantage – not least because the different communities have responded to their situations in different ways, as many stories of economic ingenuity, entrepreneurial skill and the exploitation of niche opportunities at the cost of intolerable working hours amply illustrate.

3.4   It is much the same for social life and culture in general. Class, gender and generation are critical factors. There is a growing gap between the majority of black and Asian working-class people living in inner-city deprivation, for example, and the minority moving into new middle-class careers and lifestyles.[3] Race and gender are differentiating factors that apply to all people, influencing their experience and their opportunities.[4] Racial stereotypes are systematically 'gendered'. Men and women of the same class therefore experience their ethnicity very differently. For example, African-Caribbean society is still marked by a culture of assertive masculinity, and in South Asian communities respect for traditional authority or religious leaders can be won at the cost of women forgoing their own life-choices in marriage or education.

3.5   There is a process of reciprocal influence between migrant and host cultures that changes them both.[5] Young people who have been educated in British schools often have more in common with their white peers than with their parents – they reinterpret themselves not only in terms of their origins but also in terms of the surrounding culture. Continuity with the past provides an essential resource for survival, but it exists alongside interaction across a wide spectrum of daily activities. Young people have developed the capacity to manoeuvre between distinct areas of life (it has been said that they are skilled 'cross-cultural navigators'). Such cosmopolitan skills are not restricted to the young, however – everyone has the chance to develop them if they are given the chance to do so. Inevitably, therefore, there is a degree of long-term dilution in commitment to the original culture. Hybrid cultural forms have emerged, especially in music and the arts. There has been an explosion of expressive creativity – the 'styling of difference', involving the development of new forms of ethnicity, is particularly evident.[6] Numbers of mixed-race children are growing. There is no one migrant community, but a broad spectrum in which tradition and translation are combined.

African-Caribbean communities

3.6   Caribbean culture has a distinct social and geographical basis and is the product of a unique historical experience. But it was diluted by numerous cross-cultural influences, among them African, East Indian, British, Spanish, French, Dutch, Portuguese and Chinese. It cannot be traced back to one set of roots. Each of these influences, however – Africa, slavery, the plantation system, colonisation, migration – has left indelible traces. British-born African-Caribbeans are socialised through family and neighbourhood into a migrant version of this culture. Following the rediscovery of an African and slave past at home (as communicated through reggae music), and resistance to white racism in Britain, blackness has become an essential part of their self-definition. They are conscious of their subordinate, racialised place in global power systems.

3.7   Nevertheless, colonisation familiarised African-Caribbeans with many aspects of British life and institutions. Older members of the community, especially women, hold strong Christian religious beliefs, while preferring Pentecostal forms of worship. A black identity has not prevented their active involvement in social life, enhancing the younger generation's spectacular entry into mainstream urban culture. Although worryingly vulnerable in terms of jobs and education, young

African-Caribbean people in Britain occupy a prominent position in popular culture, giving rise to many wannabe white imitators for whom black is a badge of street credibility.

'Asian' communities

3.8   Asians are not a single group. The conventional terminology blurs critical distinctions between Bangladeshis, Gujaratis, Pakistanis and Punjabis; between South Asians, East African Asians and Chinese; and between Hindus, Muslims and Sikhs. South Asians vary significantly not only in terms of nationality and religion but also in terms of language, caste and class, and of whether they have come to Britain from urban or rural backgrounds. Maintaining cultural and religious traditions is critical to their sense of identity, but the meaning of tradition varies widely in practice. Traditions of origin are strongest in familial, personal, domestic and religious contexts, where there is a strong sense of extended kinship. In consequence, a stereotype has arisen of Asians being distinctively conservative, but in fact there is much internal diversity in Asian communities. There are deep divisions between parents and their children about the dangers of assimilation, for example. Traditions and beliefs are varied and dynamic, constantly reinterpreted according to circumstances. Consider, for example, the diversity of interpretations of Islam among British Muslims.[7]

3.9   Older migrants may not have developed substantial language skills in English, but families are engaged in every type of economic activity. In large cities, the corner shop, the newsagent's and the garment trade, for example, are classic examples of successful Asian small businesses. In recent surveys nearly all Asians questioned have said that religion is important to them, but it has not inhibited full participation in the wider society. Recently, Muslims have emerged as the principal focus of racist antagonisms ('Islamophobia') based on cultural difference.[8] The politicisation of Islam throughout the world has contributed to this. Often, however, what Islam means is that 'new ways of living and the process of gradually becoming a part of British society have to be ultimately justified in terms compatible with a Muslim faith'. It does not inevitably mean 'a rigid, fundamentalist, anti-western, anti-modernist religiosity'.[9] Some Asian youths have experienced a heightening of militant religious commitment, but they have also followed their African-Caribbean peers in exploring the crossover territory and the rhythms of black-influenced youth culture.[10]

Irish communities

3.10   Anti-Irish racism developed in tandem with racisms directed at people outside Europe. There are around 2 million Irish people in Britain today – by far the largest migrant community.[11] All too often they are neglected in considerations of race and cultural diversity in modern Britain. It is essential, however, that all such considerations should take their perceptions and situations into account.

3.11   Migration from Ireland to Scotland and England took place in three phases. One of these corresponded with the period of large-scale migration from the Caribbean and South Asia, about 1948–68; the others occurred in the mid-19th century and in the 1980s. There are now substantial Irish settlements in south-west Scotland, Liverpool and the

South-East, particularly London. About four-fifths of the migrants were born in a Catholic tradition. There are various ways of being Irish in Scotland and England, connected with – but not determined by – differences of class, gender and time of migration. As in all migrant communities, there are differences between those born in their country of origin and those of the second or third generation. Irishness as an identity is sometimes combined with other strong loyalties. In Liverpool, for example, there is a strong regional identity; in all parts of England and Scotland being Irish is bound up with being Catholic. In Scotland, attacks on Irish communities are labelled as sectarianism though in fact much anti-Catholicism is implicitly anti-Irish racism.

3.12   The generations of Irish born in Britain remain under-researched. However, the few available studies indicate a continuing pattern of low achievement for young Irish men and disproportionate ill health in the second generation. The position of the Irish in Britain as insider-outsiders is uniquely relevant to the nature of its multi-ethnic society. For generations, Irish experience has been neglected owing to the myth of the homogeneity of white Britain, but it illuminates Britishness in much the same way that the experience of black people illuminates whiteness.

Jewish communities

3.13   Jews in Britain are often characterised – by the media and politicians, and by some Jewish leaders – as a single community. But there are many significant divisions and differences among British Jewry. A report published in 2000 by the Commission on the Representation of the Interests of the British Jewish Community, established by the Institute for Jewish Policy Research (JPR), is entitled *A Community of Communities*. The title reflects a diversity that has existed for some centuries, for British Jewry has always consisted of communities, distinguished geographically, religiously, socio-economically, ideologically, historically and by personality.[12] But the current diversity is essentially a response to changes that have taken place since the second world war.

3.14   Jews are expressing their identity in an increasing variety of ways. Many of these forms of expression have an ethnic character. In the past, many Jews were reluctant to define themselves as an ethnic group, even though they are thus defined by case law legislation resulting from the Race Relations Act. The JPR Commission report, however, firmly advocates that British Jews should accept the description of ethnic group, which will give them a greater sense of belonging and security in both their Jewish and their British identities. However, changing ways of expressing Jewishness are creating tensions within the community. Some members embrace pluralism; others see it as undermining their religious identity. There is a fundamental debate about how to maintain Jewish distinctiveness in conditions of unprecedented freedom, acceptance and choice, and about how at the same time to play a full part, as equal citizens, in British society.

3.15 Since the second world war two new means of expressing Jewish identity in non-religious ways have emerged: attachment to Israel and remembrance of the Holocaust. Israel has been a force of cohesion in the Jewish community; it has enhanced the status and security of British Jews, and until recently it was a central aim of charitable fund-raising. For many, awareness of the Holocaust is sufficient reason to remain Jewish, for to assimilate entirely would be, as some argue, to 'hand Hitler a posthumous victory'. The importance of the event for Jews has been reinforced by the ubiquity of Holocaust references in popular culture. The Holocaust is a principal moral reference point for non-Jews as well as Jews. The opening of the permanent and major Holocaust Exhibition at the Imperial War Museum in June 2000 was a remarkable sign of state recognition of the Jewish tragedy.

3.16 Recently, however, greater emphasis has been placed on other ways of expressing Jewish identity. The Holocaust identifies Jews with a story that offers no sense of redemption and often portrays them as passive victims. Israel is less in need of charitable fund-raising, and research indicates that most British Jews feel secure and settled. Few in the Jewish community would question the significance of the Holocaust or of Israel, but many now say that the focus of communal attention must be on values, culture and religious practice, on positive images of Jewish culture and civilisation, and they are concerned with how to maintain Jewish distinctiveness in British society. Their desire for cultural recognition in a pluralist society offers probably more potential for shared goals with Asian and black people than the shared history of racist oppression.

Gypsy and Traveller communities

3.17   The kinds of tension and complexity outlined above are issues also for Gypsies and Travellers.[13] As is the case with Irish people and Jews, they are often neglected in considerations of Britain as a multi-ethnic society, or included only as an afterthought. But they too were defined in the past as an inferior race and are part of the history of British racism. A law enacted in 1530 imposed a ban on the immigration of 'Egipcions' (they were erroneously supposed to originate in Egypt), and a further law of 1554 made provision for their capital punishment if they remained in the country for more than a month. These laws were repealed in 1783, but the Turnpike Roads Act of 1822 and the Highways Act of 1835 reintroduced the term 'Gypsy' into legislation. It was not until 1967 that the law ceased to define Gypsies as a biologically distinct race.

3.18   In common with other communities, Gypsies are diverse, not homogeneous. They do not consist, as is widely believed, of a few 'real' Romany Gypsies and a range of non-ethnic, troublesome 'travellers'. Gypsies are first recorded in Britain in the early 1500s. Other travelling people who have similarly been nomadic for centuries include the Kale of North Wales, Roma from the European continent, and Scottish and Irish travellers. Some so-called 'new' travellers have Gypsy forebears or may be the third or fourth generation on the road. Each group has its own customs and mores – the Gypsy and Traveller community, like the Jewish community, is 'a community of communities', not monolithic. Some of the estimated 150,000 travelling people in Britain have intermarried with members of other groups or with settled people over the years. Many live in housing for part or all of the year.

3.19   Nomadism, it has been said, is a state of mind. Those who travel have a range of reasons for doing so, including economic and social factors; they are in any event liable to be constantly moved on owing to a shortage of legal stopping-places. Despite the great diversity between and within travelling groups, all are lumped together in the minds of settled communities. They suffer from high degrees of social exclusion, vilification and stereotyping. Anyone who does not fit the traditional stereotype (painted wagon, campfire, swarthy complexion, much gold jewellery) is assumed to be a mere traveller, to be feared and despised.

Other communities

3.20 There is not enough space here to discuss the many other communities that have been established in Britain in recent years. But they too experience tensions and pressures such as those outlined above and their diversity is frequently hidden in official statistics. The Chinese community has been formed from a range of countries and cultures. A large proportion of its members have high-level educational qualifications and are involved in management and the professions; in common with many other communities, they suffer racial stereotyping and verbal abuse. It has been estimated that there are now over 350,000 people of African origin in Britain – substantially more than the Chinese community (166,000) or the Bangladeshi community (234,000).[14] They appear in official statistics as a single group. In fact, however, their diversity is such that official statistics are virtually meaningless as a basis for analysis. They include the substantial Somali community (estimated at about 60,000 members), and large communities from Ghana, Nigeria, Sierra Leone and Uganda. About 80 per cent of all Africans in Britain live in London. Similarly, the substantial Turkish and Cypriot communities are invisible in most official statistics, and so are communities from Afghanistan, Iran, Iraq, Morocco, Romania, Sri Lanka and the former Yugoslavia. Current estimates are that there are 195,000 'other Asians' (that is, other than from Bangladesh, China, India and Pakistan) in Britain and 406,000 'other other' (that is, not from any other Asian country either). Presumably most 'other others' are from Turkey, the Middle East, North Africa and South and Central America. They do not include East Europeans, since most define themselves as white.

3.21 The shifting complexities and uncertainties outlined above illustrate that there are few stable patterns from which future projections can be made: differences in origin and development will continue to shape attitudes towards wider integration. However, all the people discussed are enmeshed in and having an impact on life around them. Like every other element in the social mix, they are busy negotiating place and space within a rapidly changing larger whole.

The future of Britishness

3.22 We argued in the previous chapter that Britishness is less unified, more diverse and pluralistic, than is normally imagined. We recognised the impact of rapid change, especially that of postwar migration, on a comparatively settled culture. However, migrant communities also turn out to be less unitary, more diverse and varied, than is normally imagined. They are familiar strangers, not an alien wedge. The prospect of all communities finding a better, more just and humane way of living together has improved in the recent past.

3.23 However, as we show in many chapters of this report, Britain continues to be disfigured by racism; by phobias about cultural difference; by sustained social, economic, educational and cultural disadvantage; by institutional discrimination; and by a systematic failure of social justice or respect for difference. These have been fuelled by a fixed conception of national identity and culture. They are not likely to disappear without a sustained effort of political will. Is it possible to reimagine Britain as a nation – or post-nation – in a multicultural way?

3.24 New communities remain strongly identified with family and cultural and religious traditions of origin. But these are also being integrated into evolving self-conceptions. A sense of identification is weaker for younger members than it is for their elders. Although many continue to express allegiance to distinctive cultural traditions and religious beliefs, there is a visible decline in actual participation across the generations. This does not mean that differences will disappear. Where settlement is dense, the majority of children in local schools are drawn from Asian and black communities. Community traditions will therefore remain a strong source of identity and solidarity and may well strengthen over time rather than erode. Black identities have been positively embraced. Difference now matters profoundly. However, differences are not necessarily either/or – many people are learning to live 'in between', it has been said,[15] or with more than one identity. The famous Tebbit cricket test is not only racially demeaning but is also out of date. People today are constantly juggling different, not always wholly compatible, identities. South Asians and African-Caribbeans support India, Pakistan and the West Indies against England but England against Australia, especially when the English team includes Asian and black players. This is just one aspect of the complex, multifaceted, post-national world in which national allegiance is now played out.

3.25 What broad strategies are shaping the ways in which people deal with this shifting situation? Hope once centred on assimilation. However, this really meant the absorption of so-called minority differences into the so-called majority – people were expected to give up everything in order to belong. But since racism has continued, assimilation has come to be seen as an impossible price to pay – blackness and Asianness are non-tradable. Cultural difference has come to matter more. The awareness that 'non-recognition or mis-recognition can inflict harm, can be a form of oppression, imprisoning someone in a false, distorted and reduced mode of being' has led to a politics of recognition alongside the struggle for equality and racial justice.[16]

3.26 This has strengthened the claims of community over both universalism and culture-free liberal individualism. Undoubtedly, any long-term strategy must involve moving towards a much greater public recognition of difference – the rights of communities to live according to their own conception of the good life, subject to certain moral constraints. However, communities today are neither self-sufficient nor fixed and stable. They are open, porous formations. It is impossible to invest totally in communities as the sole bearers of the legal right to difference. Many individuals with a strong sense of belonging and loyalty towards their communities do not intend their personal freedom to be bound in perpetuity by communal norms. The rights of communities must be balanced, therefore, against the right of individuals to move away from their community. If necessary, this right must be supported by law.

3.27 At the same time, the law protecting individuals as bearers of rights cannot hide behind a veil of ignorance where cultural difference is concerned. The cultural resources underpinning difference must be made more widely and equally available. However, it must be acknowledged that no culture can require that its continuity be guaranteed by the state in perpetuity.[17] The need for both equality and difference, and to respect the rights of both individuals and communities, appears to be beyond the compass of existing political vocabularies. The debate about British multiculturalism needs to pursue these long-term questions. It has hardly begun. This report, we hope, will be a valuable resource for it.

3.28   Does Britishness as such have a future? Some believe that devolution and globalisation have undermined it irretrievably.[18] Many acknowledge that ideally there needs to be a way of referring to the larger whole of which Scotland, Wales and England are constituent parts. But the nation-state to which they belong is the United Kingdom, not Britain. In one community in Northern Ireland, as among large numbers of Irish people in Britain, being British is not an acceptable self-description. In Scotland and Wales the conflation of Britishness with Englishness has always made being 'British' problematic. Now, with substantially more devolved political power, the term is being used less and less. The Good Friday Agreement of 1999 implies that there should be a sense of affiliation to the supranational entity known as 'these islands'. Perhaps one day there will be an adjective to refer to this entity, similar in power perhaps to the unifying word 'Nordic' in Denmark, Finland, Norway and Sweden. But for the present no such adjective is in sight. It is entirely plain, however, that the word 'British' will never do on its own.

3.29   Where does this leave Asians, African-Caribbeans and Africans? For them Britishness is a reminder of colonisation and empire, and to that extent is not attractive. But the first migrants came with British passports, signifying membership of a single imperial system. For the British-born generations, seeking to assert their claim to belong, the concept of Englishness often seems inappropriate, since to be English, as the term is in practice used, is to be white. Britishness is not ideal, but at least it appears acceptable, particularly when suitably qualified – Black British, Indian British, British Muslim, and so on.

3.30   However, there is one major and so far insuperable barrier. Britishness, as much as Englishness, has systematic, largely unspoken, racial connotations. Whiteness nowhere features as an explicit condition of being British, but it is widely understood that Englishness, and therefore by extension Britishness, is racially coded. 'There ain't no black in the Union Jack,' it has been said.[19] Race is deeply entwined with political culture and with the idea of nation, and underpinned by a distinctively British kind of reticence – to take race and racism seriously, or even to talk about them at all, is bad form, something not done in polite company. This disavowal, combined with 'an iron-jawed disinclination to recognise equal human worth and dignity of people who are not white',[20] has proved a lethal combination. Unless these deep-rooted antagonisms to racial and cultural difference can be defeated in practice, as well as symbolically written out of the national story, the idea of a multicultural post-nation remains an empty promise.

3.31   In the next four chapters we consider what needs to be done to fulfil the promise. In Chapter 4 we discuss the various forms a multicultural society may take, and commend the concept of pluralism in particular, though only if it is synthesised with liberalism. We use the term 'community of communities', already introduced in this chapter, as a possible way of describing Britain as a whole. (The term could also, incidentally, describe the United Kingdom or 'these islands' as a whole.) Then in Chapter 5 we go into further detail about the history and nature of racism. In Chapter 6 we discuss the government's agenda for tackling social exclusion and stress that it must not be racism- or culture-blind. In Chapter 7 we argue that international human rights standards contribute substantially to the ethical and legal basis of the changes we are proposing.

Chapter 4

Cohesion, Equality and Difference

> *I still think of that scene at the end of* A Passage to India, *where two characters discuss relations between English and Indian people and say 'Not yet, not yet' with regard to full understanding. I think one could say the same about relationships between all the communities in Great Britain and do not think we can hope for anything more than a distant mutual toleration.*
>
> From a response to the Commission, 1998

4.1 The present government has declared that it is committed 'to creating One Nation', a country where 'every colour is a good colour ... every member of every part of society is able to fulfil their potential ... racism is unacceptable and counteracted ... everyone is treated according to their needs and rights ... everyone recognises their responsibilities ... racial diversity is celebrated'.[1] The previous government made a broadly similar commitment.[2]

4.2 Such assertions are no more than the opening statement in a substantial debate. What do they assume as empirical fact? What do they advocate as a political programme? What values and loyalties must be shared by communities and individuals in 'One Nation'? How can we prevent them being oppressive or jingoistic? How can we recognise and celebrate diversity but at the same time set limits? Who is to determine these limits? How should disputes and incompatible values between different communities be handled? What are the respective rights and responsibilities of individuals and groups? How can we promote public-spiritedness and willingness to compromise for the greater good? How is a balance to be struck between the need to treat people equally, the need to treat people differently, and the need to maintain shared values and social cohesion?

4.3 These are perennial questions for moral and political philosophers, but they are also experienced concretely by millions of people every day. In later chapters we consider their practical implications for police services (Chapter 9), criminal justice systems (Chapter 10), education

---

Box 4.1 **Voices: belonging, cohesion and difference**

When I'm with Asian people, like at weddings, I act Indian. And when you're at work or when you've got mixed people there, you act British, you talk in English and everything. You have like two different characters.
Asian, female, London, 25–35 age group

Britain is populated with many different races but the feeling that the whites reign supreme is one that never goes away. We always seem to be reminded that we are second-rate citizens.
Mixed heritage, female, Birmingham, 16–24 age group

Being equal doesn't mean being the same. For equality to work all people – men, women, black, brown – must feel they are valued and not treated unfairly.
White, male, Manchester, 16–24 age group

I fell off the seat when that Asian family took over the corner shop in Coronation Street, but you can't recognise them as an Asian family because they're not, culturally – that's not there, it's just them, it's just the colour of the skin what's there. There's nothing about them being Asians, any traditions.
Mixed heritage, male, Birmingham, 16–24 age group

I'm Muslim ... and portrayed in the media, it's always negative, you never see anything positive, it's always fanatics, but Islam's not all about that and it sort of gives you low self-esteem, because beyond that there's a lot of positive.
Asian, male, Birmingham, 16–24 age group

When you go on holiday and they say where are you from, I say Britain or England. I wouldn't say I'm from India, no way.
Asian, male, London, 25–35 age group

I see England now, I see England as a place where the system mows everybody down.
Black, male, Manchester, 16–24 age group

Source: Focus group research, autumn 1999.

(Chapter 11), arts administrators and journalists (Chapter 12), the health service (Chapter 13), and employers and unions (Chapter 14). Here we discuss in theoretical terms the ways in which cohesion,

Box 4.2 **Cohesion, equality and difference: five possible models**

1 Procedural – the state is culturally neutral, and leaves individuals and communities to negotiate with each other as they wish, providing they observe certain basic procedures.

2 Nationalist – the state promotes a single national culture and expects all to assimilate to it. People who do not or cannot assimilate are second-class citizens.

3 Liberal – there is a single political culture in the public sphere but substantial diversity in the private lives of individuals and communities.

4 Plural – there is both unity and diversity in public life; communities and identities overlap and are interdependent, and develop common features.

5 Separatist – the state permits and expects each community to remain separate from others, and to organise and regulate its own affairs, and largely confines itself to maintaining order and civility.

equality and difference may be balanced. The purpose of such theoretical discussion is to clarify real-life situations and dilemmas – for example, the experiences of the respondent quoted at the head of this chapter – and determine how to go beyond mere toleration. Box 4.1 on the previous page evokes the everyday feelings and situations with which the chapter as a whole is concerned.

4.4   There are five peaceful ways in which societies reconcile cohesion, equality and diversity, and therefore five roles for government and five conceptions of citizenship.[3] There are also non-peaceful ways: the world is haunted by the collapse of One Nation in countries such as Rwanda and the former Yugoslavia, and by countries held together only through repression and violence. The five peaceful ways are summarised briefly in Box 4.2.

4.5   We will discuss each of the five models in turn. First, in a country where the state is culturally neutral the government machinery acts rather like a referee in a football match, interpreting and enforcing the rules but not partisan, indifferent as to who wins. All that is required of citizens is that they should know and abide by certain minimal laws. This view of government was seen in absolute monarchies and medieval kingdoms and may be called the proceduralist view of unity and diversity.

4.6 It is often argued that procedural neutrality is not enough, for no political system can be stable and cohesive unless all its members share a common national culture, with a sense that everyone belongs to, and feels loyalty to, a single whole. There must be shared symbols and ceremonies to evoke and maintain the common loyalties, and the state has both a right and a duty to ensure that everyone assimilates into the prevailing national culture. Those who do not or cannot assimilate, shedding all vestiges of any alternative culture, cannot complain if they are treated like second-class citizens. This model may be called the nationalist view.

4.7 There is a halfway position between proceduralism and nationalism. According to this third view, proceduralism is too formal to hold a society together, and nationalism is unnecessary or undesirable or both. All that is required for a unified and cohesive political system is a common political culture. Fundamental to this view is a distinction between public and private spheres. There must be unity in the public sphere of political debate and in acceptance of the rules of decision-making, but there may be tolerance for substantial diversity in people's private lives, and in the internal affairs of distinct communities. A contemporary philosopher has suggested the term 'constitutional patriotism' as a way of describing this model,[4] which may be called the liberal view. .

4.8 The fourth model is similar in many respects to the third. However, it rejects the hard and fast distinction between public and private realms, and envisages that the public realm should be continually revised to accommodate cultural diversity in society at large. Unlike the liberal view, this model does not place the political culture beyond negotiation, and it maintains that recognition, as distinct from toleration, should be a central value.[5] At the same time it envisages that there should be considerable interdependence and overlap within and between the various communities that constitute a society, and that these dynamic realities should be welcomed and protected. Much influenced by feminist theory, it seeks to protect the rights and freedoms of individuals in the private sphere as well as in the public. It goes out of its way to promote dialogue.[6] It may be called the pluralist view. This model is to be found in acknowledged multicultural societies such as Canada, Australia, Malaysia and India. It is also sometimes known as 'the community of communities' model. (We introduced this phrase in Chapter 1 and again in Chapter 3, and will continue to use it.)

4.9   Fifth, it may be argued that the state has no moral status of its own, but simply has to protect, maintain and nurture its various constituent communities, and the distinctions between them. Society in this model is seen not as a community of communities but as a loose federation. It is not envisaged that communities will overlap, or that someone may move from one to another, or that the state may intervene in a community's internal affairs. People owe their primary loyalty to their own specific community, with its own laws and customs. Only secondarily, if at all, do they owe obligations to the state. This model was to be found throughout the five centuries of the Ottoman Empire, in traditional Muslim kingdoms, and in the British administration of many of its colonies. It is sometimes known as the millet model,[7] and may also be called the imperial view.

4.10   The five views are not mutually exclusive. Nevertheless, each has a distinctive approach to issues of unity and diversity, the role of the state, the nature of culture, and the rights and obligations of citizens. The first three see unity as more important than diversity; the fifth sees diversity as more important than unity; and the fourth envisages unity and diversity in balance. All but the first see culture as important, but only the fourth sees the state as integrally related to society, both shaping and shaped by the prevailing cultural diversity. Also, only the fourth sees culture as essentially open-ended and developing, and is committed to strong forms of intercultural dialogue. In this respect its approach differs from the *laissez-faire* philosophy of the first view, the assimilationist approach of the second, the tolerant co-existence advocated by the third, and the segregation and potential fragmentation of the fifth.

4.11   All five models may be found locally in modern Britain. At the level of national policy, however, the first is logically incoherent, for a state cannot be culturally or morally neutral. The defects of the fifth model

for a country such as Britain are similarly obvious. It fragments society into isolated groupings; has a static view of human nature; reinforces prejudices and mutual suspicions; is hostile to concepts of individual autonomy and the right of individuals to pursue their lives outside the culture into which they have been born; and prevents the emergence of an interactive democracy. Only the second, third and fourth can be seriously advocated as formal policy. Over the last 50 years the second and third models, the nationalist and the liberal, have vied for supremacy. The liberal view was advocated by Roy Jenkins in a famous and much-quoted speech made in 1966,[8] and came in due course to be articulated as official UK policy.[9] It has been strongly contested, however, by leading politicians and political theorists to the right of the political spectrum, who have upheld the nationalist model, and by their supporters in the media.[10]

4.12 The essential problem with the nationalist or assimilationist model, as we argued in Chapter 2, is that it is based on a false premise of what Britain is and has been. Britain is not and never has been a homogeneous and unified whole – it contains many conflicting traditions and is differentiated by gender, class, region and religion as well as by culture, ethnicity and race. Assimilation is a fantasy, for there is no single culture into which all people can be incorporated. In any case, it seldom leads to complete acceptance, for the demand for assimilation springs from intolerance of difference, and for the intolerant even one difference is one too many. Furthermore, assimilation cannot be justified morally. It attempts to suppress difference and condemns to second-class citizenship, in fact if not in law, everyone who does not accept majority norms. A fundamental practical problem is that assimilation cannot be pursued in an age of increasing globalisation. For no government, least of all the government of a state such as the United Kingdom, can insulate its citizens from cultural, religious and intellectual influences emanating from outside the state's physical borders.

4.13   The liberal model avoids many of the shortcomings of the nationalist model. Nevertheless, it is open to substantial objections, particularly when viewed in the light of the fourth model, which advocates pluralism and 'a community of communities'. The first challenge to traditional liberal theory is that political culture and the public realm are not, and cannot be, neutral. Their values and practices can therefore discriminate against certain members of the community, marginalising them or failing to recognise them. This was seen in the *Satanic Verses* affair and in the Stephen Lawrence Inquiry, for example. The public realm must be open to revision in the interests of those it is in danger of disregarding. This point is seen with particular clarity in relation to gender issues. Equal access to the public realm for women is necessary but not enough in itself – the public realm must also be modified to take account of women's interests, perceptions and needs.[11]

4.14   A second defect of the liberal model is that its attempt to combine a monocultural public realm with a multicultural private realm is likely to undermine the latter. For if only one culture is publicly recognised and institutionalised, other cultures will be seen as marginal, peripheral, even deviant and inferior. For example, the days of rest supported by British and European law and custom are those that coincide with traditional Christian holidays rather than with the holidays of any other faith. This makes participation in public life convenient for people from Christian traditions but inconvenient for those of other religions, and it implies second-class status for all traditions other than Christian. There is no simple answer to this problem, but at least the situation must be acknowledged. Furthermore, the separation of public and private realms means that there is little or no intercultural debate, and therefore mutual learning, either in public or in private.

4.15   A third defect concerns the state's right, and indeed duty, to intervene in the private sphere to protect and promote human rights standards, based on equal respect and dignity. We stress this point further in Chapter 7. For example, the state has a duty to regulate how children and older people are treated. It exercises this duty with substantially more legitimacy if it gives public recognition to cultural diversity, and if it is seen to be sensitive to the ways in which universal human rights are realised in different specific settings.

4.16   The debate between the nationalist and the liberal models is certainly not over, particularly in the field of immigration and asylum policy (see Chapter 15). However, it needs to be increasingly replaced by debates between the liberal and the pluralist models, with a view to creating a synthesis of their best features – Britain is both a community of citizens and a community of communities.

4.17   The term 'community' usually refers to something rather amorphous, but nevertheless can have legal significance, as for example in Northern Ireland. The *Oxford English Dictionary* defines it as 'a body of people having a religion, a profession, etc, in common ... a fellowship of interests ... a body of nations unified by common interests'. This definition reflects the fact that in everyday usage terms such as the following are all fairly familiar: 'the local community', 'a valued member of the community', 'the disabled community', 'a mining community', 'the scientific community', 'the gay and lesbian community', 'the two communities in Northern Ireland'. It would be consistent with the dictionary definition to envisage Britain as a community whose three principal constituent parts are England, Scotland and Wales, and to envisage each of the constituent parts as a community, as also each separate region, city, town or borough. Any one individual belongs to several different communities. This was stressed in Chapter 3 and was vividly illustrated in a statement made to the Bradford Commission in 1996:

> I could view myself as a member of the following communities, depending on the context and in no particular order: Black, Asian, Azad Kashmiri, Mirpuri, Jat, Marilail, Kungriwalay, Pakistani, English, British, Yorkshireman, Bradfordian, from Bradford Moor ... I could use the term 'community' in any of these contexts and it would have

meaning. Any attempt to define me only as one of these would be meaningless.[12]

4.18   The meanings and implications of the term 'community' are explored in Box 4.3, using a mixture of abstract and conversational terms. These are the connotations we have in mind when we say that it is as a community of communities, and as a community of citizens, that Britain should develop. It is a goal that gets progressively closer but is never wholly reached.

4.19   Creating a synthesis of the liberal and pluralist models – Britain as both a community of individuals and a community of communities – involves devoting attention to six issues: recognition of cultural diversity in the public sphere; public institutions, bodies and services; controversies and disputes; common values; symbols and ceremonies; racism. We consider the sixth of these in the next chapter. The other five are discussed below.

Recognition of cultural diversity in the public sphere

4.20   The cultural identity of some groups ('minorities') should not have to be confined to the private sphere while the language, culture and religion of others ('the majority') enjoy a public monopoly and are treated as the norm. For a lack of public recognition is damaging to people's self-esteem and is not conducive to encouraging the full participation of everyone in the public sphere. Public respect for different cultural identities is intrinsic to democratic equality and must be two-way – the pressure to change, to compromise, to assimilate must not all be on the so-called minorities. If some groups in society are subject to insulting stereotypes, made the butts of offensive and demeaning jokes and remarks, or viewed with suspicion, they fail to develop self-esteem and hit out at the society that excludes them. Both they and the wider society are then losers.

4.21   Recognition of cultural diversity widens a society's range of options and increases its freedom of choice, for it brings different cultural traditions into a mutually beneficial dialogue and stimulates new ideas and experiences. Consider, for example, the English language. Over the centuries it has greatly benefited from the contributions of writers for whom it was not the mother tongue and who introduced into it new metaphors, images and idioms. By stretching it to accommodate new sensitivities, they have helped the language to express a wider range of human emotions and experiences. In other arts, too, the cultural life of Britain has been greatly enriched through borrowings from other traditions. We discuss these points further in Chapter 12.

Public institutions, bodies and services

4.22   It is essential, if people are to have a sense of belonging to society as a whole, that they should not feel alienated or marginalised by public bodies. They must feel that their own flourishing as individuals and as communities is intimately linked with the flourishing of public institutions and public services such as the police, the courts, educational establishments and the health service. If they feel this identification and are at home with public institutions they have a commitment to sustaining them. Such commitment is an essential building block of One Nation. It is linked to people's sense of sharing a common fate with their fellow citizens, and is greatly strengthened if they see themselves represented in public bodies, and if these bodies accord cultural communities a high degree of self-determination.

4.23   Public services are embodiments of the state – they are windows, it could be said, through which the state is seen. It is therefore essential that they are staffed by individuals of merit and integrity, that their exercise of authority is regulated by clearly defined procedures, that their actions are above suspicion, and that any acts of partiality are subjected to the severest punishment. Public institutions should assiduously cultivate an appropriate professional ethos, and be firmly insulated against ethnic, religious and cultural biases. At the same time, they should be seen to represent a wide range of cultural experience and community background. This is particularly important in the case of the police. We discuss this point at greater length in Chapter 9. High professional standards of integrity and impartiality are also required, of course, of teachers (Chapter 11), arts administrators (Chapter 12) and staff in the health service (Chapter 13).

Box 4.3 **The meaning of community**

Belonging

A community gives its members a sense of belonging, and therefore of their identity and dignity. Here in my community I am among my own people, I am at home, I know them and understand them, and they know and understand me – though also there are times of mutual incomprehension, and when I feel alienated. We speak the same language (including often the same body language), smile or laugh at the same jokes, know the same stories and music, have shared memories. I am recognised and respected, I am a somebody not a nonentity.

Care and responsibility

The members of a community take an interest in each other and have a sense of responsibility towards each other. They are prepared to pay taxes or subscriptions for the common good, or to help less fortunate members, and to donate their time to maintaining the community, whether formally or informally. I can hope to be looked after if I fall on bad times.

Gratitude and questioning

The members of a community are grateful to it, in so far as it does indeed give them a sense of belonging, identity and dignity. My gratitude may take the form of great affection and love, even self-sacrifice, but may also be expressed through criticism and questioning. Sometimes gratitude is expressed more by caring criticism than by blind devotion.

Family quarrels

Communities are not marked by cosiness alone. There are often arguments, quarrels and profound disagreements. Expulsion or secession are frequently options. But essentially quarrels are family quarrels. I have a commitment to staying. I cherish the community, and am prepared to compromise in order that the community itself may be maintained.

Personal strengths and weaknesses
Feelings of gratitude and criticism towards one's community tie in with awareness of one's own personal qualities. As I consider my own strengths and weaknesses I am aware that many were taught by or copied from my community. For my strengths I am grateful to the community that nourished them. With regard to my weaknesses, however – prejudices such as racism and sexism, narrow-mindedness, parochialism, selfishness – I am critical of my community as well as myself.

Fluid boundaries
The boundaries round a community can be quite hard and fast, making it difficult to join or leave voluntarily. But often they are fluid, unfixed. It is in any case entirely possible for someone to be a member – a significant member – of several different communities at the same time; indeed, this is usual. I have, and nearly all people have, a range of belongings, identities and loyalties, and sometimes these are out of tune with each other, or are in blatant conflict. It is not unusual, particularly in the modern world, for some of my loyalties to be transnational – I have feelings of kinship and shared interests with people in at least two different countries.

Cohesion through symbolism
A community is held together by symbols and ceremonies which broadly mean the same to all its members. All the following can have symbolic, not just functional, power, and can help bind a community together symbolically: food; buildings and monuments; rites of passage relating to birth, adolescence, marriage and death; clothes (including of course uniforms and insignia); religious worship; music – particularly, perhaps, singing; various courtesies, customs, manners and rules of procedure; and ritualised conflict in sport and games of all kinds. I belong through symbols.

Controversies and disputes

4.24 Disputes sometimes arise between a cultural community and a state institution, for example a school. Also there are disputes both between communities and within them in which the state cannot remain neutral. There are broadly four possible ways of resolving such disputes: (a) appealing to the principles of moral universalism; (b) reference to the majority's values and customs; (c) the no-harm principle; and (d) consensus through intercultural deliberation.

4.25 Moral universalism invokes the principle that there are values that exist independently of any one culture or country. At first sight, this seems an attractive approach. But in practice universal values – life, liberty and the pursuit of happiness, for example – are too abstract to guide decisions in particular cases, for they need to be related to, and interpreted in the light of, a society's traditions and history. It would not be possible to argue from universal human values that polygamy is always wrong or always right, for example, or that Sikh men should always and everywhere be allowed to wear their turbans. However, international human rights standards establish valuable ground rules for the settling of disputed issues. We expand on this point in Chapter 7.

4.26 An appeal to a society's established customs involves arguing that each society has an established way of life, expressing its distinctive values, and that it may disallow practices that offend against it. This approach again appears promising at first sight. Certainly, a society has the right to prevent practices that would lead to its disintegration, or change it into a different kind of society. But no society is static – its survival requires that it should continually redefine its identity and modify its customs and practices, including those it currently holds to be fundamental. In any case, just because a practice is widely approved does not mean that it is desirable. Inequality is a widely shared and enforced value in slave-owning, racist and caste-based societies. It is not by that token right.

4.27 The no-harm principle is largely unproblematic when physical harm is involved, but it does not provide specific enough guidance on matters such as those cited above. Concepts of moral and emotional harm cannot in practice guide any but the most straightforward cases, for what constitutes harm is itself often a matter of deep disagreement.

4.28   In practice, consensus reached through deliberation is frequently the only effective solution. Its advantage is that it shows respect for minority viewpoints, involves people in decisions that affect them, deepens understanding between communities, and leads to realistic and widely acceptable decisions. It requires ground rules, however. There must be a shared commitment to these rules, and more widely to the values of tolerance, readiness to compromise, and respect for the dignity of individuals and deliberative decision-making that underpin them. In Chapter 16 there is further reference to non-polemical forums and to deliberative, as distinct from representative, democracy. In Chapter 17 we consider in further detail the ground rules of intercultural dialogue.[13]

Common values

4.29   Like any other society, Britain needs common values to hold it together and give it a sense of cohesion. At the same time it must acknowledge that its citizens belong to a variety of moral traditions and subscribe to and live by a range of values. Therefore common values cannot simply be the values of one community, even if it is the numerical 'majority', but must emerge from democratic dialogue and be based on reasons that individuals belonging to different moral and cultural traditions can agree on. They should not be so defined that they rule out legitimate moral differences or impose a particular rule of life on all. Nor should they be seen as fixed and settled forever, as new insights and experiences are likely to call for their reconsideration.

4.30   There are two sets of values that all people in Britain can be expected to share: procedural and substantive. Procedural values are those that maintain the basic preconditions for democratic dialogue. They include people's willingness to give reasons for their views, readiness to be influenced by better arguments than their own, tolerance, mutual respect, aspiration to peaceful resolution of differences, and willingness to abide by collectively binding decisions that have been reached by agreed procedures. Substantive values are those that underpin any defensible conception of the good life. They include people's freedom to plan their own lives, the equal moral worth of all human beings, and equal opportunities to lead fulfilling lives and to contribute to collective wellbeing. Such values are not arbitrary and are not those of any one community or society. They are embodied in international human rights standards (see Chapter 7) and form part of moral dialogue in all parts of the world. On the basis of such values it is legitimate to ban female circumcision, forced marriages, cruel punishment of children, and repressive and unequal treatment of women, even though these practices may enjoy cultural authority in certain communities.

4.31   Procedural and substantive values such as those outlined above are society's moral capital, and form the basis of what all people are entitled to demand of themselves and each other. Subject to the constraints of these values, different individuals and communities should be free to lead their self-chosen lives. They may disagree profoundly about how to structure their families, how to order intergenerational and intergender relations, or about the truth of religious doctrines. So long as people do not offend against the shared basic values, such differences should be respected. Society may legitimately ban forced marriages, or those based on duress or deceit, but it should respect the custom in many cultures of basing marriages on introductions arranged by parents. It may also rightly insist that parents should not deny full-time education or opportunities for self-development to their daughters, but should respect their desire to withdraw them from certain kinds of sports. When there are legitimate disputes, and there are bound to be many, they should be resolved by a consensus based on discussion, conducted in a spirit of charity and goodwill.

Symbols and ceremonies

4.32   Although equal citizenship is essential in developing a common sense of belonging, it is not enough. Citizenship is about status and rights, but belonging is about full acceptance, being recognised as an integral part of the community and able to move around it unselfconsciously and with ease. An individual might enjoy all the rights of citizenship and be formally an equal member of the political community, and yet feel that they are not fully accepted and do not fully belong. The experience of being a full citizen yet also a relative outsider is difficult to analyse and explain, but it can be deep and real and can seriously damage both the quality of someone's citizenship and the depth of their commitment to the political community. Full acceptance is a deeper notion than inclusion. Since inclusion is offered on terms already set by the wider society, it involves assimilation, sharing current norms of what it means to be a British or a good citizen, and demands a heavy cultural entrance fee. Full acceptance, however, involves renegotiating the terms and redefining the current norms of Britishness so as to create secure spaces within them for each person's individual qualities.

4.33   For a long time there was no legal concept of a British citizen or a British national, only of a 'subject of the Crown'. Even now, citizenship is seen in dry legal terms, and there is little moral or emotional significance in wanting to be or achieving the status of a citizen. The whole matter is dealt with through postal correspondence with an anonymous bureaucracy at the Home Office. In contrast, the taking of the Oath of Allegiance in the United States is the culmination of a process of naturalisation, and the conferring of citizenship is a highly symbolic and emotionally charged civic event, with many friends and relatives present to witness and celebrate it. Such a ceremony dramatises the importance of someone being welcomed and accepted as a fellow citizen into a network of rights and mutual obligations.

4.34   A British citizenship ceremony would not necessarily copy the American model. Each country has its own sensibilities and mode of symbolic expression, and what is appropriate in one place – saluting the national flag at the start of each school day, for example – would be seen as jingoistic in another. Nevertheless, a more ceremonious form of welcome for new British citizens might help everyone to reflect on the value of citizenship and to appreciate diversity. It could involve community organisations, especially those that feel marginal to civic life, and could promote a sense of belonging among a wide circle of people, not just the individuals whose day it is. It could, therefore, be a way of increasing civic and political participation.

4.35   'I do not think', wrote the individual quoted at the head of this chapter, 'we can hope for anything more than a distant mutual toleration.' Is this hard-nosed realism or defeatist pessimism? It may be that such pessimism is realistic. Our own vision, however, is of a vibrant, interactive democracy, a democracy that recognises – not regrets or denies – diversity, giving all people a sense of belonging and ensuring that all are treated equally. Such a democracy needs constitutional guarantees. We welcome in this connection the Human Rights Act and discuss its legal and cultural implications in Chapter 7. Further, we believe that Britain's anti-discrimination legislation needs a substantial overhaul, and discuss this in Chapter 19.

4.36   Britain needs to be, certainly, 'One Nation' – but understood as a community of communities and a community of citizens, not a place of oppressive uniformity based on a single substantive culture. Cohesion in such a community derives from widespread commitment to certain core values, both between communities and within them: equality and fairness; dialogue and consultation; toleration, compromise and accommodation; recognition of and respect for diversity; and – by no means least – determination to confront and eliminate racism and xenophobia. The next chapter considers at length the various forms racism takes.

Chapter 5

Dealing with Racisms

The Rule Britannia mindset, given full-blown expression at the Last Night of the Proms and until recently at the start of programming each day on BBC Radio 4, is a major part of the problem of Britain. In the same way that it continues to fight the Second World War ... Britain seems incapable of shaking off its imperialist identity. The Brits do appear to believe that 'Britons never, never, never shall be slaves' ... [But] it is impossible to colonise three-fifths of the world ... without enslaving oneself. Our problem has been that Britain has never understood itself and has steadfastly refused to see and understand itself through the prism of our experience of it, here and in its coloniser mode.

From a presentation to the Commission

5.1 'Last week', recalled someone in one of our focus groups, 'this happened. I was at the bus stop and this yellow car was just driving past and four white lads just shouted out, "Paki, we're coming to get you" ... All I was doing was I was at that bus stop just doing the same thing as anyone else, just waiting for a bus. There was no need and it just makes you feel gutted.' Such episodes occur in Britain many times a day, every day. A Policy Studies Institute investigation in the mid-1990s found that overall about one in eight of the people it surveyed – Bangladeshi, Caribbean, Chinese, Indian, Pakistani – had experienced racist insults or abuse during the previous 12 months. It estimated that about 20,000 people suffer a physical racist assault each year, 40,000 have items of property damaged and 230,000 experience abuse or insults.[1] Only a small proportion of these incidents are reported to the police. In Box 5.1 there are further accounts by victims, showing the distress that is caused by racist harassment and violence.[2]

5.2 Racist incidents such as those described in Box 5.1 occur across a spectrum. At one end are physical assaults and major criminal damage; at the other casual and unspoken – but infuriating and depressing – rudeness and rejection. In between there is abusive language. The spectrum as a whole is often known as overt racism, but it may also be called street racism, a reminder that racist incidents occur mainly in public spaces,

Box 5.1 **Voices: living with racism**

- *A few years ago I suffered a racial attack in East London and the per-petrators have never been caught. It left me devastated and it took me a long time before I could go out and get my confidence back. The way the police handled the situation really appalled us.*
- *He swore and shouted 'Paki', something I'm used to being called. I felt that the incident wasn't significant enough to report. In fact, the police would have laughed at me had I reported it.*
- *We have a daughter and a son who are eleven and eight. When she was going to play it was 'you are a Paki bastard' and 'go and get your-self washed' every time she stepped out of the door ... I came in from work at night and my daughter was in bed crying. She asked 'why are they calling me names?' It was getting to the stage that she didn't like who she was.*
- *Two of us went shopping together, always. Two of us had to be in the house to defend the others. We used to be scared going home. We used to phone Mum and say, "Mum, I am coming round the corner. Please look out of the window." We always had to carry change for the phone in case something happened. We had to let the family know what shops we were going to so if we were late they could go and check. Everything was really organised.*
- *I still don't feel British. Because I know we haven't been fully accepted. We still walk down the street and get called a Paki.*

Source: See Note 2.

and in urban areas more than in leafy suburbs. However, rural racism – assaults and abuse in villages and market towns whenever black or Asian people visit or settle in them – is a stark reminder that street racism is not confined to cities.[3] The green and pleasant land of England, Scotland and Wales is pleasanter for white people than it is for those who are black or Asian.

5.3   Much street racism is perpetrated by white people who are themselves economically disadvantaged in relation to wider society. Therefore, long-term action to tackle it depends to an extent on greater social justice generally. We return to this point in Chapter 6, and consider the role of the criminal justice system in this regard in Chapter 10. Racism and xenophobia are also exacerbated by insecurities about national identity.[4] They have to be addressed through rethinking concepts of Englishness and Britishness (see Chapters 2–3), and through education (Chapter 11), the media and culture (12) and political leadership (16). Here we focus primarily on what the Stephen Lawrence Inquiry report, adopting a term coined in the United States in the 1960s, called institutional racism.[5] 'You can fight one-to-one racists,' said someone in one of our focus groups, 'but you cannot fight institutional racists. That's when it's bad.' In the questionnaire they filled in, three-quarters of all black and Asian participants agreed with the statement that 'in Britain much racism is subtle and hidden'. Four-fifths of them agreed that 'many people pretend not to be racist but are'. Virtually no one expressed strong disagreement with this view. The experience at the bus stop left the victim feeling, he said, 'gutted'. It is also the case that subtle and hidden forms of racism are draining and depressing, particularly when institutionalised in the structures and cultures of public bodies. Street racism and institutional racism are interrelated, not two entirely different beasts. Their origins go back many centuries.

The targets of racism

5.4   In other European Union countries it is customary to use the phrase 'racism, xenophobia and antisemitism' as a way of summarising the issues to be addressed.[6] The phrase is cumbersome and is unlikely to become widespread in Britain. It is, however, helpful as indeed are other approaches to anti-racism in Europe. It stresses that hostility which uses skin colour and physical appearance as markers of supposed difference does not represent the whole picture. There is also hostility using markers connected with culture, language and religion. The plural term 'racisms' is sometimes used to highlight such complexity. For anti-black racism is different, in terms of its historical and economic origins, and in its contemporary manifestations, stereotypes and effects, from anti-Asian racism. Both are different from, to cite three further significant examples, anti-Irish, anti-Gypsy and anti-Jewish racism. European societies, it is sometimes said, are multi-racist societies. Specific words have been invented over the years for certain types of racism directed at particular groups – the term antisemitism originated in the mid-19th century, and more recently the terms orientalism and Islamophobia have been coined to refer, respectively, to anti-Asian racism in general and anti-Muslim racism in particular.[7]

5.5   At a popular level, the plurality of racism is poignantly evoked in an American playground chant: 'If you're white you're all right, if you're yellow you're mellow, if you're brown stick around, but if you're black get back.' Academic theory distinguishes between biological racism, which typically uses skin colour as a marker of difference (as explicitly in the playground chant), and cultural racism, which focuses primarily on supposed differences of culture.[8] Either way, the variations among human beings are imagined to be fixed and final, something determined by nature and unchangeable. Another way of referring to the same distinction is to speak of north–south racism (Europe–Africa, also the northern–southern distinction in the United States) and West–East racism (Europe–Orient, or Christendom–Islam). These formulations have the advantage of being easily memorable and accessible. The latter draws attention to one of the most serious forms of cultural hostility in modern Europe – anti-Muslim racism. But of course so simple an idea can all too readily lead to unhelpful simplifications. One major objection to it, for example, is that it neglects forms of racism directed against people within Europe, for example anti-Irish racism and antisemitism.

5.6   Historical, literary and cultural studies over the last 20 years have shown that antisemitism has been a more significant feature of British society and a more complex phenomenon than many had previously thought.[9] Although never reaching the virulent levels seen in other countries, antisemitism inspired the Aliens Act of 1905, was socially acceptable in the inter-war years, and occasionally affected policy-making at high levels. Jews see themselves historically as an oppressed group. However, Jews in Britain today face comparatively little discrimination; the number of antisemitic incidents is small; the impact of antisemitic propaganda is marginal; and antisemitism has ceased to be socially acceptable. Moreover, countervailing forces have strengthened. These include the adoption of legislation making race hatred unlawful, growing awareness of the Holocaust, greater acceptance of pluralism and many decades of successful assimilation – the wisdom of which, however, many in the Jewish community now question. Yet not all Jews recognise the improvements. In 1995, 40 per cent of Jews believed that antisemitism was worse than it had been five years earlier, despite the fact that the evidence of declining antisemitism came from data collected by the body that formally monitors such issues on behalf of the community, the Community Security Trust. In view of antisemitism's murderous consequences in the past, Jewish sensitivity is entirely understandable. Since the Jewish community is long-established, is often seen as part of the white establishment, suffers no colour racism and is often held up as a model of successful assimilation, relations between it and other groups targeted by racism are rather complex. Nevertheless, in policies designed to deal with racism, antisemitism must be included – it remains an integral part of the ideological armoury of racist individuals and groups and has been called 'a light sleeper'. It would be perverse, however, not to acknowledge that, however deeply wounding and painful expressions of antisemitism are in Britain today, the racism experienced by Asian, black, Gypsy and Irish communities demands primary attention.

5.7 Anti-Irish racism has many of the features to be found in most racisms: a history of colonisation; the establishment of plantation agriculture to provide primary commodities for the metropolis; the use of indentured labour; migration to the metropolis to furnish manpower (which in the case of the Irish began more than 100 years before migrations from outside Europe); negative stereotypes about difference and inferiority; discrimination in the criminal justice system and in the provision of jobs and accommodation; and widespread experience of social exclusion. However, anti-Irish racism has been twinned in British history, at least since the mid-16th century, with anti-Catholicism, and frequently for this reason has not been adequately recognised. Until recently, it has largely been ignored by organisations promoting race equality, for since the Irish are perceived as white it is not readily imagined that they might be victims of racism rather than perpetrators. Supported tacitly by academics and other specialists, policy-makers have espoused and propagated 'the myth of homogeneity' – the false belief that the population of Britain consists essentially of one large majority or mainstream ('white people') and an array of various minorities. 'Non-white' and 'ethnic' in this mental picture are synonymous.

5.8 Anti-Muslim racism has been a feature of European culture at least since the Crusades, but it has taken different forms at different times. In modern Britain its manifestations include discrimination in recruitment and employment practices; high levels of attacks on mosques and on people wearing Muslim religious dress; widespread negative stereotypes in all sections of the press, including the broadsheets as well as the tabloids; bureaucratic obstruction or inertia in response to Muslim requests for greater cultural sensitivity in education and healthcare; objections and delays to planning permissions to build mosques; and non-recognition of Muslims by the law of the land, since discrimination on grounds of religion or belief is not unlawful. Furthermore, many or most anti-racist organisations and campaigns appear indifferent to the distinctive features of anti-Muslim racism and to distinctive Muslim concerns about cultural sensitivity. Silence about anti-Muslim racism was particularly striking in relation to the Stephen Lawrence Inquiry report. 'Where's the Muslim', asked a headline in the Muslim magazine *Q News*, 'in Macpherson's Black and White Britain?' The magazine welcomed the report but described it as a two-edged sword: 'As most of us are from visible minorities, we want racism to be firmly dealt with. But as victims of Islamophobia, we know that any attempts to tackle racism without also tackling Islamophobia will be futile ... Much as Muslims want to confront racism, they have become disillusioned with an anti-racism movement that refuses to combat Islamophobia and which, in many instances, is as oppressive as the establishment itself.' An editorial in *Muslim News* commented that 'the real litmus test of whether the lessons of the Lawrence tragedy have been learnt will be if ... a Muslim youngster dies in an Islamophobic attack and his murder is not treated in the same way'.[10]

5.9   The essential point to stress is that over the centuries all racisms have had – and continue to have – two separate but intertwining strands. One uses physical or biologically derived signs as a way of recognising difference – skin colour, hair, features, body type, and so on. The other uses cultural features, such as ways of life, customs, language, religion and dress. The two strands usually appear together, but they combine in distinct ways, with one or other prominent at different times and in different contexts. Jews were vilified in medieval times because they were believed to be the murderers of Christ, and because they practised a strict but alien code of dietary law and social behaviour. But they also came to be represented as physically different – with hooked nose, ringlets and a swarthy complexion. In the antisemitic iconography of

Nazi Germany they were consistently portrayed as subhuman. Similarly, Gypsies have been discriminated against because of both their
nomadic lifestyle and their 'non-Caucasian' physical appearance. Most
Muslims are recognised by physical features as well as by their culture
and religion, and the biological and cultural strands in anti-Muslim
racism are often impossible to disentangle. In the 19th century the Irish,
who had always been regarded by the British as less civilised, were
racialised – represented in the press and popular cartoons as ape-like, a
race apart.[11] This tradition continued in the mainstream press into the
20th century. As well as Jews, Gypsies and the Irish within Europe, the
targets of racism over the centuries have included peoples and civilisations beyond Europe's boundaries, including, of course, the colonised
peoples.

5.10 Race, as is now widely acknowledged, is a social and political construct,
not a biological or genetic fact. It cannot be used scientifically to
account for the wide range of differences among peoples. There is more
genetic variation within any one so-called race than there is between
'races'. In reality the human species shares a common gene pool, and a
particular genetic combination is to be found in any large population.
This does not mean that racism is a myth, for although it does not have
a scientific basis it does create social and political realities – those things
that men and women believe to be true, it is often said, are true in their
consequences; that is, they have real effects. Groups are characterised
exclusively in terms of what makes them different, and differences are
reduced to a few simple either/or distinctions – a fixed set of oppositions between 'us' and 'them', those who belong and those who do not.
Difference and inferiority become all but synonymous. Individuals are
then seen and judged in terms of the group differences, and 'we' have
the right to exclude 'them' from access to scarce material and cultural resources. Racism, in short, involves (a) stereotypes about difference and
inferiority and (b) the use of power to exclude, discriminate or subju-
gate. It has existed and continues to exist in all societies. Chinese and
Indian attitudes to outsiders, and African attitudes to Asians, and so on,
show its influence. Here, we concentrate on European racism.

5.11 From classical times Europe had a well-developed set of ideas and
images about its own internal 'others'. The further away from the
centres of 'civilisation' – Greece, Rome, the Mediterranean and the

western provinces – the more it was believed that Europe was peopled by strange and monstrous species: the 'wild' men and women of the forests of the north, the 'barbarians' who could not speak Greek or Latin, the wild hordes or armies of the night, rumours of whose advance struck terror into the hearts of ordinary folk. Distant places were believed to be inhabited by what classical writers like Herodotus and Pliny called the monstrous races – bizarre combinations of human and animal forms, at one and the same time wondrous and threatening. Anyone who did not belong within the known and familiar communities – fools, beggars, nomads, witches, the very poor, widows, the insane, even peasants from remote settlements – was vulnerable to negative stereotyping. It was over and against these negative images of its internal, monstrous 'other' that European civilisation first defined itself. The cosmology was much expanded and refined during the Middle Ages. The 'internal other' now included Jews (betrayers of Christ), Muslims (the infidel enemies of Christian Europe) and the Irish. When, from the 15th century onwards, Europe eventually began to encounter peoples much further away, as a result of voyages of exploration, this internal template of monstrous races was transferred and applied to the new peoples encountered. For example, such ideas and images were a consistent point of reference in the accounts provided by the explorers of both the 'old' world (Marco Polo and Sir John Mandeville) and the 'new' (Columbus, Vespucci and Sir Walter Raleigh).

5.12   Mandeville's account of the Holy Land and parts further east was widely influential. It conveyed as descriptive fact the most exotic and bizarre images of people, mainly featuring physical deformities of hybrid human/animal elements. The New World explorers were also struck by physical differences. But what most drew their attention was differences in custom, culture and conduct. They described the 'monstrous races' of America as distinguished by their animal-like behaviour, cannibalism, the practice of sodomy, nakedness, the apparent lack of familial, religious and governmental institutions and of any vestige of what the Europeans regarded as civilisation. Within a decade Europeans were debating before Charles V, king of Spain, whether the Amerindians were indeed human at all – did they have souls and, if so, could they justifiably be enslaved? The papal view that they did have souls and could not be enslaved contributed to the growth of the alternative slave trade from Africa. The belief that other peoples belonged to different species and that there had been several different creations lasted a long time. It continued to be held even by some later Enlightenment scholars, who tried to develop systematic ways of categorising the 'races of mankind'.

5.13   The image of the African was influenced less by direct knowledge of Africa and more by the wider context of the slave trade. It was based on contact with the sellers of slaves and with the slaves themselves. Though varied in their detail, these views entailed 'one universal assumption' – that African skin colour, hair texture and facial features were associated with both the African way of life and the status of slavery. Once this association was made, prejudices about class, race and culture blended with a long-standing iconography in European Christian thought, and imagery that counterpoised the goodness of white (the light) against the degradation and evil represented by black and darkness. In the face of the growing anti-slavery movement, racialised ideas of African slaves and slavery became more systematically codified. By the 18th century this general view of the physical differences and cultural inferiority of the African, and the negative social, cultural and cognitive meanings associated with black skin, represented the common-sense opinion of the great majority of the slave-owning planter class and their supporters, as also of scholars and thinkers such as Hume, Kant and Hegel.[12]

5.14   In the 18th century European trade enclaves began to develop on a more systematic colonising basis in the East, and territorial sovereignty was gradually established over substantial parts of India and South-East Asia. At both scholarly and popular levels, a set of stereotyped views of how and why the peoples of the Orient were different and inferior developed. These were based on a set of unbridgeable oppositions between East and West – 'and never the twain shall meet', as Kipling infamously put it. As in relation to Africa and the New World, physical characteristics played an important part in alerting Westerners to oriental difference. But there was a much stronger emphasis on cultural difference within the various types of anti-Asian racism – the East/West divide was delineated primarily by divergences in social customs, sexual mores, social etiquette, family culture, religion, language, dress, cuisine and the rituals of the life cycle. Scholars contrasted the development of modern civilisation in the West with the backward and tradition-dominated East, an opposition that persists today. Where African men were stigmatised as violent and sexually aggressive, and the women as openly promiscuous, oriental men were seen as feminine, wily and devious, and the women as seductive. But the two strands in racism – the biological and the cultural – continued to interweave. A character in E. M. Forster's *A Passage to India* captured this accurately when he imagined the English in India saying: 'Here is a native who has actually behaved like a gentleman: if it was not for his black skin we would almost allow him to join the club.'

5.15   The success of the anti-slavery movements in the 19th century represented something of a high point in efforts to contest extreme racist opinion. However, after the middle of the century a new and more virulent form of racism began to emerge in Europe, spearheaded by figures such as Carlyle and Gobineau. It claimed scientific respectability for the idea that human beings belonged to distinct and separate species. Each race was seen as a self-reproducing biological group whose characteristics were fixed for ever with its own distinctive 'blood' and 'stock'. A scientific basis was similarly claimed for the principle of arranging races into a hierarchy, and physical and anatomical differences were measured so that groups could be mapped on a neo-Darwinian evolutionary tree, from primitive to civilised. Biological reproduction within each group should be regulated, eugenicists maintained, so as to allow only the physically most superior to procreate, thereby improving the racial stock.

5.16   These theories were closely aligned with increased European nationalism and with rising competition between the European nation-states for a monopoly of markets, raw materials, colonial possessions and world supremacy. Scientific racism spanned the period of high imperialism and two world wars – racial sentiments were valuable supports for military mobilisation and essential ingredients of jingoism. This race-based nationalism interacted with a race-based imperialism. In Britain, for example, the Empire was frequently celebrated as the achievement of 'an imperial race'. The revival of rabid antisemitism, leading to the pogroms against Jews in central and eastern Europe and Hitler's Final Solution, was the product of this pan-European trend.

Interconnections of race and gender

5.17 Racism exacerbates, and is exacerbated by, sexism – they reinforce each other in vicious circles and spirals, and intertwine to the extent that it is impossible to disentangle them. Racism involves believing 'races' are essentially distinct from each other, as a matter of nature. Similarly, sexism involves seeing all differences between women and men as fixed in nature rather than primarily constructed by culture. In both racism and sexism the dominant group holds much the same self/other stereotypes. The self (the male, the white person) is seen as rational, reliable, consistent, mature, capable, strong. The other is perceived and treated as emotional, untrustworthy, feckless, childish, wayward – a threat if not kept under strict control.

5.18 Sexual rivalries in sexist and patriarchal contexts exacerbate fears and fantasies among white people about the supposed sexuality, promiscuity and fecundity of people believed to be racially different. Racist stereotypes are then strengthened, particularly those that hold black and Asian people to be closer to nature, unreason and instinct, lacking in integrity and trustworthiness, and needing to be kept under control. White men perceive Asian men as effeminate. Stand-offs between white male police officers and black youths on the street, or between white male teachers and black pupils in secondary schools, are imbued with a combination of sexual rivalry and racism.[13] In all communities such stereotypes and tensions increase the oppression of women and the policing of sexuality. In racist contexts, white people see black and Asian people not only as sexually threatening but also as exotic, mysterious and exciting. The exoticisation and sexualisation of 'non-Western' people is a frequent theme in modern advertising. It has the appearance of being non-racist, perhaps, since at least a black or Asian person is visible in a high-profile way. In fact, however, such imagery may reflect and reinforce both racism and sexism.

5.19 Struggles for race and gender equality can illuminate and strengthen each other. However, there are significant differences between the two, for in most contexts the experiences, interests and perceptions of women are different from those of men. This was true in colonial contexts and continues to be true today. The impact of empire on women, both colonisers and colonised, was different from its impact on men. If the likelihood of differential impacts is not recognised it can happen – notoriously – that race equality initiatives benefit mainly black and Asian men, and that gender equality initiatives benefit mainly white women. It follows that whenever a public body engages in policy appraisal it must separate ethnicity and gender, for the impact of a policy on women may well be different, either subtly or blatantly, from its impact on men. It follows that all community consultation – an essential component of policy appraisal – must be with women as well as with men. All too often, however, so-called consultation involves men only.

5.20   Similarly, all monitoring on grounds of ethnicity – of attainment in schools, for example – must always be undertaken by gender as well. It is matter of great regret in this latter connection that the massive data collection exercise undertaken in early 1999 by the Department for Education and Employment (DfEE) in connection with the new Ethnic Minority Achievement Grant (EMAG) made absolutely no reference at all to gender differentials. Statements about how many black and Asian local councillors there are nationally, or about how many black or Asian people are employed in the upper echelons of the civil service, are of limited value if they do not distinguish between women and men.

5.21   Asian and black women bring distinctive insights and experience to both feminism and anti-racism.[14] But they frequently find that they have to struggle not only against sexism and racism within society generally but also against racism within white feminism and sexism within anti-racist projects. They have to counter the view that all women are affected by sexism and gender inequality in much the same way, regardless of issues of race and ethnicity. At the same time, they have to counter forms of anti-racism which assume, explicitly or implicitly, that men are affected by racism more seriously than women are. They are also affected by processes within Asian and black communities that involve perpetuating traditional gender roles and traditional stereotypes relating to womanhood and manhood. Lastly, they are affected indirectly, but nonetheless powerfully, by the racism encountered by their partners, fathers, brothers and sons. Similarly, men in these communities are affected by the racism experienced by women.

Institutional racism

5.22   Cabinet papers from the period 1945–50 show that government ministers made strenuous efforts to prevent the migration of 'coloured'
people, for they and their senior civil servants were imbued with the
beliefs, outlined above, that such people are essentially different and inferior. If allowed in, they would mongrelise the national stock, it was
claimed, for white working-class women would find black men irre-
sistibly attractive. In 1953 a Home Office working party produced a document on *Coloured people seeking employment in the United Kingdom.*[15] The
title was misleading, for in fact the remit of the working party was 'to
examine the possibilities of *preventing* [emphasis added] any further increase in coloured people seeking employment in the United Kingdom'.

5.23   The working party had commissioned a survey on the conditions of the
'coloured' population and its suitability for work, relying largely upon
information provided confidentially by the police. Most black and
Asian people were said to live in housing conditions that were 'primitive, squalid and deplorable ... Many police reports say that coloured
people seem to live in these bad conditions from choice.' The men were
said to be 'physically unsuited for heavy manual work' and 'volatile and
potentially violent', and the women 'to be slow mentally'. Indians were
'mainly hardworking though unscrupulous'. Pessimistic conclusions
about future developments were drawn with regard to drugs, living off
immoral earnings, national assistance take-up and social disorder.

5.24   By the late 1990s racist views such as these were no longer explicit in
official policy documents. The Stephen Lawrence Inquiry report,
however, found such views implicit in the policies and procedures of
many public bodies, and in this respect gave wider currency to the
concept of institutional racism, already well-known to specialists. 'We
accept', said Sir William Macpherson and his team, 'that there are
dangers in allowing the phrase [institutional racism] to be used in order
to try to express some overall criticism of the police, or any other organisation, without addressing its meaning ... We must do our best to
express what we mean by those words, although we stress that we will
not produce a definition cast in stone, or a final answer to the question.'
They formulated a statement that they hoped would be acceptable both
to the police and to the police's critics, and would therefore enable

dialogue and partnership to take place. The statement has been widely quoted as if it were a strict definition, and in consequence there is a danger that it will be treated not in the way the panel hoped, as a stimulus for further reflection, but as a final answer, something indeed cast in stone. It referred to 'the collective failure of an organisation to provide an appropriate and professional service', and to 'unwitting prejudice, ignorance, thoughtlessness and racist stereotyping'.

5.25 Not all racist language and behaviour are 'unwitting', of course, as has been shown in this chapter; they can be entirely explicit and intentional. Nor is unwittingness an excuse. If officials do not predict the discriminatory consequences of established policies and routine practices, they are failing in elementary duties of professionalism and care. Not knowing the consequences of their actions is no defence, either legally or morally – though the fact that all their colleagues think and act the same on such and such a point may be a mitigating factor when the actions of any one individual are under scrutiny. Certainly, if institutional racism is to be tackled it is the occupational culture that must be addressed, as well as the actions and attitudes of individuals and the biases of prevailing practices and procedures. Macpherson himself made this point as follows:

> Unwitting racist language and behaviour can arise because of lack of understanding, ignorance or mistaken beliefs ... from well intentioned but patronising words or actions ... from unfamiliarity with the behaviour or cultural traditions of people ... from racist stereotyping of black people as potential criminals or troublemakers. Often this arises out of uncritical self-understanding born out of an inflexible police ethos of the 'traditional' way of doing things. Furthermore such attitudes can thrive in a tightly knit community, so that there can be a collective failure to detect and to outlaw this breed of racism.[16]

5.26   The report did not set out a detailed theoretical framework. Its acknowledgement of institutional racism, however, was a major step forward. For 30 years British officialdom had consistently denied that it had any meaning when applied to Britain. Now, however, it has become part of the conceptual vocabulary of substantial numbers of people. It recognises that, to thrive, racism does not require overtly racist individuals, and conceives of it rather as arising through social and cultural processes.[17] Culture regulates conduct. Behavioural norms are dictated by an occupational culture and are transmitted and sustained in informal and implicit ways through routines and everyday practices. The culture of an organisation is far more powerful than formal instruction in indicating how staff are expected to behave.

5.27   In this connection the report stressed the concept of professional discretion. In policing, as in many other areas of public service, an individual employee is often required to exercise his or her professional judgement on the spur of the moment. Frequently, or even typically, employees act not in accordance with explicit formal guidance, for formal guidance has not been issued, but in accordance with what they understand to be the norms of their profession. And it is from the occupational culture of their profession, not from specific or formal training, that they have developed an intuitive, tacit understanding of how to interpret their role in relationships and interactions with others. In the case of the police service, relationships are with employees, colleagues, managers, subordinates, witnesses, victims, suspects and members of the general public.

5.28   In all professional relationships a fundamental principle is that an official should show respect. But whether respect is indeed shown rests on the perceptions of members of the public, not on those of the official. Communication of respect depends on a range of non-verbal behaviours as well as, and often instead of, on words alone – body language, gesture, facial expression, physical closeness or distance, the spatial surroundings, and so on – and this adds to the complexity. Further increasing the complexity is the fact that every piece of communication (and miscommunication) is part of a history, and is interpreted in the light of past experience, and of conflicting memories. There is such a thing as organisational body language, it may be said, as well as personal body language.

5.29   It is relevant to consider the distinctions frequently made between:
- 'attitudes' (or 'hearts and minds', or, in more academic terms, 'narratives and discourse');
- behaviour, including not only discrimination and violence but also institutional inertia and various kinds of rudeness and insensitivity in personal encounters;
- structures and patterns of exclusion/inclusion and inequality.

5.30   Common sense suggests that there is a simple chain of cause and effect between these three: (a) prejudiced attitudes lead to (b) discriminatory behaviours and (c) exclusion and inequality are the result. This widely held view can be shown visually as in Figure 5.1.

Figure 5.1 **A common-sense view of cause and effect**

Prejudice ━━━━▶ Discrimination ━━━━▶ Exclusion and inequality

5.31   However, common sense is here a simplistic and insufficient guide. More complex relationships between cause and effect need to be considered, for each of the three main components of racism is both cause and consequence of each of the others, as briefly visualised in Figure 5.2.

Figure 5.2 **Towards a more complex view of cause and effect**

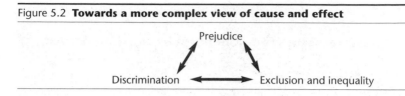

5.32 Consider, for example, the two-way arrow in Figure 5.2 between discrimination and prejudice. It expresses the idea that discriminatory behaviour can create, and not just be the consequence of, prejudiced ideas and beliefs. Police officers, like everybody else, are socialised into particular ways of behaving; only subsequently do they imbibe from their professional culture the range of negative stereotypes and beliefs which they use to explain what they do. Similar dynamics occur in many other occupational and professional settings, as well – for example, in the education system.[18]

5.33 Similarly, a set of power relationships, summarised in Figure 5.2 in the phrase 'exclusion and inequality', can generate the very beliefs, attitudes and behaviours that then act to reinforce them. It cannot be stressed too strongly that all racisms have in common that they arose and developed, and are nowadays maintained, in the context of unequal power relations. 'Slavery was not born of racism,' runs a well-known dictum. 'Rather, racism was the consequence of slavery.'[19] The unequal power relations between police officers and members of the public, teachers and pupils, health professionals and patients, employers and employees, and so on, are fertile ground for a wide range of prejudices and negative stereotypes, particularly at times of stress and conflict.

5.34 The term 'institutional racism', then, refers to a range of phenomena, not all of which may be present in any one situation, and not all of which are obvious. It focuses not only on the processes of an organisation but also on its output – the benefits or penalties which customers, clients, service users and members of the public get from it, and the extent to which, as a result, it causes more inequality or less in its surrounding environment. The various interacting components of institutional racism are summarised in Box 5.2 overleaf.

5.35 Racism awareness training was developed in the United States in the 1970s and was fairly widespread in Britain in the 1980s. It was then largely

Box 5.2 **Interacting components of institutional racism**

Indirect discrimination
Members of black and Asian communities do not receive their fair share of the benefits and resources available from an organisation, and do not receive a professional, responsive and high-quality service. They do, however, receive more than their fair share of penalties and disadvantages.

Employment practices
Members of black, Asian and Irish communities are not recruited to the extent that could reasonably be expected, or, having been recruited, receive less than their fair share of promotion, training and career development opportunities.

Occupational culture
Racist arguments, stereotypes and assumptions go unchallenged in everyday conversation and affect how the organisation treats members of the public. There is cynicism about so-called political correctness, and little or no emphasis on reducing inequalities and valuing diversity. Muslim, black, Asian and Irish staff feel that they do not really belong in the culture of the workplace, for their world-views, cultures and experiences of racism are not acknowledged.

Staffing structure
Senior management positions are disproportionately held by white people.

Lack of positive action
Few or no efforts have been made to recruit Asian and black people to senior positions or to involve them in major decision-making.

Management and leadership
The task of addressing institutional racism is not regarded as a high priority for leaders and managers, either personally or professionally, and is seldom or never considered in mainstream decision-making.

Professional expertise
Few members of an organisation's staff have skills in intercultural understanding and communication, and in handling and defusing situations of actual or potential conflict and tension.

Training
Few staff have received relevant high-quality training. They do not understand the concept of institutional racism, and do not know what they themselves can do to address it.

Consultation
Organisations do not listen to, let alone seek out, the views and perceptions of black and Asian people.

Lack of information
Organisations do not systematically examine the impact of their policies and practices in order to judge whether or not they have a negative impact on Asian and black communities.

---

dropped.[20] The Stephen Lawrence report brought it back into prominence, with seven separate recommendations concerning its use. The term 'awareness' is problematic, for the aims of training must embrace understanding, skills and practical action, not just awareness. This chapter has stressed that training should address the two main strands of racism – cultural and biological – and should take account of its roots in imperialism, anti-Muslim hostility and the slave trade, and in often strident opposition to immigration. It has stressed also that it should focus on the interacting components of institutional racism, as summarised in Box 5.2, and should therefore address the practical actions that participants need to take in their own personal spheres of responsibility. In later chapters we apply the points outlined in Box 5.2 to a range of institutional settings, and in Chapter 20 they form the basis of a discussion of organisational change.

Chapter 6

Reducing Inequalities

Rather than concentrate on minorities based on ethnicity or religion, should we not urge Government increasingly to counter the emergence of an underclass, whose deepening exclusion – known to every youth magistrate – is a matter of shame to the whole nation? Of course this underclass has black, Asian (mainly Muslim) and white minorities within it – but it is the pains, injustices and problems of the underclass as a whole which require fundamental action. It is here that the questions of racism, equalities etc. take on their sharpest edge.

A correspondent in Birmingham

6.1 If Britain is to develop as a successful community of communities, as argued in Chapter 4, there must be a reduction in inequalities, both between communities and within them. Differentials in income and life-chances between black, Asian and Irish people and the rest of the population must be tackled. Also, entirely independently of ethnicity, there must be progress to cut differentials in the general population between regions and neighbourhoods. The government that came into power in May 1997 has made several high-profile commitments on this subject, including introduction of the national minimum wage and the working families tax credit. Its own preferred term, to summarise its policy and programme as a whole, is 'tackling social exclusion'. The policy is rooted, it maintains, in a theory of the equal value of every individual.

6.2 The concept of combating social exclusion entered the public policy agenda in Britain in the early 1990s. It was derived from EU projects, themselves influenced by a theoretical framework developed by Jacques Delors and his political colleagues in France in the 1980s.[1] It received a powerful boost with the publication in 1995 of the Dahrendorf Report for the Liberal Democrats,[2] and became widely known when the current government set up the Social Exclusion Unit in the Cabinet Office in autumn 1997,[3] and with the establishment in due course of the Scottish Social Inclusion Strategy. The concept has a range of advantages or potential advantages as a means of obtaining a fresh take on perennial issues – intergenerational poverty, long-term unemployment, crime, multiple deprivation, socio-spatial segregation, political marginalisation and disempowerment, and homelessness. It also has a range of disadvantages when compared with, for example, concepts of equality and inequality, and of social justice and injustice. We shall briefly review here the advantages and disadvantages, and then consider the implications for issues of race equality and cultural diversity.

6.3 First, it is relevant to recall the overall picture. Between 1979 and 1997 the number of individuals in poverty – defined as below half the average income level (adjusted for family size, after housing costs) – rose from 5 million to 14 million, a quarter of the population. The number of working-age people on means-tested benefits fell by 10 per cent between 1995 and 1998, but the number on very low incomes, defined as below 40 per cent of average income, rose over that period from 4.3 million to 5 million before housing costs, and from 7.3 million to 8.4 million after housing costs.[4] It is important to stress that the definition is of relative poverty, therefore of inequality, not of absolute poverty. Unemployed households are the most likely to be poor, followed by lone-parent families. Elderly people constitute the greatest proportion of the poor. Another indicator of the extent of poverty is the number on income support, the means-tested minimum income. In February 1999, 3.8 million received income support. Including partners and dependants, the number in poverty by this measure was 6.7 million. Another 1.3 million were receiving job-seekers' allowance. Thus, in total, 8 million depended on the state's help. There is substantial evidence that African-Caribbean, Bangladeshi, Irish, Pakistani and refugee communities are disproportionately affected by poverty as thus defined.

6.4 In Chapter 5 we recalled the distinction sometimes made between institutional racism and street racism. The latter, involving verbal and physical assaults and criminal damage, is principally perpetrated by white people who are themselves economically disadvantaged and politically disempowered in relation to wider society.[5] The Metropolitan Police has declared that it wishes to make London 'a hostile environment for racists'.[6] There is a limit, however, to what a police service can do in this respect. For the environment in which street racism flourishes is economic inequality within the white population. Street racism, despite the best efforts of the police, will not be substantially reduced until there is less social exclusion within the white population. So for this reason too the government's social exclusion agenda is centrally relevant to the concerns of this report. One of our correspondents put the issue as follows:

> Most acutely disenfranchised is probably the poor white section, because it has been robbed of its root values, its identity and of hope. I use the word robbed advisedly ... Sustained policies and efforts to rebuild beliefs, values and institutions are needed, as well as much sustained funding. It is the juxtaposition of this poor white section with the increasingly ghettoised Pakistani concentrations that should pressure even our selfishly materialistic society into action. This, if not for justice's sake, then for enlightened self-interest!

6.5   Concepts of inclusion and exclusion, in the context of this report, have four main advantages. First, the notion of inclusion is already well known in a range of other fields and runs with the grain of common sense and intuition. There is general agreement that language should be inclusive, for example, as distinct from sexist. Newspapers seek to be inclusive of a wide range of interests. A skilled public speaker, through the use of illustrations, anecdotes and casual references, reckons to include the whole audience. The curriculum of schools should be inclusive of pupils' life experiences and will not otherwise engage their attention. Many people have childhood memories of the pleasures of being included in teams and friendship groups, and of the distress caused by being excluded, or anxiety about the possibility of being excluded.

6.6   Second, precisely because the concept appeals to common sense and deep intuitions, it can mobilise substantial political support from a wider segment of the political spectrum than is readily available for the same policies and measures if the terminology is of, for example, reducing inequalities or redistribution of resources. The concept of inclusion is itself, therefore, relatively inclusive. This is a particularly important consideration for a government that wishes to pioneer a third way between socialism and the market, and to retain the electoral support of middle England, middle Scotland and middle Wales. Third, concepts of inclusion and exclusion invite and justify holistic approaches to the issues under consideration – joined-up thinking conceptually, joined-up collaboration and co-ordination between different government departments, and joined-up funding and practical projects. Forcing different

departments and disciplines to work together appears to be one of the
Social Exclusion Unit's principal initial achievements.[7]

6.7   Fourth, the concept readily leads to monitoring and statistical analysis.
Is it indeed the case that certain communities – Asian, black, Chinese,
Irish, for example – are excluded from certain spheres of society? Do
they suffer more than others from unemployment, poor health, poor
educational qualifications, poor housing? Are they more likely to lose
their freedom by being imprisoned? Are they more included and less excluded than they were 10 years ago? How do certain cities or towns
compare with each other, in terms of the inclusion and participation of
their various communities? How do different spheres of society
compare? All such questions can be answered with reasonably precise
statistics, and the statistics themselves can be used to energise and focus
policy. In later chapters we cite many findings from recent research.

6.8   However, there are also four principal disadvantages in the concept of
inclusion/exclusion, as currently envisaged in the United Kingdom.[8]
First, it inherently focuses on marginality and boundaries, and therefore fails to address problems at the core. Its concern with
inside/outside may in consequence have no impact on the centre of
society, or on its overall structure and dynamics – no impact, for
example, on dismantling institutional racisms and transforming occupational and professional cultures. The policy thrust is typically to
enable excluded people to cross a boundary, or else to move a boundary
slightly so that people who formerly were outside are now inside. Certainly, it is frequently preferable for any one individual to be inside
rather than outside if this is the only choice. For example, it is better to
be on an electoral register than to have no vote at all, above the poverty
line rather than below and at liberty rather than in prison. But if a focus
on the margins and boundaries means that there is no pressure for
change at the centre, or in society's principal power relationships and
hierarchies, the benefits of inclusion may be slight.

6.9   As well as collecting statistics by ethnicity in relation to social exclusion,
therefore, it is essential to collect them in relation to inclusion. We refer
to this important point frequently in later chapters. For example, we
note that benchmarking information should be collected and analysed
in relation to involvement in law and justice, about judges, magistrates,

barristers, solicitors, court officers and probation officers, similar in detail and quality to the data already collected and published annually on the prison and police services (Chapter 9); education, about teachers, governors, lecturers, administrators, inspectors, academics and textbook writers (Chapter 11); the arts, about creators, performers, critics and administrators; the media, about reporters, editors, producers and columnists (Chapter 12); the health service, about senior managers and consultants (Chapter 13); and politics and government, about candidates, elected members, activists and staff, and members of public bodies (Chapter 16). In the context of this chapter it would be particularly relevant to monitor involvement at senior management levels of Asian and black professionals and activists in urban renewal and regeneration programmes, and indeed in all projects aiming to combat social exclusion. Such monitoring needs to be undertaken at national, regional and local levels: in relation to the Social Exclusion Unit; members and staff of the regional development agencies; and project managers and consultants in specific neighbourhoods. The results of such monitoring should be readily available on websites and in print.

6.10 Second, the problem is not primarily that some people are outside society, but that there are continua and gradations of inequality. The concern with boundaries is inherently, as mentioned above, a concern with either/or situations: you're in or you're out. But actually a sense of nuances and gradations is needed. There is a substantial body of research in the health field, for example, showing that inequality contributes to mortality and morbidity rates among the least affluent, not (above certain minimal material levels, for example the need for clean water) actual poverty.[9] In some fields of social policy the government has readily acknowledged that inequality rather than poverty is the issue, not least in its acceptance that poverty should be defined in relative terms. For example, its pledge to reduce child poverty is in effect a pledge to reduce inequality. Nevertheless, it is unfortunate that the concept of social exclusion displaces and de-emphasises concerns about inequality and relative poverty. In the context of this report, account must be taken of facts such as the following.

- Only one in 20 black and Asian people live in a district of low unemployment. This compares with one in five white people. More than half of African-Caribbean and African people live in districts with the highest rates of unemployment, as do more than a third of South Asian people.

- Sixty per cent of people of Bangladeshi or Pakistani origin live in poverty. In the case of Pakistanis, poverty is more severe in the West Midlands and northern England than in Glasgow, London and the South-East.
- Within specific communities income is not evenly distributed. For example, the average earnings of Chinese households are higher than the national average, but also the proportion of poor Chinese households is above the national average.
- Africans, Bangladeshis and Pakistanis are two and a half times more likely than white people to have no earner in the family, after taking into account the effects of age and family structure.
- Most of the Irish-born population are concentrated among the most deprived social classes and have lower than average rates of upward mobility. In terms of car ownership, an overall measure of standards of living, Irish-headed households were well below the national average in the 1991 Census. Irish men experience above-average unemployment rates and their health in middle age is consistently poorer than national averages.

6.11 A third disadvantage is that the concept of social inclusion apparently does not admit of cultural recognition and respect. 'Social exclusion is not simply about differential levels of income, health, educational achievement,' said someone in a presentation to us. 'An Asian business-man who is rated highly on objective measures of income and health can feel marginalised and excluded from full participation in society.' If the concept of cultural inclusion is not combined with that of social inclusion, the price of inclusion for many individuals will be too high. Black teenagers will not wish to be included in the education system if such inclusion inherently requires them to 'act white', that is, to deny their sense of themselves as black people, with distinctive personal and community experiences and perception of history. Nor will black and Asian people wish to be included in the police service if the occupational culture is inimical to their interests and perspectives, and does not recognise their distinctive experience and identity – for example, their first-hand knowledge of racism. Religious believers will not wish to be included in public administration and services if there is no recognition of, or even accommodation for, their religious identities and observance.

Box 6.1 **Combating social exclusion: why colour-blind and culture-blind approaches don't work**

Spatial distribution of poverty
Black, Asian and Irish people will not, of course, benefit from measures that target areas where they do not live – the North-East, for example, or former mining communities, or seaside towns, or housing estates on the outskirts of large cities.

Housing tenure
Renewal and regeneration programmes that target council estates are of little benefit to Pakistani people, since they live mainly in owner-occupied or privately rented accommodation.

Overt racism
Anti-poverty measures that fail to reduce levels of street racism are of limited value to people who cannot take advantage of new employment, training or recreational opportunities because of fear of violence or harassment. Generally, street racism has an extremely damaging effect on the lifestyle and quality of life of those who are attacked.

Institutional racism
The cultures and structures of regeneration projects and local partnerships must be rigorously reviewed if they are not to perpetuate some of the very inequalities they are seeking to address.

Cultural preferences
Different communities have different preferences and priorities in relation to matters such as household size, marriage, the upbringing of children, gender roles and the division of labour, personal independence, physical and emotional space, the maintenance of tradition and cultural identity, self-employment, and what constitutes a worthwhile job. Anti-poverty measures predicated on a narrow range of cultural norms will inevitably disadvantage certain communities.

Discrimination
There is discrimination in employment practices. Therefore increasing

the marketable skills of black, Irish and Asian people will not in itself ensure that they find jobs appropriate to their qualifications.

Labour market changes
Most Asian, black and Irish communities in Britain developed in response to specific labour market needs. Where industrial restructuring has reduced or even removed such needs, they have been disproportionately affected.

Education and skills levels
Different communities have different educational and vocational qualifications and therefore cannot take equal advantage of new employment opportunities.

Reasons for claiming benefits
There is great diversity within the low-income population overall – lone parents, pensioners, those afflicted by unemployment or long-term illness, and so on. In each community the pattern of reasons for claiming benefits is distinctive. Income maintenance policies and targeted initiatives (for example, the New Deal for Lone Parents) are therefore not equally appropriate for all communities.

Political influence
Asian, black and Irish organisations and communities are less likely than others to be present as equals in key deliberative and decision-making forums, less likely to have contacts and information, and less likely to have developed familiarity with formal committee procedures.

Source: See Note 13.

African-Caribbean and (in London) Bangladeshi people live in social housing and frequently are confined to poor-quality housing. The social housing system is designed to alleviate disadvantage, but in practice it can institutionalise disadvantage through lack of housing choice and educational opportunity, perhaps into several generations. The most certain way of breaking the cycle is to increase household income by reducing unemployment. (See Chapter 14.) Pakistani and (outside London) Bangladeshi people live principally in owner-occupied terraced housing. This is often of poorer quality than social housing. Problems are exacerbated by overcrowding – 24 per cent of all Pakistani and Bangladeshi households are overcrowded, compared with 2 per cent of all households.[15] If these living conditions are to be ameliorated, assistance is needed in improving existing homes or moving to larger, affordable, good-quality homes. There is potential in this respect for combining savings and loans schemes with self-build and self-development housing schemes.[16]

6.15   The victims of racist attacks live mainly in poorer neighbourhoods. Also, as mentioned above, the perpetrators of racist attacks live mainly in such neighbourhoods, though not necessarily the same ones. Yet although street racism is clearly connected with issues of housing and public places, it is seldom addressed in considerations of housing policy. 'Confusion continues to reign on the ground', someone wrote to us, 'about whether landlords, local authorities or the police are best equipped to act against perpetrators. Arrangements for reporting incidents continue to be ad hoc ... Support for victims continues to be minimal. Self-help is still the order of the day.' Priorities for action must include robust, quality-controlled reporting systems; timely and effective action against perpetrators, including civil action by landlords as well as prosecutions by the police; material and moral support for those who are attacked; and widespread sharing of successful experience.[17]

6.16   Experience in other European countries as well as Britain shows that three main approaches to combating social exclusion must be combined: (a) improving physical infrastructure; (b) using welfare-based measures; and (c) pursuing labour market strategies to improve underlying economic potential and performance.[18] A single-pronged attack will not work. Within this overall framework key tasks include securing long-term financial and political support for projects in specific local areas; achieving and sustaining inter-agency working; empowering local communities; capacity building; avoiding activist burn-out; addressing institutional racism in white-dominated organisations and bodies; cultural and religious sensitivity; redirecting main programmes and resources; providing access to credit; striking the right balance between area-based projects and conurbation-level measures; striking the right balance between central government initiative and local responsibility; and engaging the private sector. Box 6.2 on the next page provides a case study of common problems.

6.17   If measures are not to be colour-blind, the following points must be borne in mind.

- In regeneration partnerships wider involvement of Asian, black and Irish people is essential. Genuine participation should be a condition for funding. Out of 555 successful bids in the first three rounds of the Single Regeneration Budget, only four were led by Asian or black organisations.

- There is a place for flagship projects that explicitly celebrate diversity and oppose racism. The thinking behind such a project in Tower Hamlets, east London, has been outlined as follows: 'Every city, every region, every nation is a blend of cultures, peoples and communities and that blend will become more intense as time goes on. We can face this with fear or open-mindedness. We can retreat into our shell or acknowledge it with a sure touch. We can communicate or be in conflict. The time is right for an era of inclusiveness, tolerance and empathy, because by mixing we can unleash untold energies.'[19]

- There must be a long-term commitment to empowering local communities.

- Throughout all stages of the process there must be an information base that takes due account of diversity.

6.18   It is frequently invaluable if different cultural groups and communities have to co-operate and negotiate with each other on a common task. For example, two tenants' organisations on an estate in east London had to form an alliance with each other to create a Tenant Management Co-operative to gain access to much-needed capital funds. One organisation was wholly white and the other wholly Bangladeshi. It was reported that 'racial harassment on the estate is now virtually non-existent and although the two communities may not exactly be in each other's arms all the time, they cohabit the same space in a friendly and peaceful fashion'.[20]

6.19   The notion of 'cohabiting the same space in a friendly and peaceful fashion' is taken up in many other chapters in this report – see, for example, the discussion of national identity in Chapter 2, disputes and

Box 6.2 **Toxteth, Liverpool: a case history**

The Commission has made two visits to Liverpool. During the first, one Commissioner met a group of local black activists working on youth sports and arts projects in Toxteth. Subsequently, a plan was developed to convert one of the local Toxteth churches into a 'Social Centre of Excellence': a concept designed to provide training and personal development as well as facilities for sports and performance arts. During both visits the Commissioners were convinced of the need for such a centre. The area in which it is to be based is demonstrably exceptionally deprived, and unemployment is high and morale low. The Commissioners were also impressed by the enthusiasm and personal commitment of the local black activists working on the project.

However, during the second visit, after a gap of a year, three Commissioners visited the proposed centre and were dismayed by the state of dilapidation into which the church building had fallen. Although there had been expressions of support from national organisations such as English Heritage and the Department of Culture, Media and Sport as well as Liverpool Council, it had been vandalised and looted of much fine carved stone, and the roof and exterior had deteriorated.

At the meeting there was a sense of considerable frustration with Liverpool Council. The activists believe the Council's expressions of support to be insincere given its refusal to provide the initial funding that would enable the building to be secured and weather-proofed. A representative of the Council insisted later that for their part they welcome the project and are waiting for fully developed funding applications and a properly constructed management plan.

The Commission is left with the impression that much of the frustration and disillusion stems from the fact that the black activists believe the Council is not seriously committed to improvements in a 'black' area of the city and would rather spend money in deprived 'white' areas. Representatives of the Council insist this is not the case. However, it is hard for black residents to feel that they have any influence in local government decisions when virtually all senior officers in the Council are white. By the end of 1999 there was reasonable diversity among Council employees overall – black and Asian representation had risen from 0.7 per cent in 1981 to 4.5 per cent. However, these staff were overwhelmingly working in lower grades. Even more significantly, out of 99 elected councillors all but two in mid-2000 were white.

The Commission has no final view about the rights and wrongs of this particular example, except to point out that where there is inadequate representation of different cultural groups at senior decision-making levels it is hardly surprising that suspicion arises if local government officers appear to be obstructive when limited local resources are being allocated. We urge local parties to take this into account when they are designing selection processes for local candidates. We also urge chief executives in local government to treat as a priority the promotion of Asian and black people to senior decision-making positions.

controversies in Chapter 4, deliberative democracy in Chapter 16 and the open/closed distinction in Chapter 17. The legal and ethical framework for such negotiations is provided in part by human rights standards. These are the subject of the next chapter.

Chapter 7

Building a Pluralistic Human Rights Culture

> *Human rights, being universal by definition, are not the privileges of citizens but the entitlement of all individuals ... It is not a shared passport which motivates individuals to respect human rights and the corresponding responsibilities but a shared humanity.*
>
> From a submission to the Commission

7.1 In the previous chapters we have argued that Britain should develop as a community of communities in which there are shared values but also recognition of differences (Chapter 4), with vigorous action taken against both overt and institutional racism (Chapter 5). We have stressed that shared values are maintained through dialogue and negotiation, that they are relevant to both public and private life, and that equal citizenship means an equal sense of belonging as well as equal rights. Such a sense of belonging cannot rely on formal procedures alone. It also depends on how individuals are treated daily by the other people they meet, and on a culture of mutual respect. It is also the case that negotiations over contested issues – for example, the content of the national curriculum, sensitivity to cultural diversity in the health service, the wearing of religious clothing at work, equality for women in the home – cannot take place in an ethical vacuum. They require ground rules that provide a minimum guarantee of protection for individuals and a framework for handling conflicts of interest.

7.2 Our argument in this chapter is that such ground rules are provided in part by international human rights standards, for example those enshrined in the European Convention on Human Rights (ECHR) and the UN Convention on the Rights of the Child. These standards provide a framework within which to negotiate conflicts between the rights of individuals, and between the rights of an individual and those of society. For example, they balance the right to free speech and the right to freedom from incitement to racial hatred, or the right to individual privacy and the rights of the community to prevent crime through the use of CCTV surveillance. Human rights are thus rarely absolute but can be limited in order to protect the rights of others. Crucially, restrictions on rights are legitimate only if such restrictions are proportionate to the harm they are trying to prevent. Human rights standards provide a framework for negotiation and minimum guarantees to prevent the worst abuses. The protection of all women from domestic violence illustrates the value of a non-negotiable bottom line.

7.3   Human beings are not only individuals but also culturally embedded. Therefore human rights should not be equated solely with the rights of individuals defined in narrowly individualistic and abstract terms, for it is essential to recognise the rights that people have as members of religious, cultural and linguistic groups. Examples include the right to worship, to bear religious insignia, to express cultural identity, and to transmit language and culture to the next generation. Human rights need therefore to be interpreted and applied in a culturally sensitive manner and may sometimes entail different responses in different individual cases. When rights conflict with each other, disputes can be resolved only within the context of a democratically determined and widely shared conception of collective wellbeing. This cannot be based on human rights alone. The logic of multiculturalism qualifies and informs the logic of human rights, just as the logic of human rights qualifies the logic of multiculturalism. Human rights lay down the moral minimum, but they cannot define the whole of public morality.

7.4   International human rights provide not only ground rules in law for protecting minimum standards and negotiating conflicts of interest, however, but also an ethical code on how individuals should minimally treat their fellow citizens – for example, respecting their privacy, their freedom of religion or belief, or their right to a fair hearing. They are therefore central to achieving an equal sense of belonging. The Home Secretary has said of the Human Rights Act that it is 'an ethical language we can all recognise and sign up to, a ... language which doesn't belong to any particular group or creed but to all of us. One that is based on principles of common humanity.'[1] The incorporation of the ECHR into UK domestic law through the Human Rights Act, and the government's stated intention that the Act should lead to a wider respect for human rights and the responsibilities they entail, is the specific historical context for the discussions in this chapter.[2]

7.5   The term 'human rights' has come to be widely used only since the second world war, when experiences of state terror and ethnic cleansing strengthened determination to develop a body of international law to prevent their recurrence.[3] The Universal Declaration of Human Rights, adopted by the UN in 1948, has subsequently been complemented by a range of international and regional instruments, including the ECHR, covering not only civil and political rights (such as the right to a fair trial and to free elections) but also social, economic and cultural rights such as the right to adequate housing and to work. Of great importance in the context of this report, they also include obligations on governments to promote equal representation in public life and to create the conditions in which diverse cultures can flourish. Significantly, the standards cover behaviour not only in the public sphere but also in the private home. For example, the UN Convention on the Rights of the Child – the most widely ratified of all UN conventions – provides protection for children against parental abuse, and requires parents to give children greater autonomy as they grow up. Box 7.1 lists some of the key rights in international human rights agreements.

7.6   Specific conventions, for example the Council of Europe Framework Convention on National Minorities and the UN Convention on the Elimination of all forms of Racial Discrimination (CERD), provide detailed protection for the rights of minorities. CERD was ratified by the UK in 1969. It requires the government to implement a comprehensive policy to eliminate racial discrimination within and beyond government and public authorities, and to ensure that the full range of civil, political, social and economic rights can be enjoyed by everyone, unhindered by discrimination.[4] The UK is required to report to the UN regularly on its compliance, but has so far refused to sign up to the procedure for consideration of individual complaints. In recent years the UN has been critical of the UK's record on deaths in custody, immigration and asylum policy, discrimination in employment, its reluctance to introduce legislation on religious discrimination, and exclusions from school. Box 7.2 on page 94 lists the key equality provisions in CERD, and also in several other international agreements.[5]

Box 7.1 **Social, economic and cultural rights**

International human rights agreements include the right to:

- work;
- fair wages and equal pay for work of equal value;
- safe and healthy working conditions;
- rest, leisure, and paid holidays;
- join a trade union of choice;
- social security;
- an adequate standard of living;
- the highest attainable standard of health;
- take part in cultural life;
- freedom from discrimination in the enjoyment of these rights.

Limitations and strengths

7.7 The limitations of the international covenants and conventions lie partly in their drafting but primarily in the weakness of their enforcement mechanisms. Individuals can rarely challenge their treatment by governments; rather, governments simply report at regular intervals on their compliance with the agreements. The reporting procedures are not well known and governments may feel little need to give the reports priority. In some cases, as with CERD, a complaints procedure for individuals does exist, but governments may deny their citizens access to it. In Chapter 19, when making recommendations about legislation and enforcement, we propose that the UK government permit individuals access to the UN complaints system. The ECHR has been an exception to the general rule, for individuals have been able to take cases to the European Court of Human Rights in Strasbourg to challenge UK legislation, policy and practice, and they have done so successfully on more than 50 occasions. Under the Human Rights Act, the Convention rights are enforceable in the UK's domestic courts for the first time.

7.8 The strengths of the international standards lie first in the breadth and depth of the commitments that successive governments have made with regard not only to civil and political rights but also to social, economic and cultural rights. People in the UK often think of human rights as limited to the civil and political arena – and the decision to make only

Box 7.2 **Equality provisions in international human rights agreements binding on the UK**

- Each national government shall take effective measures to review governmental, national and local policies, and to amend, rescind or nullify any laws and regulations which have the effect of increasing or perpetuating racial discrimination wherever it exists.
- National governments shall ensure equal treatment in the administration of justice; equal political rights, in particular the rights to participate in elections … [and] to take part in the government as well as in the conduct of public affairs at any level and to have equal access to public service; equal economic, social and cultural rights, in particular the rights to work, to free choice of employment and protection against unemployment, to housing, medical care, social services, education and training.
- National governments shall adopt immediate and effective measures in teaching, education, culture and information to combat prejudices which lead to racial discrimination.

UN Convention on the Elimination of All Forms of Racial Discrimination,
1966

- National governments shall take measures to create favourable conditions to enable persons belonging to minorities to … develop their culture, language, religion, traditions and customs, except where specific practices are in violation of national law and contrary to international standards.
- National policies and programmes shall be planned and implemented with due regard for the legitimate interests of persons belonging to minorities.

UN Declaration on the Rights of Persons Belonging to National or Ethnic,
Religious and Linguistic Minorities, 1992

- Persons belonging to minorities have the right to enjoy their own culture, to profess and practise their own religion and to use their own language in private and public, freely and without interference or any form of discrimination.

Vienna Declaration, World Conference on Human Rights, 1993

- The law shall prohibit any discrimination and guarantee to all persons equal and effective protection against discrimination on any ground such as race, colour, sex, language, religion, political or other opinion, national or social origin, property, birth or other status.

   International Covenant on Civil and Political Rights, 1966

---

the ECHR enforceable in the UK may intensify this misconception. The commitments that successive UK governments have made on socio-economic and cultural rights are not well known. Nor are the reports that the government periodically makes. The government should give greater priority to fulfilling its obligations under international human rights agreements, and to making the public aware of the commitments it has made. Its regular reports to the international bodies that supervise these agreements should be widely distributed and published on government websites, and should be drawn to the attention of Parliament.

7.9   The standards also have strength because the commitments are legally binding between states, albeit difficult to enforce. Further, their legitimacy derives from having been negotiated and agreed by people of diverse cultures, faiths and ideologies. They go beyond codes of ethics agreed within only one nation or religion – they are the language of global citizenship. Also, their strength is in providing a balanced package of rights and responsibilities – not absolute rights (with rare exceptions, such as freedom from torture) but rights tempered by respect for the rights of others. The core idea in human rights is balance, not assertion. It is in this sense that international human rights standards provide a framework for negotiating difference, for balancing the rights of one individual (for example, to liberty) against that of another (for example, to freedom from harm). Lastly, the strength of the international standards lies in their being living instruments. Their interpretation can legitimately evolve over time, as public attitudes change; the fundamental principles are non-negotiable, but their interpretation provides scope for negotiation between and within communities.

Human Rights Act 1998

7.10 The Human Rights Act is the most significant human rights legislation ever enacted in the UK, and should lead to a new culture of respect for human rights that will prove of particular value for race equality. Formally, the Act requires public authorities throughout the UK to conduct themselves in a way that is compatible with the rights and freedoms enshrined in the European Convention, and provides remedies for individuals through the courts if they fail to do so. 'Public authority' is widely defined to include private and voluntary organisations that fulfil public functions, and thus covers companies like Group 4, which runs private prisons, and charities that run residential homes.

7.11 If primary legislation is enacted which breaches the Convention rights, the courts can make a declaration of incompatibility, requiring the government and Parliament to consider amending it. Secondary legislation, such as immigration rules, can be struck down by the courts, as can legislation enacted by the Scottish Parliament and the Northern Ireland Assembly, under separate provisions in the devolution legislation. The first purpose of the Act is thus to impose responsibilities on government and public authorities and to provide stronger rights for individuals.

7.12 The rights and freedoms protected by the Act are broad and significant, ranging from freedom from degrading treatment to rights to marry and found a family. They are listed in Box 7.3. They impose positive obligations on the government, for instance to protect the right to life. The Act requires that all the rights and freedoms in the Convention shall be enjoyed without discrimination on any grounds including race, colour, language, religion, national or social origin, or association with a national minority.

7.13 Some of the rights protected by the Convention may be of particular benefit to black and Asian communities in Britain. The right to family life, for example, may enable family members to challenge their separation by immigration controls or deportation. Freedom from degrading treatment may provide an additional ground on which to challenge discriminatory treatment or harassment, and freedom of religion may help individuals whose employers restrict their ability to observe their reli-

---

Box 7.3 **Human Rights Act 1998**

The rights enshrined in the European Convention on Human Rights, which became domestic law when the Human Rights Act came into force on 2 October 2000, are to:

- life;
- freedom from torture, inhuman or degrading treatment or punishment;
- freedom from compulsory labour;
- freedom from arbitrary arrest or detention;
- a fair hearing;
- respect for private and family life;
- freedom of thought, conscience and religion;
- freedom of expression, including freedom of the press;
- freedom of association;
- marry and found a family;
- peaceful enjoyment of possessions;
- education;
- participate in free elections for Parliament;
- freedom from discrimination in the enjoyment of these rights.

---

gion at work. Freedom of expression may assist individuals who are not allowed to wear clothing at work or school which is important to them for religious or cultural reasons. The Act also protects people from racial or religious discrimination in the enjoyment of these rights. It may therefore be possible to challenge the denial of state funding for schools of a particular religious tradition, or disproportionate use by the police of stop-and-search powers.

7.14 As stressed above, the Convention rights and freedoms protected by the Act are not absolute. In certain circumstances, provided for in the Convention, public authorities will be able to argue that it was necessary to restrict certain rights in order to protect those of others, and judges and sheriffs will need to decide if this is the case. Crucially, the infringement will have to be proportionate to the harm that the authority is trying to prevent.

A pluralistic human rights culture

7.15   Beyond the letter of the law, however, the Act should have a wider importance, because the long-term goal is that it should affect attitudes and
behaviour, both within public authorities and among the public at large.
The Home Secretary has said of the Act: 'A rights and responsibilities
culture really is our goal. It's what we want the whole public service in
this country to move towards.' He went on to explain that by culture he
meant: 'the habits of mind, the intellectual reflexes and the professional
sensibilities which are historically ingrained and typical of the behaviour
of a particular group of people ... the unconscious understandings and

assumptions concerning politics, social life and justice'.[6] The Act will change thinking within the public sector because it will require staff constantly to ask themselves whether what they are doing is compatible with the Convention. In the words of a government minister:

> Every public authority will know that its behaviour, its structures, its conclusions and its executive actions will be subject to this culture. It is exactly the same as what necessarily occurred following the introduction of, for example, race relations and equal opportunities legislation. Every significant body, public or private, thereafter had to ask itself with great seriousness and concern, 'Have we equipped ourselves to meet our legal obligations?' That caused a ... transformation in certain areas of human rights. The same is likely to follow when this Bill becomes law.[7]

7.16   The Home Secretary has said that 'in time, the language of the Convention will be the language in which many of the key debates are settled. The language you need to speak to win an argument. And that's a real culture change.' We point out at length in Chapter 15 that there are policies and statements emanating from the Home Office, particularly in relation to asylum, which do not currently reflect human rights principles. Nor have the vital service departments, those responsible for health and education, for instance, been eager to embrace the Human Rights Act or the new culture it heralds. Nevertheless, the stated intention behind the Act is significant.

7.17   There is a direct connection between the introduction of a human rights culture within public authorities and the parallel drive to eradicate institutional racism.[8] Initiatives to implement the Lawrence Inquiry recommendations are designed to ensure that individuals are treated equally by the police and other public services regardless of their ethnic background. This is undoubtedly a human rights objective, even though it is not couched in human rights language. Both the Act and the Lawrence Report action plan aim to restore confidence in the key institutions of the state. The Home Secretary has said:

> The Act points to an ethical bottom line for public authorities. It's what you call a fairness guarantee for the citizen ... This new bottom line, the fairness guarantee, should help build greater public confidence in our public authorities. And that's a vital part of our strategy for getting more public participation. For building the society we want to see.

7.18 The strategy is not mere aspiration. The price of the fairness guarantee for government is that people can sue public authorities if their rights are infringed. The cultural shift that the Act is expected to foster is, however, not limited to public authorities. It is intended to change the behaviour of individuals and groups towards each other, and to promote shared understandings and values:

> Consider the nature of modern British society. It's a society enriched by different cultures and different faiths. It needs a formal shared understanding of what is fundamentally right and fundamentally wrong if it is to work together in unity and confidence ... The Human Rights Act provides that formal shared understanding.[9]

7.19 Equality and diversity principles will thus necessarily be a central part of human rights culture. This is not to say that equality and diversity should be seen only as human rights issues, but it does mean that human rights have much to offer in the realisation of these principles. Their relevance to equality is not questioned in other parts of the world, but the argument is less familiar in the UK. Despite the fact that the motivation to develop international human rights standards after the second world war arose from the ill-treatment of minorities, race equality issues in the UK have not usually been addressed within a human rights framework. A consequence has been that race discrimination has been seen as a comparatively minor problem rather than as a challenge for society as a whole.

7.20 Recognition that race is a human rights issue is now, however, on the agenda in the UK. The 1990 Trust, for example, set up a human rights programme in 1997 whose co-ordinator became a member of the Home Office Task Force on implementation of the Human Rights Act. The Commission for Racial Equality (CRE) said in its annual report for 1998 that it 'expects to develop closer working relationships with the other statutory and non-governmental organisations to promote racial equality within a human rights culture, and to explore possible legal challenges for a breach of Convention rights which includes discrimination on racial grounds'. The chairman of the CRE said in 1999: 'The Human Rights Act will offer further scope to make Britain a fair and just society and the CRE can foresee many vital areas where the promotion of racial equality and the promotion of human rights will overlap.'[10]

7.21 Acknowledging the significance of a human rights perspective does not mean that specific measures needed to address race discrimination and promote equality should lose their focus. At both a philosophical and a political level, the perspective recognises that black and Asian people share mutual rights and responsibilities with the rest of society which have been endorsed by the international community and which successive governments have promised to uphold. In practical terms, it means that those addressing race equality issues should work closely with those involved in other human rights issues, including those of gender and disability, with each ensuring that they reflect both race equality and wider human rights principles in their work. There is a useful analogy here with the environmental field. At one time people working on, say, wildlife protection, global warming or industrial pollution operated entirely separately. Now they see themselves as part of a single environmental movement. Far from losing their individual focus, they have been strengthened by working together, recognising what unites them as well as their own distinctness.

7.22 We consider the practical implications of a human rights perspective in Chapter 19. The Human Rights Act is unlikely to achieve its potential, either to protect rights or to foster a human rights culture, if there is no statutory body to drive progress forward. Just as the government in the 1970s saw the need to establish the CRE and the Equal Opportunities Commission (EOC) in order to enforce the anti-discrimination legislation – and just as the Disability Rights Commission has now been set up to do the same in relation to disability – so there must be an effective body to promote and enforce human rights. Northern Ireland has a Human Rights Commission, and at the time of writing the Scottish Executive is considering proposals for such a body with all-party support. We list the functions of a Human Rights Commission in Chapter 19. In line with the CRE's own view, we recommend that a Human Rights Commission and the CRE work closely together.

7.23 The Act is relevant to the introduction of citizenship education into the national curriculum in England from 2002, and for parallel initiatives in Scotland, Northern Ireland and Wales. Human rights principles must be taught and experienced, and pupils and students must appreciate the importance of equality and respect for difference. In Chapter 11 we recommend that an understanding of human rights principles, and their relevance to everyday life, be part of the citizenship curriculum taught in every school, for children of all ages.

7.24 Within public authorities, preparations are taking place to ensure that policies and procedures comply with the Human Rights Act. At the same time, as recalled above, steps are being taken to tackle institutional racism following the Lawrence Inquiry report. In Whitehall, and within the devolved administrations, officials are implementing the statutory requirement to carry out a human rights audit of proposed legislation and policy to ensure that they comply with Convention rights. At the same time, separate officials conduct voluntary procedures for assessing compliance with discrimination law and the impact of the measures on particular communities. The Welsh Executive, in which responsibility for human rights and equality issues is centred within the same unit, is the exception. Neither set of initiatives and procedures should lose its focus; but both address discrimination, and organisations should at least recognise the overlap and ensure that each complements the other. In Chapter 19 we recommend that officials in central, devolved and local administrations consider the relationship between their human rights and equality procedures, and assess whether the established structures are sufficient for them to complement each other effectively.

7.25 The overlap between human rights and equality must also be apparent in Parliament, not least in the role of the new Joint Select Committee on Human Rights at Westminster. It could play a vital role in calling the government to account on race equality issues, and the importance of a focus on race equality should not be lost within its wider human rights focus. The Committee should also ensure that it monitors the UK's compliance with international human rights standards, particularly those outlined in Box 7.2.

7.26 We have stressed the value of the European Convention as a living instrument, the interpretation of which is open to negotiation. It follows that it must not be interpreted in the courts only by white, male judges whose lives bring them into minimal contact with the cultural values they are required to consider. The Human Rights Act thus necessitates reform of the appointment of judges, magistrates and tribunal members, by the establishment of an independent body for that purpose – a point to which we return in Chapter 10. An independent judicial appointments system must be established to ensure transparency and equality of opportunity in the appointments system.

Chapter 8

Summary of the Vision

8.1 'Stories', writes Ben Okri, 'are the secret reservoir of values: change the stories individuals and nations live by and tell themselves and you change the individuals and nations.' He continues: 'Nations and peoples are largely the stories they feed themselves. If they tell themselves stories that are lies, they will suffer the future consequences of those lies. If they tell themselves stories that face their own truths, they will free their histories for future flowerings.'[1]

8.2 In the opening chapters of this report we have argued that some of the dominant stories in Britain need to be changed – stories about the past, the present and the future. With regard to the past we have recalled a range of myths: that the history of Britain goes back many centuries; that it has always been a basically peaceful and lawful place, untroubled by internal dissent or strife; that there is a single true version of the national story; that until recently Britain was culturally homogeneous; that the sea round Britain aptly symbolises its independence and isolation from the rest of the world. These myths feed the imaginations of millions of people. As long as they are dominant in British recollections of the past the country cannot be a just and inclusive society in the present, for from these myths large numbers of people and many experiences are omitted.

8.3 If nations and peoples tell themselves stories that face their own truths, says Okri, they 'will free their histories for future flowerings'. We have recalled in previous chapters the truth that Britain is a recent creation, and that colonialism and empire were integral to its making. Therefore virtually all current citizens of the United Kingdom are part of a single story – though their ancestors, of course, engaged with it in a range of different ways. A second truth is that there are several versions of the single story, several truths. There are different versions in England, Ireland, Scotland and Wales; and according to class, gender, region and religion; and depending on whether British greatness was experienced

at the centre or from the periphery. A third truth is that these islands
have always been a place marked by unceasing dissent and argument. In
1948 the *Windrush* did not dock in a culturally homogeneous country or
in a foreign country. The journey was an internal one, from one part of
a single system to another. Nor did the *Windrush* dock in a country that
was politically and ideologically united. It came to a land riven by
debates and disputes that pre-dated its arrival by many decades. Similarly, Africans, Bangladeshis, Indians, Irish, Pakistanis and many others
came to a country that was already culturally and ideologically diverse,
with a range of different self-understandings and stories.

8.4   Stories are true or false not only about the past but also about the
present. We have argued that the picture of Britain as a 95/5 society –
where 95 per cent are said to belong to one vast majority since they are
white and 5 per cent to various minorities since they are not – is not an
accurate one. Homogeneity in the so-called majority is a myth, not a
true story. So is the idea that so-called minorities have more in common
with each other than they do with people in the so-called majority.
Britain is more appropriately pictured, we have said, as a community of
communities. It is about a community of communities that true stories
need to be told.

8.5   The fundamental need, both practical and theoretical, is to treat people

equally and to treat them with regard and respect for difference; to treasure the rights and freedoms of individuals and to cherish belonging,
cohesion and solidarity. Neither equality nor respect for difference is a
sufficient value on its own. The two must be held together, mutually
challenging and supportive. Similarly, neither liberty nor solidarity is
sufficient on its own. They too must be held together, qualifying and
challenging each other, yet also mutually informing and enriching.

8.6   To say that Britain should be pictured as a community of communities
is to refer, first and foremost, to relationships between its three constituent parts, England, Scotland and Wales. But it is also to maintain
that each of the constituent parts is in itself a community of communities, not a monolithic whole. Each contains many identities and affiliations; each is in a process of development, with its own internal
tensions, arguments and contradictions; each overlaps with several
others. Everyone belongs to more than one community; every community influences and has an impact on, and in turn is influenced by,
others. None is self-sufficient, entire of itself. 'Britain' is the name of the
space they all share. Some have far more weight and power than others,
but no group, no community, owns Britain. It is no one's sole posses-
sion.

8.7   If Britain is to be a successful community of communities it will need to
combine the values of equality and diversity, liberty and solidarity. In
the language of political theory, the ideals and principles of both liberalism and communitarianism have to be pursued and realised. Achieving this synergy will certainly not be easy, not least because of the legacy
and current realities of racism – or, more accurately, racisms. We have
distinguished between institutional racism, street racism and violent
racism; colour racism and cultural racism; the racism of beliefs and attitudes and the racism of behaviour and structures. We have recalled also
that racisms have been an integral strand of the weft and warp of British
history. They have to be addressed directly, explicitly, vigorously. A
softly, softly approach will not work. Good cannot be done here by
stealth.

8.8   The three tasks of (a) reimagining Britain's past story and present identity, (b) balancing equality and difference, liberty and cohesion, and (c)
confronting and eliminating racisms need to go hand in hand, we have

Box 8.1 **The way ahead: seven fundamental principles**

Three central concepts: equality, diversity and cohesion
People must be treated equally but also with regard to real differences of experience, background and perception, and to the need for common values and social cohesion. These concepts need to be consistently and constantly central in government policy- and decision-making. High-profile statements of ideals by senior politicians and civil servants are important. They remain mere paper commitments or rhetoric, however, if they are not fully incorporated into all mainstream agendas and programmes.

Demonstrable change at all levels
The concepts of equality and diversity must be driven through the government machinery at national and regional levels. Responsibility for making them real must be devolved to the local levels at which theory becomes practice, where real change does or does not take place. Verbal and financial commitments from the government are essential. But the test of real change is what happens on the ground.

Addressing racisms
There must be a sustained and fearless attack on all forms of racial injustice. Such injustice threatens the very basis of citizenship. Street racism and violent racism must be dealt with, but so also must institutional racism. Among other things, the latter is a major factor in the environment in which street racism and violent racism go unchecked. Attention must be paid to racism's different targets: anti-black racism, anti-Muslim racism, anti-Gypsy racism, anti-Irish racism, antisemitism, and so on.

Tackling disadvantage
Street racism and violent racism arise and flourish in situations of economic disadvantage and inequality. This is one major reason why social exclusion must be addressed; another is the fact that it disproportionately affects some (though not all) black, Asian and Irish communities.

Colour-blind approaches do not work
There must be a commitment to go beyond the racism- and culture-blind strategies of social inclusion currently under way. Programmes such as the New Deal for Communities are essential. They must, however, have an explicit focus on race equality and cultural diversity.

Empowering and enfranchising
There must be vigorous commitment to recognising cultural diversity through, for example, the systematic representation of black, Asian and Irish communities on public bodies.

A pluralistic culture of human rights
Human rights standards provide both an ethical and a legal basis for the changes required, but must include respect for cultural difference.

---

said, with two further tasks. These are to do respectively with (d) reducing material inequalities and (e) building a human rights culture. In the next part of our report we consider what these five tasks mean in specific areas of policy – policing (Chapter 9), criminal justice (10), education (11), culture (12), health (13), employment (14) and asylum and immigration (15).

8.9   In Part 3 of the report we consider the implications for the authorities in Cardiff, Holyrood and Westminster, and for organisations and institutions in cities, towns, boroughs and shires. Several recurring principles or threads run through both Parts 2 and 3. They are derived from the previous five chapters, and are summarised in Box 8.1.

Part 2

Issues and Institutions

Chapter 9

Police and Policing

In a recent speech to chief constables and chairs of police authorities the Home Secretary described the police service as 'a can-do organisation'. The description is an accurate one. Chief constables are oriented towards doing rather than thinking carefully about and clarifying the ideas that inform their policies and actions. His description, however, could have the unintended consequence of sustaining a very undesirable situation in which the police do much but understand little about the ideas underpinning their actions.

From a presentation to the Commission

Please note

The criminal justice system in Scotland is different from that in England and Wales. The discussions and recommendations in this chapter are not equally relevant to both.

9.1 Shortly after the publication of the Lawrence Inquiry report the chief constable of a police force in northern England approached a local law centre and asked for a meeting to discuss the report's implications. The law centre declined to meet without first consulting its contacts and clients, and circulated a questionnaire. About a quarter of the respondents were adamant that the meeting would serve no useful purpose from the centre's point of view and would merely be a public relations exercise for the police. The comments of some of these, and also some comments from those who were in favour of the meeting, are quoted in Box 9.1.

9.2 For black, Irish and Asian communities, contacts with the police are a microcosm of their contact with the state, for the police have more impact on the everyday lives of communities than any other single agency. They can engender a sense of security and justice, but also much distrust and anger – racism is 'rampant in the police force', 'intrinsic endemic racism ... is pervasive both in the police force and in the city as

---

Box 9.1 **Voices: shall we meet the police?**

No

It is obvious that individual racism and institutional racism are rampant in the police force. Why should anyone give him the chance to say he has been 'consulting' the community while doing nothing about the racism? It would just turn out to be another token effort that would take years and in the meantime the racists continue to hide under his tunic tails. Tell him to get stuffed.

If the chief constable is met … he would use this as a publicity stunt and this would encourage the status quo to perpetuate their rhetoric. Until he acknowledges the intrinsic endemic racism which is pervasive both in the police force and in the city as a whole, the situation will not change.

I don't think meeting with him will have any effect on the operational police at street level and will benefit police public relations more than anyone else.

There is racism in the police force, both institutionalised and overt. We are aware of this because we and our friends/family have experienced it. There can be no way forward until this is admitted, only then can we work towards solving the problem.

Yes

If we don't meet, how are they to know the true feelings of the community and the rest of the country, how we truly feel towards the police and how they treat us and go about solving the crimes against us by whites and ourselves against each other?

To try to influence the police to have a more positive attitude to black people and to take strong action against members of the police force who are racist.

Because anything that will stop the same thing happening as Stephen (and other less publicised incidents) can only do good and pave the way for eventual desegregation and better relations with the police.

Source: Responses to a law centre survey, 1999.

---

a whole', 'racism in the police force [is] both institutionalised and overt', 'tell him to get stuffed'. The anger is about both heavy policing and police neglect – criminalisation and harassment on the one hand and inadequate attention to racist crime and behaviour on the other. Such feelings show that Britain is a long way from being a community of communities, at ease with its own diversity and with confidence in public authorities. Moreover, evidence of great variation in policing practice and priorities – between forces, between town and country, and between the two legal systems of Britain[1] – indicates that there is still much progress to be made. Nonetheless, many of the law centre's contacts wanted to believe that they would be heard. Their feelings of cautious optimism show that ways forward are possible. In this chapter we discuss both the optimism and the anger. In general terms, most of our observations are relevant throughout Britain. In certain specific respects, however, they are not relevant in Scotland. For example, the Police and Criminal Evidence Act does not apply in Scotland, nor does the ministerial priority relating to policing, which the Home Secretary established following the Lawrence Inquiry report.

9.3   'Most agencies have ignored the matter', a racial equality council (REC) wrote to us, 'and seem to think that the recommendations and government strategy are actually for someone else.' The matter in question was the Stephen Lawrence Inquiry report. We had written to all RECs in England, Scotland and Wales, enquiring about responses to the report in their area. Several said that their police service had responded positively, at least at senior levels, and at least in comparison with other sections of the criminal justice system and with other public bodies. The following quotations from correspondents show the perceptions expressed:

> In the northern half of Scotland the impact of the Inquiry has been profound on the police and procurator fiscal service. The change has been deep-going with real impact at street level.
>
> [The report] has had a great effect on the police in this area and on the local authority. We shall be pushing for a checklist with timetabled implementation from the local authority. At least the concept of institutional racism is being discussed, which has been very useful.
>
> There is no doubt that the police have moved forward in respect of policy, but it is as yet too early to say what effect this will have on practice, for example stop and search. In respect of reporting racist incidents ... there has been an improvement in reporting and understanding. The problem is now switching to the Crown Prosecution Service and the courts – who still have some difficulty in dealing with racist incidents effectively.

9.4   Positive remarks such as these about the police and the impact of the
      Lawrence Inquiry report need to be balanced by different views from
      other sources. On the first anniversary of the report's publication the
      chair of the National Black Police Association said of the police service:
      'They haven't even got to the first hurdle. Though there's a lot of frenetic
      activity now, there's a hope within forces that this issue will go away.
      There's no evidence that things have improved for black officers.'[2] At
      the same time, a specialist in police training estimated on the basis of re-
      search undertaken in eight forces that only a third of police officers were
      'switched on and willing to learn'. Another third were said to be 'con-
      fused and resentful but not actively resistant'. The remaining third were
      described as being 'very resistant to change. They don't think there is a
      problem, they can't see the connection between race equality and
      service delivery.'[3]

9.5   Those who are hostile to the report have received much encouragement
      from certain sections of the media. For example, a recurring allegation
      has been that as a consequence of the report police officers make less
      use of their stop-and-search powers 'in case it upsets anyone'.[4] One jour-
      nalist wrote: 'Sir William's silly charge of "institutional racism" has put
      a torpedo through the effectiveness of urban forces across the country.
      An epidemic of muggings is Sir William's main legacy to the rule of
      law.'[5] Another: 'A significant number of the 550,000 people violently at-
      tacked last year [1999] can fairly blame Sir William and his stupid
      report. The man has blood on his hands.'[6] A banner headline referred to
      the 'Rise of the New McCarthyism', the subheading stating that 'an in-
      sidious new witchhunt threatens Britain'. The ensuing article described
      'wild claims' about institutional racism in the Lawrence report and
      averred that because of such claims 'crime is rising, recruitment tum-
      bling'. It added: 'Our other public bodies, especially education, local
      government and social work, have seen standards collapse through the
      fixation with absolute equality.'[7]

9.6   Media comment such as this affects the climate of opinion within the
      police service, as well as the assumptions and expectations of people
      with whom the service comes into contact.[8] Language of the kind
      quoted ('silly', 'stupid', 'wild', 'witchhunt', 'fixation') makes it all the
      more difficult for senior officers who are 'switched on and willing to
      learn' to have an impact on their colleagues. Also, equally seriously,

such remarks increase the difficulty of fulfilling the ministerial priority for all police forces in England and Wales 'to increase trust and confidence in policing among minority ethnic communities'.[9] Performance is to be measured by four indicators: the numbers of recorded racist incidents; the use and effects of stop-and-search procedures; levels of recruitment, retention and progression of Asian and black staff; and surveys of public satisfaction. There is no statutory mechanism for Scottish ministers to set priorities or performance indicators for the Scottish Police Service. However, the Scottish Executive accepted the basic principle that a national priority should be set and advised chief constables accordingly.

9.7   The impact of the priority and performance measures remains to be seen. Meanwhile, it is relevant to note that substantial inertia in the police service in relation to issues of race and diversity has been documented in recent years by Her Majesty's Inspectorate of Constabulary (HMIC). A January 2000 report on the Metropolitan Police, for example, found that there was still a lack of empathy among officers for the plight of victims of racist crime: 'Response and investigation officers and their supervisors must understand that to be a victim because of skin colour multiplies the emotional and psychological hurt well beyond that of the physical pain.'[10] Further, the report indicated that the force's recent emphasis on tackling racist crime was seen by many officers as providing preferential treatment to black and Asian people, and was widely resented.

9.8   An earlier report published in autumn 1999 was similarly critical of inertia in the Metropolitan Police.[11] It noted 'insecurity, low morale and cynicism' among officers in relation to the Lawrence report, and stated that some officers 'take a narrow and negative view of the public they deal with', and that many feel 'a deep sense of personal injustice [in relation to the Lawrence report], perceiving their integrity systematically and relentlessly being called into question'. It claimed there was no evidence of a rise in public confidence in the police; rather, the police had lost confidence in themselves. It criticised senior management for not providing clearer leadership and guidance, and for sending mixed messages about whether the use of stop-and-search powers was a permissible performance indicator. Officially, the use of these powers as a performance indicator was abandoned in 1997, but in practice, officers felt that they were still under an obligation to pursue quantity rather than quality. There was also substantial criticism of unnecessary aggression, sarcasm and lack of basic politeness among some officers, particularly younger ones, and of their poor interpersonal skills in handling provocation and defusing confrontation. The use of stop-and-search as a means of social control – for example, to break up groups of young people in a public place – was reinforcing hostility to the police in the African-Caribbean community and leading to growing disaffection in some of London's Asian communities.

9.9   The report did not, however, gloss over the difficulties of policing in areas of high unemployment and social exclusion. Economic inequality and disadvantage are not, of course, of the police's own making. Yet 'the frustration that feeds on restricted opportunity can place ethnic minority people in real or potential conflict with police. The police service is the visible symbol of a society that fails to deliver benefits but is perceived as being quick to deliver injustice.'[12] In these circumstances there are often displays of macho bravado among young members of the public. They take pleasure in baiting or provoking police officers – 'winding them up'. Dealing with deliberate provocation and defusing confrontation are certainly not easy. Problems in this respect are exacerbated not only by the anger of some members of the public but also by a long legacy of bad professional practice on the part of the police themselves. Less confrontational styles cannot be established overnight, even if individual officers would like them to be. A sergeant put the issues as follows:[13]

> We're reaping the rewards of a lot of our colleagues' behaviour in the past. I've seen behaviour in the past that was absolutely atrocious. In relative terms, the police service is now more professional, more ethical etc. than ever – anywhere. Some officers really deserve commendations. But others don't – and it only takes a couple of people to destroy all the good work. But the culture of the police is changing fast. I've seen PCs now take colleagues to one side and say: 'Listen, pal, you're out of order. If you want to behave that way it's not all right, because it's causing me problems.'

9.10   'The police service is more professional, more ethical than ever,' asserts the officer just quoted. 'The culture is changing fast.' If indeed a cultural shift is taking place it needs to be codified in statements of principle and aspiration. One of the first and most influential such statements was

Box 9.2 **Policing in a multi-ethnic society: principles and intentions**

1 Dignity and respect
All members of the community with whom we come into contact will be treated with dignity and respect. They will not be subject to discourtesy, bullying, victimisation or unfair discrimination.

2 Equality and difference
In our organisational structures and decision-making processes, and in our ways of working, communicating and managing, we intend to treat all people equally and fairly. We intend also to recognise and respect differences, and therefore to behave with due sensitivity to diversity of experience, perspective, culture and religion.

3 Dealing with racism
We accord racist incidents a high priority, for they are attacks not only on individuals but also on communities. We encourage the reporting of racist incidents; provide information, support and assistance for victims, and for their families and communities; and do our best to take firm action against perpetrators.

4 Other public bodies
We work in partnership with other public bodies whenever appropriate and seek dialogue with them. We welcome challenge, criticism and suggestions and in our turn offer challenge, criticism and suggestions to others.

5 Consultation and openness
We seek opportunities to learn the views of the communities we serve, and their perceptions of our work; for example, in relation to our behaviour when investigating crime and providing support for victims, and in crime prevention.

6 Recruitment, retention and promotion
We wish all communities to see the police service as providing a worthwhile career, and wish our own staffing structure, at all levels of seniority, to contain people from the full range of communities we serve. We make special efforts to attract applications from black and

Asian people, and to provide black and Asian officers with full professional support. We work closely with the National Black Police Association.

7 Complaints
We deal swiftly with complaints against our staff and keep complainants informed of the action we take.

8 Institutional review
We are aware that there is institutional racism in the police service. We keep our structures and procedures under critical review, in order to identify and remove all features of our organisation which unfairly discriminate against people because of their race, colour, religion or culture.

9 Evaluation
We use a range of quantitative and qualitative methods to evaluate our progress in fulfilling the principles and intentions in this declaration. We publish much of the information we gather, in order that others may form judgements about our performance.

10 Training
We provide training and professional development measures for all staff in order that they may increase their knowledge, understanding and practical expertise in relation to the topics and issues in this declaration of principles and intentions.

Source: Compiled from similar declarations drafted in Leicestershire, Nottinghamshire, Reading and Rotterdam.

drawn up by 120 experts from 17 countries at a conference in Rotterdam in 1996.[14] In Britain, more recently, valuable statements have been drafted in the wake of the Lawrence report in, among other places, Leicestershire, Nottinghamshire and Reading.[15] In Box 9.2 we outline a composite statement drawn from these sources. *We recommend that a formal declaration about principles of good policing practice in a multi-ethnic society be drafted and agreed in every town or city.*

9.11   Such declarations of principles have many advantages, including:

- providing a focus for police training and a means of relating training to operational practice;
- establishing criteria for use in recruitment and promotion procedures, and in supervision and appraisal;
- providing the basis for practical action plans, targets and indicators, and for assessing progress;
- requiring collaboration and partnership between the police service in any particular locality and other public agencies, and the non-governmental sector;
- if they are drafted after a process of consultation, officers have a feeling of identification with them;
- providing a reference point for campaigning and complaining, and for watchdog-style activities by non-government organisations.

Stop-and-search

9.12   When police services seek to fulfil the aspirations summarised in Box 9.2 they come under the microscope in two particularly sensitive ways. If they fail in either or both of these ways the credibility of all other measures is vastly diminished, and the chances of complying with the ministerial priority on trust and confidence are negligible. The service must deal with racist crime with the utmost vigour, but it must also use its discretionary powers to stop and search with the utmost professionalism and the minimum of damage to wider relationships and public trust.[16] We consider the first of these two points in the next chapter, since it involves the whole criminal justice system, not just the police. With regard to the second, we summarise some key points in Box 9.3, and introduce them with the conclusions of a research study published in 1999:

> Stop and search as used at present is a massive and blunt instrument, costly to maintain and grossly inaccurate in its impact. Its effects are counterproductive, its yield largely of minor crimes and its necessity unproven.[17]

Box 9.3 **Stop-and-search: some key issues in England and Wales**

- There is widespread agreement that the powers of the police under Section 1 of the Police and Criminal Evidence Act 1984 (PACE) are required for the prevention and detection of crime. Crime that might otherwise go undetected is identified and intelligence that feeds into tackling crime more generally is collected. There are both direct and indirect impacts on crime prevention. The essential question is not whether to use the powers but how, and to what specific purposes.

- By their nature, searches are conducted in public places and are frequently observed by bystanders. This can increase a sense of injustice and humiliation in the person being searched and lead to an altercation, which in its turn leads to arrest. It can also encourage a confrontational style in officers, in reality or in the perception of others.

- There is pressure from sections of the media, claiming to speak for respectable middle Britain, for the powers to be used more widely, targeting black people in particular. A journalist wholly unsympathetic to this pressure has commented: 'One paper has run the same story three times, that police are so scared of being labelled racist that they are using stop and search powers less against black people ... It was claimed the result was a rocketing in street crime such as muggings. The subtext is not that subtle; if you take your foot off their windpipe for just a second, they jump up and mug you.'[18]

- Irish people as well as African-Caribbean people are disproportionately affected.[19]

- There is a real disproportion in its use, certainly, and this must definitely be addressed. But so must more general and fundamental questions about manner of use and specific purpose.

9.13   With regard to how stop-and-search is used, the Lawrence Inquiry made several constructive and potentially far-reaching recommendations. The Home Office accepted all these in principle and set up a range of action research projects to investigate exactly what would be involved in practice in implementing them. These concerned how officers make the decision to carry out a stop-and-search; the qualities of officers who are successful, in terms of both arrest rates and not using a counterproductive approach; profiles of street populations, that is, of those 'available' to be stopped, to assess the extent of disproportionate use; the contribution of stop-and-search to the detection and prevention of crime; and an evaluation of measures already under way to improve its management and operation. The Home Secretary has said that the outcomes of these studies will be considered at a seminar.[20] This is not sufficient. *We recommend that the results of action research on improving the use of stop-and-search be widely published and considered, and that advice be sought on what further research is needed.* In line with the Lawrence Inquiry conclusions and those of other recent studies, *we further recommend that:*

- *Records categorised by ethnicity be made of all stops under any legislative provision, not just PACE, and that these include 'voluntary' stops.*
- *Police authorities undertake publicity campaigns to ensure that the public knows the purpose and correct procedure of stops and is aware of its own rights.*
- *Evaluation of the use of stop-and-search powers take the arrest and conviction rate into account and focus on the more serious types of crime. Crimes of a minor nature, and especially those that result from an altercation arising from the stop itself, should be weighted lightly.*[21]
- *Local commanders systematically examine how the powers are currently used. They should deploy officers on the street to this end, and resulting improvements should be linked to specific objectives within the local crime strategy.*[22]

Training

9.14   In 1971/72 the House of Commons Select Committee on Race Relations and Immigration recommended that all police officers should have 'a wider knowledge of immigrants, their culture, background, history and nature'. Training programmes were accordingly instituted. But the training was based, observed inspectors caustically in due course, 'on

the premise that imparting information about immigrant [sic] groups would in itself improve relations with them. It did little to change underlying attitudes and behaviour. At best, it ensured that prejudiced people were better informed. At worst, it reinforced their stereotypes.'[23] Similar criticisms could probably be made of training in other parts of the criminal justice system. In Chapter 20 we itemise the essential features of effective race equality training for all professions. These are taken largely from publications about police training.[24]

9.15   *We recommend that relevant authorities specify the competencies and core skills required in relation to race and diversity for all practitioners in the criminal justice system, and ensure that these are systematically considered in initial and continuing training, in recruitment and promotion systems, and in all staff appraisals.* Further, in view of HMIC findings that training has not been adequately evaluated, *we recommend that the Home Office commission evaluation and action research with regard to the effectiveness of specialist training on issues of race and diversity for practitioners in the criminal justice system, and disseminate the findings to all interested parties and individuals.* In view of the importance of strong leadership in the police service, *we recommend that all candidates for appointment to Association of Chief Police Officers (ACPO) and Association of Chief Police Officers*

Scotland (ACPOS) status posts should have taken an accredited training module on issues of race equality and cultural diversity.

Deaths in custody

9.16   In 1998/99 there were 65 deaths in police custody in England and Wales. This compared with 53 the previous year and 46 in 1995/96.[25] Six of the 65 deaths were of African or African-Caribbean people, which is about four times more than might be statistically expected. Research into the causes of all deaths in police custody in the period 1990–97 showed that for black people a higher proportion than for others occurred when actions by the police themselves might have been a contributory factor. Conversely, a higher proportion of white people's deaths were attributed to an underlying medical condition.[26] In 1999/2000 there was an overall reduction in deaths in custody, partly because of changes in police procedures.[27]

9.17   For the grieving families of those who have died, distress is greatly aggravated by current procedures. There is often no sense of moral support from official sources. 'In essence,' recalls the sister of a man who died, 'you're not the victim, the victim is dead.'[28] There is also the fact that the investigating officer's evidence is not disclosed; the trauma of the inquest, which may be the first time that the bereaved family hears, along with the press and members of the public, the harrowing details of how their loved one died; the fact that it is the coroner alone who decides who should be called as witnesses and what the range of questions should be; and the lack of funds for legal representation (though the police and any other concerned public bodies do have ready access to professional representation). Later, there is distress occasioned by delays in the body being released for burial. *We recommend that:*

- *every death be independently investigated when it occurs;*
- *in cases where it is considered that the actions of officers and other staff may have contributed to the death, they be suspended from duty pending and during investigation;*
- *legal aid be available for families during investigations;*
- *there be full disclosure to families of all evidence and documents;*
- *information be provided about organisations that provide specialist counselling, advice and moral support to bereaved families.*

Accountability and discipline

9.18 Over the years there have been several well-publicised breakdowns in police discipline and failures to investigate racist crime with sufficient vigour. Substantial damages have been paid to members of the public in respect of wrongful arrest or assaults by police or prison officers. However, it has been a matter of serious concern that the officers responsible have frequently not been identified, or else have left their employment before disciplinary action could be taken against them.

9.19 In Chapter 10 we discuss complaints procedures in the wider criminal justice system. This is as applicable to the police as to other services. It is particularly essential in the case of the police that the complaints system should be independent and open. Proposals for independent investigation have been made at least since 1929, on the grounds that, in the words of the Lawrence Inquiry report, 'investigation of police officers by their own or another police service is widely regarded as unjust, and does not inspire public confidence'. An independent body would help to root out malpractice in the police. It would also increase public confidence and would be in the best interests of the police themselves. Models of independent investigation have been proposed and a formal consultation exercise has been initiated.[29] *We recommend that an independent body to investigate complaints against the police be established.*

9.20 The Stephen Lawrence Inquiry report and HMIC reports have acted as valuable stimuli to review and change. It is essential that the momentum should be maintained, and that there should be public scrutiny of annual reports on progress in implementing the recommendations in the Lawrence Inquiry report. For it is not sufficient merely for the Home Secretary to issue a report, important though such reports are. There must be thorough examination. 'I am more than a little sceptical', someone wrote to us, 'about the update in regard to recommendations 32–37 regarding the Crown Prosecution Service. Are the CPS really consulting victims as suggested by the Lawrence Inquiry? Is there really no plea bargaining in any racist crimes?' Further, in view of the evidence we have cited that there has been substantial inertia and resistance in relation to the report, *we recommend that, in association with HMIC, the Home Office commission independent audit and examination of progress in implementing the recommendations in the Stephen Lawrence Inquiry report, and ensure that its findings are widely disseminated.* In addition, *we recommend that HMIC's Winning the Race inspection be continued annually, with the involvement of local communities in each force area.*

9.21   'Every constable on the beat', it has been said, 'acts as a shop window for the police service.'[30] In its turn the police service acts as a shop window for the wider criminal justice system. It is not only the window and the store that need attention, but also the chain to which the store belongs. There is a need for more 'practical cop things to do' – a phrase used in presentations about the Metropolitan Police's Project Athena, concerned with implementing recommendations about policing in the Lawrence Inquiry report.[31] The practicalities need to be supported by substantial and expert training at all levels, and by vigorous leadership and supervision, as urged in the HMIC reports.[32] This is not in question. But 'practical cop things' will have limited success, we have argued in this chapter, unless they take place within a substantial overhaul of the total system. There is a limit to what the police themselves can do. In the next chapter we look at the wider system of which the police service is only one part.

Chapter 10

The Wider Criminal Justice System

Notoriously, more young black men in the USA now go to prison than go to college, and in some cities the percentage of young black men under criminal justice system control has reached levels of 40 per cent. What has happened is not that crime has disappeared from the streets of America but that a whole generation of young black men has become inured to the experience of imprisonment. Although UK penal policy is not (yet?) as draconian as that of the US, and although the figures of black male imprisonment are not so massive, some of the same trends are apparent here. There has been the same tendency to substitute penal policy for social policy.

From a presentation to the Commission

> **Please note**
>
> The criminal justice system in Scotland is different from that in England and Wales. The discussions and recommendations in this chapter are not equally relevant to both.

10.1   On the evening of 13 February 1998 Imran Khan, a Glasgow schoolboy aged 15, was stabbed during a fight in Midlothian Drive, Pollockshaws. He died eight days later in hospital. His friend Burhan Ilyas was also stabbed. Two white youths, twins aged 16, were charged with the murder of Imran and the wounding of Burhan. They pleaded self-defence. One was detained for seven years for attempted murder, the other for two years for assault. The fight was between rival gangs of Asian and white youths and it was known that the two white youths had been expelled from school (the school also attended by Imran and Burhan) for racist harassment. They were heard to say immediately after the fight that they had 'stabbed the Pakis'.

10.2   'Who is to blame for this laddie's death?' asked the defence counsel at the trial. His answer was that inadequate care at the hospital was to blame. There was 'not a scrap of evidence', he said, to show that racial prejudice had played a part on either side. In his address to the jury the judge said: 'There has been no evidence to suggest that this was a racist attack. This case again demonstrates the dangers inherent in young men going about with knives.' This produced a headline in the *Daily Record* the following day to the effect that 'Knives are not Racist'. Another newspaper argued as follows:

> We should guard very carefully against rushing too readily to accept the view that racial tension played no part in this tragedy. 'No racism here' is a glib and complacent slogan but it is little more than that. Furthermore, it is a perception which is not shared on the streets of Glasgow's south-side. There is a widespread belief there, notwithstanding the judge and counsels' comments, that racist motives played a significant part in this affair. Furthermore, there is a clear and unmistakable belief that racial tension is no myth but a very definite fact of life ... Pretending that racism does not exist is not an option.[1]

10.3   Throughout Britain there is a perception in Asian, black and Irish communities that the criminal justice system is not just. As discussed in the previous chapter, the complaints start with policing. But the case of Imran Khan reveals resistance to recognising and dealing with racism within the wider system, not just in the police. This comprises failures to investigate complaints; structures dominated by white people from a small social pool; a lack of interest in widening the recruitment base; and a reluctance to become more accountable. Not least, distrust of the system is founded on the growing body of data (albeit almost exclusively collected in England and Wales) which shows that black and Irish people are differentially treated at all stages of the criminal justice process, and that they are disproportionately likely to be imprisoned.

10.4   In all three countries there have been initiatives to implement the recommendations of the Stephen Lawrence Inquiry report. The Scottish Executive's action plan is broadly similar to the Home Secretary's,[2] and a statement by Scotland's Lord Advocate has its parallels in England and Wales:

> The starting point for all of us in response to the Macpherson report should be one of diligent self-assessment ... If there is discrimination, it is our duty as prosecutors to identify the difficulty and remedy the situation so far as possible. Failure by us to do so ignores the fact that Scottish society is multi-cultural and that Scotland is the richer because of the varied ethnic origins of her citizens ... The challenge of the Lawrence Inquiry is one for all of us at a personal and professional level.[3]

10.5   However, there are significant differences between the legal system in Scotland and that in England and Wales. Beyond a certain point, therefore, generalisations that are true of one system are often not true of the other. Many significant Acts of Parliament and legal measures do not apply in both systems; the hierarchies of courts and law officers differ; constabularies and police forces are organised differently; statistics are collected and published separately. There is no equivalent in Scotland of the annual Home Office report *Statistics on Race and the Criminal Justice System*, published under Section 95 of the Criminal Justice Act 1991. Publications that claim to be about the whole of Britain, the *British Crime Survey*, for example, are in fact only about England and Wales. The separateness of the two systems was highlighted by the fact that the European Convention on Human Rights was introduced a year earlier in Scotland than in England and Wales. Reflecting substantial differences of approach, each system has its own distinctive legal terminology: the accused/the defendant; advocate/barrister; avizandum/reserved judgement; sheriff officer/bailiff; interdict/injunction. We seek to take account of such differences in this chapter, but are aware that there is less published data for Scotland than for England and Wales.

Racist attacks and incidents

10.6   The number of racist incidents reported to and recorded by the police in England and Wales rose from 13,878 in 1997/98 to 23,049 in 1998/99, an increase of 66 per cent.[4] It is impossible to estimate how much of the increase is due to greater confidence on the part of Asian and black people that their reports will be taken seriously, how much to improvements in police recording procedures and how much to a real increase in attacks. It is, however, known that far more incidents take place than are reported.[5] New guidance on recording racist incidents was issued by the Home Office in summer 2000 and has the potential to promote substantial improvements.[6]

10.7   Hate crime in general, and racist crime in particular, has a character that distinguishes it from other kinds of crime. The difference lies not only, and not primarily, in the offender's motivation,[7] but in the greater harm done.[8] The working definition of a racist incident proposed by the Lawrence Inquiry is helpful, as is the fact that it has been taken on board energetically by associations of senior police officers – ACPO[9] in England and Wales and ACPOS in Scotland. It is also important that practitioners throughout the criminal justice system see clearly what lies behind the definition. The distinctive feature of racist crime is that a person or household is attacked not as an individual, as in most other crimes, but as the representative of a community. This has three particularly serious consequences.

- Other members of the same community are made to feel threatened and insecure as well, and are less inclined to walk the streets of their neighbourhood,[10] so it is not just the individual who suffers a curtailment of his or her freedom and security. Policies aiming to build Britain as a community of communities, as advocated throughout this report, are pointless if some people are virtual prisoners in their own homes, afraid to venture into public spaces because of racist violence or cultural or religious prejudice.
- Since racist attacks affect a community as well as an individual, they are experienced as attacks on the values, loyalties and commitments central to a person's sense of identity and self-worth – their family, honour, friends, culture, heritage, religion, community, history. Racist, cultural and religious abuse is accordingly more hurtful, as indeed its perpetrators consciously know and intend, than most other kinds of abuse.
- Racist attacks are committed not only *against* a community but also, in the perception of offenders themselves, *on behalf of* a community[11] – offenders see themselves as representative of their peer group, and by extension of white Britishness generally. Even more than in the case of most other crimes, it is therefore essential that mainstream public opinion shows solidarity with and support for victims, and takes care not to provide any kind of comfort or encouragement to the offenders or to the community to which they see themselves as belonging. The representative of mainstream opinion, in the first instance, is the criminal justice system.

10.8   We have stressed elsewhere in this report that racism uses not only physical but also cultural and religious markers of difference.[12] However, there is no reference to culture or religion in guidelines currently (summer 2000) being considered by the Sentencing Advisory Panel in relation to racially aggravated offences. It would be valuable to investigate those convicted of racist crime, in order to identify the conditions that engender such activity and the circumstances in which it is most likely to occur. Such research would also help establish the role of religious and cultural factors in these offenders' motivations. *We recommend that research be commissioned into the characteristics of persons convicted or cautioned for racially aggravated offences under the Crime and Disorder Act 1998. Such research should identify the strategies most likely (a) to reduce the levels of racist incidents and (b) to be effective in the programmes being developed and applied by the prison and probation services for dealing with offending behaviour.* In this latter regard we note that the Home Office's explicit intention is that offending behaviour programmes should involve 'planned interventions over a specified period of time which can be shown to change positively attitudes, beliefs, behaviour and social circumstances'.[13] It would also be valuable to conduct action research on community mediation approaches, of the kind pioneered in a range of European cities in recent years, including Frankfurt.[14] Further, there needs to be dissemination of successful projects undertaken in boroughs such as Tower Hamlets, where the civil law has been used to reduce levels of racist harassment on and near housing estates,[15] and where there has been beneficial youth work.[16]

Penal processes and policy

10.9 Black and Irish people are differentially treated at all stages in the criminal justice system, from policing on the streets, as described in the previous chapter, through to sentencing and imprisonment, where they may be subjected to racism by both prison officers and other prisoners.[17] The key facts are summarised in Box 10.1.

10.10 There are various explanations for the differences summarised in Box 10.1. For a start, there is ample evidence that patterns of criminal behaviour are closely related to the social background and circumstances of offenders.[18] A comparatively high rate of offending could statistically be expected from the degree of social disadvantage, exacerbated by racism in its various forms, experienced by black and Irish people. Furthermore, many of the crucial judgements affecting how an individual is treated by the justice system are influenced by criteria connected with social background and circumstances – home, family relationships, school record and experiences, employment situation, peer-group

---

Box 10.1 **Criminal justice processes: some key facts**

- Black suspects are more likely than white suspects to be dealt with by arrest rather than summons and by prosecution rather than caution. They are more likely to be remanded in custody than released on bail.

- Black people are more likely than white people to be charged with indictable-only offences and therefore to be tried in crown court; to elect for trial at crown court rather than magistrates' court for either-way offences; and to plead not guilty. They are less likely to be the subject of a pre-sentence report. They are more likely to be acquitted, but the other factors mentioned here expose them to the likelihood of a more severe sentence if they are convicted.

- Black people are six times more likely than white people to be in prison.

- Black people are given longer sentences than white people.

- Irish people are classified as white for statistical purposes, but their experience is closer to that of black people than to that of other white people. This means that not only are specific concerns and issues for the Irish community ignored, but also official statistics underestimate the difference between black people's experience and that of the white British.

Source: See Note 17.

---

influences, life-story, and so on. Such judgements include decisions about the granting of bail, the risk of reoffending as assessed in pre-sentence reports, the weight that a court gives to a plea in mitigation and the sentence someone eventually receives.[19] They may be affected by stereotypes which assume that the circumstances and difficulties of black and Irish people enhance rather than mitigate their blameworthiness.[20] Different consequences may also reflect the quality of representation by defence lawyers, and the effect of reluctance on the part of some black defendants to offer guilty pleas or to engage in plea or sentencing bargaining.[21]

10.11   The policies and practice of criminal justice in Britain have for several years been influenced by developments in the United States.[22] In the words of the quotation at the head of this chapter, the shift has been from social policy to penal policy. Imprisonment is used for both its deterrent and its incapacitating effects, and there is 'zero-tolerance' policing. The claims made for American penal policy appear exaggerated and to be politically and commercially motivated. Undoubtedly, they have a disproportionate effect on the criminalisation and social exclusion of black and Hispanic people. They are associated with the claim that civilised or legitimate society is threatened by a dangerous criminal and welfare-dependent underclass whose members have been corrupted by social benefits and 'soft' criminal justice measures.[23] As a partial consequence of such theorising, England, Scotland and Wales now have a higher proportion of their populations in prison than almost any other European country.[24] As a sombre reminder of the likely consequences of continuing American influence, Box 10.2 summarises some recent American statistics.[25]

10.12 Differential treatment continues after arrest and conviction. A thematic inspection by Her Majesty's Inspectorate of Probation, undertaken in 1999, found many substantial weaknesses in probation services. The inspection involved an audit of all 54 services and then detailed studies of 10 of them. Interviews and discussions were held with staff at all levels of seniority, a questionnaire was distributed to Asian and black staff, and a wide range of documentation was studied, including pre-sentence reports (PSRs). The report, published in summer 2000, showed clearly how the interacting components of institutional racism (see Chapter 5) operate in one particular public service. It demonstrated that Asian and black offenders receive a poorer service than white offenders, for example in terms of the inadequate quality of PSRs and of staff confidence and knowledge in dealing with them. Staff training is inadequate and Asian and black officers are not given sufficient professional support – a high proportion fail their probationary year. Large numbers of white staff are ignorant about racism and lacking in confidence in their own ability to deal with it, and the services are weak in relation to racially motivated offenders. Monitoring by ethnicity is unsatisfactory and information is not used even when it is collected. Management and leadership at all levels, including the most senior levels, are poor.

10.13 There is no similar information publicly available about the Prison Service, although the Service's own RESPOND programme, which we

Box 10.2 **The shape of things to come? Penal policy and practice in the United States**

- During the 1960s the US prison population was shrinking and in 1975 it stood at 380,000. Ten years later it had risen to 740,000. By 1995 it was in excess of 1.6 million. It has grown by 8 per cent annually through the 1990s. In 2000 it reached 2 million.

- At any one time almost one in three of all African-American males is either in prison or under some form of penal supervision.

- The US prison system also contains individuals on probation or parole. In 1995, 3.1 million were on parole and 700,000 on probation. In total, 5.4 million Americans were in the prison system. They accounted for one in 20 of all men aged over 18 and one in five of all male African-Americans.

- Over a lifetime an African-American male has a one-in-three chance of spending at least a year in prison. A white man has a chance of one in 23.

- It is estimated that the prison system in the US has cut male unemployment figures by at least two percentage points – partly by creating new jobs for prison and probation staff and partly by incarcerating people who would otherwise be unemployed.

Source: See Note 25.

fully endorse, acknowledges the need for constant vigilance. *We recommend that HM Chief Inspector of Prisons carry out an urgent and thorough thematic inspection of race equality in prisons, similar to the inspection of the probation service completed in 1999/2000 by HM Chief Inspector of Probation.* Such an inspection would focus on staffing and training issues. One story[26] can stand for many. In the early 1990s a black prison officer in South London reported a number of incidents of what he considered to be unacceptable behaviour. In one a group of white officers attacked a black prisoner, and in another a black woman prison officer was deserted by white colleagues when she was attacked by a group of white visitors. The officer who made the report was then subjected to a long campaign of harassment and discrimination by colleagues, involving loss of overtime, malicious accusations of misconduct and adverse appraisals. In 1995 an employment tribunal found that he had been unlawfully discriminated against and awarded him substantial damages. The prison service appealed but this was turned down. He then brought a further case alleging victimisation; this was settled in return for an undertaking by senior management that it would take steps to protect him. Nevertheless, the victimisation continued, and the officer took a third case to the tribunal. In a judgement in April 2000 the tribunal found that two of the three governors involved had sought to mislead it during the course of their evidence under oath. A third 'exhibited outright hostility' towards the officer. The tribunal found that the officer had faced prejudice not only from colleagues in the original case but also from relatives of these colleagues who were employed at the prison. The whole episode vividly illustrated the interacting features of institutional racism.[27]

10.14 It is clear that training of probation officers and prison officers, at all levels of seniority, is a major issue. In Chapter 9 we discussed aspects of police training and in Chapter 20 we discuss the generic features of race and diversity training for all professions and public services. *We recommend that a national committee or forum be set up on the training of probation officers and prison officers on issues of race and diversity.* It would establish standards on content, methodology and evaluation and its agenda papers would be publicly available.

Grievances and complaints

10.15 Effective grievance and complaints procedures are an essential component, among others, of action against institutional racism. For not only are they ethically right, they also highlight aspects of an organisation that are not working properly, and can provide an invaluable impetus for organisational change.[28] It behoves the justice system more than any other to ensure that it acts swiftly, energetically and with transparent fairness when complaints are made against it, whether from members of the public or from its own staff. In the previous chapter we discussed complaints against the police. The same considerations apply to all employees in the criminal justice system. There are valuable provisions in the Access to Justice Act 1999 that extend the powers of the Law Society to act on complaints against solicitors, widen those of the Legal Services Ombudsman and enable the appointment of a Legal Services

Complaints Commissioner. These provisions must be used in ways that will help to promote race equality and respect for cultural diversity. *We recommend that the government review all procedures for dealing with complaints about racism in the criminal justice process to ensure that:*

- *an independent element is included in the investigation;*
- *investigators have an accredited qualification in dealing with issues of race and diversity.*

10.16 It is totally unacceptable that serious cases of racism should be investigated and substantiated but not followed by criminal or disciplinary outcomes of any kind, or that officers should be able to escape such action on technical grounds. *We recommend that the government review the disciplinary procedures for public servants working in the criminal justice system to ensure that they cannot evade responsibility for racist conduct by means of technical or procedural devices.* At the same time criminal justice services should develop the use of restorative procedures for dealing with complaints and loss of confidence, especially where criminal or disciplinary proceedings may not be practicable. Such procedures are already being developed in several parts of the criminal justice system. A fundamental aim is to use complaints constructively so that they help to improve confidence, relationships and practice.

10.17 In the criminal justice system, as in all public bodies, it is always important to receive a complaint sympathetically; to understand what lies
behind it and the context in which it is made; to be sensitive to power
and status differences between complainants and those who receive the
complaint; and if appropriate to make clear that action will be taken to
prevent the causes of the complaint recurring. If a complaint is not resolved locally, procedures should allow for it to be independently investigated by an individual or a team not drawn wholly from the same
professional group as the person against whom the complaint is made.
The action to be taken should always include prosecution or disciplinary action against the person responsible if it is justified.

Staffing

10.18 Those who define, administer, enforce and judge in matters of law and
criminal justice are still overwhelmingly white. Numbers of Asian and
black people are gradually increasing in the magistracy, the probation
service and the practising legal profession, but are still extremely low at
senior levels. 'From the point of leaving university,' a senior police
officer pointed out to us, 'there is not one selection process between law
student and high court judge which has an element of transparency and
therefore fairness. To have crucial positions within a system which supposedly delivers justice decided on methods such as "secret soundings"
is totally unacceptable. It is a breeding ground for discrimination. The
absence of any black people or Asians at senior levels in the judiciary
confirms this. Radical reform of the entire system, from pupillage to
barristers to QCs to judges, is required.' *We recommend that a Judicial
Appointments Commission be established to oversee all appointments and
promotions within the magistracy and the higher judiciary, and to Queen's
Counsel, and that it seek to ensure that the judiciary is more diverse in terms
of community background.*

10.19 The Home Office has set recruitment and progression targets for services for which it has responsibility.[29] This is commendable, certainly.
But there is concern that the targets will not be met, or will be rendered
worthless by early resignations, resulting in disillusion and frustration.
In any case, training for judges and magistrates is of utmost importance. In this respect the approach of the Ethnic Minorities Advisory

Committee (now the Equal Treatment Advisory Committee) of the Judicial Studies Board has been courageous and successful and should be better known.[30] There is further discussion of training issues in the previous chapter, and a summary of principles in Box 20.3 in Chapter 20.

10.20 Issues relating to appointments and training were included in a wide-ranging survey by the National Association for the Care and Resettlement of Offenders (NACRO) published in early 2000.[31] The survey covered many further topics discussed in this chapter. It also made recommendations relating to the work of the Criminal Justice Consultative Council and the local strategy committees; to effective communication and consultation with Asian, black and Irish communities and their representation on boards and committees; to the preparation and use of pre-sentence reports; to the provision of hostels and other accommodation; to vigorous application of the RESPOND programme in the Prison Service;[32] to work by the prison and probation services with the perpetrators of racially motivated offences; and to energetic action to promote understanding of core values and principles in the legal profession. We support the recommendations in this report and hope that they will become widely known and will be acted on.

10.21 In principle, the Crown Prosecution Service (CPS) plays a crucial role in ensuring that the criminal justice system is just – it is expected to be a beacon of fair play and impartiality. Research has shown that for black defendants it is more likely than for white to discontinue certain cases, to reduce the charges brought by the police, and to offer no evidence in court. This is particularly so for defendants charged with affray, violent disorder or theft. However, black and Asian defendants prosecuted by the CPS are also more likely to be acquitted in magistrates' courts because of insufficient evidence. As an employer, the record of the CPS is particularly poor. A report published in May 2000 found strong evidence of institutional racism. It referred to 'the persistent pattern of under-representation of ethnic minorities at higher grades', the dominance of a clique of white managers, the discriminatory conduct of promotion boards and a lack of sensitivity by management to race issues. Policy statements and action plans by management were said to lack coherence, and to be 'heavy on ambitious declarations of intent' but lacking substance. When managers were confronted with statistical evidence about inequalities within the service, 'their first reaction was to seek an "innocent" explanation'. The report continued: 'It is a matter of concern that there was a noticeable reluctance on the part of some managers to contemplate the possibility of a serious problem.' Elsewhere it referred to 'a tendency within the service to overreact and panic in the face of allegations of race discrimination'.[33]

Recent government policies and measures

10.22 The present government's reforms have crucial implications for race equality. Examples of the reforms include the array of new orders (especially the anti-social behaviour order) made available to the courts under the Crime and Disorder Act 1998; the measures to reduce crime and disorder set out in the Crime and Disorder Reduction Strategy and the Best Value targets for the police; the new arrangements for youth justice introduced by the Crime and Disorder Act 1998 and the Youth Justice and Criminal Evidence Act 1999; the proposals in the Criminal Justice and Court Services Act 2000 to intensify the effect and tighten the enforcement of community sentences; the application of targeted and intelligence-led policing; the widening of the definition of terrorism in the Terrorism Act; the various procedures for assessing, managing or avoiding risk, for example in connection with pre-sentence reports or discretionary release from prison; and the proposed new powers to detain persons suffering from severe personality disorder. All these developments may be affected in practice by the Human Rights Act.

10.23 In many of these reforms the emphasis is on protecting the public and managing risk. To the extent that the measures succeed in their avowed overall aim of protecting the public as a whole, Asian, black and Irish communities should benefit. But if the criteria for the various discretionary judgements are correlated with personal or social situations in which Asian, black and Irish people are disproportionately represented, the effects will be discriminatory. The evidence on which the criteria are established, and on which programmes are evaluated, is thus critical.

10.24 It will also be essential to ensure that the Legal Services Commission set up under the Access to Justice Act 1999, the Legal Services Consultative Panel, the Community Legal Service and the Criminal Defence Service all operate in ways which guarantee that members of all communities can rely on fair and equal access to justice. This applies whether they are defendants or witnesses in criminal cases, parties in civil cases, or practitioners making their way in the legal profession. Other concerns arise from the impact on black, Irish and Asian communities of the government's proposal to restrict access to trial at crown court, and therefore to trial before a jury, in the Criminal Justice (Mode of Trial) Act.

10.25 Much will depend on the spirit in which the new measures are put into practical effect; the spoken and unspoken assumptions made about individuals and situations; the conscious and unconscious expectations brought to critical situations and events; and the professional culture within which the courts and operational services go about their work. The assumptions, expectations and professional culture will in their turn be influenced by public opinion, or more accurately by what public opinion is perceived to be; by media reporting of specific events, and general coverage of crime and justice; and by the quality and style of the country's political leadership. They will also be influenced by the day-to-day experience of professionals throughout the criminal justice system, and by their relationships and interactions with each other. Rigorous monitoring and constant vigilance will be necessary to ensure that actions flowing from the new initiatives do not reflect and perpetuate racist stereotypes, and that the end result of their implementation is to sustain and strengthen the safety and confidence of all parts of society. Therefore, *we recommend that the government, the courts and the criminal justice services:*

- *extend the use of ethnic monitoring to those existing functions of the criminal justice system not already covered, for example sentencing, criminal appeals and the work of the Criminal Cases Review Commission;*
- *ensure that ethnic monitoring is systematically applied to the new functions and procedures introduced under recent legislation such as the Crime and Disorder Act 1998, the Youth Justice and Criminal Evidence Act 1999, the Access to Justice Act 1999, the Criminal Justice and Court Services Act 2000, the Terrorism Act 2000;*
- *make the results available for public discussion and for independent inspection, audit and research;*
- *ensure that monitoring is carried out rigorously and with integrity, and that staff in central government and throughout the system have the expertise to draw the correct conclusions, and apply them to the formation of policy and the development of professional practice;*

- *prepare and publish appraisals of the effects of its policies and measures.*

10.26 The information should be made public and widely discussed. Statistics need to be published and disseminated, not only in their current form but also in forms that are more user-friendly. In particular, it is important that community organisations and watchdog bodies should be able to use them to scrutinise and challenge criminal justice agencies in their locality. It is equally essential that the statistics should be collected not only for England and Wales but also for Scotland. In particular, they should include Irish and Gypsy/traveller as categories; cease using 'ethnic appearance' as a classification in instances where it is possible to establish ethnic origin; provide breakdowns of the categories of 'black' and 'Asian'; and include data on religious and cultural identity in the statistics on the prison population and on the ethnicity of victims of racist attacks. *We recommend that the government review and improve the quality of the data included each year in* Statistics on Race and the Criminal Justice System.

10.27 It is also essential to collect qualitative data. To what extent do Asian and black people believe themselves to be treated unfairly because of colour or cultural racism institutionalised in the criminal justice system? To what extent are professionals in the system, including all court personnel, aware of the kinds of action on their part likely to give rise to perceptions of injustice? *We recommend that qualitative research on perceptions of fairness in the criminal justice system be undertaken, with particular regard to race and diversity issues.*

Accountability and legitimacy

10.28 Many of the concerns we identify in this and the previous chapter are part of a wider set of questions about the accountability and legitimacy of the criminal justice system, and about the role and authority of the state and its institutions.[34] The values of community, citizenship, social inclusion and human rights, and the balance between cohesion and difference and between equality and diversity, discussed in Chapters 2–7, can all be either sustained or undermined by the way in which a country arranges and runs its criminal justice system. They demand a system that has the confidence and respect of the population as a whole, towards which people feel a sense of ownership and of responsibility. The system must be accountable in the sense that it can be held up to public scrutiny, and must be required to justify and if necessary improve its performance. It must be legitimate in the sense that people accept, respect and abide by its decisions even when they are adversely affected by them.

10.29 We consider general questions of accountability and legitimacy in Chapters 18–20, the last section of our report. In the case of the criminal justice system, services are in some respects more accountable than they were, say, 10 years ago. This has been brought about by the processes of inspection and audit, the setting and monitoring of performance indicators and targets, and the publication of reports. It will be further enhanced by the Human Rights Act. All this we welcome. But there has also been an increase in the number of appointed authorities, with considerable powers, not directly accountable to Parliament or indeed to any electorate, and therefore not in any formal sense to the communities they serve. Such bodies include the Youth Justice Board; the Legal Services Commission and its Consultative Panel; police authorities and – of critical importance – the new police authority for London; probation boards set up in a new form under the Criminal Justice and Court Services Act; the Criminal Cases Review Commission; and longer-established bodies such as the Police Complaints Authority and prison boards of visitors. All these bodies will in future have a positive duty under the Race Relations (Amendment) Act to promote race equality. They must also be seen as able, and determined, to act on behalf of society as a whole and all its diverse communities. *We recommend that the criteria for appointment to all public bodies, especially those set up under recent legislation, include a requirement that they demonstrate their ability to understand and act in the best interests of all sections of the communities for which they have responsibility.* In addition, *we recommend that such organisations be required to specify in their reports the action they have taken to promote race equality.*

10.30 However, an increase in accountability can be accompanied by an increase in direction by central government, diminished influence of elected local government, and an absence of any significant or effective sense of local ownership. The result is that local communities do not feel any genuine responsibility for the services provided on their behalf, and that any remaining local influence is concentrated in the hands of established interests and organisations. There is then less chance of black, Asian and Irish voices being heard, and a loss not only of accountability but also of legitimacy.

10.31 Following Imran Khan's death in 1998, a leader of the Asian community in Scotland wrote in the *Herald*: 'The new Asian Scots have been brought up here and are not prepared to "turn the other cheek" and rightly expect to be treated as the equals of white Scots. Young Asians in today's Scotland also complain that this is not happening ... It is not good enough for those in authority to merely pay lip service to the laws governing racial discrimination. People in positions of power must really believe, in their hearts and minds, that black and white are equal.'[35] This belief in equality must be reflected in, and reinforced by, strong structures of accountability and legitimacy, at local as well as national levels. Such structures are required not only in the criminal justice system, of course, but throughout all areas of social policy. They need to interlock, and therefore to be built from local levels upward, not imposed from above. Only in this way will a community of communities thrive. In the next chapters we consider accountability and legitimacy in a range of other policy contexts, starting with Britain's education systems.

Chapter 11

Education

'What's wrong with you, miss? Why are you always smiling?' the students at my black-majority school ask me. 'I smile because I see you,' is my habitual reply. But what I want to say is something like this:

'I smile to salute you, to salute all the learners here, who continue to hold tight to their dignity and self-belief in the endless and ugly face of racism, rejection and poverty. I smile to salute our teachers who work more hours than there are, before and after school, in holidays and at weekends, to struggle beside our students to try, through mentoring, after school classes, residential courses, to restore the balance and open the doors in a closed and unbalanced world.' That's what I hope they hear in my smile.

But even that ignores the poignancy of their question, their subtext that says a smile – respect, recognition, affirmation – is so unexpected as to be a symptom of illness, of deviance, their message that announces that there is nothing to smile about.

From a correspondent in London

Please note

In significant respects England, Scotland and Wales have different education systems. The discussions and recommendations in this chapter are not equally relevant to all three systems.

11.1   In 1988, when the new national curriculum began to be established in England and Wales, the Secretary of State for Education requested the National Curriculum Council to issue guidance on ways in which the curriculum should 'take account of the ethnic and cultural diversity of British society and the importance of the curriculum in promoting equal opportunity for all pupils, regardless of ethnic origin or gender'. Three years later, when reporting to the United Nations Convention on the Elimination of all forms of Racial Discrimination (CERD) committee on measures taken to combat racism in UK society, the government mentioned this request as one of its achievements.[1] However, the report to CERD was economical with the truth. For although guidelines were produced they were never published, apparently because of opposition by senior civil servants and ministers.[2] It is still the case today, in Scotland as well as in England and Wales, that there is inadequate direction from government on issues of equality and diversity in education.[3] The gap has to an extent been filled by teachers' organisations – particularly the Educational Institute of Scotland (EIS), the Association of Teachers and Lecturers (ATL), the National Union of Teachers (NUT) and the National Association of Schoolmasters/Union of Women Teachers (NAS/UWT)[4] – and by a range of other bodies. These include the Centre for Education for Racial Equality in Scotland, the Development Education Centre in Birmingham, Race On The Agenda in London, the Runnymede Trust and the Early Years Trainers Anti-Racist Network, as well as many local authorities.[5] Although valuable, such piecemeal developments are no substitute for national leadership. They have no statutory force and their documents are unlikely to be read and used by those who most need them.

11.2 In preparing for this chapter we wrote to about 200 contacts in the field of education with a set of questions about current issues. One of our correspondents arranged for a group of students from refugee backgrounds to express their views. They paid tribute to individual teachers and head teachers but felt also that the education system as a whole had failed them. Box 11.1 on the next page contains some of the points they made and serves as a backdrop to the discussions that follow.

11.3 Ideally, all relevant authorities in England, Scotland and Wales, and also individual schools, colleges and universities, should be able to demonstrate, with statistically valid data, that gaps in the achievements and life-chances of learners from different communities are closing. Information should also be readily available about the composition of the teaching force and the administrative staff in schools, colleges and universities, broken down by ethnicity, gender, seniority and remuneration.[6] It should show that the three education systems are becoming steadily more inclusive.

11.4 As long ago as 1981, the Rampton Report urged that such monitoring should take place.[7] There is still a dearth of straightforward information, however. In England a fundamental practical problem is that no attempt has been made nationally to go beyond the ethnicity categories

---

Box 11.1 **Voices: refugee pupils talk about their education**

I was given extra English support and the teacher was great. The trouble was that it wasn't linked to any of the topics I was covering in class … There was no attempt to integrate it. In history, geography and English no attempt was made to integrate me.

We had a black head who was tough but fair. You felt he really cared what happened to you. I went through a bad time. I was separated from my family, I was picked on and there was a lot of bullying. I wasn't able to express how I felt so I took matters into my own hands. I was suspended on a number of occasions … You need a range of role models in a school that show the complexity and diversity of people's lives. My head teacher was a positive role model for me.

There was a lot of name-calling and fights. There were no black teachers at the school and no acknowledgement of black experience. No black history was taught, for example.

There was setting in maths and it was bad. It sent the wrong messages – of lower expectations for certain groups. You don't get stretched. You need to be challenged in school. You need excitement and external influences.

There was nothing I could relate to at school about my ethnic identity and me … This came through English and history lessons. I felt they projected a negative image of my country of origin and this affected my status in the school.

Source: A project organised by Save the Children, 2000.

---

used in the 1991 Census. There are comparable problems in Scotland and Wales. The terms 'black African', 'black other' and 'other minority ethnic group' are useless for monitoring purposes; the terms 'black Caribbean' and 'black other' are used in different ways in different authorities and schools. Thus aggregating figures from two or more authorities is often of dubious validity, as is making comparisons. The term 'African' covers such a wide range in terms of culture, socio-economic situation and migration experience that it is almost entirely unhelpful. The term 'Indian' fails to distinguish between the large Punjabi and Gujarati communities, and does not take account of certain smaller communities with roots in India which are culturally, religiously and socio-economically different from the larger groups. There is inadequate information about – among others – Gypsy/traveller, Irish, Nigerian, Somali, Sri Lankan, Turkish and Vietnamese communities.

11.5   It has been estimated that less than one school in 200 has commendable arrangements for monitoring by ethnicity.[8] Twenty years after the Rampton Report had called for the collection, analysis and use of valid and reliable statistics, inspectors in England reported that 'a longstanding obstacle to progress is the reluctance of schools and LEAs [Local Education Authorities] to monitor pupil performance by ethnic group'.[9] The inspectors added that 'nor, until recently, has a strong lead been given in this respect by successive governments. In the absence of such performance data, it is all too easy to turn a blind eye to ... underachievement and for scarce resources to be dissipated on the wrong priorities.' It was a trenchant criticism of everyone involved, from successive governments to all schools and local authorities. However, the inspection regimes themselves have never given a strong lead, either by offering clear advice or by example. They do not require individual schools to collect adequate statistics, let alone to analyse and use them. Detailed guidance to schools on inspectors' expectations and requirements on this matter has never been provided.[10] In most communities the achievements of girls are higher than those of boys, but statistical breakdowns by both gender and ethnicity are rare.[11] Few of the available statistics on ethnicity and school achievement take account of the key variable of social class. There are no publications nationally providing essential information about race equality and education similar in detail to the annual reports provided in England and Wales about the criminal justice system. *We recommend that national authorities require local authorities and individual schools to maintain substantially more detailed and helpful statistics on ethnicity than hitherto, and ensure that there is high-quality training available on how such statistics are to be analysed and used.* They should lead by example as well as by exhortation.

11.6   Several local authorities and individual schools have, of their own accord, already developed systems better than those used by the national authorities. The latter should therefore draw on their experience and expertise. Further, since the inspection systems are highly influential in terms of what schools deem to be important, *we recommend that inspectors provide detailed guidance to schools on how they should collect, analyse and use statistical information broken down by ethnicity.*

11.7   Despite the poor quality of the information available, as summarised above, broad pictures can be sketched. The general situation in England appears to be as follows.[12]

- African-Caribbean children start school at the age of five at much the same standard as the national average. By the age of 10, however, they have fallen behind. The difference is greater in mathematics than in English. At the age of 16 the proportion of African-Caribbean students achieving five higher-grade GCSE passes (grades A*–C) is considerably less than half the national average. This is even worse than implied by the government's own figures, based on the National Youth Cohort study.[13]

- At Key Stage 2 (age 11) in English and mathematics and at GCSE (16) generally, Gujarati and Punjabi (that is, 'Indian') pupils achieve results above the national average. The differential at GCSE is even higher than at Key Stage 2.

- Bangladeshi and Pakistani pupils achieve below the national average, but steadily close the gap between themselves and others in the course of their education. In some authorities they perform at or above the national average at GCSE.

11.8   Averages can hide substantial polarisation. For example, young people of Bangladeshi and Pakistani backgrounds are well represented proportionately in terms of entry to university, especially in London and Scotland, but are also over-represented among school pupils aged 16 with the poorest qualifications.

11.9   Gypsy and Traveller pupils are particularly at risk. Although some make a reasonably promising start in primary school, by the time they reach secondary level their generally low attainment is a matter of serious concern. In 1996 it was estimated that as many as 10,000 Gypsy and traveller children of secondary school age were not even registered for education in English schools.[14] 'Often schools do not want them,' it has been said, and 'often Gypsies themselves do not want the schooling that is on offer'.[15]

11.10 The information available in England and Wales for A level and entry to higher education is of a higher quality than that for education up to the age of 16. It also gives a more promising picture than do the (inadequate) figures for attainment in schools. For some years the Universities and Colleges Admissions Service (UCAS) has collected, and more recently has begun to publish, detailed figures on the ethnic background of all UK-based students (a) who apply for and (b) who are accepted for undergraduate degree courses. The figures[16] show that the A level participation rate for all Asian students (that is, those with Bangladeshi, Chinese, Indian or Pakistani backgrounds), as also for most black students (that is, with African or African-Caribbean backgrounds), is much the same as, or appreciably higher than, the national average. The one exception is the case of African-Caribbean men. It is striking that, contrary to a prevalent stereotype, the participation rate among young women of Bangladeshi and Pakistani backgrounds is higher than that of white young women.

11.11   For entry to university the national average is exceeded by Indian, Pakistani and African-Caribbean women and by Indian, Pakistani and Bangladeshi men. The achievements of these groups are all the more remarkable given that the socio-economic status of their parents is lower overall than that of the white population. Sixty-seven per cent of white students enter university from middle-class backgrounds. The proportion in all other communities is much lower – only 36 per cent of Bangladeshi women undergraduates, for example, are from these backgrounds. Higher proportions of African and African-Caribbean students than others enter higher education after the age of 24 and from the further education sector rather than schools. This point is significant for both schools and colleges, and also reflects well on the hard work, commitment and perseverance of the students themselves.

11.12   Data from the Higher Education Statistics Agency show that 18–24 year-old people from all Asian and black communities are over-represented in higher education, in the sense that their proportions in higher education are greater than their proportions in the general population. (See Table D in Appendix D.) Students of African backgrounds are three times as likely to be in higher education as might be expected from their numbers in the general population, and those of Indian backgrounds more than twice as likely. However, such general statements mask gender differences, and also differences relating to the esteem in which universities are held. About 70 per cent of African-Caribbean and 60 per cent of Indian, Pakistani and Bangladeshi students pursue their degree studies at universities that were formerly polytechnics. Only 35 per cent of white students do so. Surveys of employers have shown that they much prefer to recruit from the older universities.[17] A further issue that needs highlighting is the experience of Asian and black students in higher education. Common problems include isolation; the possibility of indirect discrimination in assessment procedures, for example, in clinical examinations for medical degrees where students are directly assessed by their tutors; curricula and programmes of study that do not reflect Asian and black experience and perceptions; assessment regimes that are not appropriate for mature students; timetabling arrangements that are culturally insensitive; lack of sensitive pastoral support for students experiencing difficulties associated with colour or cultural racism; and a lack of Asian and black lecturers and tutors.[18] *We recommend that all institutions of higher education review and improve their arrangements for ensuring that potential students from Asian and black communities apply for a wide range of courses.* This is particularly important in the case of the older and most prestigious institutions and applies to both young and mature students. In addition, *we recommend courses and syllabi be reviewed with a view to making them culturally more inclusive wherever appropriate.* There are at present no Asian or black vice-chancellors or pro vice-chancellors, and few senior administrators, such as deans or registrars. *We recommend that all institutions of higher education review and improve their arrangements for the recruitment and retention of academic staff, particularly at the most senior levels.*

Curriculum content and access

11.13   The education system is pivotal in terms of providing entry to employment, as outlined above, and for participation in social, political and cultural affairs. It is also uniquely well placed to promote the understandings, values and practical skills associated with the building of what we have called 'a community of citizens and communities'. (See Chapter 4, and also the references to deliberative skills in Chapter 16 and open/closed views of self and other in Chapter 17.) Such learning must start with children at nursery and infant schools. 'So often it appears', someone wrote to us, 'that decisions about the importance of working with young children are in the hands of men with little knowledge or valuing of this period in children's lives ... It almost begins to smack of sexism.' Another correspondent, confirming long-standing research findings, wrote, 'Young children are not colour-blind. As young as two or three years old they are aware of differences between the people around them and are developing positive and negative feelings ... It is important to build resilience in each child, so that every child can intervene if they see others being hurt or abused, and that all children have the emotional and verbal tools to defend themselves.'

11.14 Since government authorities in England, Scotland and Wales do not seem inclined to provide authoritative guidance to schools on what this involves in practice, *we recommend that a voluntary organisation, in co-operation with other organisations, produce a handbook for schools on issues of race equality and cultural diversity.*[19] Such a handbook would be closely related to the revised curricula recently introduced in England, Scotland and Wales; would draw on the discussions about national identity, racism and cultural differences provided in the first part of this report; and would provide guidance on both the content and pedagogy of multicultural and antiracist education. *We recommend that education for citizenship include human rights principles; stress on skills of deliberation, advocacy and campaigning; understanding of equality legislation; and opposition to racist beliefs and behaviour.* The importance of political literacy with an anti-racist perspective was stressed in the 1980s by the Swann Report, and also by *Murder in the Playground*, the Burnage Report.[20] It is still apposite in this regard to recall the observations of a researcher for the Swann Report, after he had spoken to white sixth-formers:

> Only now [in the sixth form] have they come to realise they have been subjected to outdated, insular and often indefensible sets of values and attitudes. What disturbed them most was that they ... were in the fortunate position of being able to modify implanted attitudes but many of their contemporaries had left school with little incentive or opportunity to have their opinions altered. A further bone of contention was that they felt that education had denied them access to political ideas and that they would leave school politically illiterate and easy prey to the first political pressure group that confronted them.[21]

11.15 In its official response to the Stephen Lawrence Inquiry report, the Department for Education and Employment (DfEE) claimed that the new Ethnic Minority Achievement Grant (EMAG) scheme in England would have a significant impact. The scheme replaced the Section 11 arrangements administered by the Home Office since 1966. It began a few weeks after inspectors had reported that:

> the reduction of Section 11 grant has weakened schools' capacity to provide the amount and quality of support needed. The short-term nature of the funding and the resultant lack of a career structure has exacerbated the difficulty of recruiting and retaining well-qualified teachers. In general, the quality of Section 11 teaching is too variable, the extent to which Section 11 support impacts on the whole school is generally limited, the commitment of mainstream teachers to these issues is inconsistent and the amount of specialist training for this work has all but evaporated.[22]

11.16   The evidence submitted to us implies strongly that EMAG has not been an improvement on Section 11, even though some of its ideas are in principle sound.[23] Indeed, the stringent criticisms of Section 11 quoted above seem even more pertinent in relation to EMAG. There has been a decline in resources for many schools; considerable insecurity among staff; a continuing loss of experienced and expert teachers; even less provision of specialist training; lack of informed leadership by head teachers; and scarcely more attention to the plight of African-Caribbean pupils than in the past. It appears unlikely that the grant will have a substantial impact on the patterns of underachievement summarised above. In Scotland there is no equivalent of Section 11 or EMAG, but here too many specialist teachers feel unrecognised and under-used.

11.17   When EMAG was introduced, the government announced that it would be independently evaluated. Tenders were invited from university-based researchers, but after many months' delay the proposal was apparently dropped. It is nevertheless essential that the scheme should be properly inspected and evaluated. *We recommend that work financed under the auspices of the EMAG grant be independently evaluated. Particular attention should be paid to the grant's impact on raising the achievement of African-Caribbean, Bangladeshi and Pakistani pupils and reducing their experience of exclusion.* Further, in view of the judgement by inspectors quoted above that specialist training for teachers of English as an additional language has 'all but evaporated', *we recommend that there be a substantial programme of certificated training for specialists in teaching English as an Additional Language.*

11.18   There are also several other urgent training needs. *We recommend that in England a specific Standards Fund grant be created and used for in-service training in race equality and cultural diversity.* Many individual LEAs and schools have mounted valuable training courses in recent years, and many have set up working parties to consider their response to the Stephen Lawrence Inquiry report. These various local initiatives would benefit from liaison among themselves, and from a high-profile lead from the relevant national authorities. Further, *we recommend that issues of race equality and cultural diversity be properly covered in initial teacher training, and that they be mandatory in all major programmes of management development for head teachers and deputy heads.* In the 1980s there was a valuable programme entitled Training the Trainers, focusing on staff in universities and teacher education. Such training is again urgently needed. *We recommend that funding be provided for a systematic programme of Training the Trainers courses.* The subject matter would be based in part on this report. In Chapter 20 we discuss issues of content, methodology and organisation.

Ethos and relationships

11.19   The most successful multi-ethnic schools are 'listening schools':

> Schools which took time to talk with students and parents; which were prepared to consider and debate values as well as strategies; which took seriously the views students and parents offered and their own interpretations of school processes; and which used this learning to reappraise, and where necessary change, their practices and to build a more inclusive curriculum.[24]

11.20   Schools that demonstrate such respect for their pupils and the pupils' parents are less likely to use exclusion from school as a sanction. Staff in such schools have strategies and skills for preventing disruption and 'disobedience', and for dealing with them in ways that defuse and de-escalate tensions rather than exacerbate them. They also have skills and strategies for addressing the tendency of some pupils to resort to violence when 'settling' disputes among themselves. In such schools the principles of citizenship education are taught not only by the formal curriculum but also by the ethos and general atmosphere.

11.21 African-Caribbean pupils are considerably more likely than others to be excluded. In some authorities and schools there also appears to be a worrying increase in exclusions of Bangladeshi, Pakistani and Somali pupils. But the government's targets in England for reducing exclusion rates do not mention the disproportionate numbers of exclusions of pupils from particular community backgrounds. There is far more to reducing exclusions, of course, than simply setting numerical targets and performance indicators. But since numerical targets are so influential in demonstrating what the government believes to be important, and in affecting therefore the climate of opinion, it is important that they should be used. For this reason, *we recommend that the government set targets for reducing nationally the numbers of exclusions experienced by pupils of particular community backgrounds. The targets should refer to fixed-term exclusions as well as to permanent exclusions. Further, we recommend that pilot schemes be established in certain schools to investigate the implications of moving towards a no-exclusions policy. Appropriate funding should be provided, and research should identify the lessons to be learned.*

11.22 The best practice in reducing exclusions, and in reducing the disaffection underlying their prevalence, has been developed in individual schools and authorities. This was acknowledged in the report for the DfEE quoted above. If generally applied, best practice would have a dramatic impact on exclusion rates and on their current discriminatory effects. Therefore *we recommend training for all members of governors' disciplinary committees and appeal panels; in-service training in non-confrontational approaches to discipline and conflict resolution; that a member of the governing body serve as an advocate for any student facing permanent exclusion, or that a student be represented by an advocate of their choice; and that procedures require head teachers to explain and justify how and why necessary support has not been provided.* There is evidence that being supported by an independent and well-informed advocate can make a crucial difference to whether or not a student is reinstated.[25] *We recommend that the national authorities fund independent bodies of trained advocates.*

11.23 There are many vigorous supplementary schools. They vary in their philosophies and immediate concerns, but most have in common that they are self-funding and depend on large numbers of volunteers.[26] For a range of reasons, local authorities and mainstream schools have difficulties even in contacting them, let alone in working with them as equal partners. It is essential, however, that strong links are established. *We recommend that schools and local authorities develop closer working relationships with local supplementary schools, parents' groups and community organisations.* Generally, schools and authorities need to attend more closely to the perceptions, experiences and outlooks of Asian and black parents and communities. We return to this point in Chapter 20, when discussing the notion of a 'listening organisation'.

Inspection of schools

11.24 At a major conference in Edinburgh in early 2000, Her Majesty's Inspectorate (HMI) was identified as 'critical to mainstreaming race equality issues within Scottish education'.[27] Delegates were disappointed, however, by what they perceived as a lack of HMI commitment. They noted that the Inspectorate is predominantly male and white, and maintained that reports do not sufficiently reflect issues of equality. However, HMI in Scotland has published clear guidance on equal opportunities in general, and this could readily be adapted to focus on race equality in particular.[28] Similar documents are urgently needed in England and Wales.[29] Discontent with Ofsted's poor record on race issues is reflected in Box 11.2. *We recommend that all inspection reports include the heading 'Race Equality and Cultural Diversity', and that high-quality training be provided for all inspectors.*

11.25 There need to be forums in which the inspection systems are publicly accountable in relation to issues of race equality and cultural diversity. Such forums would consider reports on individual schools and local authorities, and thematic reports about national situations. They would discuss and comment on the criteria and methodology used by inspectors, and ways in which the findings of reports could be widely disseminated. Accordingly, *we recommend that in each country a national working party be set up to examine and evaluate the impact of the inspection system on issues of race equality and cultural diversity in schools and local authorities.*

Box 11.2 **Voices: the inspection of schools**

In this borough the hard data on achievement shows clearly that pupils of African-Caribbean heritage are achieving very significantly worse than pupils from other ethnic groups. The baseline assessment data, however, shows that they enter schools at or slightly above the average achievement of their peer group ... Since the start of Ofsted inspections I have read almost every Ofsted report in my authority, and some 60 from other authorities. I cannot recall reading a single one where this issue was commented upon.
LEA officer

The middle school in whose inspection I participated was located in an area in which two British Movement cells were operative. The 'race' attitudes of the school's almost exclusively white pupils were conspicuously negative. I drew the lead inspector's attention to this as something that the governors, head teacher and staff should address as a key issue for action. I was advised that the school might be resentful if issues for action were identified that they felt unable to remedy. The inspection team's final report contained no reference to the issues I had raised.
Inspector

Members of our union worry that the 'Ofsted curriculum' does not give sufficient priority to the more affective areas of education. One teacher commented that her Ofsted team was only interested in 'sums, sentences, and good behaviour' – in spite of the fact that much work had been devoted to developing anti-racist policy and practice in the school.
Union official

The inspection team showed very poor understanding of equality issues and were clearly not in a position either in terms of conceptual understanding or methodology to undertake a more significant assessment of the LEA's work. In particular, some of the new members of the HMI team showed no understanding at all of the issues and were wholly ill-equipped to inspect the LEA.
Chief education officer

Source: Letters to the commission.

Recent trends, measures and policies

11.26 If the bodies responsible for education are serious about issues of equality and diversity they must commission high-quality and independent research, to be widely disseminated, on the impact of government policies and initiatives since 1988. The research will deal in particular, but not exclusively, with issues of race and diversity. It will investigate the possibility that measures intended to benefit all pupils may in fact have had differential impacts, and may have widened inequalities of opportunity and outcome. We have already indicated in this chapter that we have doubts about aspects of the new national curriculum ('Curriculum 2000') in England. In the following paragraphs we outline concerns about overall administration and management.

11.27 Under the provisions of legislation in England and Wales since 1988, school budgets are determined by student numbers; numbers for their part are affected by, or are even dependent on, parental choices and therefore schools' reputations. In effect (as also most certainly in intention in the early 1990s), education has become increasingly a market. Research in other countries demonstrates, however, that a major result of this approach to organising educational provision is that there is increased segregation, in any one urban area, along lines of class, 'race', ethnicity and culture. It appears that this is also happening in Britain.[30]

The playing field, to borrow a well-known metaphor, is increasingly unlevel. In some areas, African-Caribbean, Bangladeshi, Pakistani and refugee children are disproportionately educated in schools that have lower levels of resourcing, because of their falling numbers, and that are less able to attract the best-qualified staff. Such schools were often once non-selective secondary modern schools, in name or in effect, and have a long history of being at a competitive disadvantage.

11.28 'The key question in education', someone said to us, 'used to be, "What can a school do for its pupils?" Now the key question is, "What can pupils do for their school?"' A pupil commented to researchers recently: 'They want us to do well in this so their league tables are all right. They don't seem to care about what we want to do for ourselves. Just seem to care about us on the league table.'[31] Secondary schools select desirable customers, those who will prosper in the A–C economy. Also, and most worryingly, they engage in tiering, also known scathingly as *triage*. Pupils judged likely to obtain the much-coveted A–C grades at GCSE are identified, and in effect given preferential treatment, sometimes as long as two years before they sit the exams. Research has shown that this disadvantages black students and those for whom English is an additional language, and that part of the problem is that schools use racist stereotypes and assumptions when trying to predict who is and who is not likely to enhance the school's reputation through the league tables.[32] The tiering of GCSE exams means that students sitting the same subject are entered for different examination papers, each with a restricted range of possible grades. For students entered on the lowest tier the best they can usually attain is a grade C – although the situation is even worse in mathematics, where the bottom tier has an upper limit of grade D. *We recommend that the Qualifications and Curriculum Authority require that all exam boards offer only syllabuses in which it is possible to gain at least a C grade at each tier, and that all schools monitor tier entry by ethnicity.*

11.29 The policy of targeting failing schools, together with derogatory media campaigns, is in many cases a classic example of blaming the victim.[33] Some 700 schools have been placed under special measures since 1993, and about 70 per cent of these have been attended largely by black, Asian and refugee pupils. If naming and shaming them led to their being 'turned round', then the pupils may well have benefited. (Though it is not self-evident that the process was to their advantage, or that the same advantage could not have been attained for them more cost-effectively in another way. In this respect, as in so many others, research is needed to study the impact, including the unintended impact, of trends, decisions and policies.) But the naming and shaming of schools with large proportions of black, Asian and refugee pupils arguably leads to further scapegoating and stigmatisation, and to further white flight and segregation. *We recommend that independent research be commissioned to assess the impact on issues of race equality and cultural diversity of recent initiatives intended to benefit all pupils, but which may have failed to benefit, or have actually disadvantaged, pupils from certain communities.*

11.30   If and when such research finds that the impact of recent trends, measures and policies has been negative for many black, Asian (particularly Pakistani and Bangladeshi), Irish and refugee pupils, the government will be unable to say that it was not warned. Ever since Kenneth Baker's Education Reform Bill of 1987, there have been warnings from academics and campaigners that the reforms would work to the disadvantage of certain communities. Nor will the government be able to say that it has never received authoritative advice. The Rampton and Swann reports in the early 1980s laid out clearly what the government needed to do, and not do.

11.31   One problem is that there has never been a forum in which academics, campaigners and government officials could sit down together and review what is happening, and what is likely to happen. A potential forum was set up in England in 1996 on the day the report *Recent Research on the Achievements of Ethnic Minority Pupils* was published by Ofsted. But it was short-lived and under-resourced; arrangements for appointment to it were not clear; it was not allowed to play the role of watchdog or critic; its agenda papers were not publicly available; its deliberations were not reported; and it was in due course wound up without publicity or protest. Nevertheless, a forum reminiscent of that group is needed, but without its structural weaknesses. The Race Equality Advisory Forum in Scotland has the clear potential to develop into the kind of body we have in mind. *We recommend that in each system a forum be set up or developed in which government officials, academics, practitioners and representatives of non-governmental organisations can jointly review developments in education that have an impact on issues of race equality and cultural diversity.* We envisage that such a body would have at least some independent funding, so that it would not be dependent solely on the government; that some of its meetings would be in public, and would take the form of hearings; and that its agenda papers and minutes would be publicly available, both in print and on a website. It would be a national body, but it could have regional or local branches.

11.32 The United Nations CERD committee, mentioned in the first paragraph of this chapter, receives its regular reports from the UK government as a whole, not from the four national administrations separately. For this reason, as for others, there should be closer contact between the four of them on issues of race and diversity, particularly in the field of education. The four education systems have sufficient in common to make joint reflection on experience valuable, and for comparisons and contrasts to be fruitful. The agenda would include the cultural fabric of each country separately, as also that of the UK as a whole. It is to this topic, cultural fabric, that we turn in the next chapter.

Chapter 12

Arts, Media and Sport

*Acts of racism, racial violence, racial prejudice and abuse do not exist in a
vacuum. They are not isolated incidents or individual acts, removed from the
cultural fabric of our lives. Notions of cultural value, belonging and worth are
defined and fixed by the decisions we make about what is or is not our culture,
and how we are represented (or not) by cultural institutions.*

From a presentation to the Commission

12.1 In Jane Austen's *Mansfield Park*, set in early 19th-century England,
Edmund Bertram reproaches his cousin Fanny Price for not talking
more to her uncle. 'Did you not hear me ask him about the slave trade
last night?' replies Fanny. 'I did,' says Edmund, 'and had hopes the question would be followed up by others. It would have pleased your uncle to
be inquired of farther.' 'And I longed to do it – but there was such a dead
silence!' In 1999 the dead silence was confronted by a new permanent
exhibit at the National Maritime Museum, Greenwich. It showed a Jane
Austen-like figure sipping tea with a sugar bowl on the table beside her.
From beneath the floor at her feet a manacled black arm reached out as
if from the hold of a slave ship, and as if to show the source of her
comfort and wealth. The exhibit drew bitter criticism from sections of
the media. The display, it was said, aimed 'at depriving the British
people of any aspect of their history in which they can take justifiable
pride'. The museum's director responded by maintaining that
'museums are not just there to perpetuate the old view. We want galleries to be challenging.'

12.2 Through such episodes and arguments the cultural fabric of a country is
questioned and re-formed. Who should or should not receive funding
for artistic and recreational activities and projects? Whose experiences,
perceptions and stories should be included, and how should they be included, in the narratives and images that appear on television and in the
press? Who should have opportunities to develop skills in various competitive sports, and to represent their neighbourhood, town or country?
Who should receive resources to express themselves, and gain access to

platforms where they will be heard, through literature, film, painting and music? Who should or should not be represented in the collections of art galleries and museums, the repertoires of theatre companies, the programmes of local arts centres? These are the questions that cultural policies have to address.

12.3 Decisions on such questions are taken by a wide range of governmental and private bodies, at national, regional and local levels. They inherently reflect and perpetuate views of the past – embodied in terms such as 'heritage', 'canon' and 'mainstream' – at the same time as they fashion the present and lay the foundations for the future. Funding and resourcing policies should consciously attend to issues of cultural recognition, inclusion, identity and belonging, and therefore question many customary criteria of quality and aesthetic value. Appropriate infrastructures must be created or developed to ensure that this attention is given.

12.4 In this chapter we consider Britain's cultural fabric under the three conventional headings of arts, media and sport. The distinctions between these three appeal to common sense, and are embodied in the structures of the lead government department for cultural policy, the Department of Culture, Media and Sport (DCMS). (Confusingly, the DCMS uses the term culture instead of arts, thus implying that media and sport are not key aspects of the country's cultural fabric.) There are significant overlaps between the three, however, and it is misleading to discuss each separately. Certainly, many of the general comments we make in this chapter about any one of the three are true also of the other two. All have in common that they reflect and mould images and assumptions relating to the kind of society Britain is and has been, and relating to who is and is not included in the national story.

12.5 Box 12.1 summarises some of the issues that need to be addressed.

12.6 The arts and media are currently affected by rapid technological and commercial change: the synthesis of information technology with satellite and cable television, and commercial mergers concentrating decision-making power in the hands of a small number of companies. Companies think and plan globally rather than nationally or locally. Britain's diverse communities and cultures mesh with global networks of great economic significance. It is as yet too early to predict with

---

Box 12.1 **Arts, media and sport: summary of concerns**

- Of the first £2 billion spent on the arts from the National Lottery, no more than about 0.02 per cent was allocated to organisations representing black and Asian artists.

- Media coverage of African, Asian, Caribbean and Irish communities and individuals in Britain is frequently negative, distorted or patronising – or else the communities are simply invisible, not represented at all.

- African, Asian, Caribbean and Irish people enjoy sport as much as everybody else, but in a wide range of popular and high-profile sports they feel unwanted and unwelcome as spectators and supporters.[1]

- The first major annual report from the DCMS, published in 1999, made absolutely no reference, in its substantial introductory overview of policy aims and concerns, to issues of cultural, ethnic and religious diversity in modern Britain.

- The same report asserted that the DCMS is firmly committed to equal opportunities but indicated also, without a shred of embarrassment or regret, that of the top 20 posts in the department (those paying salaries over £40,000 in 1998), every single one was held by a white person.

- At senior decision-making levels in Channel 4, ITV and the BBC there were even fewer black and Asian people in 2000 than there had been 10 years earlier.

---

confidence what these changes will entail, but certainly they will have a substantial impact on whether countries such as Britain are able to develop, in their cultural fabric, as communities of communities. They offer exciting possibilities, but could also lead to fragmentation.

The arts

12.7   At present, there is scant recognition of Britain's cultural and religious diversity in funding policies for the arts in England, Scotland and Wales. Inadequate attention is paid to issues of race, racism and whiteness in British culture, and there are insufficient representations, through the performing and visual arts, of the increasingly hybrid society that Britain now is. *We recommend that a national cultural policy be developed through widespread participation and consultation. It should pay particular attention to issues of cultural inclusion and identity.*

12.8   This policy will have to address six main issues.[2] First, the whole mainstream canon needs to be reinterpreted. Just as individuals, families and groups turn the random incidents of their lives into coherent narratives, so a nation creates – and continually re-creates – its national story. The arts are a critical element in this process. Like personal memory, social memory is inherently selective, and by its nature seeks and imposes patterns. Beginnings, middles and ends are defined, as also are chains of cause and consequence. Events are highlighted or denied, placed centre-stage or left in the background. Selectivity is inevitable, but it is also a matter of human choice. The function of such selectivity is to explain and justify aspects of the present. The essential question is: Who feels included in the national story, and who does not? (See Chapter 2.) Arts institutions and funding organisations play a key role as gatekeepers in this selective process. For they either open doors or create barriers to the production, promotion and distribution of creative talent. Their decisions have the effect of maintaining the status quo and excluding diverse cultural voices from the artistic mainstream. All too often they seem to be working from inherited assumptions which have not been questioned in the light of Britain's growing internal cultural diversity and its rapidly changing relationship to the outside world.

12.9   In recent decades, many museums have become more inclusive in terms of class and ideology. The lives, artefacts, houses, workplaces, tools, customs and oral memories of ordinary people have begun to take their rightful place in the national heritage. Local and family history, oral history and personal memorabilia have encouraged new views of what is and is not worth conserving. The agrarian and industrial revolutions are essential parts of the national story, as are the struggles for decent working conditions, universal franchise, the abolition of slavery, freedom of speech, religious freedom, sexual equality, the rights of children, and so on. This greater inclusiveness needs now to be extended to embrace Britain's diverse communities and the lifestyles, experiences, identities and creative work of its newer citizens.

12.10   Historical events have to be seen through more than one pair of eyes, and narrated within more than one story. It is increasingly recognised that no individual, group or institution has the right – or, indeed, any longer the power – to define the culture and stories of others. But this democratising approach to heritage and the arts has so far stopped short of addressing the issue of racism, of confronting Britain's selective amnesia about its former empire, and of reflecting the diverse composition of its present population. Notable and courageous exceptions include the Liverpool Museum on the Slave Trade and the National Maritime Museum's evocation of slavery as an essential contributory factor in the prosperity of 18th- and 19th-century merchants.[3]

12.11   The requirement here is not so-called political correctness – it is not, to borrow a well-known phrase, about the airbrushing out of dead white males (though certainly arts administrators will have to withstand complaints about alleged political correctness). Rather, it is a question of recognising the experiences and contributions of those conventionally omitted, and of seeing colonisers and colonised as sharing a single intertwined history.[4] Increasingly, artistic influences are international and flow across boundaries. Artists from Britain's diverse communities play a key role in sustaining cultural networks that make the British artistic mainstream increasingly cosmopolitan and are of enormous potential benefit to the country as a whole. This is not just a moral and aesthetic imperative, but also of substantial economic importance. In an increasingly global yet diverse world, it is societies that know themselves to be internally diverse, and are at ease with their internal differences, which stand the best chance of economic success. Similarly, it is individuals who have a broad repertoire of cultural skills, and for whom culture shocks are welcome and interesting rather than traumatic and paralysing, who are most readily able to navigate the turbulent waters of contemporary life.

12.12   Second, there needs to be greater clarity about what the notion of reflecting and respecting cultural diversity involves in practice. All too simplistically, it is assumed to mean recognising 'ethnic' traditions, separate from the mainstream 'Western' canon. According to this interpretation, hard and fast distinctions are to be made between Western and so-called ethnic, and between mainstream and minority. Furthermore, the focus is typically on conservation and valuing the past rather than on promoting new creativity in the present, although undoubtedly there is a place for the conservation and celebration of traditions, as, for example, when there is an exhibition of African sculpture or Islamic art at a national or municipal gallery, or a concert of South Asian music at the Proms.

12.13 It is essential that 'Westerners' should know far more than they do about the arts, philosophy and religions of other civilisations. Equally, it is essential that British people who have family links to traditions outside Britain should have opportunities to know and feel at home with these aspects of their inheritance.

12.14 Equally crucial, however, is that changes and reinterpretations currently taking place within various cultural traditions, not least as a result of their continually rubbing up against each other, should be reflected. Relationships are constantly being renegotiated – between women and men, the younger and older generations, faith and secularism, the spoken and the written word. Traditions originally predating 'the West' now co-exist with hybrid cultural forms. These are frequently affected not only by each other but also by memories and experiences of colonisation, oppression and marginalisation, and of resistance, emancipation and liberation. Furthermore, it must be remembered that modernism is not a purely Western phenomenon, but has been pursued and developed throughout the world and in migrant communities within the so-called West. For example, artists from overseas made a significant contribution to British modern art before and after the second world war; so-named Commonwealth writers have made an outstanding contribution to postwar fiction and poetry in English; there was an explosion of creativity in the visual arts in the 1980s and 1990s, including photography, film and multimedia; until the recent decline of regional and independent theatre there was a lively and innovative theatrical tradition involving Asian and black actors and directors; and commentators are beginning to speak of a Muslim renaissance spearheaded by Muslim artists.[5] No single programme could adequately represent such depth and range. The agenda itself will have to be diverse, therefore, and will have to respond to reciprocal influences that refuse to stand still. There are many different but complementary ways of being included and represented, just as there are, and always have been, many different ways of being British.

12.15 Third, attention needs to be paid to contemporary history. Selective amnesia applies not just in relation to empire; there is widespread denial or wilful ignorance in relation to events and episodes within living memory. One crucial topic that needs to be embraced in the culture as a whole is the migrant experience itself – the decision to leave home, the farewells, landfall and culture shock, encounters with both overt and subtle racism, the building of a new life. There is rich evidence in oral testimonies, family stories and memories, photographs, documents and letters, certificates, souvenirs, possessions. It is important that such material should be collected and exhibited – in museums, galleries, libraries and other public spaces, and in books, film and theatre. 'The people in this book,' writes a young author who worked on an oral history project with her parents' generation in the late 1990s, 'like so many thousands of others, have triumphed in the face of adversity. They have not been broken and they have not given up. They have persevered in the face of signs in boarding houses reading, "No Blacks, no Irish, no dogs". They have stood their ground and, whether acknowledged or not, they have made Britain into a better place to live.'[6]

12.16 Also part of the whole migrant experience are a great number of specific projects, campaigns, tragedies, organisations, defining events, struggles and confrontations, key personalities and seminal publications. Many stories of the last 40 years are well known nationally: Kelso Cochrane, Quddus Ali, *Murder in the Playground*, the Deptford fire; Grunwick, Scarman and Macpherson, the anti-sus and anti-bussing campaigns; the Guildford Four and the Birmingham Six; the 1976 Race Relations Act, and much illiberal legislation; the building of gurdwaras, mandirs and mosques; *The Satanic Verses*, and ensuing feelings of anger, isolation, solidarity and assertiveness.[7] Most stories remain local, in individual cities, towns and boroughs. Yet in their own place they are powerful templates for understanding the present, anticipating the future and mobilising energy for change. All such stories, whether national or local, are material for the full range of the arts. One of the finest explorations of contemporary history in this connection was the play *The Colour of Justice*, based on transcripts of the Stephen Lawrence Inquiry.[8]

12.17 Fourth, there is a whole raft of funding priorities in the arts not intrinsically concerned with race and cultural identity issues but nevertheless relevant to the subject matter of this report. They include a greater emphasis on supporting and promoting the creation of new works, as distinct from the conservation of tradition and heritage; the funding of the means of production as distinct from the commissioning of new work (for example, the funding of community video equipment and related training); an emphasis on the role of the arts in the corporate life of local communities; the widening of access to entertainment and news from other cultures, countries and continents, and measures to widen access to those arts usually thought of as elitist, particularly theatre and classical music, and most museums and galleries.

12.18   Fifth, there must be a redistribution of funding. More money must be specifically targeted at the objectives of (a) promoting art that explores Britain's new cultural diversity and (b) revisiting and reinterpreting the past. Money alone is not enough, certainly, although it is essential. We are proposing a major culture change – indeed, a cultural revolution. It would be absurd to suppose that this could take place without a significant redirection of resources. We stress that a retargeting of resources is required rather than, necessarily, the creation of new resources. *We recommend that organisations funded by public bodies lose some of their funding if they do not make changes in their staff and governance, and do not* demonstrably *make their programmes and activities more inclusive.*

12.19   Sixth, institutional obstacles must be addressed in all the main arts bodies. There is an operational inertia – a preference for business as usual – which discourages key professionals from re-examining their practices from scratch and from trying to alter the habits of a professional lifetime. Institutional racism, as summarised in Box 5.2 in Chapter 5, is widespread. It is also, however, denied. 'The arts and media sectors do not see any implications for themselves in the Macpherson report,' someone wrote to us. 'In other words, they do not believe that institutional racism in any way permeates their domains ... If your report does not address this misapprehension, then the arts and media sector will simply ignore its recommendations and findings.' Over the years, there have been a number of potentially valuable initiatives, such as special traineeships and fast-tracking schemes for Asian and black staff. But these have not been adequately monitored, evaluated or documented. In relation to race and cultural diversity issues, *we recommend that every major arts organisation should commission an independent audit of its programmes, output, employment profile, representation of wider society and financial investment.*

The media

12.20 The six components of change outlined above in relation to the arts are all relevant also to television and the press. The media have an essential role to play in reinterpreting the mainstream, and in representing Britain as a community of communities rather than as a 95/5 society. They should depict the traditions and heritages of African, Asian, Caribbean and Irish cultures, but even more importantly should show these cultures as dynamic and developing, and in constant interaction with other cultures, both borrowing from and influencing them. They should address contemporary history. Developments that democratise and demystify the media and resist standardisation and dumbing down should be encouraged. There should be a redirection of resources and profound cultural changes in the institutions of the media and in the mindsets of all senior staff.

12.21 Over the years, substantial research has been conducted on the ways in which various communities are represented in the print and electronic media. The findings on TV representation are summarised in Box 12.2.

12.22 Problems of representation, summarised in Box 12.2, are connected with organisational and employment issues behind the scenes. The number of high-profile black and Asian television presenters gives a false picture of the industry as a whole. The situation off-screen is considerably more white. The first need in this respect is for basic information. *We recommend that broadcasters and franchise-holders be required to provide statistics broken down by ethnicity and gender in relation to grades and categories such as producer, editor and camera operator, and by management level.* Such information must be published. It is not in itself sufficient, however, to guarantee change. *We recommend that contracts and franchises depend on the production of plans (a) to increase black and Asian staff at all levels and grades; (b) to commission more work from black and Asian producers; and (c) to ensure that a proportion of programmes tackle issues of race equality and cultural diversity.*

12.23 Throughout the media and the arts there are gatekeepers who play a key

Box 12.2 **Images on television: summary of research findings**

- Representation of African, Asian, Caribbean and Irish communities and individuals is predominantly negative and/or simplistic. Communities are seen as homogeneous and unchanging. The complexities of multi-layered identities and cultural mixes are neglected. Ignorance, prejudice and negative stereotyping in wider society are compounded.

- Local media generally provide a better service than national channels. Also, imported programming, particularly from the United States, carries a greater range of positive images and role models than British channels.

- Television lags behind society itself. Audiences are more aware of cultural diversity and complexity, from their own lived experience, than media depictions show or imply.

- People actively look for representations of themselves on television, and these representations are vividly remembered. But people do not just want to be visible to themselves. They also want to be seen by others; they want mainstream television to show the true nature of contemporary society. It is not sufficient just to provide 'minority' programmes at unsocial times.

- Characterisation of African, Asian, Caribbean and Irish people is often weak. They are depicted as one-dimensional, and seem to be introduced to make a point or raise an issue or 'a problem', not as an integral and natural part of the plot. Actors from these communities have to bear a burden of representation – 'to act their skin colour' – rather than deploy the full range of their skills. There needs to be much more colour-blind casting.

- African, Asian, Caribbean and Irish people are generally depicted as being connected to, or as themselves being the cause of, social problems. They are seldom seen as social assets.[9]

role in enabling or obstructing access to opportunities – editors, producers, critics, agents, curators, arts funding officers, and so on. In the television industry they include commissioning executives, production managers, casting directors and heads of department. Many of them work on freelance contracts to tight schedules. Inevitably, they often use people they already know rather than take risks. There are therefore substantial dangers of indirect discrimination, and there is a disinclination to tackle sensitive subject matter. Problems of access are compounded by the fact that major broadcasters issue fewer open-tender documents than in the past. In order to address problems inherent in the way the industry operates, *we recommend that:*

- *the BBC should make the employment and contracting of black and Asian staff and producers an integral part of its latest reviews;*
- *broadcasters should seek to encourage the promotion of black and Asian people to commissioning editor and management posts;*
- *broadcasters and other bodies should find and develop ways of improving networking opportunities for black and Asian people in the industry;*
- *broadcasters should use their websites to provide open-tender documents;*
- *programming targets should be set similar to those that exist for countries and regions;*
- *large established production companies should occasionally be required to work in partnership with smaller companies which have developed distinctive expertise in creating programmes about race and cultural diversity.*

Media bias

12.24 Any one news story is interpreted by the reader or viewer within the context of a larger narrative, acting as a kind of filter or template. If the larger narrative is racist – or, more benignly, representative of a 95/5 society – then the story is likely to be interpreted in a racist or majority-biased way, regardless of the conscious intentions of reporters, journalists and headline-writers.[10] For example, any reference to Muslims is likely to switch on the notion, implanted by numerous other stories, that most Muslims are terrorists and/or 'fundamentalists' in their interpretation and practice of their faith. It is difficult or impossible in these circumstances for a single news item to be absorbed on its own merits. The difficulties are compounded by certain recurring juxtapositions of words. A study by the *Guardian* of its own coverage of Islam in a particular period in 1999 found that the adjective 'Islamic' was joined with 'militants' 16 times, 'extremist or extremism' 15 times, 'fundamentalism' eight times and 'terrorism' six times; in the same period the adjective 'Christian' was joined, in so far as it appeared at all, to positive words and notions or to neutral ones, such as tradition or belief.[11] Constant juxtapositions such as these have a cumulative effect on the consciousness of all readers, to the point where it is exceedingly difficult, for journalists and readers alike, to unlearn the assumptions and stereotypes they perpetuate. There are similar subliminal or overt associations in the news media between African-Caribbean people and street violence, and between asylum-seekers and scrounging.

12.25 However, certain negative stereotypes have been unlearned by the media. Most obviously, it would be unthinkable nowadays for any newspaper or broadcast to contain the kinds of antisemitic message prevalent earlier in the century. More recently, coverage of Islam has become less virulent in at least some newspapers. Among the reasons for this was the high-profile report on Islamophobia published by the Runnymede Trust in 1997, which named and shamed a wide range of newspapers, including those that pride themselves on their openness and liberalism. More importantly, it is due to the carefully focused efforts of bodies such as the Muslim Council of Britain. For example, when the *Express* ran a large front-page headline reading MOSLEM THREAT TO BOMB LONDON in September 1998, the Council made an immediate approach to the editor, pointing out that the headline was inflammatory and distressing. The next day the *Express* ran an apology, which was both educative for *Express* readers and set out the ethical and professional standards by which the paper was happy to be judged:

> There is a danger that whole communities, sometimes whole races, are deemed at worst guilty, at best suspicious, because of the actions of a few of their members. It is wrong to suggest that all Muslims are extremists ... In our headline yesterday on the arrest of several men in London by anti-terrorist police it was not our intention to cause offence to the Muslim Community. We're sorry.

12.26 It would be valuable if the professional ethics implied in this apology were to be codified, at least by each newspaper individually, but preferably by the National Union of Journalists generally. It would also be valuable if as many organisations as possible, not just the Muslim Council of Britain and its many supporters, were to complain formally and concertedly whenever coverage of a community is palpably unfair and inaccurate. Even a small number of phone calls or letters can make a difference. *We recommend that voluntary-sector organisations seek funds to set up media monitoring projects, so that they may complain regularly about coverage they find offensive. Newspapers and television companies should be named and shamed in high-profile ways.* Through a combination of professional self-regulation by journalists and constant pressure by the public, the worst stereotypes will be removed and new rules of engagement will be drawn up. The report on Islamophobia mentioned above proposed the following to summarise the values the new rules would embody:

> The right to freedom of political speech and public debate is essential but is not an absolute right which has no limits. There are other fundamental democratic values. Because of the vital importance of promoting equality of opportunity and respect for everyone, of respecting the human dignity of everyone and of discouraging group prejudice and the scapegoating of minorities, the right to freedom of speech must not be abused, in the competition for readers and viewers, by exploiting or encouraging racial, religious or cultural prejudices. Media coverage must not only be honest, truthful and lawful; it must seek to avoid, whether blatantly or covertly, stirring up prejudice, or encouraging racial or religious discrimination.

12.27 The development of a new code of ethics will be facilitated by the recruitment of more African, Asian and Caribbean journalists at influential levels. A survey undertaken in early 1999 found that of over 2,000 people at such levels in the daily and Sunday press, only 43 were black or Asian.[12] Of these, more than half were on just four papers: the *Guardian* (eight), the *Express* (six), the *Financial Times* (six) and the *Independent* (five). The papers with the worst records were the *Daily Mail*, the *Mirror*, the *Observer* and the *Sunday Telegraph* (all two), the *Daily Telegraph*, the *Sun*, *The Times*, the *News of the World* (all one) and the *Mail on Sunday* and the *Sunday Mirror* (none at all). There are substantial implications in these dire figures for the papers' recruitment and promotion policies, and for all bodies connected with journalists' training and career development. *We recommend that every newspaper publish, both in its pages and on its website, a breakdown of its staff by gender, ethnicity and seniority. The breakdowns should be regularly updated and accompanied by statements of the paper's plans to increase the employment of black and Asian staff.*

12.28 Measures to deal with inclusion, representation and employment will be implemented in the midst of profound technological changes and commercial restructuring. These will also have an immense impact on the capacity of the media to represent Britain as a community of communities, with new material creatively exploring the issues that both divide and unite the country. The new technologies involve high-speed cable or broadband links, the merging of television, telephone, radio, print and the Internet, and the possibility of accessing material from all over the world, in the home or the workplace or through the mobile phone network, 24 hours a day. Many commentators fear that the commercial restructurings, bringing together broadcasting, print and Internet companies, mean that control over what can in practice be produced, disseminated and accessed will be concentrated in a small number of global corporations, integrated both vertically and horizontally, with constant cross-promotions within their own massive spheres of influence. 'Content may be king,' it is said, 'but access to the home [or anywhere else] is king-maker'. *We recommend that the regulatory framework for digital TV include, at least in the short term, protection for programme suppliers which offer channels targeted at particular cultural interests.* Further, *we recommend that the implications and workings of the new digital universe be closely monitored.*

Sport

12.29 In *The Satanic Verses* there is a character who watches cricket matches with a vivid sense of the history of imperialism:

> When the England cricket team played India at the Brabourne Stadium, he prayed for an England victory, for the game's creators to defeat the local upstarts, for the proper order of things to be maintained. (But the games were invariably drawn, owing to the featherbed somnolence of the Brabourne Stadium wicket; the great issue, creator versus imitator, coloniser against colonised, had perforce to remain unresolved.)

12.30 Rushdie's distinctions (coloniser/colonised, creator/imitator, originator/upstart) set the context for the Tebbit test of loyalty (1990), John Major's declaration that county cricket grounds are quintessentially part of Britain's cultural fabric (in his speech on St George's Day, 1993), and *Wisden*'s[13] claim in 1995 that black British and Asian British cricketers are culturally and biologically incapable of giving to England 'that little bit extra' needed to go 'beyond the call of duty' in order to win

matches. His references also contextualise the ostracism faced by black and Asian players at recreational levels.[14]

12.31   There are comparable problems in all sports. For example, there is widespread ostracisation of Asian footballers, at all levels, from recreational to professional.[15] Exclusion from the pitch or the terraces is tantamount to exclusion from major sources of local pride and identification – a sense of belonging to their own town, city or conurbation is at least as important for many people as a sense of belonging to a country. Sport is part of a place's cultural fabric. Among other things, it provides (at least for men, and particularly younger men) a huge reservoir of talking points, and of shared memories, jokes and allusions, which transcend the rivalries that are an inherent part of sport. For there are shared values – the rules of the game, admiration for skill and teamwork, the concept of 'foe-honouring'. Sport is an essential element in the daily business of 'putting the world in order' through continuous chat and social interaction.

12.32   In many parts of the country the situation appears to be improving, particularly with regard to football. There are anecdotal accounts – not yet confirmed by research – of substantially greater involvement of young

Box 12.3 **Aspects of football**

In 1997 Celtic Football Club was contacted by one of our 53,000 season ticket holders who asked if the Club would consider flying the flags of Pakistan and India in recognition of 50 years of independence ... His own background was Indian and his wife was Irish and ... his children take great pride in their joint Indian, Irish and Scottish identities ... Celtic, as a club founded in 1888 to help the Irish integrate into Scottish life, but importantly not at the expense of their own cultural identity, was delighted to fly the flags and celebrate the culturally diverse society that Scotland enjoys. The warm response Celtic received from around the world for this small but meaningful gesture was very encouraging.

From a letter to the Commission

(1) The Club needs to be seen to own the project. (2) Supporters need to accept responsibility for their role in opposing racist abuse and making Asian and black fans welcome. (3) Ways need to be found to involve supporters actively in campaigns, rather than merely adopting a moral 'don't do it' approach. (4) Projects need to involve all relevant agencies – local authorities, police, community groups, youth clubs and schools, and Football in the Community schemes. (5) Resources are needed – to pay staff, produce materials, set up coaching schemes, and so on. (6) It is valuable to use informal means of communication familiar to supporters, for example fanzines and fans' forums. (7) It is prudent to be careful when dealing with the local media, for race sells papers, or so the editors think. (8) Don't despair – there is strong support for anti-racist campaigns among all kinds of fans.

From a review of Football Unites Racism Divides,
Sheffield United Football Club

black and Asian people in sport at recreational levels. High-profile projects initiated in professional football seem to have had a marked effect on reducing levels of racist abuse on the terraces. At the very least, such projects have put the concept of racism on the agenda. The Kick Racism out of Football campaign was set up by the Commission for Racial Equality and the Professional Footballers Association and now has the support of nearly all bodies and interests involved in the administration of football. Among the notable projects it has developed or inspired are

Bhoys Against Bigotry, run by Celtic; Red, White and Black at the Valley, run by Charlton Athletic; Football Unites Racism Divides, run by Sheffield United (see Box 12.3); and Leeds Fans United Against Racism and Fascism. The success of such projects, based on a combination of sponsorship from commercial sources and innovative use of publicity materials such as supporters' magazines, provides a model of good practice that other sports would do well to emulate. *We recommend that there be further pooling of experience from the range of anti-racist projects that have been implemented in football clubs, and that lessons for other major sports be learned.*

12.33   In addition, *we recommend that all sports organisations be required to draw up and publish equal opportunity policies to show how they intend to increase the numbers of black and Asian people involved as managers, administrators, coaches and officials. Further, we recommend that all sports organisations be required to publish anti-racist statements and monitor their effectiveness.*

12.34   The problems are great, but so are the opportunities. At the highest levels, sportsmen and women represent their country not only in the conventional sense but also by portraying an image of it. They therefore have a powerful effect on society's cultural fabric, and it is thus of profound importance that policies on the arts, media and sport be thought of holistically. *We recommend that the administrations at Cardiff, Holyrood and Westminster issue policy statements on the interconnections between the arts, media and sport in the development of Britain as a multi-ethnic society.*

Chapter 13

Health and Welfare

> *Mainstream British people seem to believe that non-English speakers and different dress codes are inferior. In mainstream health and social services there are little or no provisions for language interpreting. Not only children, but also cleaners are often used for interpreting in serious matters of health even in major hospitals ... One hospital was rather surprised when I sent them an invoice following a six-hour interpreting session on a serious case involving complicated diagnosis and treatment. They said they never paid for interpreting as they have no budget for such things. When I asked how they managed with translations, 'we use relatives' was the reply. 'And if there are no relatives?' I enquired. 'We use cleaners,' said the head nurse.*
>
> Letter from a Somali organisation, London

13.1 In summer 1998 a patient in a critical condition was admitted to an intensive care unit in the North of England.[1] Brain stem testing established that he was dead, and his body was put on a life support machine. As is customary in such cases, his relatives were asked if they would agree to his organs being used to save other lives. They agreed in principle and signed a form authorising removal of heart, kidneys, lungs, liver and pancreas. They added in a written note: ' Family consent is conditional upon recipients being white (that is, not of ethnic origin).' This condition was accepted by the hospital.

13.2 Tests showed that the man's heart and lungs were not suitable for transplantation. The liver was given to a local transplant unit and the kidneys were offered to units throughout the country, under the auspices of the UK Transplantation Service Support Authority (UKTSSA). The initial telephone conversation between the hospital and the UKTSSA was tape-recorded. 'These organs cannot go to anyone who is not white,' said the hospital's transplant co-ordinator. The duty officer at the UKTSSA replied: 'You've got to respect it, I suppose.' A second duty officer, however, telephoned a manager for advice. 'If [the co-ordinator] completely guaranteed ... that that was the stipulation,' said the manager, 'I think you have to stick by it.' The duty officer then worked through the national waiting list, ringing hospitals in order of priority. But he skipped the third and fourth priority patients, who were both children with Asian-sounding names. Eventually, the kidneys were transplanted into two white people. Both the hospitals concerned knew of the stipulation that the kidneys were not to be given to black or Asian people, and did not object. Defending the behaviour of the UKTSSA, its chief executive was quoted as saying that the authority was simply 'a message handling bureau'.[2]

13.3 The episode was a graphic example of the complex interplay between individual and institutional racism.[3] It showed that the NHS is capable of treating black and Asian people less favourably than white people, even in emergencies and on life-and-death issues, and that there are health professionals at all levels of seniority who see nothing wrong with colluding with a particularly crude form of biological racism. At fault were the norms of the occupational culture of the NHS and a range of established customs and procedures, not just the actions of certain individuals. Progress has since been made within the health service to tackle institutional racism, we are aware,[4] but much remains to be done. The scale of the task ahead was well documented in reports published by the Department of Health (DoH) in autumn 1999 and March 2000, and by the British Medical Association (BMA) in January 2000.[5] Likewise it is implicit in the recommendations and principles of *New Life for Health*, the April 2000 report of the Commission on the NHS set up by the Association of Community Health Councils for England and Wales.[6]

13.4 In this chapter we review the twin roles of the NHS as (a) a provider of services and (b) an employer. The roles are linked in a striking paradox. The NHS depends, and for several decades has depended, on the contributions of Asian, black and Irish doctors, nurses, managers and ancillary staff. At the same time, patterns of mortality and morbidity are more serious in Asian, black and Irish communities than in the population as a whole, and there is much insensitivity in the NHS to their distinctive experiences, situations and requirements.

The NHS as service provider

13.5 We argued in the opening chapters that public bodies should treat

Box 13.1 **Health and social care: facts and issues**

Poor health is associated with poverty. Certain black and Asian communities, particularly Bangladeshi and Pakistani communities, are more likely than the rest of the population to live in deprived districts, be unemployed, have low incomes, live in poor-quality accommodation and be the victims of crime.[7]

The Irish community, under-researched and rarely appearing in ethnically sensitive monitoring, suffers from health problems linked with poor housing and poverty. Research shows that Irish migrants' health has deteriorated since migration, and that death rates among the Irish living in Britain are worse than for Irish people who remain in Ireland.[8] It also shows that worse-than-average health continues among the children of Irish-born migrants. The invisibility of the Irish as a distinct community has led to the neglect of their specific health problems.

Racism – the experience of harassment and actual and threatened violence, and the stress of living in a hostile society – directly harms health. American research has suggested that high blood pressure may be a clinical response to racist abuse, rather than an inevitable biological characteristic of black people. Similar explanations may be applicable to mental health disorders.

Racist harassment from within the health service itself is an issue highlighted in 2000 by the government's Mental Health Act Commission.[9] A disproportionate number of black patients are forcibly detained in mental hospitals (an issue we return to below). Once there, many experience racist harassment from both staff and fellow patients.

Access to appropriate healthcare for refugee communities is a serious issue, for refugees by definition are fleeing trauma, persecution, dislocation and often torture. However, some material on support for refugees is now available.[10]

Communities formed through migration face additional poverty, and therefore health risks, as they age. For the pension system depends on lifelong contributions – an impossibility among people who migrated as adults and who have worked intermittently and for low earnings.[11]

Some diseases disproportionately affect certain communities (see below). The expression of these diseases varies from one community to another and demonstrates the diversity of Britain's population and the need for culturally specific healthcare and knowledge. For example, health workers are not usually aware that people from South Asia are at risk of thalassaemia and so do not offer carrier screening, genetic counselling or prenatal diagnosis.

High blood pressure and stroke
In African-Caribbean people in England and Wales death rates from stroke are 76 per cent higher in men and 110 per cent higher in women than in the population as a whole.[12] Other communities suffering higher-than-average mortality rates from strokes in people under the age of 65 include Bangladeshis, Pakistanis and the Irish.[13] There is a higher prevalence of high blood pressure among African-Caribbeans, with one in four women and one in six men reporting a diagnosis.[14]

Suicide
Suicide rates among some communities (Pakistanis and Bangladeshis) are lower than the average for Britain as a whole. However, particularly high rates are found among the Irish; indeed, they are higher than for any other group. Higher-than-average rates are also reported among young Indians and Africans.[15]

Cancer
Irish men and women experience considerably higher rates of lung cancer than all other groups.[16] Uptake of cervical screening among Pakistani and Bangladeshi women was low in a national survey, and half the non-attendees lacked basic information about cervical smears.[17] Yet a study carried out in east London found that Asian and black women were enthusiastic about cervical cytology screening once they understood the purpose of the test and its procedures. Low-cost interventions such as training GP reception staff improved breast-screening uptake, particularly among Indian women in east London.[18] Administrative and interpretation barriers were important factors in preventing participation in the screening programme, as was the inadequacy of surgery premises.

Diabetes
A Policy Studies Institute survey reported the highest rates (7.5 per cent) of diabetes among Bangladeshi and Pakistani people. The overall rate of diabetes for all South Asians and African-Caribbeans was 5.9 per cent, compared with 2.2 per cent for Chinese and white people.[19]

Sickle cell disease
There are an estimated 6,000–9,000 people with sickle cell disease in Britain. Almost all are of African or Caribbean origin. Management of painful crises varies from the best in some teaching hospitals in London and the Midlands to inadequate in some GP clinics and accident and emergency departments of district general hospitals.

---

people both equally and differently. The need for both equal and different treatment is seen particularly clearly in services providing health and social care. The realities to which services have to respond are summarised in Box 13.1.

13.6   A health service committed to reducing inequalities and to taking action against racisms must acknowledge and address all the factors summarised in Box 13.1. Policy and practice must not be colour- or culture-blind. Documents such as the *National Performance Framework*[20] and the *National Priorities Guidance*[21] must have an explicit race equality dimension, and targets must be set to reduce inequalities in health between different communities. There are some signs that this process is beginning. The *National Service Framework for Diabetes*, to be published in 2001, 'is to ensure that policy development and implementation encompasses and is sensitive to the health needs of members of minority ethnic groups'.[22] The *National Service Framework for Mental Health*, published in September 1999, includes a number of targets aiming to reduce inequality.[23] There must be focused training for professionals; targeted campaigns to provide information and promote awareness of risk; and targets relating to improvements in access. For example, on the last point, the provision of proper interpretation services (see below) and the appointment where appropriate of female health professionals should be set as performance indicators.

Research and impact appraisal

13.7   The Cabinet Office advice is unequivocal, though not yet widely known, let alone heeded. The approach to impact analysis and equality could not be clearer: 'When you present policy proposals they must include an impact analysis which clearly brings out the effect on particular sections of the population and how you have addressed any relevant data. If necessary commission new data, ensuring that statistics are separated by race, as far as it is possible to do so.'[24] The DoH is looking at how to implement this approach. According to the 1999 DoH report: 'Officials will pilot an approach that calls for building proposals from the perspectives of black and other ethnic minority groups and testing out how these can be shaped to also meet the needs of the white population, that is, the reverse of current practice.'[25]

13.8   The government papers quoted above accept that research and data analysis, thus far, have not adequately examined the distribution of benefits and resources. To be inclusive, provision must be based on secure data. At present, however, there are problems in both research and data collection. Research into the health needs of black, Asian and Irish communities has so far been qualitative rather than quantitative, and short-term project-funded rather than long-term. Such research needs to adopt a higher profile. In Wales, the Health Committee of the National Assembly's funding for two development officers to look at 'black and minority ethnic health issues' is welcome. *We recommend that there be substantial black, Asian and Irish representation, both professional and lay, on the Service Delivery and Organisation Research and Delivery programme.* Further, *we recommend that research into the impact of racism on health be given a high priority within the health research programme.*

13.9   Black, Asian and Irish representation could help to ensure that the impact of racism on health is properly researched and recognised and appropriate action taken. It could also help to ensure that links are made between, for example, high rates of exclusion from school of African-Caribbean young men and involvement, or not, in school health programmes. This is not, of course, to say that the burden of race equality action should fall on black, Asian and Irish people, but rather to affirm the crucial importance of direct experience. As a research report commissioned by the NHS Executive concluded: 'the inclusion of a minority consumer perspective tended to widen the focus of attention to include issues of discrimination in employment and housing, and racial harassment'.[26] The DoH acknowledges that the statistical base for analysing access and results by ethnicity is currently unreliable. Through the National Health Service Information Strategy, and as electronic patient records and electronic health records become more widespread, there should be no technical reasons for insecurity of data.

13.10   It is vitally important that proper monitoring by ethnicity should take place throughout the health and welfare systems. All services should be monitored for ethnicity, language and religion by nationally prescribed categories, to ensure consistency for comparative purposes. It should be a requirement that all primary care trusts[27] provide information to their local health authority about the ethnicity and religion of those registered with them. Health authorities should be required to return reports to a central monitoring unit at the DoH, and they should also be required to report results to their local communities.

13.11   There should be annual audits and analysis of this information. Who is using the service? Who, more importantly, is not, and why not? If members of particular communities are not using services, what is preventing or discouraging them from doing so? Authorities should have a duty to show that everybody they are responsible for has access to and is using all their services. If services are not being used they should make sure that they are satisfied with their explanations as to why not. The recently introduced Health Improvement Programmes provide a good opportunity for setting targets and reporting progress in reducing ethnically as well as regionally based health inequalities.

13.12   The present government's intention to reduce infant and adult mortality from specific causes by quantified amounts is laudable. *We recommend that similar targets be applied to other care issues, for example, the provision of interpreting services throughout the health service and culturally specific food in hospitals and residential care homes. Targets should not be colour-blind. For example, waiting lists should not just be monitored, but monitored by ethnicity and religion as well.* How can it be ensured that authorities implement policy as intended? *We recommend that record-keeping and monitoring by ethnicity, use of the data to set targets and race equality audits using appropriate categories be established, as they are an essential part of any efficient management system, in both health and social services. Specific results must be sought, which must be qualitative as well as quantitative.*

13.13   To repeat, access to healthcare is crucial to inclusion. Yet such research as does exist suggests that access is far from equal for all peoples and all communities. The first place most patients go for help is their doctor's surgery. Access to GPs is therefore basic to healthcare. Yet a study in Birmingham found that people with South Asian surnames were almost four times as likely as others to be excluded from practice lists.[28] Research among Chinese people working in catering in Oxfordshire found that although they had serious rates of long-term illnesses, one in five were not registered with GP practices. Information and communication must be available in community languages.

13.14   Trained interpreters are necessary so that people can use health services effectively. This is a particular issue in mental health, where a government commission found that although almost 25 per cent of black, Asian and other minority patients in the 104 mental health and learning disability units visited by Mental Health Commission representatives spoke English as an additional language, there had been almost no recourse to interpreting services during their detention. As a result, according to one commissioner, some mental health units do not even know what needs their patients have.[29] Welcome recognition of this issue is to be found in the May 2000 consultation document on the review of the Mental Health Act (Scotland),[30] which acknowledges the specific needs of black, Asian and other minority communities and accepts that these are possibly not yet being properly met. The review refers to interpretation, information in community languages and 'religious or cultural imperatives', and asks whether such services should be provided as a matter of law.

13.15   Children should not be used to interpret conversations between service users and professionals. Despite official recognition of this, children are still used as interpreters for their parents. This bad practice places extra stress on patients for whom English is an additional language, as well as on the informal interpreter and health professionals. Furthermore, it breaches confidentiality between professional and patient. Interpreters should understand all the related topics that may crop up in discussions between medical staff and their patients, such as community care arrangements and how the hospital appointments system works. Ideally, interpreters should also be able to put time aside to work with individual patients outside the doctor's office, making appointments with consultants, hospitals, social workers or other elements of the social services system.

13.16 For districts where numbers are too small for it to be practical to provide regular face-to-face interpreting in all relevant languages, there should at least be access to a properly trained and certified telephone interpreting service. No patient in any doctor's surgery should be told that there is no access to an interpreting service; in every health authority some form of interpreting service should be available 24 hours a day. *We recommend the training and appointment of more interpreters.* Further, *we recommend that all NHS primary care trusts be required to have a contract with a telephone interpreting service.* This good practice already exists in London.[31]

13.17 Thought should be given to the location of new healthcare services. During its consultation period, the Commission visited a new health centre on the Broadwater Farm estate in Haringey, London. The contribution made by the centre to its local community's sense of security and general quality of life is partly because of its central location on the estate. It is a model of how the planning of services should be implemented, particularly when targeting districts with unusually high levels of social distress.

13.18 A disproportionate number of children living in poverty are members of African-Caribbean, Bangladeshi, Irish, Pakistani or refugee communities. In poverty there are arguably even greater barriers to an improved quality of life for children than there are for adults, as children are more dependent. Children living in poverty and in overcrowded conditions suffer from poor health. They have more childhood illnesses, in particular the respiratory illnesses associated with damp and poor ventilation. Child poverty and the problems that poverty brings are foremost among the inequities facing today's children. Therefore, *we recommend that child benefit, linked to each individual child, be increased significantly, to give every child living in poverty, from whatever background, a better chance in life.* We welcome the above-inflation increases in child benefit introduced in 1999 and 2000 and hope that similar or greater increases will be instituted in the future.

13.19 The workings of the child protection system are a source of concern within black, Asian and Irish communities, but the experience of children from these communities within the system is under-researched. An NSPCC report concludes that lack of research may be attributable to 'elements of racism in the research process itself'.[32] There is evidence that African-Caribbean children and mixed-ethnicity children are disproportionately represented within the system for children in care, and Asian children are under-represented. However, record-keeping is often inadequate, reinforcing once again the need for proper monitoring throughout the welfare state. Research has found that care plans are missing for many children, and that information about their cultural background, for example their religious affiliation or linguistic heritage, is not recorded.[33]

13.20 The same research shows that Asian and African-Caribbean parents are the least likely to apply to the social services for help, although a significant number of parents of mixed-ethnicity children do. These are mostly single white mothers, living in conditions of extreme vulnerability, with absent co-parents, in poor housing and socially isolated. A significantly greater number of African-Caribbean children than white children are taken into care quickly, which indicates how the social services regard black parenting and/or the behaviour of black children. It has been noted that 'training for staff and carers on equal opportunities and anti-racist practice was very sparse and lacked any impetus'.[34] Social services departments dealing with children at risk of being taken into care must be required to provide a proper linguistic environment, with trained interpreters. This is particularly important in formal situations such as child protection case conferences. *We recommend that the DoH require social services departments to record information about the ethnicity, religion and home language(s) of all children receiving direct services of any kind.*

13.21 The voluntary sector, as well as initiatives such as Newpin and Sure Start, offers valued support to families. Parents who have only recently

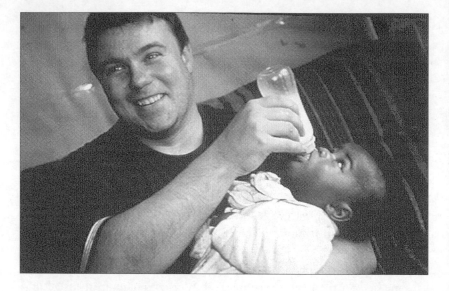

come to Britain may not have networks of support among their own family or friends living near by, and may need specific advice on legal obligations and rights. The voluntary and community sector in particular has earned the trust of communities where statutory agencies may be viewed, in the words of one contributor to the Commission, as people 'who criticise you and take your kids away'. Particular support may be needed by parents who find themselves alone. Some men are separated from their families by Britain's lengthy immigration procedures – in these cases women may in effect be lone parents for many years. It is very difficult as a single parent to combine paid employment and satisfactory childcare; however, the introduction of the working family tax credit may partially alleviate this problem. Employment practices in Britain are not child-friendly, and the longer hours now worked by those in employment are making the problem worse. This is another area where poor people, on low earnings and sometimes with only one (working) adult in the household, struggle disproportionately. These parents cannot afford private childcare, and they may work unsocial hours incompatible with a child's day, let alone with school holidays. Few organisations offer childcare. Such parents are also likely to live in poor housing and work in the informal economy, which lacks any organised working practices.

13.22 African-Caribbean and South Asian groups are concerned by the high unemployment rates among young men, which can lead to associated problems of poverty, stress, alienation, use of addictive drugs and mental ill health. There is growing concern about the number of men living outside family structures, who are more likely to be unemployed and to suffer from bad health. Men should be encouraged to participate in parenting and family life and to feel valued as members of families. *We recommend the wider establishment of one-stop shops for health issues, including parenting education. All parenting advice should be available to both mothers and fathers, and men should be encouraged to participate.*

13.23 Demographic changes mean that there will be a substantial increase in the numbers of older people from diverse groups who will be users of a care system that has until now been indifferent to cultural sensitivity towards clients. There is a need for investment in the care of black and Asian older people, for, as a paper written for the Commission notes, 'they were regarded as marginal on three levels; mainstream agenda, mainstream-age agenda and in race relations'.[35] There are many issues concerning the treatment of the ill, the dying and relatives of the dying, where religious and cultural practices may be of vital importance to those involved and may be approached with casual indifference or worse by healthcare professionals. For example, there are differences in the way death itself is treated, in mourning practices, and in the whole question of burial or cremation. *We recommend that all those employed in the health and social welfare services be trained in cultural awareness and sensitivity.* Current NVQ care training has an anti-discrimination element and this should be extended. In social work training the curriculum includes 'awareness of racism' as a universal and mainstream element, but this is not the case with health professionals, for whom it has always been perceived as an optional extra. The issue of cultural sensitivity should be integrated into the core training of all doctors, nurses and other health service professionals.

13.24 Extended family households are more common among some communities, principally South Asian and Chinese, than they are in the population at large. *We recommend that, because of the benefits of mutual support, greater priority be given in housing allocation to helping members of families to live with or near each other.* The benefits system works in ways that are detrimental to large or extended below-average-income family households, which are common in Pakistani and Bangladeshi communities. A member of such a household who becomes unemployed will not be able to get housing benefit unless they are personally liable to pay rent to a landlord outside the family. If this household member does claim housing benefit, then this benefit is reduced because other members of the extended family live in the household. In some cases, claimants can lose their housing benefit completely. Current policy therefore militates against extended families living together when some members are unemployed and some low-paid employed, yet this is a common pattern in Bangladeshi and Pakistani households. Also the payment of housing benefit to the elderly should not depend upon them living independently. The state should recognise the advantages of extended families and the support they can offer to the old, the young and the infirm. If benefits were linked exclusively to individuals, whether adults or children, there would be no penalty in living together and caring for family members.

13.25 African-Caribbean people are diagnosed as psychotic out of all proportion to their presence in the population. Research has found an incidence of diagnosed psychosis around 75 per cent above that diagnosed in white people.[36] Treatment is an acute issue. One research project found that the rate of compulsory detention for African-Caribbeans was five times that of the white population, whereas the incidence of psychosis among those detained was only twice as high.[37] Incarceration rates alone raise major issues about who is penalised and disadvantaged within the health service. Young black and Asian men are over-represented in the 'care and youth justice systems and being sectioned under the Mental Health Act, 1983'.[38] The over-representation of black people in secure units, special hospitals, electroconvulsive therapy and drug treatments, and 'challenging behaviour' units[39] is likewise an issue of acute concern. The one area of mental health treatment where black people appear to be under-represented is in counselling. *We recommend co-ordinated inter-agency action to cut the numbers of young black and Asian men held in state institutions, and that targets be set for this.*

The NHS as employer

13.26 The vast majority of black and Asian employees in the NHS are to be found in the lower grades.[40] For example, black nurses are greatly under-represented at senior levels.[41] Black and Asian nurses account for 8 per cent of the nursing workforce, yet under 1 per cent of directors of nursing. 'Nurses, midwives and health visitors from black and ethnic minority groups are poorly represented in service positions, and many do not have the same access to education, training and career development opportunities as colleagues with similar experience and qualifications.'[42]

13.27 Racism damages students applying to medical schools,[43] students sitting exams,[44] the career progress of medical staff,[45] the fate of people who are the subjects of complaints,[46] and remuneration prospects through the system of distinction awards for consultants.[47] Analysis of membership of the councils of the various Royal Colleges indicates an almost total absence of Asian or African surnames. In the face of the accumulated evidence the pioneers of research in this area concluded that, despite a number of initiatives, 'little seems to have changed, and it is an indictment of our profession that we still seem to tolerate a situation in which people's careers and livelihoods are jeopardised simply because they have the wrong name (and hence the wrong colour of skin)'.[48] *We recommend monitoring by ethnicity of short-term contracts; external as well as internal advertisement of all DoH posts; medical recruitment advertising in the black and Asian press; training in equalities issues in recruitment and selection for all medical recruitment panel members; and acceptance of the recommendations of the 'Recruitment of Doctors' guidelines produced by the BMA in January 2000. Further, we recommend that the DoH undertake a thorough review and overhaul of the consultant distinction award system to ensure that issues of equity and diversity are central to its operation, and that targets be set for black and Asian membership of the councils of all Royal Colleges.*

13.28 Medical and nursing schools are the key gatekeepers for the clinical workforce in the NHS, but the gates are not yet equitably open. *We recommend targets for black and Asian representation on education and training consortia and Healthwork UK, and urgent action to achieve these.* In 1998 the Council of Heads of Medical Schools agreed to initiate action to address the possibility of discrimination at the admissions stage;[49] there is scope for the DoH to influence this through its sponsorship of student doctors. *We recommend that the DoH provide guidance for medical school candidates to encourage those coming from family backgrounds other than medicine. We further recommend that the DoH use its sponsorship of student*

Box 13.2 **Voices: working in the NHS**

Black employees should feel lucky if they reach the status of ward or service managers as not many make it beyond that. Even then there is a price attached. While white managers feel that their rights to manage are well earned, black managers are made to feel privileged when reaching that position. ... For many, the only way to grow into the job is through undying loyalty to those who pull the strings. Of course, that means distancing themselves from any blackness and to be seen to be tough on people of the same racial background so as to show that racial affinity is not going to get in their way. Black managers who go against the grain are grounded and their heads will be the first to roll when a financial crisis arises. Frankly, it scares the hell out of me to see how divided we are among ourselves.

From a paper submitted to the Commission

While it is difficult and potentially dangerous to abuse the white doctors, the timid, helpless overseas doctors become an easy target.

From a letter in Hospital Doctor, 1999

I am a trade union officer who has been fighting racism in every which way one can imagine since I joined the NHS more than a decade ago. What has happened to me is well beyond belief because I am made to pay for forcing management into complying with delivering the equal opportunities policies that had been sitting in its drawers for so long. My employer is denying me my civil rights to perform my duties as specified in my contract.

From a letter to the Commission

doctors to support the anti-racist drive of the Council of Heads of Medical Schools' action programme against discrimination in admissions.

13.29   The statistics in the DoH report[50] reveal some progress. For example, in 1996 only 4.8 per cent of consultants holding distinction awards were from black and Asian communities, although these communities made up 13.9 per cent of consultants. However, 6.2 per cent of distinction awards granted in 1998 went to black and Asian doctors.[51] Likewise black and Asian representation on health boards and committees has more than doubled, from 5 per cent to 11.9 per cent.[52] The report celebrates these statistics and, with gentle understatement, comments that 'there may be some value in examining the success factors behind these appointments and transferring the learning across to the Department's role as an employer and service provider'.[53]

13.30 In 1995 the Policy Studies Institute discovered that two-thirds of black and Asian nurses reported racist harassment from patients and from their white colleagues. The Manufacturing, Science and Finance (MSF) union maintained that 'racial discrimination operates at all levels in the NHS, right from the processing of application forms through to top jobs. It presents a concrete ceiling, which keeps talented and qualified ethnic minority staff from the positions they could be filling. Racism operates also at other levels, be it racial harassment or abuse from patients, or unequal disciplinary measures applied to ethnic minority staff.' The programme 'Tackling Racial Harassment in the NHS' is a result of this research. It is important that the programme is properly audited so that success (or lack of it) may be accurately assessed. 'Working Together', launched by the DoH in September 1998, contains targets to combat harassment. NHS employers are obliged by April 2000 to have instituted policies and procedures to address harassment by staff and patients, as well as monitoring and reporting arrangements in order to assess progress.[54]

13.31 Many of the employment issues discussed above are to be found in other areas of society as well. The next chapter considers them in further detail.

Chapter 14

Employment

A lot of employment places recognise equal opportunities, but it's like just a procedure thing ... it's not really put forward in action.

We came here because they brought us over here to do the jobs that they didn't want to do and now that we've made something of our life they're cursing us for it. I can't understand that. They want us to go back because they've finished with us ... We're not going to accept that, we're going to make ourselves better. We're going to strive to make our community better than what it is already. And we're always going to do that.

If your name's Patel and they've got Harvey Wrinkleworth-Smith, Harvey's a couple of steps ahead of Patel. Even if Patel has got greater qualifications. So there it is. The old school network.

From transcripts of the Commission's focus group research

14.1 The postwar migration to Britain was a direct response to the demand for labour in certain specific sectors of the economy. The new workers from the Caribbean, Ireland, Africa and South Asia were needed in foundries in the Midlands, textile mills in the North, transport industries in major cities and throughout the health service. They generally occupied the low-paid jobs avoided by the white working class, and for many employers were seen as a workforce of last resort. There are, of course, exceptions to this generalisation. For example, the 'African Asians' (mainly Gujarati Indians) who came to north-west London and Leicester in the early 1970s were not labour migrants but refugees with substantial resources. They could and did set up a wide range of business enterprises. Similarly, other refugee communities were established because of war or persecution in their countries of origin, not in response to labour market needs in the places to which they came. In all the new communities established in the 1950s and 1960s there were academics, teachers, doctors, engineers and business people.

14.2 Many but not all of the descendants of the original labour migrants continue to be employed in a comparatively restricted spectrum of occupational areas; are over-represented in low-paid and insecure jobs; have lower wages than the national average; and often work antisocial hours in unhealthy or dangerous environments. Many are not working at all. The underlying causes include industrial restructuring and a range of discriminatory practices by employers. Among individuals who are in work, many have good or excellent qualifications. They nevertheless have greater difficulty than white people with the same qualifications in gaining the most sought-after jobs – the top 10 per cent of jobs are denied to them by various subtle glass ceilings.[1] This is also the case for those whose parents or grandparents came originally from and to middle-class careers.

14.3 Particularly for the more competitive posts, individuals from black and Asian communities have to be not just as good as but better than their competitors in order to get the job. There is, it has been said, an 'ethnic penalty' to be paid by everyone in these communities, regardless of their qualifications and their position in the jobs hierarchy. The ethnic penalty has been defined as 'all the sources of disadvantage that might lead an ethnic group to fare less well in the labour market than do similarly qualified whites'.[2] For example, statistical analysis of census data has shown that Asian and black graduates, including those who appear to be doing well, have worse jobs than white graduates. People of Indian, African and Chinese backgrounds are generally better qualified than white people, but nevertheless have difficulty in gaining access to prestigious jobs.[3] This is not because they are new to Britain or have overseas qualifications, as the second generation experiences the same pattern and magnitude of penalties as the first generation. In short, the penalty is not a short-term problem and things are not getting better. However well qualified people are, they still meet substantial discrimination in the labour market.

14.4 Broadly, then, in the context of this report, there are two substantial tasks to be addressed: (a) to reduce unemployment and underemployment for all those who are affected; (b) to eliminate glass ceilings and ethnic penalties. The tasks have practical implications for the government at national, regional and local levels; for employers in the public, private and voluntary sectors; for unions and professional associations; and for those who provide financial and advisory support to new business enterprises. In this chapter we consider the full range of practical implications, focusing in particular on the role of government. First, we recall and stress that there is substantial diversity among and within different communities, and that the labour market itself has changed substantially over the last 20 years, and we review the research evidence relating to discrimination.

Diversity, disadvantage and polarisation

14.5   Within the overall picture sketched above there is great diversity, for different communities engage with the labour market in substantially different ways. The diversity is increasing, and in all communities there are marked differences in the experiences of women and men. There is also substantial internal polarisation within each community, and this too is increasing. Key facts and trends include the following.

- African-Caribbean and Bangladeshi men are half as likely as white men to be working as professionals – the proportions are 4 per cent and 8 per cent respectively.

- Indian and Chinese people are better qualified than white people. For example, they are substantially more likely to take A level exams.[4] However, they do not benefit proportionately from their qualifications.

- In 1998 the employment rate among white people of working age was 75.1 per cent. The average for all black and Asian people was only 57 per cent. This average obscured the facts of even greater disadvantage for people of Bangladeshi and Pakistani backgrounds – the respective figures were 35 per cent and 41 per cent. Rates for women in these communities were lower still.

- No community is systematically and comprehensively disadvantaged, for in all there are success stories as well as unemployment and poverty. When communities are compared with each other, and with themselves over time, attention must be paid to the extent of internal polarisation between high and low achievers. The degree of polarisation is currently lower among Indians than among Bangladeshis and Pakistanis. It is high among African-Caribbeans.

- Irish-born men's occupations are similar to those of the whole population. Irish women, however, are more strongly clustered into particular occupational groupings. Much higher than average proportions of Irish women are in occupations such as nursing, and

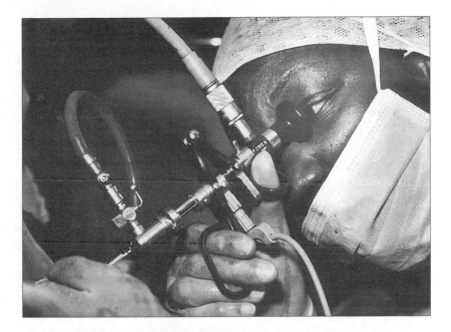

domestic and catering work. This is consistent with a general dual pattern of labour migration from Ireland: highly trained professionals for whom there is a skill shortage, and low-paid manual workers in jobs rejected by the indigenous population.[5]

- The average hourly earnings of Indian men and white men in 1998/99 were almost identical (£9.34 for Indian men, £9.29 for white men). They were about £1 an hour more than the earnings of black men and £1.50 an hour more than those of Bangladeshi and Pakistani men. Women of all backgrounds earned less than men. The highest earners were black women (£7.78 an hour), followed by white women (£7.50), Indian (£6.84) and Bangladeshi/Pakistani (£6.33).[6]

14.6   Facts such as these have to be seen against the backdrop of wider economic and industrial change. A dramatic feature of employment variation in Britain during the last two decades has been the contraction of full-time employment for men and the growth of part-time employment for women, for example. This shift is connected with major technological changes, and a move from primary and manufacturing industries to service industries – a move that is both geographical and cultural, in terms of the skills and aptitudes required. Among men, the incidence of part-time employment is greater for Asian and black communities than for white people. It is much higher for all women than for men, but more common among white women than among black and Asian women. Overall, more than two-thirds of Asian and black women in work are full-time employees, compared with 55.6 per cent of white women. Full-time employment is most common among African-Caribbean women, with over three-quarters of those in work employed full time.

14.7 There are also marked differences between communities and genders in terms of sectors of the economy. In the population as a whole, men are most commonly employed in engineering, construction, distribution, transport and communications, and in banking, insurance and business services. Women, however, work mainly in distribution, public health and education, miscellaneous services and banking, insurance and business services. In the case of black and Asian communities, the distribution of female employment is similar to that of white women. Men from many of these communities, however, are much more likely than white men to work in textiles and clothing, distribution, transport and communications and public health, and much less likely to work in the construction industry.

14.8 One of the most dynamic features of employment in the 1980s was the growth of self-employment, strongly encouraged by government policy. Black communities are substantially under-represented in self-employment, whereas South Asians are more prominent. In the case of black people, the percentage of the working population that is self-employed is barely more than half the national average.

Discrimination

14.9 There are seven separate kinds of research evidence that demonstrate or imply that inequalities in employment are caused by discrimination. These are census and survey statistics; discrimination testing, that is, special experiments using actors or fictitious applications; interviews with gatekeepers, for example the staff of employment agencies; interviews and surveys studying the experience of Asian and black people in the labour market or the workplace; the actions of aggrieved employees;

investigations conducted by the Commission for Racial Equality (CRE); and incidents that come to light at employment tribunals. In summary, the evidence from these sources is as follows.[7]

- Labour force surveys have shown that Asian and black school-leavers have less success in gaining employment than white people. This is the case even when all relevant variables, such as educational attainment, are held constant. The New Deal for 18–24 year-olds, which started in 1998, has so far produced significantly worse results for black and Asian young people than for white. The Modern Apprenticeships scheme has recruited barely half the black and Asian trainees to be expected from their numbers in the age group.
- Discrimination tests show that people can be rejected at the first stage of applying for a job simply by having an Asian or African name.[8] If candidates state their ethnicity on the application form there is the possibility of discrimination against other communities as well. In a study in the North of England and Scotland in 1996, white candidates other than Irish were found to be three times more likely to be called for interview than Asians, and five times more likely than African-Caribbeans. Irish candidates fared better than Asians and African-Caribbeans but less well than other white people.[9]
- Gatekeeper studies reveal that some employers operate with racist stereotypes and prejudices, and may take account of the racist preferences of their white workforce. Although generally concealed, this can be demonstrated by the instructions given by employers to external agencies such as the careers service when seeking recruits. Gatekeeper studies have also identified a number of routine and institutionalised recruitment practices which can severely reduce the chances of success of black and Asian applicants.[10]
- Research undertaken on employment agencies has identified further routines of exclusion. For example, agency employees who anticipate the rejection of their clients and thereby avoid submitting them to apparently racist employers perpetuate the processes of exclusion without a specific act of racial discrimination by an employer actually occurring.[11]
- Interviews with Asian and black people offer individual insights into the processes of exclusion. In one recent study young people were conscious of the extra difficulties they faced or were likely to face when putting themselves forward for opportunities. This awareness

constrained their job-seeking behaviour, so that again the very antic-
ipation of rejection on racial or ethnic grounds meant that, over
time, processes of exclusion continued to operate without individual
acts of direct discrimination taking place.[12]

The role of government

14.10 Experience in Northern Ireland in the 1980s showed that when compliance with fair employment legislation remained voluntary very few employers took serious steps to implement equal opportunities practices.
Change came only after a campaign began in the United States to put
pressure on corporations and others with investments in Northern
Ireland to make sure that their subsidiaries adopted anti-discrimination
and affirmative action practices. Largely as a result of this, the legislation was amended in 1989 to impose an obligation on employers to undertake monitoring and periodic reviews so as to ensure fair
participation of Catholic and Protestant communities in the workforce,
and the Fair Employment Commission was given extensive enforcement
powers. The House of Commons Northern Ireland Affairs Committee
reported in 1999 that these measures have led to considerable improvements in equality-based employment practices, and that there has been
a reduction in employment segregation, in the under-representation of
Catholic communities in specific areas, and in the unemployment differential between the communities.[13]

14.11 For Britain, as distinct from Northern Ireland, the government's Better
Regulation Task Force advocated in 1999 that voluntary methods should
be used in the first instance.[14] Only if these failed should any form of
compulsion be used. Similarly, the Policy Action Team on Jobs spoke of
'persuading' businesses and 'providing encouragement' rather than
making requirements, and specifically stated: 'The task is primarily one
of persuasion. Regulation would be costly and counter-productive.'[15]
However, the distinction between voluntary and compulsory is in our
view misleading. There has to be a balance between self-generated
change and a mix of incentives and rewards. The principal source of the
latter is necessarily the government, and the range of public bodies, including regional development agencies and local authorities, through
which the government works. There are also other key actors, including

unions and professional associations, and within these various forms of black and Asian self-organisation. The government's overall aim should be to eliminate differences in the employment and unemployment rates between Asian, black and Irish people and the rest of the population.[16] Monitoring of the extent to which this aim is achieved should take into account variables of age, gender, level of qualification and geographical area. In other words, statistics must be sufficiently disaggregated to ensure that like is compared with like. It is irrelevant to compare black female graduates in their 20s in London with white non-graduate men in their 50s in the North-East. The statistics must also, of course, be disaggregated by ethnicity.

14.12 For this aim to be achieved, the government's strategy must have three main components: promoting employment equity directly; ensuring that equity considerations are taken fully into account in active labour market policies and projects; and ensuring that a range of appropriate and culturally responsive support is provided for black and Asian jobseekers. These three points are discussed below.

14.13 All public bodies and institutions, and all businesses in the private sector, should be required by legislation to develop their own employment equity plans and to adjust these on the basis of regular monitoring. The plans should include targets and deadlines, and clear statements about the ways in which the targets are to be achieved. They should be formulated in consultation with recognised trade unions and professional associations. Where there is no union, consultation should be with elected workplace representatives. Either way, steps should be taken to ensure that Asian and black staff are fully consulted. The purpose of such consultation with employees is (a) to improve the plans through involving a wide range of perspective and expertise; and (b) to secure collective or workforce agreements. Employment equity plans should be issued to the workforce, and in the case of large private-sector organisations to shareholders in company annual reports. Progress in implementing them should be independently audited by accredited consultants or by the CRE. In Chapter 19 we set out the advantages of such legislation. *We recommend that as a matter of priority the government place a statutory duty on all employers to create and implement employment equity plans.*[17]

14.14 Such plans should involve:[18]
- fair recruitment procedures, which give a wide range of qualified local people the chance to compete for jobs;
- arrangements to monitor by ethnicity and gender the workforce at all levels;
- arrangements to monitor by ethnicity and gender all applicants, shortlists and new recruits;
- arrangements to achieve and maintain fair representation of Asian and black staff at all levels and in training and staff development programmes.[19]

14.15 Such legislation should give the CRE power (a) to demand information about employment equity plans; (b) to obtain binding undertakings; and (c) to institute proceedings against businesses that have not introduced plans or have failed to implement them. Employment tribunals should have the power to order businesses to take appropriate action and, if they fail to observe such orders, to pay financial compensation. The fact of failure to adopt or implement a plan should be admissible as evidence in individual discrimination cases, from which an adverse inference may be drawn against the respondent employer.

14.16 The introduction of this legislation will take time. For this reason, as for others (discussed more fully in Chapter 19), the government should proceed swiftly with voluntary measures, including the following.
- Providing encouragement and practical help to businesses that wish, without compulsion, to formulate and implement employment equity plans. In particular, many businesses need guidance on how to engage in positive action schemes, and how to undertake effective ethnic monitoring.
- Promoting good practice more vigorously than hitherto to small and medium-sized organisations, for example, through the Department for Education and Employment's Race Relations Employment Advisory Service (RREAS), and using the kinds of high-profile campaigning that have been used to promote the New Deal programmes.
- Itself leading by example, by drawing up and implementing plans for all government departments.
- Building standards of fair recruitment and equity employment into Investors in People and the Business Excellence Model, so that employers may align positive action measures with their existing

business objectives. *We recommend that achievement of Investors in People status in future be conditional on the formulation and implementation of an employment equity plan, and that equity issues be explicitly and comprehensively covered in the Business Excellence Model's guidance materials.*

- Ensuring that employment equity issues are explicitly considered when government grants and procurement contracts are under consideration. *We recommend that guidance on public procurement and the award of subsidies for investment, such as Regional Selective Assistance, be revised to stress the importance of employment equity.*

14.17 All measures aiming to create more employment opportunities, such as those undertaken by the regional development agencies, as well as those designed to help unemployed and jobless people compete effectively for jobs, should include targets relating to the benefits for Asian and black people. Thus all such measures should be monitored by ethnicity. Furthermore, an explicit focus on achieving employment equity should be a key condition for the award of contracts to deliver programmes such as the New Deal at local levels. If inequality persists, responsibility for such programmes should be transferred to other organisations. *We recommend that all organisations delivering New Deal programmes be required to demonstrate that they are contributing positively to employment equity, and if they cannot do so, that their responsibilities be transferred to others.*

14.18 The government should ensure that the support provided for unemployed or jobless black and Asian people is sensitive to their backgrounds and aspirations, and should ensure more use of role models, personal advisers and mentors who are themselves black or Asian. *We recommend that organisations providing personal adviser services be required to ensure that persons from black and Asian backgrounds are equitably involved in their programmes as both managers and advisers.*

Self-employment

14.19 The number of self-employed people rose by 49 per cent between 1971 and 1992, the bulk of the growth being in the 1980s. The term self-employed refers (a) to entrepreneurs who run their own business; and

(b) to people who work for others as sole traders on a self-employed basis. The statistics show that African and African-Caribbean communities are substantially under-represented in the entrepreneur category but that Bangladeshi, Chinese, Indian and Pakistani people are comparatively prominent.[20]

14.20 It has been estimated that Asian and black businesses represent almost 7 per cent of the total small business stock, and that in London there are at least 15,000 such businesses – around one in five of all privately owned businesses in the capital – employing between them over 200,000 people in full- and part-time work.[21] In 1997, around 9 per cent of all new business start-ups involved entrepreneurs from Asian or black backgrounds. The Bank of England has estimated that in 1996 the contribution of black and Asian people to gross domestic product was around £37 billion. The Office for National Statistics does not collect data on the contribution of Asian and black firms to UK gross national product or UK trade balances. We stress in Chapter 15 that such data would be valuable for counteracting media misrepresentation and ignorance relating to immigration and asylum policies. *We recommend that research be commissioned on the contributions of Asian and black firms to UK gross national product and UK trade balances.*

14.21 There is evidence that Asian and black small businesses encounter more severe problems than do others at start-up and growth stages, but that they make less use of business support services.[22] *We recommend that the Department of Trade and Industry (DTI) and the Small Business Service (SBS) commission research into Asian and black business start-up and survival patterns, with a view to formulating local targets and contributing to SBS national strategies.* Further, *we recommend that targets be set at SBS national council and local council levels for increasing the take-up of support by Asian and black small businesses.* This will involve, but not be limited to, increasing the numbers of Asian and black people represented at every level in business support services. Further, *we recommend that the Banking Code and the Mortgage Code include undertakings on non-discrimination.*[23] A review by the Bank of England has stressed that there is a perception among Asian and black businesses that they meet institutional racism in the provision of financial services.[24] Therefore, *we recommend that all providers of financial services monitor and improve their procedures and ensure that key staff receive race and diversity training.* (For fuller discussion of institutional racism see Chapter 5, and for notes on racism awareness training see Chapter 20.) The Bank points out that the problems encountered by Asian and black small businesses may be owing to the sectors in which they operate (for example, independent retailing, catering and taxi driving), or to business location or lack of collateral, rather than to discrimination by lenders. However, it adds that 'whether or not discrimination exists, the steps that need to be taken by banks and other finance providers to counteract either actual or perceived discrimination are the same in both cases – perception of a problem may be as important in practice as the reality'. In the light of this, *we recommend that there be monitoring by ethnicity of lending decisions by financial institutions.*

14.22 Many Asian and black businesses are substantially involved in import/export.[25] Their advantages include language and intercultural skills, and family and community networks that cover African countries and North America as well as Asia and the Caribbean. At present, many British Trade International and Business Links initiatives are geared towards large companies and are inappropriate for the Asian and black business sector. Therefore, *we recommend that British Trade International and Business Links partnerships set targets for working more closely with the Asian and black business sector, and for highlighting the possibility of international trade as a mechanism for encouraging growth.*

14.23 Asian businesses make a substantial contribution to independent retailing – the 'corner shop', known technically in statistics as the confectionery, tobacconist and newsagent (CTN) sector. It has been estimated that around three-quarters of all independent newsagents in London are owned by people of Asian origin.[26] Local shops respond to customers' special requests and preferences, help to revitalise the areas in which they are located, and play a vital role in maintaining a sense of community and continuity. The greater the use of local streets and public spaces, the greater is the sense of safety and community spirit. The sector is now under intense pressure, however, from one-stop supermarket shopping and out-of-town shopping centres. It is also affected by reluctance on the part of the next generation to join the family business,[27] not least because of the long hours and the prevalence in some areas of racist abuse and attacks. A study by the Asian Business Initiative found in 1999 that 'a sense of hopelessness ... pervades this sector' and suggested that 'long hours and low margins are not conducive to managing the external environment actively and planning the business proactively'.[28] *We recommend that business support agencies develop their expertise in advising and assisting the independent retail sector, and that all agencies involved in urban regeneration and business development recognise the value of independent retailers.*

14.24 The issues discussed in this chapter have links with sections of several other chapters, particularly policies to reduce material inequalities (Chapter 6), the acquisition of qualifications and entry to the labour market (Chapter 11), the need for new equality legislation (Chapter 19), institutional racism (Chapter 5) and organisational change (Chapter 20). We have also mentioned that there is a need for much better data on the contributions of Asian and black people and their enterprises to gross national product. Such data would be invaluable for economic planning, and would be relevant to policies on refugees, immigration and asylum. These are the subjects of the next chapter.

Chapter 15

Immigration and Asylum

> *I'm afraid that it will, alas, be necessary to make elementary points about the benefits of immigration, given that the atmosphere is once again being poisoned by deeply prejudicial statements about refugees and asylum seekers, taken up first in the media and now (to their shame) by politicians. I understand how tedious it is to have to restate arguments with which all of us are familiar. But since there is currently a vacuum of leadership on this issue, an authoritative statement is all the more necessary.*
>
> From a letter to the Commission, April 2000

15.1   When the letter quoted above was written, it looked as if immigration would be an election issue for the first time since 1983, and that each of the main political parties would signal its readiness to take harsh decisions in order to stem a perceived flood of new arrivals. The scenario was by no means new. Postwar British history is littered with legislation and regulations passed swiftly, and by both parties, to counter such perceived threats. Examples include the 1968 Commonwealth Immigrants Act aimed at keeping out East African Asians, and the racially and sexually divisive marriage rules brought in by the first Thatcher government (see below). There are three problems with this approach. First, the sense of panic the issue instils and the subjectivity with which it is discussed lead to bad law that does not work even in its own terms, giving rise to challenges both in UK courts and among international human rights bodies. Second, it prevents or obstructs an objective and forward-looking examination of the need for, and benefits of, immigration. Third, it undermines Britain's development as a cohesive but diverse society, for it implies or indicates that politicians are not genuinely committed to addressing all forms of racism.

Nationality

15.2   The definition of who is and is not British has two important corollaries. On the one hand it provides superior and exclusive rights for those who have full citizenship; on the other it reflects the national self-understanding – it states who 'we' think we are. Citizenship carries with it many rights and responsibilities. But the fundamental right, governing the exercise of all of the others, is a person's right to live in, and return to, their country. The UK is the only democratic country in the world to have granted forms of citizenship that carry no right to live anywhere, and which are in reality disguised forms of statelessness. These second-class citizenships are almost exclusively held by people targeted by colour racism. (See the discussion of colour racism in Chapter 5.)

15.3   In 1960, all people in Commonwealth countries and the remaining British colonies were British subjects and had an unrestricted right of access to the UK. Subsequently, as countries became independent, this right of entry was restricted. One possible approach would have been to restrict the entry rights of those who had acquired citizenship of independent countries, and who therefore had somewhere they belonged, but to retain full entry rights for those whose British status was their only nationality. This is what other former colonial powers in Europe did. The UK is the only country in the EU to have dealt with the problems of decolonisation by creating virtually worthless second-class citizenships for some of its ex-colonial nationals.

15.4   Some of the people who had British nationality and no other – the East African Asians, for example, or the people of Hong Kong – were denied entry to the UK. At the same time people who were not British at all, but who had a UK-born parent or grandparent, retained virtually free right of entry. Almost all the former were black or Asian, almost all the latter white. These distinctions were then written into the 1981 British Nationality Act, which provided for five different categories of British nationals,[1] of which only one, British citizens, have the right to live in the country of their nationality. However, Commonwealth patrials retained their rights of entry, and they were joined by people from Gibraltar and, after 1983, the Falklands. The definition of nationality – of who 'we' are – is therefore grounded in a distinction that is fundamentally racially and ethnically based.

15.5   The number of second-class British nationals is declining, for such nationality can only rarely be acquired by birth. The present government has taken, or promised, remedial action for some of these people. Just before the return of Hong Kong to China, the problem of British nationals who were not ethnically Chinese, and would therefore not have Chinese nationality, was belatedly tackled. The small number who by then remained in Hong Kong were given the opportunity to register as full British citizens. The vast majority had no intention of leaving Hong Kong; but they did want an effective nationality, guaranteeing them the right to live somewhere else if forced to do so. In 1998, the government also promised to take action to grant full British citizenship to people from the few remaining British dependencies, most of which are too small to be viable independent states. This too is welcome, and the government's detailed proposals are awaited.

15.6 However, there is one remaining blot upon British nationality law – the position of thousands of people who were promised and took British nationality and protection when the countries where they lived became independent. In almost all cases, they are members of minorities in these countries – South Asians in East and Central Africa, for example, and Chinese in the Malay Straits. Some have the right to citizenship in the independent country where they live. Others, in particular many of the remaining East African Asians, do not. Although holding British passports, they are effectively stateless. Giving people passports, it has been said, 'is about as effective a remedy against statelessness as airlifting luncheon vouchers to relieve famine'.[2]

15.7 The situation also casts a blight on the UK's international reputation and human rights record. The UK has not signed the Fourth Protocol of the European Convention on Human Rights (ECHR), which guarantees citizens the right to re-enter their country of nationality. It has also made a wide-ranging reservation in respect of other international human rights conventions as they affect UK nationality law. The reservation to the most widely signed UN convention, the Convention on the Rights of the Child, which also allows UK nationality law to discriminate against children born outside marriage, was criticised by the Convention's supervisory committee on the grounds that it undermines such basic provisions as the right of every child to a nationality.

15.8 There are certainly practical difficulties in granting rights of entry to many thousands of people. However, the UK does accept continuing responsibility for some of the people from its former colonies. For example, it is estimated that 20,000 white Zimbabweans who can claim British nationality, and many thousands of others with British ancestry, have the right to come here if they should need to. This is precisely the same safety valve that other British nationals overseas are seeking. The point is not lost on public opinion. It reinforces the image of a country where white people are naturally imagined to belong, but black and Asian people do not. In principle, the granting of nationality should always involve a commitment to grant entry. In practice, the right is most clearly essential for those who belong to no other country. *We recommend that the UK government take action to bring British nationality law into line with international human rights standards, and to deal with the statelessness and racial and ethnic divisions that have been created by its present policies.* This should involve:

- as a minimum, granting full British citizenship to all British nationals who do not have the right to any other nationality;
- examining closely the position of British nationals with dual nationality, or the right to another nationality, to see whether safety-net arrangements, similar to those for Commonwealth citizens with British ancestry, need to be made;
- signing up to the Fourth Protocol of the European Convention on Human Rights and removing the nationality reservations applicable to other international instruments, particularly the International Convention on the Rights of the Child.

Immigration

15.9　During the late 1960s and 1970s, the emphasis in immigration control shifted from workers, whose entry was by then tightly controlled, to the family members of those who had already entered. The rules that governed the entry of family members, for settlement or visits, were on the face of it race-neutral. In practice, however, relatives of black and Asian people experienced delays, indignities and separation that would not have been tolerated had they been imposed on white families. Provisions for family reunion, involving dubious medical techniques and intrusive questioning, even of small children, were interpreted so as to cast doubt on the paternity of Asian children and the validity of Asian marriages. African-Caribbean or West African single parents who had left children to be cared for temporarily by relatives at home were

separated from their children on the grounds that they did not have 'sole responsibility' for them. Relatives who simply wanted to visit for important family events were often refused. Where entry was allowed, it was frequently delayed – Home Office officials in the 1980s admitted that the long queue for entry of relatives from Bangladesh, India and Pakistan was a hidden quota system.[3]

15.10 One of the clearest examples of such provisions was the 'primary purpose' marriage rule. Originally, it applied to British women and women settled in the UK whose right to live in the UK with a foreign husband was qualified by the need to show, even if it was accepted as genuine, that the marriage had not been entered into primarily for immigration reasons. Its immediate target, and its primary use, was to exclude young men from Bangladesh, India and Pakistan. By 1990 the initial refusal rate for such men had reached 60 per cent of applications.

15.11 The European Court of Human Rights accepted that the marriage rules were sexually discriminatory, but rejected a claim of race discrimination, largely because race was not written into the rules. The UK government then removed the element of sex discrimination by applying the rule to men as well as women, but continued to apply it selectively: for example to Filipina women. Refusals of American, Australian or Swiss spouses were virtually unknown. Nationals of other EU countries resident in the UK did not need to go through these hoops to bring in their spouses, of whatever nationality, because under EU law they have a right to family reunion that British people, in their own country, lack.

15.12 In 1997 the new government made the welcome decision to abolish the primary purpose rule, and to bring in some rights of appeal for refused visitors. However, there are continuing problems. The marriage rules are still leading to disproportionate refusals of black and Asian spouses. People no longer have to prove why they married, but they still have to prove that they intend to live together, and that spouses can be supported without the use of public funds. Those who are unemployed, looking after children, on low incomes, or without their own accommodation will find it difficult or impossible to be joined by their spouses from overseas. This can create a vicious circle. For example, a lone parent may remain unemployed precisely because the other parent cannot enter the UK and assist with childcare. Visitor appeal rights have still not been finalised and are likely to be expensive to exercise. There was even a proposal that a bond, of thousands of pounds per visitor, be posted by the friends or relatives of suspect visitors from certain selected countries, including Bangladesh, India and Pakistan. Both for families in the UK and for people visiting them there is a danger that what was principally a race trap is also a poverty trap. Since Asian and black people are disproportionately affected by poverty (see Chapters 6 and 14), they will continue to be adversely affected by immigration policy.

15.13 Family reunion is a fundamental right. It should not be subject to intrusive investigation and in principle should not be means-tested. As a minimum, *we recommend that the UK support and sign up to a new EU directive extending and protecting family reunion rights.* Over and above this, *we recommend that the public funds requirement be removed for the spouses and children of British citizens and permanent residents, and time-limited for all other family members.*

15.14 The area of the government's immigration policy that has attracted most criticism is deportation, and in particular the removal of rights of appeal for those who have been in the UK for lengthy periods. Appeal rights for those who had overstayed their leave to remain in the UK, but had been here for less than seven years, were restricted by the Conservative government in 1988. This is widely held to have led to an increase in asylum applications, since it was the only way to gain an effective right of appeal before removal. The incoming Labour government was urged to restore full appeal rights, so that compassionate circumstances could always be argued at appeal. Instead, the new Immigration and Asylum Act has taken away all pre-removal appeal rights for overstayers, unless they have an asylum claim or a claim under the Human Rights Act. It will be for the Home Secretary, not the appellate system, to decide whether compassionate circumstances, such as length of stay and family and community links, should preclude expulsion.

15.15 The decision to expel a person from a country, and separate them from their home and community environment, is momentous for those directly affected. In practice, it bears particularly heavily on Asian and black people, since they are more likely to be subject to immigration control. Of course, breaching immigration laws is a serious matter, which rightly has serious consequences. So is criminal activity, and yet criminal proceedings are hedged around with judicial safeguards, and even those convicted can plead mitigation in sentencing before a court. People facing removal may similarly have mitigating circumstances to offer. For example, they may have overstayed unknowingly because an agent or a spouse misled them, or for compelling personal reasons. Appeals under the Human Rights Act are welcome, but can only succeed in certain narrowly defined circumstances. Even the existence of a family or of UK-born children may not be sufficient.

15.16 The process of forced removal will be painful, in personal and emotional terms and in the way it is carried out, since it may involve physical restraint or detention. The perception that it can be undertaken arbitrarily and without proper appellate rights will add to the community anger that enforcement action is likely to engender. The Race Relations Act, even after the amendments made in 2000, will continue to permit particular ethnic or national groups to be targeted for enforcement action (see below). Moreover, the absence of effective appeal rights may well lead to less rigorous decision-making. Therefore the removal of appeal rights for overstayers is likely to have a damaging effect on the perceived, and perhaps the actual, fairness of decisions to remove people who have been in the UK for long periods. *We recommend that appeal rights relating to deportation be fully restored.*

15.17   The immigration debate in the UK has always been conducted on the assumption that immigration is a problem, not an opportunity. In contrast to the situation in other countries, including Canada, Australia and Germany, no detailed economic and social studies have been carried out in the UK into the effect of, or the need for, immigration. However, recent reports have highlighted the fact that western Europe will soon face a shortage of young workers, owing to declining and ageing populations.[4] There are signs that this has begun to influence the political judgements and the public rhetoric that surround immigration policy. However, consideration of these factors is a matter of great urgency. Recognition of the benefits of immigration – indeed, of its necessity – would for the first time allow key issues to be discussed objectively and imaginatively, and could help to break the vicious circle that links race with immigration and immigration with threat. *We recommend that the government carry out and publicise research into the economic impact, and the potential economic benefits, of immigration.* Such research should take full account of recent forecasts of skills and worker shortages.

Asylum

15.18   Asylum-seekers have for some time been in the eye of the immigration storm, stimulating three major Acts of Parliament over six years, and a series of increasingly vitriolic press campaigns. Targeted groups have included Tamils, Turkish Kurds and Somalis. Most recently, odium has been focused on Roma from central and eastern Europe. The consequences of a failing asylum system, and the racist and xenophobic attitudes engendered by the media and encouraged by many politicians, are extremely damaging both for individual asylum-seekers and for the security and dignity of Asian and black communities in general.

15.19   The perception of asylum-seekers has changed greatly over the last 15 years. Until the early 1980s, they were seen as brave people fleeing persecution, in contrast to the workers and families against whom immigration control was directed. In the context of this report, it is important to note when, and in relation to whom, the perception changed: it was when young Tamil men from Sri Lanka began to seek asylum from persecution in the mid-1980s. Single young men from

South Asia were precisely the people against whom UK immigration control had been targeted for 30 years. Tamil asylum-seekers were characterised as 'bogus' and in the UK, unlike in other European countries, they were hardly ever given full refugee status.

15.20 The same culture of disbelief informed official attitudes to asylum-seekers from other countries of the South and East who followed the Tamils – Kurds, Zairois, Somalis and, initially, Kosovar Albanians. These all came from countries or regions where ethnic persecution and civil upheaval were endemic, leading to economic as well as political instability and affecting large numbers of people. However, the attitudes of official decision-makers to the new generation of asylum-seekers were geared much more towards preventing 'abuse' and discouraging arrivals, than to providing protection. Officials used to a role of detecting 'bogus' family members or marriages were easily able to adapt to the new task of identifying so-called bogus asylum-seekers, and deterrent measures were put in place to prevent or discourage arrivals.

15.21 Visa regimes were the first deterrent. They were imposed on countries producing asylum-seekers, backed by penalties on airlines that carried people without visas. As visas are not issued for asylum, those needing to flee their country or region could do so only by paying 'agents' to provide the false documentation they needed. The growth of an international trade in people-smuggling was a direct result, and has led to asylum-seekers paying thousands of pounds for dangerous journeys across the world. A second deterrent measure was detention. Administrative detention under immigration laws could be authorised for an indefinite period, without judicial supervision. In 1998, the UN Working Party on Arbitrary Detentions examined the UK's detention system and characterised it as arbitrary, and therefore in breach of international human rights standards. A third measure was to reduce the support available for asylum-seekers, in the belief that such support acts as an incentive for those who have no valid asylum claim. The Conservative government's attempt to remove social support altogether was partially thwarted by the courts, where judges robustly stated that no civilised society should require people to choose between persecution and starvation.

15.22 Particularly seriously, the culture of disbelief became the enemy of good and effective procedures. All claims were scrutinised minutely for inconsistency and a lack of 'credibility'. Asylum recognition rates plummeted from around 80 per cent in the 1980s to less than 20 per cent in the 1990s. Yet lengthy delays occurred before the making of initial decisions, which were themselves often unsupported by proper reasons and were then challenged in a series of appeal and judicial processes. By 1997, a 70,000 backlog had been created through a lengthy process which not only demoralised those whose claims were accepted but also made it difficult, if not impossible, to remove those who were rejected. A report by refugee and human rights groups in 1997 pointed out the urgency of dealing with this to avoid asylum-seekers taking the blame for defects in the system.[5] It identified initial decision-making as the key to fairer and more effective asylum procedures, and urged that resources should be front-loaded to ensure that decisions were taken fairly and effectively. This view was later echoed by internal and external reviews commissioned by the Home Office itself and by other independent bodies.[6]

15.23 The government readily accepted that there were defects in the asylum system it had inherited and initiated a process of consultation, with the support of many asylum and immigration groups, to reform it. Procedures were put in place to clear the backlog and there was a marked increase in the success of asylum applications. However, as work proceeded on a new asylum and immigration bill, major problems began to appear. The first was administrative – the inability of the newly computerised decision-making system to cope with its workload. As a result, a new and bigger backlog replaced the one that had been cleared, and decision-making virtually ground to a halt during part of 1999. The second was legislative and political – the decisions to create a new asylum support system, based upon support in kind at a lower level than basic income support, and to disperse asylum-seekers throughout the country. The new system required the creation of a huge new Home Office agency, complex and untested legislative provisions, a new currency (the asylum voucher) and the establishment of a nationwide network of housing providers.

15.24 The impact of these two factors on the integrity of the system, and on the dignity and rights of asylum-seekers, cannot be overstated. Although clearly it was the system itself that was failing to deal effectively with applications, it was asylum-seekers themselves who were scapegoated. Furthermore, the attitudes that underpinned decision-making did not substantially change. A report on those conducting asylum interviews at ports found that: 'The most commonly held perception is that asylum is simply a means to an end and that the majority of those who claim asylum are actually economic migrants who are able to abuse the asylum system to gain entry to the UK.'[7] There also remains considerable resistance to the early involvement of competent legal advisers, recommended by almost all independent commentators as an aid to good decision-making.

15.25 Instead of political and administrative energy being directed where it was most needed, into the creation of an effective early decision-making process, it was diverted into the huge task of creating the parallel universe necessary for the new support system. Priorities were entirely the wrong way round, for the key to defusing support problems is to minimise the need for support by creating a quick and effective decision-making system. Yet both the main political parties have focused their attention on the systems for supporting asylum-seekers (the voucher and dispersal system, or reception/detention centres) rather than the systems for determining applications. Once again, it is asylum-seekers who have suffered the consequences: the indignity of subsisting on vouchers and being bussed around the country to communities that are often ill prepared and hostile, and the lack of proper financial, educational and community support. Problems of inadequate support in dispersal areas were predicted during consultations on the Immigration and Asylum Act 1999. A report by the Audit Commission in summer 2000 confirmed that the warnings had been well founded: the dispersal areas do not have sufficient resources and expertise to meet the housing, education, medical, language and legal needs of asylum-seekers.[8] Of all the communities in the UK, asylum-seekers are the most obviously and damagingly socially excluded. The fact that this is not accidental, but the consequence of deliberate official policy, is bound to have an effect on the way they are regarded in public opinion generally.

15.26 Even more seriously, the social exclusion of asylum-seekers during their first critical months undermines what should be one of the principal aims of asylum policy: the successful settlement of those whose claims are accepted, so that their talents and skills can be properly used to the benefit of the whole community. This must be one of the key aims of a multi-ethnic and fair society, and is recognised by the Home Office itself in a recent consultation document: 'Integration is not only essential for the refugees themselves, but also in the wider context of the Government's policies on social inclusion generally, community and race relations.'[9] Yet the dispersal and voucher scheme that the same department is implementing could hardly be more at odds with such aims. The system itself undermines economic and social self-sufficiency. Moreover, those who are eventually granted asylum may be swiftly decanted, without any support, English language training or settled accommodation, into a benefits system that expects them immediately to be 'job-seekers'. The same Home Office team that is responsible for dispersal is now also tasked with moving on those whose applications are successful. Refugee agencies fear that its resources will be concentrated on the former, and point out that its proposals for 'integration' are so far undeveloped and largely exhortatory, depending to a great extent upon 'coordination' of already underfunded local initiatives. As well as failing refugees and asylum-seekers, the scheme places unacceptable levels of stress on schools, health services, and housing and social service departments, to the detriment of other users of these services, who, once again, will be inclined to blame asylum-seekers and refugees for problems absolutely not of their own making.

15.27   The successful settlement of those granted protection in the UK is critical to the development of a successful multi-ethnic Britain and ought to be one of the key aims of government policy. It should have a much higher government priority: the task of promoting joined-up approaches and joined-up funding could be undertaken by the Social Exclusion Unit, or a similar body, with the close involvement of the refugee communities themselves and the self-help organisations they have established. *We recommend urgent action to remedy defects in the systems for determining asylum claims and supporting asylum-seekers, and to provide better settlement services for those granted asylum. This should involve:*

- *improving the initial decision-making process to ensure that asylum-seekers have the opportunity properly to present their cases, with appropriate legal advice, to decision-makers who are properly trained and well informed, and providing sufficient resources to improve quality and minimise delays;*
- *government support for asylum-seekers so that those whose claims are*

accepted have the best chance of successful settlement; this could best be achieved through cash support (at not less than the basic income support level) and a choice of available housing, and must include language and skills training and social orientation;

- *a co-ordinated approach to the settlement needs of those granted asylum, so that the Social Exclusion Unit, or a similar body, with the help of refugee community organisations, can identify needs and develop a national strategy for meeting them.*

A new basis for immigration and asylum policy

15.28 We have dealt above with remedying the effects of what we believe to be unfair and divisive immigration and asylum policies, rooted in past assumptions and laws. We go on to set out what we believe should be the foundation of an immigration and asylum policy for a multi-ethnic 21st-century society. Such a policy should be founded on four pillars: the promotion of equality and the elimination of discriminatory treatment; adherence to the principles and requirements of human rights; public acceptance of and welcome for the diverse, multi-ethnic society that has been created as a consequence of immigration; and the development of policies at EU level that strengthen these principles at regional level.

15.29 Following the Stephen Lawrence Inquiry, the government took action to bring all activities of central government, including the police and immigration service, within the ambit of the Race Relations Act. This targets both direct and indirect discrimination, and will allow individual immigration officials to be challenged if they apply official policies in a racially or ethnically discriminatory way. However, there is an exemption for immigration, nationality and asylum law, which allows the Home Secretary himself to discriminate on grounds of nationality, or national or ethnic origin, or to authorise his officials to do so by way of guidelines or instructions. Immigration law by definition discriminates on grounds of nationality, of course. But the exemption goes further than this, specifically permitting institutionalised discrimination on grounds of ethnicity or national origin, without the need to justify differential treatment. It will permit instructions to be issued to officials to examine the claims of people from certain backgrounds more closely or sceptically, or to target them for detention or enforcement action.

Arguments that it is necessary to provide protection for certain ethnic groups, such as Kosovar Albanians as opposed to Kosovar Serbs, are unfounded. Where positive discrimination is necessary and can be justified (for example, to allow swift entry of members of a persecuted ethnic group) this could be provided for in the legislation.

15.30 It will be unlawful for the police to act upon perceptions that certain ethnic or national groups might be disproportionately involved in criminal activity, yet lawful for the immigration service to be instructed to act on such perceptions in relation to immigration control. Many of the problems faced by Asian and black communities arise from such stereotypes and from rules that appear to be race-neutral but that in practice adversely affect particular groups. A vicious circle will be set in motion and will be legitimised by the new legislation – a high degree of official and ministerial suspicion of certain ethnic and national groups will lead to a high rate of refusals, and this in turn will lead to greater suspicion. *We recommend the removal of the exemption in the Race Relations (Amendment) Act permitting discrimination on grounds of ethnic or national origin.*

15.31 Immigration and asylum decisions and procedures, like other actions of public authorities, will need to comply with the Human Rights Act 1998, discussed in detail in Chapter 7. The Act provides important safeguards – a bottom line below which officials and policy-makers cannot safely go – and these will be of particular benefit to groups such as asylum-seekers, who cannot necessarily rely on the democratic process alone. There are several areas where the Human Rights Act is likely to affect, or to mitigate, official policies and procedures. They include widening the grounds for appealing against refusals of asylum; providing a framework to challenge arbitrary or unnecessary detention; allowing challenges to removal decisions that breach the right to family or private life; prohibiting discrimination on grounds of race, nationality or ethnicity in the exercise of any of the ECHR rights; and requiring a basic minimum standard of decency and dignity in asylum support arrangements.

15.32 Some of these provisions have already led to changes in law or practice, and others will be used as the basis of legal challenges later. However, the Human Rights Act, and the human rights culture that it is designed to create, should do more than provide a legal basis on which to challenge executive decisions and policies. If that were the only consequence of the Act, it could be counterproductive, for ministers and the press might implicitly or even explicitly blame the courts for subverting political and democratic processes. It is therefore important that human rights standards also infuse the administrative systems that determine immigration and asylum applications, and that they are used to change the decision-making culture. This will involve not only a programme of training but also the development of new criteria for making and justifying decisions. Human rights also need to underpin the law-making process. The government is required to examine new laws to see whether they comply with the Human Rights Act. There has been considerable criticism, in relation to the Immigration and Asylum Act, of the government's reluctance to engage with the arguments of expert critics who have challenged the broad statement that the whole of the Act is human-rights-compliant. *We recommend that independent experts examine all existing legislation, rules, procedures, guidelines and decision-making criteria for their compliance with the Human Rights Act.* This should form the basis of remedial action, and of a programme of training for immigration and entry clearance officers, developed and delivered with the assistance of these experts.

15.33   'Illegal immigrants, asylum-seekers, bootleggers and scum-of-the-earth drug-smugglers', declares an editorial in a Dover newspaper, 'have targeted our beloved coastline. We are left with the back-draft of a nation's human sewage and no cash to wash it down the drain.'[10] Such language could have been transposed, with scarcely any alteration, from migration scares of previous decades. It feeds the kinds of street and violent racism discussed in Chapter 5, and political leaders have distinctive responsibilities not to collude with it – indeed, to dissociate themselves explicitly from it. (See Chapter 16.) During the passage of the Immigration and Asylum Act, there was an all-party agreement to deal sensitively and objectively with the issues it raised, and not to use them to inflame racist or xenophobic attitudes. The consensus quickly appeared to break down, however. Neither of the main political parties publicly countered the overtly racist statements appearing in the media; both took them as an invitation to attack, or to defend, policies on the basis of whether they were sufficiently 'tough' or too 'soft'. The territory of debate was thus defined by media coverage, with asylum-seekers seen as undesirable and undesired. The Audit Commission report mentioned above stressed that 'in some areas community tensions have been raised by emotive and sensational media reporting', and called for positive public relations strategies at local levels. The report also highlighted the need for central government to take a lead – 'more positive messages would help to abate the overwhelmingly negative media coverage'.[11] The next chapter discusses in greater detail the playing of the race card by politicians, and suggests measures to reduce it. *We recommend that the government accept responsibility for encouraging and leading a positive debate on asylum and immigration through its own publicity mechanisms, and by commissioning research and providing information.*

15.34 The UK is no longer the sole, or even perhaps the most important, focus of decision-making on immigration and asylum policies. Following the Treaty of Amsterdam, the European Union now has power to develop and enforce minimum common standards for the entry, stay and treatment of migrants and asylum-seekers. The UK obtained an 'opt-out' during the treaty negotiations, which leaves it free to decide whether or not to adopt any common policies agreed upon.

15.35 New directives (the EU equivalent of legislation) are currently (summer 2000) being drafted on common criteria for deciding on asylum applications and common standards for the reception of asylum-seekers; and on common criteria for family reunion applications, and increased rights for 'third country nationals' (non-EU citizens legally resident in the EU). Once accepted by member states, these will be binding requirements under the jurisdiction of the European Court of Justice, which is also, under the Amsterdam Treaty, charged with interpreting EU law in the light of human rights and constitutional standards.

15.36 However, the UK's opt-out means that it can effectively cherry-pick which of these directives it wishes to implement. Already, there are indications that it will opt out of those that grant greater rights than are presently available under UK law (such as the enhanced family reunion rights in the draft directive), but may sign up to those that make the enforcement of immigration and asylum law easier (such as binding common asylum criteria, which facilitate the return of asylum-seekers to other EU countries, and which may restrict interpretation of the Refugee Convention). Developments in EU law are likely to define regional immigration and asylum policy for the 21st century. It is important that the UK is at the heart of policy-making, and that it uses its influence positively. *We recommend that the UK use its best efforts to promote an EU immigration and asylum policy that is aligned with the principles and recommendations of this report and with international human rights standards; and that it welcome EU initiatives, such as the enhancement of family reunion and third country nationals' rights, which move towards these goals.*

15.37 Immigration, nationality and asylum laws are among the most contentious issues that face European governments. Moreover, the enforcement of immigration controls is always likely to be divisive, and to affect those who are easily marginalised and potential targets of racist attacks. Immigration and asylum controls are needed but must be operated fairly, openly and without ethnic or racial discrimination. Our recommendations are designed to shift UK (and ultimately EU) policy away from the overt or implicit racist base on which it was developed, and towards a system that reflects and endorses the kind of society outlined in Part 1 of this report. Given the political sensitivity of the issues involved, and the institutional and media resistance they may provoke, this will be a difficult transition to make. There is therefore a need for strong and independent voices outside government, with the ability to monitor, research and report on the effects of immigration control within the context of multi-ethnic Britain.

15.38 At parliamentary level, it would be helpful to have a specific and continuing focus on immigration and asylum issues. For example, the Home Affairs Select Committee should set up a subcommittee on these issues, as it did during the 1980s; and the new Joint Human Rights Committee should examine the operation of human rights standards within immigration and asylum law as one of its earliest inquiries. Outside Parliament, resources should be given to the Commission for Racial Equality, whose remit can now include immigration matters, to monitor and report on recent changes in immigration and asylum law and practice in the light of their impact on race relations and social exclusion. In the longer term, this monitoring and reporting role should fall to the Human Rights Commission, whose establishment we advocate in Chapter 19. In addition, *we recommend that an independent commission on all aspects of immigration, nationality and asylum be established.* It would examine the economic and social needs of Britain over the next decades, monitor and review the implementation of current immigration and asylum policy, identify areas of the economy where immigration needs to be encouraged and put forward recommendations for change. It would involve defining long-term national interest by democratic deliberation, as distinct from leaving sensitive issues to the mercy of narrow electoral calculations by political parties. The importance of deliberative democracy is stressed in the next chapter.

Chapter 16

Politics and Representation

The proportion of ethnic minority electors as compared to the total electorate is tiny. But so is the thumb as a physical proportion of your body. But try picking up your pen without the aid of your thumb. It is its strategic position that gives it a disproportionate importance.

From a paper submitted to the Commission

16.1 'It's midday. I'm sitting in a basement pub, forcing crisps down my throat and draining the last dregs of my cigarette. Two grease-stained sheets of paper lie in front of me, covered with insane scribblings on British politics, liberalism and ethnic minority politics.' The author of this diary entry has applied to take part in a project giving Asian and black people an opportunity to shadow the day-to-day work of MPs and peers at Westminster.[1] The diary continues: 'According to the constitution of the Liberal Democrats, their purpose is to "create and maintain a fair, free and equal society, based upon the values of liberty, justice and equality and where no one is enslaved by poverty, ignorance or conformity." The number of times I've read that today, I'll be saying it on my deathbed.'

16.2 Directly or indirectly, the work-shadowing project explored many issues. How to generate sufficient interest in party politics among Asian and black people so that more of them would see politics as a worthwhile career. How to promote organisational change within political parties, and to confront institutional racism in their spheres of influence. How to get more Asian and black people to register as voters, and to use their electoral muscle to put race and diversity issues higher on the political agenda. How to sustain interest not only in electoral politics but also in deliberative democracy, the making of decisions through reflective discussion rather than through the force of majorities.[2] How to ensure that Asian and black people are represented not only on elected bodies but also on those whose members are appointed.

16.3　Appointed bodies control substantial resources. These bodies include the wide range of non-departmental public organisations known as quangos, health authorities and trusts, regional development agencies, the governing bodies of schools, and local partnerships between public sector and community organisations. There are also consultative mechanisms such as citizens' juries, policy panels, advisory forums, and liaison, watchdog and focus groups. All political bodies, whether elected or appointed, operate within a landscape that is currently undergoing a series of potentially seismic shifts: elected devolved government at Holyrood and Cardiff; the Greater London Assembly and London Mayor; the modernisation of local government and establishment of cabinets and scrutiny committees; substantial changes in the membership of the House of Lords; a democratic deficit in the English regions and the likelihood of increased demand for directly elected regional assemblies; the incorporation into the legal systems of England, Scotland and Wales of the European Convention on Human Rights, and the increased power of the judiciary; and the increasingly powerful role of the European Union.

16.4　These shifts could lead to increases in accountability and legitimacy at all levels. There is no guarantee, however, that their influence will be for the better. In so far as the new political bodies fail to be accountable and to secure legitimacy, their existence may not only perpetuate the marginalisation of black and Asian communities but also provide a fertile breeding ground for political movements with explicit racist policies.[3] In 1999 no Asian or black people were elected to the Welsh Assembly or the Scottish Parliament, and in 2000 none were directly elected to the Greater London Assembly.

16.5　If Britain is to flourish as a community of citizens and communities (see Chapter 4), its democratic institutions should have four features. First, political leaders should shape, not pander to, public opinion on issues relating to race and diversity. They should relate a national story that includes everyone (Chapter 2), and should take and make opportunities to speak and act against all forms of racism (Chapter 5). Their legitimate desires to maximise their own electoral support and to diminish the attractions of their opponents should never involve playing the race card, either openly or covertly. Second, black and Asian people should be more fully involved than at present in the party political system at local and national levels, as both elected representatives and party activists. If this is to happen the parties will need to address institutional racism within their own structures and procedures. Third, black and Asian people should also be fully involved in unelected bodies. Such bodies should be representative in the sense of exhibiting a spectrum of perspective and experience, and aspire to be deliberative and non-polemical in style. Fourth, both elected and unelected bodies should be strenuously and explicitly concerned with the themes discussed in Part 1 of this report and, as appropriate, with the recommendations made in Part 2.

The race card and political leadership

16.6 First, a brief working definition: a political party plays the race card when it colludes with racist views and attitudes among white people in the hope of gaining their electoral support. It involves emotive and untrue or partial assertions about minorities, immigrants and asylum-seekers, and exploiting unfounded popular anxieties for political purposes. Further, it involves claiming that strict immigration controls contribute to 'good race relations'. In the 1950s and 1960s the race card was played by some politicians and newspapers entirely openly and with crude language[4] – from the top of the pack, as it were. Nowadays the playing is more subtle, artful and coded, and the card is frequently part of a hand rather than played on its own. It gains strength and resonance from the company it keeps – hostility to Europe, ridicule of political correctness, and punitive approaches to law and order.[5]

16.7 Even extremist parties now take pains in public to maintain that their agenda is not racist. It is instructive in this connection to note the mayoral election address for the British National Party, which was delivered to every home in Greater London in April 2000 at the government's expense: 'Opposition to immigration is not a matter of "racism" or "hate" against other peoples. What we oppose is the destruction of the traditional identity of the British people in our homeland ... We ask for our culture, freedoms and our traditions to be respected, and for the majority to have the right to run our country as they wish.' The address also stated that 'politically correct "diversity policing" must be replaced by impartial law enforcement', that education authorities should be pushed 'into dropping multicultural indoctrination and concentrating on discipline and the three Rs', and that 'positive discrimination in favour of "minorities" is ... racist against whites'.

16.8   The BNP candidate came nowhere near to being elected – although he was the first or second preference choice of almost 5 per cent of all who voted, a result that is certainly not negligible.[6] But there was barely a phrase in the party's election address that could not have come straight from the editorials of certain mass-circulation newspapers. The race card was played at all general elections up to and including that of 1992. The 1997 election, however, appeared to break with the tradition. The *Compact on Free Speech and Race Relations in a Democratic Society*, endorsed by all the main political parties, is said to have been influential in this respect.[7] A more cynical view, consonant with our discussion of current government policies on immigration and asylum in Chapter 15, would be that the Labour Party took pains to ensure that there was no gap between its own policies on immigration and those of its principal opponent, the Conservative Party. In 1995 a senior Labour politician was reported as having said that the Labour Party should not allow 'so much as a cigarette card' to come between the Labour Party and the Tory Government over immigration.[8]

16.9   Also in 1995 the research director at Conservative Central Office recalled the strategies used by his party in 1992:

> Immigration, an issue which we raised successfully in 1992 and again in the 1994 Euro-elections campaign, played particularly well in the tabloids and has more potential to hurt. Then there is the 'loony left' and political correctness. Voters can't define it, but they don't like it and Labour councils are the arch exponent.[9]

16.10   The implication was that immigration and political correctness were two separate campaign issues. The two are not the same, certainly, but each can act as a code for the other, and as code words both tap into a range of other anxieties and themes. This was clearly seen in a strategy paper issued by the deputy chairman of the Conservative Party in 1994.[10] It was based on professional market research among potential Conservative supporters and reported that 'there is a feeling of powerlessness and insecurity about jobs, housing, health service, business, family values, crime, etc, and no vision of where we are heading'. Many people with such anxieties are 'natural Conservatives', for they have 'very right-wing views on crime and immigration', 'deep disapproval of scrounging on social security', 'deep fear of loony lefties', and 'distrust of politically correct, liberal-minded do-gooders'. The incorporation of immigration within a broader package demonstrated the campaigning strategy to be adopted. The party's answer to feelings of powerlessness, insecurity and loss of vision in its heartlands would be to castigate its opponents' softness on three specific issues – immigration, crime and welfare – as well as their association with the amorphous phenomenon of political correctness. ('Voters can't define it, but they don't like it.') [11] The party's campaigning strategy should use vivid and concrete stories rather than abstract arguments:

> While ABC1s can conceptualise, C2s and Ds often cannot. They can relate only to things they can see and feel. They absorb their information and often views from television and the tabloids. We have to talk to them in a way they can understand.

16.11 A politician wanting to 'talk to people in a way they can understand' may well turn to the 1997 Eurobarometer survey,[12] which found that 32 per cent of British people described themselves as very or quite racist. In winter 1996/97 the Institute for Public Policy Research conducted qualitative research into attitudes on race, identity and immigration issues.[13] The findings were consistent with the Eurobarometer survey, and with the conclusions outlined in the Conservative Party memorandum quoted above about powerlessness and loss of vision: 'Increasingly, white people of all classes are feeling deep anxieties about the loss of white identity as we go into the next century and into further integration with Europe. Many are now identifying themselves as English rather than British because, as one of the interviewees said, "A Chinese person could be British, but I am English." White A/B men, usually assumed to be confident in their identity, are beginning to have their doubts.' Typical comments included those quoted in Box 16.1 on page 229. They show how anxieties about race and immigration belong to a package along with anxieties about national (specifically English) identity and political correctness.

16.12 When a rival plays the race card, a political party has, broadly speaking, four options:
   • try to beat them by playing a card of higher value – 'no, we're not

Box 16.1 **Voices: Englishness and political correctness**

Increasingly we are English. It's a feeling of being beleaguered.
Man, A/B

They have brought Britain to its knees.
Woman, C1/C2

Britain was a world leader before we had ethnic minorities.
Man, A/B

Someone comes over here and tries to run their country inside ours.
Man, A/B

They get hand-outs we can't get – the second they get off the plane.
Man, C1/C2

We should be more picky.
Woman, C1/C2

You can't even say blackboard now. It is ridiculous.
Woman, C1/C2

Source: Focus group research by IPPR, autumn 1998; further details in Note 13.

---

soft, we're hard, we're even harder than you';
- denounce them for being racist;
- deconstruct their claims, nail the myths and provide accurate facts;
- confidently present a coherent overall policy on race equality and cultural diversity, at the same time recognising and responding constructively to voters' anxieties about identity, economic insecurity and political correctness.[14]

16.13 It is the fourth of these options we urge parties to adopt. Within its framework, they should by all means embrace the second and third options as well, but if they go for these without the wider framework their efforts may well prove counterproductive – they open themselves to the accusation of being merely politically correct. Our report as a whole shows what the framework should be. Specifically, political leaders should:
- lead the country in reimagining Britain as a community of communities, and in ensuring that the national story is inclusive of everyone;

- recognise that many white people have anxieties about national identity, economic insecurity and cultural change, but stress that these are caused by much wider issues than immigration and asylum;
- avoid collusion with the claim that 'good race relations' (that is, acceptance by white people of race equality legislation) depends on tough immigration policies;
- appeal to voters' idealism and decency – middle Britain is arguably much less insecure and ungenerous than some politicians and newspapers appear to think;
- lead the country in discussions of fundamental principles in relation to immigration and asylum policy;
- stress the benefits of multiculturalism and immigration.[15]

16.14 *We recommend that each political party draw up and publish a statement showing how it will avoid playing, or appearing to play, the race card in local and national elections. The statement should be quoted in the party manifesto, and brought to the attention of all candidates and party workers.*

Membership and involvement

16.15 In 1991 there were 78 parliamentary constituencies with more than 15 per cent black and Asian people. Of these, 25 had over 30 per cent. It is estimated that there are now more than 125 parliamentary constituencies in England where the proportion of black and Asian people is over 10 per cent. The 1991 Census showed that 100 local wards had a proportion of over 43 per cent. The locations and concentrations mean that black and Asian people are statistically important in the political process. There are at least 50 constituencies, for example, where the black and Asian population is larger than the current MP's majority.[16] However, a substantial majority of black and Asian people have voted over the years for a single party, the Labour Party – overall, between October 1974 and May 1997, four out of five black and Asian votes were for Labour.[17]

16.16 A number of black and Asian candidates stood for the main political parties between 1974 and 1983,[18] but with the possible exception of Hemel Hempstead in 1983 none contested a safe or winnable seat. In 1987 four black and Asian candidates were elected, all Labour. In 1992 there were 23 black and Asian candidates (nine Labour, eight Conservative and six Liberal Democrat) and six were elected, five Labour and one Conservative. In 1997 there were 37 black and Asian candidates but only nine were selected for safe or winnable seats. All nine were elected; all were Labour. Since then the organisation EQ has been set up to increase the number of Asian and black candidates put forward by the Labour Party. It will promote positive action to identify, develop and fast-track individuals of special promise and provide grants and bursaries accordingly. The project is promising, and similar initiatives should be taken in all parties.[19] *We recommend that each party conduct an audit by ethnicity of its own membership, and draw up and publish plans on how it proposes to ensure that more Asian and black candidates are selected for safe and winnable seats.* Parties should particularly aim to include Asian and black candidates on shortlists in constituencies where at least 25 per cent of the electorate is Asian or black.

16.17   There is frequent disillusion among black and Asian people who have tried to make a mark by being elected to a borough, county or city council.[20] Eighty per cent of black and Asian local councillors, in a study undertaken in the early 1990s, agreed with the statement that 'the political parties are more interested in ethnic minorities' votes than their opinions'.[21] In interviews, councillors expressed views such as those quoted in Box 16.2. The quotations are evidence of institutional racism in political parties and suggest that one of the strands in such racism is the fear of alienating middle Britain.

16.18   The Royal Commission on the Reform of the House of Lords argued against an elected second chamber. Nevertheless, it stressed that the new chamber should be broadly representative of the United Kingdom and that all people 'should be able to feel that there is a voice in Parliament for the different aspects of their personalities, whether regional, vocational, ethnic, professional, cultural or religious, expressed by a person or persons with whom they can identify'. The chamber should be 'a relatively non-polemical forum for national debate, informed by the range of different perspectives which its members should have'. Members should, among other things, have 'the ability to bring a philosophical, moral or spiritual perspective to bear', 'a non-polemical and courteous style', 'the ability to take a long-term view'. These quotations evoke the aspirations of many other unelected bodies as well.

Box 16.2 **Voices: experiences in party politics**

*One always hears that the Labour Party is the natural party for ethnic mi-
norities, but it isn't and it is very sad really. Because the Labour Party is
looking more towards the middle class and attracting that particular
section of the community. It feels that the ethnic minority will have no
choice but to support them, whether they like it or not. Because if they
don't support the party, then they are the ones who are losers. We are left
out to fend for ourselves within the political arena if we don't co-operate
with the Labour Party.*

*Their reluctance to allow black people voice, an independent voice ... at
the end of the day it is about votes and elections, a fear of white backlash
if the party appears to be giving power to blacks.*

*They [the Labour Party] are moving towards the centre, and because they
are moving towards the centre, they have to appease the electorate at the
centre. And the electorate at the centre couldn't give a damn about black
people.*

Source: Research undertaken in the mid-1990s; details in Note 21.

16.19 The Royal Commission recommended that an Appointments Commission for the new second chamber be set up, under a statutory duty to
ensure that at least one-third of new members each year are women,
with the aim of making steady progress towards gender balance over
time. It also recommended that the commission 'use its best endeavours
to ensure a level of representation for members of minority ethnic
groups which is at least proportionate to their presence in the population as a whole'. The notion of best endeavours is not satisfactory. *We
recommend that the appointments commission have a statutory duty to
ensure that the second chamber is more representative of the country in terms
of ethnicity.* Further, *we recommend that in any one year, during at least the
next five years, about one-sixth of new members be drawn from Asian and
black community backgrounds.* The pool of available talent is substantial.
Since the present group of black and Asian peers is severely unbalanced
in terms of gender, *we recommend that a least a third of newly appointed
black and Asian peers in any one year be women.* We would also expect at
least 30 per cent of new white peers to be women.

16.20 The Royal Commission's report did not discuss principles and practicalities for appointing Asian and black members of the second chamber, other than to say that their numbers should be at least proportionate to their numbers in the UK as a whole. The new appointments commission will need to quantify this requirement in guidelines and a code of practice. The difficulties it will meet are already familiar in many other spheres, and it will benefit from suggestions and reflections from public bodies and community organisations which have already been wrestling for many years with how to compose deliberative forums that are adequately accountable and legitimate. A valuable starting point is provided by the Commission's expectation that people should be able to feel that there is a voice in Parliament for the 'different aspects of their personalities ... expressed by a person or persons with whom they can identify'.

16.21 The number of black and Asian life peers tripled between 1997 and spring 2000, from six to 18. Fourteen of them were Asian, four black. They represent all three parties between them, though the majority are Labour. In January 2000 they made common cause in connection with the Race Relations (Amendment) Act during its committee stage, and forced a significant addition to it from the government. Their success was striking confirmation, if confirmation were needed, that even quite a small number of black and Asian people, if they are present when major issues are being debated and settled, can make a substantial difference to the parliamentary process as a whole. Appointments to the House of Lords are to an extent part of the overall honours system. The award of honours should be monitored by ethnicity, and criteria should be reviewed and publicised to ensure that substantially more Asian and black people are nominated and considered. For example, the criteria should recognise contributions made over the years to the Asian and black voluntary sector.

16.22 All appointments to unelected bodies, whether national bodies such as the reformed House of Lords or local area committees of the kind proposed for new structures of local government,[22] need to take into account the importance of the black and Asian voluntary sector. It was created on a self-help basis and developed because there was a widespread awareness that both the public sector and the wider voluntary sector were neglecting the needs of the newer communities. Neglect and indifference in central and local government were replaced in due course by what is sometimes termed the 'district commissioner mentality' – the approach of a colonial officer who favours men rather than women, elders rather than the young and tradition rather than development; and who distributes grants, patronage and favours, the effects of which are to maintain dependency and to foster wasteful competition. The main problems faced nowadays by many organisations are the suspicion, mistrust and insensitivity they encounter in public bodies and in the wider voluntary sector. For example, they feel that they have to operate under intense scrutiny from funders. This has sometimes led to an escalation of mistrust.[23]

16.23 Genuine deliberation involves acknowledging the realities of such mistrust and taking conscious steps to reduce it. Democracy is more than just a system for organising the election of governments. It is also a theory that all citizens are of intrinsically equal worth and that all should be able to participate in the making of decisions that affect them. All therefore should have the necessary communicative and deliberative skills, and all should have access to platforms where issues are debated, and to the forums and tables where decisions are made. True deliberation requires of people an open-mindedness, a willingness to listen and to weigh up, to give reasons and agree principles, and a 'civic magnanimity'[24] that recognises the moral seriousness of those with whom they disagree. In cross-cultural situations it critically requires of people a certain cultural literacy – an awareness of their own biases and of how they may appear to others, and a capacity to attend to others' views without being distracted by, and making unsound judgements about, cultural difference. Decisions made through deliberation are more just and more principled, and therefore of more benefit to the disadvantaged, than those that depend on electoral power alone. In the next chapter we consider not only political disagreement but also other areas of society where citizens have profound differences of outlook and world-view.

Chapter 17

Religion and Belief

> *There is a tendency in western democracies to believe that secular society provides the best public space for equality and tolerance ... [but] secular society tends to push religion ... to the margins of public space and into the private sphere. Islamophobia and antisemitism merge with a more widespread rejection of religion which runs through a significant part of 'tolerant' society, including the educated middle class and the progressive media.*
>
> From a letter to the Commission from a Christian organisation, 1998

> *There was a newspaper ... article about racism. It asked a hundred white people about it – and most hated was Asians, Muslims ... That makes me realise I'm walking around now and people are looking at me in a different way.*
>
> From the Commission's focus group research, autumn 1999

17.1 Faith communities and religious organisations play significant roles in civil society. They engage the energies of substantial numbers of people, mainly on a voluntary basis and at local levels, and motivate them to work for the greater social good. Their use of ethical arguments, grounded in their role as providers of ritual at times of stress, anxiety or celebration, enables them to command a hearing in secular forums, and to mobilise substantial support from their own members. They possess considerable material assets, including buildings where they can accommodate meetings, and run many welfare and educational services, thereby performing some of the functions of public bodies. For these reasons, singly and jointly, they are readily able to engage in negotiations with the public sector. The previous government recognised their importance by establishing the Inner Cities Religious Council; the present government has issued guidance on involving them as partners in regeneration programmes,[1] and has commissioned research into the effects of religious discrimination.[2] Article 13 of the Treaty of Amsterdam provides a legal basis for the European Union to take action against discrimination based not only on 'racial or ethnic origin' but also on 'religion or belief ',[3] thus recognising the importance of religious identities in modern Europe. There is similar recognition in the Scotland Act 1998 and the Greater London Authority Act 1999.[4]

17.2 In every religious tradition a broad distinction may be drawn between nominal or community involvement and active membership. But each tradition makes this distinction in its own way. In Christianity, for example, active membership usually includes public worship as a high priority, and both women and men are expected to attend. In other religions, active membership gives greater relative weight to private devotion and to observance in the home, and there are different expectations of women and men. For these reasons, statistics about religious affiliation cannot be more than rough estimates, and comparisons between different religions may be misleading. We welcome the inclusion of a question about religious affiliation in the 2001 Census. In consequence of it, valuable and precise statistics will in due course become available. In the meantime, rough estimates are better than nothing at all. According to one such estimate, the nominal or community membership of Christian denominations includes 26.2 million Anglicans or Episcopalians, 5.7 Roman Catholics, 2.6 million Presbyterians and 1.3 million Methodists. Black-majority Pentecostal and Holiness Churches probably have a community membership of around 500,000.[5] With other religions, the proportion of active members is higher.[6] It has been estimated that overall (that is, both nominal and active) there are between 1.2 million and 1.5 million Muslims, 500,000 Sikhs, 500,000 Hindus and 300,000 Jews. Smaller faith communities include around 50,000 Buddhists, 25,000 Jains, 6,000 Baha'is and 5,000 Zoroastrians. The growth of religions other than Christianity in Britain between 1960 and 2000 has been substantial: from around 259,000 active members to 1.46 million; from 548 groups or congregations to 2,650; and from 814 individual leaders in 1960 to 6,385. Fuller details are given in Table C in Appendix D.

17.3 The historic commitments of religious traditions to race equality are reflected in the work of, among many others, the Churches Commission for Racial Justice (CCRJ), the Islamic Human Rights Commission and the Jewish Council for Racial Equality. However, theoretical opposition to racism and other forms of oppression is not consistently embodied by religious believers and communities in practical action. In all traditions, religious claims and rituals may be used to legitimise power structures rather than to promote ethical principles, and may foster bigotry, sectarianism and fundamentalism. Notoriously, religion often accepts and gives its blessing to gender inequalities. This legitimising role is usually less blatant nowadays in the case of race equality issues. Nevertheless, it can be significant, particularly when clearly racist policies claim to be motivated by Christian beliefs. A piece of racist propaganda recently circulated in Britain called on the government to use the army to remove all mosques, temples and synagogues from 'this Christian land'.[7] When racism uses a religious justification, anti-racism has to adopt distinctive strategies. However, most race equality organisations are broadly secular, not religious. It is perhaps for this reason that they frequently appear insensitive to forms of racism that target aspects of religious identity. For example, they are widely perceived by British Muslims to be insensitive to distinctive Muslim concerns, by Jewish people to be uninterested in antisemitism, and by Irish people to be indifferent to sectarianism and anti-Catholicism. People with Indian cultural backgrounds and ties to Sikhism or Hinduism similarly feel that anti-racist organisations have little or nothing to say about their religious affiliations and identities. Further, there is little recognition in the secular race equality community of the work and importance of black-majority Churches.

17.4   The Christian Churches undertake a range of anti-racist programmes, focused ecumenically each year on Racial Justice Sunday and co-ordinated by the CCRJ. But such projects are typically separate, both intellectually and structurally, from those concerned with inter-faith relations and dialogue, and they address the biological strand in racism more than the cultural. (See Chapter 5 for discussion of this distinction.) It is unfortunate that Christian anti-racism is too often isolated from inter-faith issues, and that Christian involvement in these issues, conversely, ignores or underplays colour and cultural racisms and the need to address them. The split is to an extent caused by the fact that Christian anti-racism has two separate aspects: combating institutional racism within Church structures, and speaking and acting against racism in wider society. In other traditions, the split between anti-racism and inter-faith activity is perhaps less marked. *We recommend that in all faith communities there be closer connections between anti-racism and work to improve inter-faith relations.*

17.5   Victims of racism frequently turn to their religion for inner strength in their struggle against exclusion, abuse and non-recognition, particularly when their religion is being singled out for attack by racism as alien or inferior. 'If Islam is good enough for people to hate me because I'm a member of it,' someone said to us, in explanation of this pattern, 'I may as well believe it.' This may result in a vicious spiral of mutual hostility: cultural racism leads to increased assertiveness among those at whom it is directed, and this in turn is perceived to justify further racism. Here too is a set of issues that the race equality community all too frequently ignores. The race equality community's silence on the subject of religion was seen particularly clearly when the Stephen Lawrence Inquiry report was published. (See Chapter 5.) Box 17.1 shows the pressures on and arguments within one particular religious community. It is a case study of the issues that concern most communities.

Discrimination and non-recognition

17.6   Case law since the Race Relations Act 1976 has defined the members of two religions, Judaism and Sikhism, as belonging to ethnic groups. In consequence Jews and Sikhs have been privileged over other faith communities by gaining legal protection from discrimination in employment and the provision of services. The protection extends to cultural or secular Jews and Sikhs as well as those who are observant in their practices and beliefs. Similarly, in Northern Ireland it is recognised that the terms Roman Catholic and Protestant refer essentially to cultural background and tradition, not to religious belief and practice. In Chapters 3 and 4 we stressed that non-recognition of cultural identities is unjust, and may be as distressing for those affected as are discrimination and harassment.

17.7   The government acknowledges that there are anomalies and injustices in the present situation, but it has stated that simply adding a reference to religion in existing anti-discrimination legislation would cause more problems than it would solve: 'The Government is sympathetic to religious groups on this issue, but there is no straightforward solution. It is not a simple case of amending the legislation to simply add religion. There are considerable difficulties in defining religion without including groups which would be better described as cults.'[8] The government

Box 17.1 **Voices: pressures on and arguments about religious identity**

I come from a Muslim family, but Islam has never done anything for me, it's only ever caused me problems and aggro. In school everyone used to slag off my Muslim name, Yousaf, but when I called myself John they changed their attitudes and accepted me and now all my best mates are Scottish. I feel like one of the boys.

From day one we are bombarded with alien ideas and values and made to feel that this is what we should aspire to ... The national curriculum is Eurocentric. You are taught about great scientists, philosophers, writers like Newton, Plato, Byron, Wilde, etc., all white Europeans. You never get taught that when Europe was in the dark ages the Islamic empire was the most advanced and civilised in the world ... Islamic scholars set the basis for most modern-day science and thinking.

It is left to individuals to find out about their Islamic origins and who they really are, because the current system is failing them. This leads to confusion, alienation and inter-generational conflict.

At school ... I always felt really embarrassed to be myself, 'cos all the kids would treat you like a weirdo if you acted different. None of them really understood or knew anything about the real me.

Aye, just because I live like a typical Scot most of my community treat me like an outcast.

As Muslims in this country we are being forced by the system to make a choice, either integrate, therefore compromising ourselves, our cultures and our beliefs, or separatism, whereby we create our own institutions and educational systems.

Aye, but if you split up from the rest of society that will just cause more tension and racism.

The government and schools ...feel threatened by Islam. It's up to us to take the initiative.

Source: Presentation to the Commission when it visited Stirling, June 1998.

fears that members of cults, as distinct from religions, would claim protection under the new legislation, but that some of the practices and beliefs of such cults would be morally objectionable. When the House of

Lords Select Committee on the European Union debated EU proposals to combat discrimination under Article 13 of the Treaty of Amsterdam, it expressed reservations about the vagueness of the phrase 'religion or belief' and maintained that 'if protection on these grounds is to be extended beyond the employment field, a clearer definition, or a list of examples, will be required'.[9]

17.8   These issues need to be publicly and thoughtfully debated, and claims and counter-claims should be given respectful, as distinct from polemical, attention. For example, it is surely not necessary to define in law the difference between a religion and a cult – although a possible definition was proposed in a debate in the House of Lords in October 1999.[10] A report from the Council of Europe has declared that 'it is not for public authorities to determine which beliefs should not be considered as "religion". It is rather for them to determine which activities, manifestations, practices or claims are consonant with public policy, with due regard to the basic human rights.'[11] It is not, it follows, necessary to distinguish between a religion and a cult. The requirement rather is to distinguish between practices that are and are not compatible with basic human rights. We discussed human rights in Chapter 7 and intercultural dialogue and negotiation, in the settling of disputes, in Chapter 4.

17.9   In the field of employment, a distinction has to be drawn between fair treatment in recruitment and fair treatment in the workplace, for example in relation to holidays and festivals, clothing and insignia, prayer times, dietary observances, and so on. Many public bodies – including police, health and local authorities – have formally declared that they will not discriminate on grounds of religion, in either recruitment or the workplace.[12] Such authorities have not met insurmountable problems, for example in relation to the distinction between a religion and a cult, or in terms of unreasonable demands by employees. The concepts of 'reasonable adjustments' and 'reasonable accommodation', already well known in relation to disability issues, are applicable to issues of religion and culture.

17.10   *We recommend that legislation be introduced in Britain prohibiting direct and indirect discrimination on grounds of religion or belief.* Employers, schools and other institutions should be under a duty to make reasonable adjustments to accommodate a person's religious observance or practice, provided that this can be achieved without undue adverse effects on the employer's business or on the general conduct of the school or other institution. Since many employers and schools do already make reasonable adjustments, the good practice they have developed should be evaluated and shared more widely. *We recommend that a statement of general principles be drawn up on reasonable accommodation in relation to religious and cultural diversity in the workplace and in schools, and that case-study examples of good practice be provided.* The initiative on this could be taken by the Department for Education and Employment (DfEE), the Commission for Racial Equality (CRE), an employers' organisation, a union, or a voluntary organisation, but of course the faith communities themselves should be fully consulted. The principles would also clarify instances where discrimination on religious grounds would not be unlawful, for example in the making of certain appointments.

17.11   The Crime and Disorder Act 1998 imposes higher penalties when an assault is judged by the court to have been motivated, in part or entirely, by racism. The definition of racism does not include a reference to religion, however. A possible consequence is that assaults on Jews and Sikhs, and desecration of their sacred buildings, will be punished more severely than assaults and desecration targeted at other religions. A number of police forces have included a reference to religion in their definition of hate crime, and the new Home Office guidance on recording racist attacks (April 2000) refers to those that occur in the vicinity of religious buildings. *We recommend that a study be made of police responses to hate crimes containing a religious component.* It would also be valuable if monitoring projects and advice services, including citizens' advice bureaux, were to make a point of collecting reports of attacks and discrimination where religious factors are believed to have been relevant.[13]

17.12   The right of faith communities to found and run schools is enshrined in law. With certain conditions – relating to curriculum, staff qualifications, standard of buildings, and so forth – state funding for such schools is in principle available. There are around 4,800 Church of England schools, 2,140 Roman Catholic, 28 Methodist, 24 Jewish and 2 Muslim. Opposition to state funding for Muslim schools has been fuelled over the years by anti-Muslim prejudice,[14] but it has also come from those who believe that faith community schools are divisive and that all state education should be secular.[15] But state-funded Muslim schools now exist and they are likely to increase in numbers in the years ahead. Several schools are also likely, in certain respects, to become Muslim in their ethos, though not in their legal status, as a consequence of making 'reasonable accommodation' (see above) for the vast majority of their pupils. These trends are welcomed by many, not feared, as important components in a community of communities. Safeguards are needed, however, to prevent fragmentation and separatism. Schools with a religious ethos must be encouraged and enabled to play a full part in the wider educational community.

Religion and public life

17.13   We argued in Chapters 2–4 that public life should recognise a wider range of cultural identities than it does at present. A widening of recognition will involve reconsidering symbolic connections between Englishness and Anglicanism, and between Scottishness and Presbyterianism, for these connections arguably exclude large numbers of people from a full sense of belonging – members of all other Churches are excluded as well as atheists and agnostics and the adherents of Buddhism, Hinduism, Islam, Judaism and Sikhism. In his lecture at the Edinburgh Festival in August 1999 the composer James Macmillan outlined his dream of 'a genuinely pluralistic democracy where differences are not just recognised and respected but celebrated, nurtured and absorbed for the greater good'.[16] He spoke too of 'a seemingly insurmountable hurdle' preventing the realisation of such a democracy, which he called sleep-walking bigotry, and 'a desire to narrow down and to restrict the definition of what it means to be Scottish'. He commented that 'most Scottish Catholics learn at an early age that the best self-defence mechanism is to keep one's head down. Try not to attract attention to the fact that you are a Catholic – it will only annoy them.'

17.14   A thoroughgoing review of religion in Britain would need to reconsider a wide range of connections, both legal and symbolic, between Church and state. Specifically it would need to examine the Act of Settlement 1701, which the Scottish Parliament has declared to be offensive and discriminatory; the Bishoprics Act 1878, which will in any case have to be reformed if the recommendations of the Royal Commission on the Reform of the House of Lords are implemented;[17] the Prisons Act 1952;[18]

and the Marriage Acts 1949–96,[19] which are widely felt to privilege Anglicans in England over other denominations and faiths; customs related to civic religion, for example daily prayers at Westminster and various religious ceremonies, including memorial events, in local government;[20] the law of blasphemy; and the coronation oath.

17.15   For some commentators, a review of such issues would lead to disestablishment of the Church of England.[21] An alternative view is that the privileges should be shared, not removed entirely.[22] Holders of this view welcome the fact that the Church of England speaks on and influences public affairs well beyond its own pulpits and has a sense of responsibility for all people, locally as well as nationally. It also fosters civic responsibility in its own members and those who look to it for leadership; provides shared rituals at times of collective emotion; helps to ensure that pastoral care and counselling are available in hospitals and prisons; and plays a part, often in unsung ways, in promoting respect for the religious world-views of people who are not its own members. These contributions to society should be shared formally by a wider range of faith communities, it is said, not abolished.

17.16   It is now 30 years since relations between Church and state were last systematically considered by a commission.[23] The time has come to revisit the issues in the context of the religious pluralism and increased secularism of the present time. Such issues include chaplaincy arrangements in prisons, hospitals, higher education and the armed forces; the involvement of religious bodies in the registration of marriages; recognition of, for example, Islamic law in matters of inheritance, marriage and divorce; ceremonies in local and national government; the role of Parliament in regulating the Church of England; representation in the House of Lords and other deliberative assemblies; and the governance of Church schools that have substantial proportions of pupils from backgrounds other than Christian. These issues need to be widely debated within and among faith communities and in interaction with society at large. Such debates already happen in local situations and are often valuably promoted by inter-faith co-operation.[24] *We recommend that a commission on the role of religion in the public life of a multi-faith society be set up to make recommendations on legal and constitutional matters.*

Difference, dispute and disagreement

17.17 In Scotland, it has been said that 'we must all become Jock Tamsin's bairns, regardless of creed or colour'.[25] People should see themselves as sharing a common humanity, and having a common store of metaphors and allusions to celebrate that humanity ('Jock Tamsin's bairns'), and yet also see and affirm themselves as different from each other in profound ways. The creation of such a multicultural democracy, to cite James Macmillan again, requires people to 'forgive and receive absolution for the sins and prejudices of the past on all sides, to experience the healing embrace of reconciliation, and to say to one another, again with respect and gratitude but also with compassion and even love, "I may not agree with you, but the free expression of your ideas allows me to see how things may not be as clear-cut as I had previously thought. I had not thought about it like that before."'[26]

17.18 Adherents of different world faiths and religious traditions have different theological, moral and philosophical views, and many of these are incompatible with each other. Also there are profound differences between religious believers and secular humanists. Freedom of religion is an essential value, but so also is freedom from religion. This is presumably why Article 13 of the Treaty of Amsterdam uses the phrase 'religion or belief', not 'religion' only. Dispute and disagreement are integral to democracy. When believers use religion to justify practices that others judge to be unethical, immoral or illegal, it is right that they should be challenged.

17.19 Religious disagreements – whether between adherents of different faiths or between believers and agnostics – are a paradigm of cultural and intellectual disagreements more generally.[27] The alternative to hostility and hatred is not necessarily agreement but rather a reasoned approach to difference and disagreement. This involves, it has been said, 'willingness and ability to articulate our disagreements, to defend them before people with whom we disagree, to discern the difference between respectable and disrespectable disagreement, and to be open to changing our own minds when faced with well-reasoned criticism'.[28] To repeat, such qualities are needed in a wide range of deliberative forums, not just in discussions of religion.

17.20 When the Runnymede Trust Commission on Islamophobia published a consultation paper in 1997 it quoted from an article by a prominent journalist. Islam was once, he had said, 'a great civilisation worthy of being argued with'. But latterly it had degenerated into 'a primitive enemy fit only to be sensitively subjugated'.[29] Seeing himself quoted in this context, the journalist immediately published a defiant response. He entitled it 'I believe in Islamophobia' and concluded: 'To worry about contemporary Islam is not mad. It would be mad to do otherwise.'[30]

17.21 The term 'Islamophobia' was coined by way of analogy to 'xenophobia'. Its use involves distinguishing between unfounded ('mad') hostility to Islam and reasoned disagreement or criticism. In this connection, distinctions may be drawn between closed and open views. The Commission on Islamophobia listed and discussed eight main ways in which these two sets of views differ. For example, it noted that closed views see

Islam as monolithic, static and unresponsive, whereas open ones see it as diverse and developing, with internal differences and disagreements. It recommended that the eight differences between closedness and openness be used in analysis of media reporting, and as ground rules for handling disagreements. The eight features are shown in Table 17.1. The table does not refer specifically to hostility towards Islam, however, but to all hostility towards 'the Other', all forms of cultural racism. The duty to view others and to hold one's own beliefs in an open manner applies to everyone, including, of course, religious believers themselves. The openness they legitimately expect from others should also be a feature of their own outlook and behaviour.

17.22 This is the last chapter in Part 2 of the report. It is fitting that this section should close with Table 17.1, as the distinctions between open and closed views of the Other are centrally relevant to many other discussions in the report: different perspectives on national history (Chapter 2); the maintenance of cohesion and shared values in a diverse society (Chapter 4); combating cultural racism (Chapter 5); the formation of a human rights culture (Chapter 7); citizenship education in schools (Chapter 11); the responsibilities of the media (Chapter 12); and the playing of the race card by politicians (Chapters 15 and 16). What we have called an open approach to disagreement can and must be promoted by the government of the day. The leadership tasks of government, and the structural and strategic tasks that flow from them, are considered in Part 3.

Table 17.1 **Closed and open views of the Other**

Distinctions	Closed views of the Other	Open views of the Other
1 Monolithic/diverse	The Other seen as a single monolithic bloc, static and unresponsive to new realities	The Other seen as diverse and progressive, with internal differences, debates and development
2 Separate/interacting	The Other seen as separate: (a) not having any aims or values in common with the self; (b) not affected by it; (c) not influencing it	The Other seen as interdependent with the self: (a) having certain shared values and aims; (b) affected by it; (c) enriching it
3 Inferior/different	The Other seen as inferior to the self: e.g. barbaric, irrational, 'fundamentalist'	The Other seen as different but of equal worth
4 Enemy/partner	The Other seen as violent, aggressive, threatening, to be defeated and perhaps dominated	The Other seen as an actual or potential partner in joint co-operative enterprises and in the solution of shared problems
5 Manipulative/sincere	The Other seen as manipulative and deceitful, bent only on material or strategic advantage	The Other seen as sincere in their beliefs, not hypocritical
6 Criticisms of the self rejected/considered	Criticisms made by the Other of the self are rejected out of hand	Criticisms of the self are considered and debated
7 Discrimination defended/criticised	Hostility towards the Other used to justify discriminatory practices and exclusion of the Other from mainstream society	Debates and disagreements with the Other do not diminish efforts to combat discrimination and exclusion
8 Hostility towards the Other seen as natural/problematic	Fear and hostility towards the Other accepted as natural and 'normal'	Critical views of the Other themselves subjected to critique, lest they be inaccurate and unfair

Part 3

Strategies of Change

Chapter 18

Government Leadership

My final appeal to the Commission would be not to produce another worthy document or report without any real action being taken. We have already had many worthy reports and documents which have propped up bookcases, shelves or doors. We need to have clear aims and aspirations as a society, reflected through ... political processes, resources, actions and media and at individual and community levels.

From a response to the Commission, 1998

18.1 Government has four principal functions: to provide political leadership; to allocate resources; to manage its own departments in ways that are both efficient and exemplary; and to formulate and implement legislation, with support, regulation and enforcement as necessary. We consider the first three of these functions in this chapter. The fourth, that of enacting and enforcing legislation, is considered in Chapter 19. Measures by the authorities in Cardiff, Holyrood and Westminster are necessary, certainly, but not in themselves sufficient. If momentum is to be maintained there must also be a process of change in each individual city, borough, shire and district, and in each individual organisation and institution. At local as well as national levels there must be both accountability and legitimacy. A community of citizens and communities has to be built from the bottom up as well as through government action. In Chapter 20 we consider the momentum of change at all levels.

18.2 The Labour Party manifesto that preceded the 1997 general election contained a commitment to introduce new legislation on racist violence and harassment. Subsequently, this commitment led to a consultation paper and to clauses in the Crime and Disorder Act 1998. Otherwise, in its 177 commitments, the manifesto made no direct reference to issues of race equality and cultural diversity. Likewise, there was almost no reference to race and diversity issues in the speeches of Tony Blair published a few months before the election, or in any of the other key texts outlining New Labour's general thinking.[1] The tacit assumption was that measures intended to benefit the whole of society would automatically benefit Asian, black and Irish communities at the same time. This colour- and culture-blind approach to social policy continued to be dominant at least until the end of 1999.

18.3 There was initially no reference to race and diversity issues in the government's strategies to combat social exclusion; no explicit focus on them in the raft of new educational measures and initiatives; and no reference in early documents about cultural policy. The government's wide-ranging programme of public service modernisation[2] seemed to take for granted that modernisation was bound to benefit all sections of society equally. Nor was there reference to these issues in the Business Excellence Model that the government adopted from the private sector, or in the early documentation issued about the Performance and Innovation Unit (PIU). The Treasury's Public Service Agreements (PSAs) with other departments required clear policy objectives, broken down into targets and performance indicators. However, there was no requirement in the first round of PSAs to consider race equality objectives, or to take into account cultural diversity. Likewise, there was no reference in the 1998 white paper on local government[3] or in the founding documentation about the best-value regime for such government.

18.4 During 1999 the government began to drop its colour- and culture-blind approaches to social policy and modernisation. By early summer 2000 it was able to itemise a number of specific and significant developments, including the following.

- First steps in the creation of a race equality performance management framework, involving a 'basket' (the government's own term) of race equality performance indicators for many government departments.[4]
- The announcement that all public authorities are to be put under a statutory duty to promote race equality; that the police and immigration services will be subject to the Race Relations Act; that all the functions of public bodies, including regulatory functions not previously covered, will be subject to the Act; and that the concept of indirect discrimination will therefore be more widely applied to public services than ever before.[5]
- The introduction of race equality recruitment targets for the police,

fire and probation services; for the civil service as a whole, but in particular at senior levels; for the armed forces; for public appointments; and for several individual departments.[6]

- The inclusion of the Commission for Racial Equality's standards in the best-value regime for local government.[7]
- A strong emphasis on equality issues in reform of the civil service. The Cabinet Office will help ensure that departments' individual targets are met, and for senior posts will create a central pool of potential secondees from under-represented groups. There is to be equality-proofing of all recruitment, appraisal and promotion processes.[8]
- Acceptance of the majority of the recommendations in the Stephen Lawrence Inquiry report, including the adoption of a ministerial priority to increase confidence in policing among black and Asian communities. Performance against this priority is to be measured by four key indicators: the numbers of recorded racist incidents; the use of stop-and-search procedures; levels of recruitment, retention and progress of Asian and black staff; and surveys of public satisfaction.[9]
- Issuing of clear and helpful guidance on race equality issues in New Deal for Communities partnerships[10] and of a wide-ranging set of recommendations relating to neighbourhood renewal.[11]
- Setting up the Race Relations Forum, and seeking advice from it about the establishment of new government structures and machinery.
- The creation of a grants programme for black and Asian voluntary organisations, intended to improve the infrastructure of this part of the voluntary and community sector.[12]

18.5   The Scotland Act and the Government of Wales Act reserved equal opportunities as a Westminster responsibility. However, they also empowered the new authorities in Scotland and Wales to promote such opportunities, and in this respect the Scotland Act adopted a wider definition than that operating in England: 'the prevention, elimination or regulation of discrimination between persons on grounds of sex or marital status, on racial grounds, or on grounds of disability, age, sexual orientation, language or social origin, or of other personal attributes, including beliefs or opinions, such as religious beliefs or political persuasions'.

18.6   The Scottish Parliament established an equal opportunities commit-
       tee as one of eight mandatory standing committees, and ensured that
       its rules of procedure required all legislative proposals presented by
       the Executive to be accompanied by a statement about their impact on
       equality issues. The Executive committed itself to developing an equal-
       ity strategy, to doing this through a process of public consultation,
       and to reporting annually on progress. It set up a special unit, the
       Equality Unit, to ensure momentum. In early 2000 the Unit issued a
       consultation paper containing statements of general intent and com-
       mitment, and 14 questions on which opinions were invited. These in-
       cluded the following: What do you think constitutes good practice in
       the equality field and can you supply the Executive with examples of
       good practice? How do you think the Scottish Executive can promote
       a better understanding of the needs of specific groups? How could
       data and information on equal opportunities be improved? What ex-
       perience do you or your organisation have of effective consultation
       and how do you think the Executive can develop and improve its con-
       sultation methods and mechanisms on equality? Such questions have
       the potential to engage large numbers of people in crucial debate. The
       ensuing strategy and resourcing proposals stand a good chance of
       being widely embraced and understood, and of contributing to the
       Executive's action plan for implementing the recommendations of the
       Stephen Lawrence Inquiry.[13] If the consultation process proves to be
       successful in these respects, significant lessons will be available for
       such projects in the rest of Britain. For example, it would be appropri-
       ate to consult widely on the performance indicators the Home Office
       outlined in its publication of March 2000. There is further discussion
       of this below.

18.7   The National Assembly for Wales set up a standing committee on equal-
       ity of opportunity whose remit is to monitor how the Assembly pro-
       motes such equality. The committee's first main activity was to conduct
       an audit, and the results of this were published in April 2000.[14] The
       report referred to 'the very low starting point that the Assembly is start-
       ing from', 'the need as a matter of urgency to review or replace existing
       recruitment practices and procedures', 'a need for greater equality
       awareness training within the Assembly even for those who profess not
       to need it', and 'the enormity of the task ahead'. In the light of the audit,
       the committee set itself three priorities: raising awareness, especially in

terms of impact appraisal; studying the implementation of the Stephen Lawrence Inquiry report; and considering how to encourage black, female and disabled recruitment both in the Assembly itself and in the appointments it makes to public bodies and boards.

18.8   The Westminster government is to be commended for dropping its initial colour- and culture-blind approach, which it inherited from all previous administrations. The new authorities in Cardiff and Holyrood are similarly to be commended for attending explicitly to equality issues from the outset. These moves towards greater explicitness break with several decades of inattention and insensitivity on the part of most government departments most of the time. The changes are still, however, a long way from being irreversible and institutionalised. The criticisms and reservations set out below are intended to be supportive of the general trend of thinking and action. Our concern is that the three administrations should proceed with greater vigour and determination.

18.9   The following observations and recommendations are addressed as appropriate to the administrations based at Cardiff, Holyrood and Westminster. Some clearly relate to Britain as a whole, but others are relevant as phrased only to England. The patterns of devolved and reserved powers are such that statements that are true in one country are not necessarily true in others, unless at a high level of generalisation. Terminology varies between the three countries, reflecting different administrative structures as well as different conceptual approaches.

Leadership of public opinion

18.10   Official documentation continues to project an image of Britain as consisting essentially of one large white majority (this term is used frequently in the Home Office paper of March 2000 on public services) and various minorities that all have more in common with each other than with anyone else. The Social Exclusion Unit, for example, conceptualises race equality as essentially a 'minority ethnic issue',[15] as does the Department for Education and Employment (DfEE).[16] A further problem is that the documentation is almost entirely concerned with equality as distinct from diversity issues,[17] and with addressing colour racism rather than all forms of racism. The opening declaration in the March 2000 document is in this respect significant: 'Every colour is a good colour.' The reference is to racism based primarily on physical appearance and therefore disregards phenomena such as anti-Muslim and anti-Irish racism. The term 'diversity' does appear in the opening declaration, but the adjective applied to it is 'racial', not 'cultural'. We have argued throughout this report that equality and diversity are both significant values, and that neither can be reduced to the other. Similarly, we have argued that both colour and cultural racism must be addressed. It is important that follow-up documents from the government should widen the terms of debate.

18.11 There is an even more serious respect in which the government has failed to provide high-profile leadership, which we highlighted in Chapter 15 – it has failed to lead public opinion on immigration and asylum issues. In Chapter 16 we noted that policy in this sphere is formed with electoral considerations in mind rather than rational or ethical principles, or the requirements of international law. The recommendations about immigration and asylum made in Chapter 15 need to be implemented as a matter of priority if the government and the Labour Party are to maintain the credibility of their race equality agenda more generally. Similarly, the recommendations made in Chapter 16, about race and political representation, must be taken on board by all political parties.

The need for co-ordination

18.12 Although significant, progress has been patchy. For example, employment targets have been set for services administered by the Home Office but as yet there are no equivalent targets for the education system, the health service and arts institutions. If target-setting and performance management are important in some spheres of government influence, then they are in all. There is already considerable scepticism as to whether the targets for the police service can in fact be achieved. Such scepticism is magnified by awareness that the education system, for example, has no targets at all. The guidance provided is similarly uneven. The Department of the Environment, Transport and the Regions has issued sound guidance on New Deal for Communities partnerships, which is thoughtful, challenging, conceptually sound and practitioner-friendly.[18] A welcome can also be accorded to the RESPOND project from the Home Office, but other government departments have yet to offer guidance of similar quality.

18.13 It is to an extent inevitable that different government departments should display different levels of understanding and commitment. But beyond a certain level, differences imply lack of central control and political will. All governments lead indirectly by example as well as directly through their words and actions. If a government appears unfocused or disorganised on equality and diversity issues, this signals that in its view the issues are of little or no importance. Consequently, other public bodies will not bother with them either. If, however, its approach is purposeful and co-ordinated, others will be in no doubt about what they are expected to do, and how they are expected to do it.

18.14 Joined-up thinking and cross-cutting structures are well established in tackling social exclusion. They are also needed when addressing issues of race equality and cultural diversity. In Whitehall the Home Office is generally thought of as the lead department on equality and diversity issues, since it has responsibility for the Race Relations Act. But it does not have substantial influence on, for example, the measures adopted by the DfEE in relation to education and employment, or those adopted by the Department of Health in relation to health services, or the work of the Department of Culture, Media and Sport, and so on. In Scotland, however, the Equality Unit does have a formal co-ordinating role, as mentioned above.

18.15 The best structural arrangements will become clearer in the light of further deliberation about how co-ordination should be ensured. We suggest that they are likely to have six key components.
- A lead or 'champion' minister with overall responsibility.
- A lead minister in each department.
- A cabinet committee comprising the lead ministers in each department.
- A management group of senior civil servants.
- A strategic unit similar in its range of tasks to the Social Exclusion Unit.

- A subcommittee of the Human Rights Select Committee, concerned specifically with race and diversity issues.

18.16 The tasks of the lead minister and the cabinet subcommittee, supported by the strategic unit, would include promoting the development of action plans and targets in each government department; working with other units, for example those concerned with gender equality, social exclusion, human rights and disability issues, on the development of legislative options and future structures of enforcement; ensuring that rigorous impact assessments are made of new policies and measures; consulting with a wide range of communities and with representatives of the private, public and voluntary sectors; ensuring that there is a shared and co-ordinated approach across departments to issues and methods of data collection and use; co-ordinating arrangements for periodic reports to the United Nations Committee on the Elimination of Racial Discrimination (CERD); and co-ordinating approaches to accountability, and to regulation, inspection and advice. Further, the unit would service the substantial consultative forum that we outline later.

Enforcement, support and inspection

18.17 The government needs to rethink and revise its approaches to enforcement, as well as to the right balance between legislative and non-legislative measures, and between self-regulation and external coercion. There must, in short, be sanctions and rewards to drive change forward. The government wishes to 'avoid unnecessary and burdensome regulation' and to 'promote, encourage and support progress through non-legislative means'.[19] We argued in Chapter 14 that it is necessary, and would not be a disproportionate burden, to require all employers to formulate employment equity plans. We indicated in outline what such plans should contain. In Chapter 19 we discuss regulation with regard to the need for new legislation. We do not believe it is sufficient to do no more than promote, encourage and support. It is also necessary to require.

18.18 Of course, promotion, encouragement and support are crucially important – it is not a question of either/or. One central approach to encouragement, which the government is adopting, is leadership by example, particularly with regard to performance management, and therefore to targets and indicators. Its approach in this respect was set out in the Home Office document of March 2000,[20] which did not, however, appear to have been developed through any kind of public consultation, and did not invite comment. It is nevertheless important that organisations in the voluntary and community sector, and other public bodies and academics, should respond with their detailed views.[21] The main points to spell out include the following.

- It is valuable but not sufficient to focus on issues of staffing and recruitment. There must also be performance indicators for service delivery, the awarding of grants, processes of consultation and self-review, and the commissioning and use of impact assessments. Most importantly, there must be indicators relating to results. With specific regard to employment, there must be indicators for the effectiveness of complaints and grievance procedures, and for staff retention and promotion as well as recruitment.

- There must be indicators for the collection, publication and use of high-quality data. It is seldom if ever satisfactory to refer to 'ethnic minorities' as a single homogeneous group. By the same token the categories 'Asian' and 'black' must be broken down if an adequate picture of what is happening is to be gained. The Home Office admits that much existing data is unsatisfactory. It would be wholly appropriate to set targets for improving its quality.

- There must be indicators for staff training and professional development.

- There must be indicators relating to diversity as well as to equality. The Home Office envisages that it is right to 'treat people of all races equally' and wrong 'to treat people of different races differently'.[22] We have stressed throughout this report that respect for equality is not enough. There must also be respect for diversity.

- Although it is valuable to include the perceptions of the general public in the performance indicators, it would also be appropriate and valuable to include the perceptions of public service employees, and to ask about real, not hypothetical, experience. The centrally relevant question is not 'How do you think you would be treated if you were employed in such and such a government department?' but 'How are you treated by and in the department where you work?' This would yield substantially more meaningful and usable data.

- There must be much greater consistency among government depart-

ments, and all government departments must participate. Measures to enhance consistency should themselves be the subjects of performance indicators.

18.19 Each government department is to be required to make an annual review of its progress against its own proposed targets. There should be public discussion both of the targets themselves and of the annual reports. A minimum requirement for such discussion is that information should be freely and easily available, particularly on relevant websites. Also the existing inspection regimes, such as the Audit Commission in relation to the best-value regime in local government and Ofsted in relation to education, need to be reviewed and improved. Without external inspection, institutional racism can all too easily go unchecked, and may indeed be perpetuated and strengthened rather than eroded. We mentioned in Chapter 9 that Her Majesty's Inspectorate of Constabulary has set high standards which the other inspection regimes should learn from.[23] We have also noted that the record of Ofsted in relation to race and diversity issues has so far frequently been unsatisfactory.[24]

18.20 The strategic unit proposed above should work closely with existing inspection regimes and the Commission for Racial Equality in order to:
- harmonise standards and methods as appropriate over an agreed timescale;
- create a national framework for diversity and equality inspections, and for managing a national programme of inspections of government departments, next-steps agencies, other national public bodies, and regional and local public bodies;
- provide external validations of self- and peer-evaluation processes undertaken by public bodies;
- arrange a national programme for the training and accreditation of inspectors specialising in diversity and equality issues;
- provide advice to individual bodies.

18.21 Inspections and evaluations must study employment and promotion practices; service delivery; public consultation; occupational culture and ethos; training and staff development; processes of monitoring and self-evaluation, and the use made of hard and soft data; and the nature and quality of leadership. The list of interacting components of institutional racism in Chapter 5 (Box 5.2), together with the list of questions about maintaining momentum in Chapter 20 (Box 20.1), provides a sound basis for clarifying in greater detail the topics that inspections should cover.

Pressure and advocacy

18.22 Credit for the strengths in the new explicitness must be given not only to government itself but also and principally to the groups, individuals and community organisations that have persevered in pressing the government to do far more than it was at first inclined. The Lawrence family and their supporters must be commended for getting the Stephen Lawrence Inquiry set up, and for maintaining pressure to have the Inquiry's recommendations implemented. An all-party alliance involving most Asian and black peers in the House of Lords forced the

government to rethink and radically improve its proposals for amending the Race Relations Act. Pressure from Muslim organisations forced
the government to take seriously the issue of making discrimination on
religious grounds unlawful. The basket of performance indicators on
race equality benefited from the advocacy of members of the Race
Relations Forum. Refugee organisations prevented some (though alas
not many) of the worst proposals in the Immigration and Asylum Bill
from being implemented in the ways, and to the extent, first envisaged.
Community organisations working at local levels contributed invalu-
ably to the provision of sound advice on race equality in New Deal for
Communities partnerships.

18.23 The influence of these various sources of pressure was enhanced and assisted by many agents of internal change within public bodies. Individuals and groups in the civil service and in local and regional authorities
echoed the pressure coming from outside. To summarise, credit for
what has happened must go in three directions: to the government itself,
for listening and for providing resources; to officers in public bodies for
being responsive to community concerns and giving sound advice to
their senior managers and to elected politicians; and, principally, to a
wide range of community campaigns, lobbies and organisations.

18.24 The crucial importance of community pressure must be acknowledged
with action as well as with words; such pressure must therefore be
funded. One way of ensuring that community voices are heard would be
the establishment of a much-expanded version of the current Race Relations Forum, making use of website-based discussion groups as well as
local face-to-face deliberations, and involving several thousand people.
A good model for such involvement has been provided by the People
and Parliament project in Scotland.[25] The present government set up
the Race Relations Forum shortly after it came into office. The basic
concept of such forums is sound. The dangers, however, are well known.
They can all too easily degenerate into mere talking-shops; lose touch
with the interests they supposedly represent; in consequence lose credibility and legitimacy with government itself; and be the cause of much
suspicion and bitterness. Such problems are particularly likely to
develop when the criteria for appointment to the forum are not transparent, agenda papers are not in the public domain and regular
progress reports are not published. It is entirely possible for a body to

be accountable even when it is not elected, but only if it has the following features.

- Arrangements for appointment to the forum must be transparent. Among other things, this means that there should be a public statement of criteria for appointments; that the committee making appointments is named; and that nominations and recommendations are invited.
- Even if they are appointed, not elected, members should be expected to keep themselves informed of views and concerns in a particular community of interest.
- Agenda papers must be publicly available both in print and on a website. Some of the forum's meetings should be in public and might take the form of hearings.
- The forum as a whole should make a point of consulting widely, using a range of methods. These could include small face-to-face group discussions of the kind pioneered by the People and Parliament project in Scotland and the Upsahl Commission in Northern Ireland.[26]
- It must have access to adequate resources, so that, for example, it can commission research papers and feasibility studies, and organise meetings and conferences.

Recommendations

18.25 In the light of the discussions in this chapter, *we recommend that the government:*

- *create further co-ordinating structures;*
- *require the various inspection regimes to work more closely together on issues of race equality and cultural diversity, with a view to improving their practices;*
- *arrange a programme of equality and diversity inspections of its own departments;*
- *commission impact assessments of all new policies that have the potential to exert a detrimental influence on race equality and recognition of cultural diversity;*
- *commission independent research on the impact of recent government measures that may have had a detrimental effect on race equality and recognition of cultural diversity;*

- *consult widely with interested and experienced persons and organisations on the race equality performance management framework currently being developed;*
- *set up for each department and also for the government as a whole an advisory forum on race equality and cultural diversity issues.*

Chapter 19

Legislation and Enforcement

> *By now I would have thought that there would be a move to a new piece of legislation ... the 1976 RRA [Race Relations Act] has many loopholes. Speaking from experience ... I have taken up a case against an employer with help from a local REC [Race Equality Council] and worked for them as a race equality officer and ... seen them fail twice.*
>
> From a submission to the Commission, 1998

19.1   We are convinced that the Race Relations Act 1976 has had a positive effect. Together with the Sex Discrimination Act of the previous year, which conceptually and politically paved the way for it,[1] it has helped to curb the worst kinds of discrimination in employment and the provision of services. It has also had an invaluable impact on the general climate of opinion. The amendments made in 2000 will make it applicable to the functions of nearly all public bodies[2] and will introduce, in addition to the duty to avoid discrimination, a positive duty on public authorities to promote equality of opportunity. These changes are most certainly to be welcomed. In the longer term, however, amendments are not enough. The whole legislative framework needs substantial overhaul – not only as it applies to race but with respect to other dimensions of equality as well. There are several separate but mutually supporting reasons why the present system needs to be reviewed. The recent independent review of the enforcement of anti-discrimination legislation has set out these reasons in detail.[3] For our purposes the most important points are the following.

- A major priority is to tackle institutional racism and organisational culture, as argued in Chapter 5. The new positive duty on public authorities, including the police, will be a valuable spur in this regard. It is unlikely, however, to be sufficient to ensure that all the interacting components of institutional racism in the public sector (Box 5.2 at the end of Chapter 5) are systematically addressed.[4] Moreover, the positive duty does not extend to private employers or private providers of services, and it is uncertain how far it will apply to the public/private partnerships that are increasingly important in the provision of services to the public.

- The Race Relations Act was more concerned with colour racism than with cultural racism (for example, Islamophobia), and more concerned with ensuring equality of treatment than with recognising difference and diversity. The amendments proposed[5] in 2000 do not reflect or promote understanding of the wider nature of racism, as outlined in Chapters 2–5.

- We argued in Chapter 17 that religious identities should be recognised through legislation that makes discrimination on religious grounds unlawful. Pressure for such legislation will also result from the incorporation of Article 14 of the European Convention on Human Rights (ECHR) into domestic law and by the Human Rights Act, since this prohibits discrimination on grounds of religious belief in the exercise of Convention rights. There will be further pressure if the pending Protocol No. 12 to the Convention, which provides a free-standing right against discrimination on grounds *inter alia* of religious belief, is adopted.[6] Moreover, if the draft directive on discrimination in respect of employment and occupation under Article 13 of the EC Treaty is adopted, the UK will be obliged to enact legislation in these fields against religious discrimination. This directive may also require action against discrimination on other grounds, such as age, marital status and sexual orientation. It would be possible in principle to introduce legislation against each kind of discrimination separately, but the pressure for a single comprehensive piece of legislation will be considerable.

- The original Race Relations Act was concerned essentially with negative duties – the avoidance of discrimination as distinct from actively promoting equality of opportunity and recognising diversity. An alternative approach was initiated by the 1989 Fair Employment Act (FEA) in Northern Ireland, and is embodied in the Fair Employment and Treatment Order 1998. This imposes positive duties on certain employers to achieve the fair participation of Roman Catholic and Protestant communities. There is clear evidence that it has had a significant impact on reducing inequalities in the workplace.[7]

- We argued in Chapter 5 that race and gender must frequently be considered in tandem, for otherwise measures concerned with the one may have detrimental effects on measures concerned with the other. Also black and Asian women are affected simultaneously both by racism and by sexism. In 1975 and 1976 it was politically necessary that there should be two separate sets of legislation and enforcement mechanisms.[8] The political context has now changed, however.

- The government has accepted that there needs to be greater harmonisation with legislation on disability and gender.[9]
- There needs to be greater simplicity.[10] Most of the legislation is written in complex and obscure language.
- Current means of seeking and obtaining redress are expensive financially and emotionally draining for complainants, as much personal energy has to be invested in pursuing a case through the various stages of an adversarial process. Certainly, formal complaints are frequently beneficial in acting as spurs to substantial organisational change. They are neither necessary nor sufficient, however, for such change to be set in motion. Complainants seldom have access to the statistical and other information required to prove indirect discrimination, and for this reason as for others (the inability to pay for expert legal representation, for example) sound cases often fail. There is frequently a danger of covert victimisation.
- The overall focus is on retrospective examination of the treatment of individuals rather than proactive and anticipatory steps to make an organisation genuinely more inclusive and participatory.
- In many large organisations, in both the public and private sectors, there has been a move away from command-and-control cultures towards less hierarchical authority structures and more decentralisation and localisation of decision-making. These changes have been caused or conditioned by irreversible technological developments and by the pressures of global competition. In these new employment circumstances more sensitive and flexible approaches are required to prevent discrimination taking place.

19.2   In several other countries – including Australia, Canada, Ireland, New Zealand and the United States – there is a single Equality Act, or else a Human Rights Act that includes equality matters. The advantages are that the principle of equality is recognised as indivisible, solidarity is promoted among people experiencing or facing discrimination, and inconsistencies between different statutes cannot arise. There is also the potential advantage that it is easier with a single statute to incorporate further grounds of unlawful discrimination, for example, relating to religion, if this is deemed necessary. The principal disadvantage is that the various fields have their distinctive features and constituencies. Some argue that campaigning activities might therefore lose sharpness of focus. We believe that the advantages of a general principle of equality, embodied in a single statute, outweigh the disadvantages, and that the dangers can be avoided. Therefore, *we recommend a single Equality Act in Britain. It should be supplemented by regulations and regularly updated codes of practice on specific subjects. Both the Act and its supporting documentation should be written in plain language.*

19.3   The report of the independent review of the enforcement of UK anti-discrimination legislation has proposed that there should be five principles underlying a new Act.[11] We have adapted these for our purposes in Box 19.1 on the next page.

19.4   A single Equality Act would logically require there to be a single Equality Commission to enforce it. The advantages are that the principle of equality would have a higher profile and the commission would be less likely to be perceived as serving sectional interests. It would speak with a stronger voice and give consistent advice across a range of specific issues. It could readily tackle cases of multiple discrimination and would be more convenient for employers, who at present have to relate to several different commissions. It would mirror the equality units that exist in most public bodies and private-sector companies, and administratively there would be efficiency gains. If legislation on further issues were to be introduced at some point in the future, a single Equality Commission would simply expand departmentally; this would be preferable to creating entirely new bodies.

19.5   The main fears about a single Equality Commission as far as race equality issues are concerned are that specialist expertise built up since 1976 might be lost or dissipated and campaigns on race issues might be watered down. There might be wasteful rivalries between different departments in a single commission, not least for shares of the overall budget, and the chief officer might not have the credibility required to make authoritative statements about racism. The differences between various kinds of discrimination might be neglected and the distinctive mechanics and components of racism underplayed, and the turbulence caused by major organisational restructuring could set the cause of race equality back many years. Such fears must be taken seriously and

Box 19.1 **Principles for a new legislative approach**

Twin goals and a holistic view
The goals should be (a) the elimination of unfair discrimination and (b) the promotion of equality with respect to sex, race, colour, ethnic or national origin, religion or belief, disability, age, sexual orientation, or other status.

Clear standards
The standards in legislation and codes of practice should be clear, consistent and easily intelligible.

Regulatory framework
The regulatory framework should be effective in achieving measurable targets, efficient in terms of cost and equitable in its effects. It should encourage personal responsibility and self-generated organisational change.

Participation
Everyone affected should be able to participate in processes of organisational change, including employees and their representatives, clients and customers, and campaigning groups.

Redress
Individuals should be free to seek redress for harm they have suffered as a result of unfair discrimination. The procedures should be fair, inexpensive and fast and the remedies should be effective. They should act as a spur to organisational change.

Source: Adapted from *Equality: a new framework* by Bob Hepple, Mary Coussey and Tufyal Choudhury, 2000.

carefully debated. However, providing there is a new Equality Act built on the principles summarised in Box 19.1, and providing there are carefully thought-out safeguards to maintain a sharp focus on race equality, we believe a single commission would be more powerful and effective than several smaller ones. Therefore, *we recommend that following a new Equality Act in Britain a single Equality Commission be created, covering all grounds of unlawful discrimination.* The internal structure of the commission should be the subject of substantial discussion and consultation.

There also needs to be a Human Rights Commission, as discussed in Chapter 7 and later in this chapter.

19.6 A new legislative approach will involve developing a new balance along the spectrum that runs from self-regulation at one end to enforcement and sanctions at the other. The advantages of self-regulation include the following.

- Organisations have a greater sense of engagement if they have been part of the process of diagnosing the problems to be addressed, have weighed up options and tailored requirements to their own ethos, goals, business planning methods and recent history, and have set targets and deadlines for themselves that they believe to be attainable.

- The process of creating this sense of engagement means that key concepts and ideas are internalised. Staff have a sound grasp of rationales and underlying principles, and are therefore less likely to engage, or to appear to engage, in lip-service and window-dressing.

- Grievances are more likely to be resolved in a non-adversarial manner.

- Self-regulation by organisations is more cost-effective than its alternatives from the government's point of view, since scarce resources are not tied up in inspection and policing activities, or in trying to redeem situations in which relationships have broken down, with much mutual distrust and hostility.

- Organisations are more likely to go beyond non-discrimination to the tasks of making reasonable adjustments for staff who need them and enabling under-represented groups to participate.

19.7 Voluntary self-regulation, with the benefits summarised above, was the preference of the Better Regulation Task Force in its 1999 report.[12] For some organisations it may well be sufficient. But for many, probably most, legislative measures to enforce self-regulation are required as well. The mix between self-regulation and external pressure will vary among organisations, and over time within any one organisation. The independent review of the enforcement of UK anti-discrimination legislation developed a model of an enforcement pyramid.[13] At the base of the pyramid there are self-generated policy statements and action plans. These are typically created with outside stimulus, consultancy and assistance, and with regard to good practice elsewhere. An Equality

Commission may well provide advice and guidance at this stage, directly or through its codes of practice, but essentially initiatives at the base of the pyramid come from the organisation, not an external agency. In Chapter 20 we list the principal points an organisation needs to address. For organisations that do not voluntarily create policies or targets, or that do not translate their policies into action and do not achieve real, measurable change, other levels of the pyramid become successively operative. The structure as a whole is summarised in Box 19.2.

19.8 The three faces of the pyramid may be envisaged as (a) the work and conduct of the organisation itself; (b) the work of the external agency, as the representative of the public interest; and (c) the involvement of interest groups, such as unions and staff associations, and community-based watchdog and advocacy groups. The pyramid needs to be sustained by imposition of a positive duty to promote equality. The amendments made in 2000 to the Race Relations Act will impose such a duty on public bodies but do not apply to private employers or private service providers. Experience from other countries, particularly Northern Ireland, Canada and the United States, indicates that an action plan should include monitoring of all recruitment and promotion processes; the setting of goals and targets; impact assessment; and consultation with those likely to be affected.[14]

19.9 It is of course essential that equality schemes should be externally scrutinised and validated. In contrast to Northern Ireland, it would not be practically feasible in Britain for such scrutiny of public-sector bodies to be carried out by the Commission for Racial Equality (CRE), or in due course by the new Equality Commission we propose. Nor would it be desirable, given that several inspection and audit regimes already exist – the Audit Commission, the Office for Standards in Education, Her Majesty's Inspectorate of Constabulary, and so on. Therefore, *we recommend that existing auditing bodies be given formal responsibility for inspection and audit of public-sector equality schemes, and that they require progress towards fair participation and fair access over a defined period of time. The Commission for Racial Equality, or the proposed Equality Commission, should have the power to issue compliance notices and, in the event of these not being effective, to apply to a court or tribunal for an order requiring the body in question to comply.*[15]

Box 19.2 **The levels of an enforcement pyramid**

1 Auditing and disclosure
Every organisation should audit its workforce by ethnicity and publish the results. Minimum standards for such auditing and disclosure are laid down.

2 Action plans and performance targets
Minimum standards are laid down on what these should contain. However, organisations are encouraged to go beyond them. Interest groups must be involved in their formulation and review.

3 Investigation
There is a formal investigation or inquiry by the external enforcement agency if there are grounds for believing that measures at levels 1 and 2 are insufficient. In the light of the investigation or inquiry, the organisation commits itself to certain undertakings.

4 Compliance notice
The enforcement agency issues a compliance notice if the undertakings required at level 3 are either not given or not carried out.

5 Judicial enforcement
A court or tribunal requires the organisation to take action within a specified period.

6 Sanctions
Monetary penalties are imposed for contempt of court.

7 Withdrawal of contracts
Government contracts, grants, subsidies and licences are withdrawn or not renewed.

Source: Adapted from Hepple et al., paragraphs 3.6–3.7.

19.10 In addition, companies in the private sector should be required to draw up employment equity schemes, as outlined in Chapter 14. Legislation would give the Equality Commission power to demand information about these schemes, to obtain binding undertakings and to institute proceedings against businesses that have not introduced plans or have failed to implement them. Employment tribunals should have the power to order businesses to take appropriate action and, if they fail to observe such orders, to pay financial compensation. Failure to implement a plan should be admissible as evidence in individual discrimination cases, from which an adverse inference may be drawn against the respondent employer.[16]

19.11 We welcome the EU's Race Directive of summer 2000 and the UK government's endorsement of it. The directive flows from Article 13 of the 1997 Treaty of Amsterdam and prohibits discrimination on grounds of race or ethnicity in employment, education, social security, healthcare and access to goods and services, and ensures that victims of discrimination have rights of redress through judicial or administrative procedures. It provides a common European framework across the 15 member states and therefore makes sharing of experience both more feasible and more valuable. Of particular value is its proposal that the burden of proof should be shifted in civil cases, once a prima-facie case of discrimination has been made out by the complainant and accepted by the court. This removes some of the most severe obstacles faced by victims of discrimination. The directive also valuably requires member states to report on the measures that they have adopted to reduce discrimination. It thus provides a useful check on the partisan politics of national governments and opens the way for greater involvement of non-governmental organisations, within and among countries, in scrutiny and review of government actions.

19.12 The directive will in due course help shape the new Equality Act in Britain that we have recommended. In the more immediate future it will inform the implementation of the Race Relations Amendment Act 2000, and will strengthen the case for the range of administrative and organisational measures itemised in Chapter 20. Furthermore, it should give impetus to additional amendments to the Race Relations Act 1976. The Act needs to take fuller account of institutional racism. This will involve a new legal definition of indirect discrimination; specifying the content of the new positive duty to promote equality, in order to help create appropriate organisational cultures; and enhancing the powers of the Commission for Racial Equality.

Human rights

19.13 As argued in Chapter 7, the Human Rights Act and international human rights agreements are of vital importance for the achievement of race equality and a human rights culture of mutual respect. Their potential will not be achieved, however, unless there is a Human Rights Commission to drive change forward. In the last 10 years such bodies have been created throughout the world, strongly encouraged by the United Nations. The oldest commissions, in France, Australia, New Zealand and Canada, have been joined more recently by those in, for example, India, South Africa, Latvia, Indonesia, Sri Lanka and Uganda, and most recently in Northern Ireland (1999) and the Irish Republic (2000). Almost without exception the human rights commissions in other countries have responsibility for equality issues. This may eventually be the right structure in Britain as well. We consider that at present, however, there need to be two separate commissions, for equality and human rights respectively. *We recommend that, in addition to an Equality Commission responsible for enforcing equality legislation, there should be a Human Rights Commission.* Its functions should include the provision of advice and guidance to public authorities on their responsibilities under the Human Rights Act; scrutiny of existing and draft legislation; advising on the adequacy of the arrangements for protecting human rights; legal assistance to members of the public and the mediation of complaints; the conduct of investigations and inquiries, and the promotion of a human rights culture. We welcome the decision of the Scottish Executive to issue a consultation paper on proposals for a Scottish Human Rights Commission. In more detail, the functions of a Human Rights Commission would be as follows.[17]

Guidance to public authorities
The commission would fulfil a vital role in providing information and guidance to public authorities, and to the private and voluntary bodies that have responsibilities under the Human Rights Act. It is in everyone's interest that public authorities should bring their policies and practices into line with the Act as a preventative measure, and thus avoid unnecessary court cases. The absence of a Human Rights Commission during the preparatory stage before the Act came into force in October 2000 meant that the task of advising public authorities was left to Whitehall departments. Most were not in a position to provide

appropriate literature or guidance. Much work remains to be done.

Advice on the adequacy of law
The commission would have a duty to keep under review, and advise the government on, the adequacy and effectiveness of law and practice relating to the protection of human rights, and measures that should be taken to protect them. The term human rights here refers to, but is not limited to, ECHR rights (also known as Convention rights).

Scrutiny of draft legislation
The commission would scrutinise draft legislation and advise whether it is compatible with international human rights standards. This is not a straightforward matter, for it is permissible to limit most rights in certain circumstances. Although the government has civil service lawyers to advise on compliance, Members of Parliament do not. Without an independent source of expert advice, therefore, it can be difficult for Parliament to challenge ministers who provide assurances that particular provisions are compatible with Convention rights. A Human Rights Commission could advise, for example, on whether the provisions in a new immigration bill comply with the right to family life, or whether arrangements to detain asylum-seekers constitute an acceptable denial of their right to liberty.

Advice and assistance to individuals
The commission would advise individuals and provide assistance to them in taking human rights cases to court. Without a statutory body to provide advice and assistance, many individuals will simply be unable to remedy injustice. Expert advice is particularly necessary in a fast-changing area of law. The commission would also play an invaluable mediation role in cases where individuals believe their rights have been infringed, thus reducing the likelihood of such cases reaching court.

Understanding and awareness
It would have a responsibility to promote appreciation of the importance of human rights, to which end it would undertake or commission research and educational activities.

Investigations and inquiries
The Australian Human Rights and Equal Opportunities Commission

has found that public inquiries are its most powerful tool for raising public awareness, identifying proposals for action and persuading the government to act.

19.14 The Human Rights Commission should work closely with the present CRE, so long as it remains in its present form, or with the Equality Commission if this replaces the CRE. Priorities include joint advice to public authorities on their responsibilities under the Human Rights Act and the Race Relations Act, and joint production of codes of practice; the establishment of local one-stop shops to provide guidance to employers, public authorities and individuals; ensuring that each commission, when conducting an inquiry or promoting awareness, addresses issues that are primarily the responsibility of the other – for example, an inquiry into deaths in custody by the Human Rights Commission would consider the high proportion of deaths of black people; ensuring that the Human Rights Commission, when scrutinising draft legislation, is aware of the need to promote race equality and cultural diversity. It will be valuable to learn from the experience of the Equality Commission and the Human Rights Commission in Northern Ireland.

19.15 It would be essential for the new Human Rights Commission to be in close contact with a broad range of opinion on human rights issues. One way to achieve this would be to set up an advisory committee, possibly on a statutory basis. Its members would include academics, judges, public figures, community representatives and campaigners, and representatives of the public sector.

19.16 In the light of our discussions in Chapter 7, *we recommend that the government allow individuals access to the UN complaints system if they believe that their rights under the Convention on the Elimination of Racial Discrimination (CERD) have been infringed.* Further, *we recommend that the government give greater priority to fulfilling its obligations under international human rights agreements, and to making the public aware of the commitments that have been made.* The regular reports submitted to the international bodies that supervise these agreements should be widely distributed and drawn to the attention of Parliament. It is essential that work on human rights issues in public institutions should be carried out in parallel with work on equality and anti-discrimination issues. Therefore *we recommend that officials in central, devolved and local administrations ensure that the procedures they operate with regard to human rights issues are harmonised with those relating to equality issues.* For the same reason *we recommend that the Parliamentary Human Rights Committee undertake to focus on race equality issues.* This should include monitoring the UK's compliance with international human rights standards relating to the rights of minorities, particularly CERD.

A declaration on cultural diversity

19.17 A recurring theme throughout this report has been the need not only to promote equality but also to recognise diversity. Framing legislation on this point would be difficult but not impossible. Such legislation would refer to the cultures of the UK's four constituent parts as well as to those more customarily thought of when cultural diversity is under discussion. In this connection, it would need to recognise the points made in Chapters 2–4 and in Chapter 12 about multi-layered identities, intercultural dialogue and social cohesion. It could only be successfully introduced after thorough and widespread deliberation and consultation. A relevant resource in such consultation would be the declaration on

Box 19.3 **A Declaration on Cultural Diversity – an example**

The following statement is closely based on the Canadian Multiculturalism Act

IT IS HEREBY DECLARED TO BE THE POLICY OF THE GOVERNMENT OF THE UNITED KINGDOM TO:

- recognise the freedom of all members of society to preserve, enhance and share their cultural heritage;
- recognise and promote the understanding that cultural diversity is a fundamental characteristic of the national heritage and identity and that it provides an invaluable resource in the shaping of the UK's future;
- promote the full and equitable participation of individuals and communities of all origins in the continuing evolution and sharing of all aspects of UK society and assist them in the elimination of any barrier to such participation;
- ensure that all individuals receive equal treatment and equal protection under the law, while respecting and valuing their differences;
- promote the understanding and creativity that arise from the interaction between individuals and communities of different origins;
- encourage and assist social, cultural, economic and political institutions to be respectful of the UK's multicultural character.

IT IS FURTHER DECLARED TO BE THE POLICY OF THE GOVERNMENT OF THE UNITED KINGDOM THAT ALL STATE INSTITUTIONS SHALL:

- ensure that UK citizens of all origins have an equal opportunity to obtain employment and advancement;
- promote policies, programmes and practices that enhance the ability of individuals and communities of all origins to contribute to the UK's continuing evolution;
- collect statistical data in order to enable the development of policies, programmes and practices that are sensitive and responsive to the multicultural reality of the United Kingdom;
- make use, as appropriate, of the language skills and cultural understanding of people of all origins and community backgrounds.

multiculturalism drawn up in Canada. Box 19.3 shows how this might be adapted in the UK. *We recommend that the government formally declare the United Kingdom a multicultural society, and issue a draft declaration for consultation.* The declaration would have clear implications for policing (Chapter 9), the criminal justice system (Chapter 10), the curriculum of schools (Chapter 11), cultural policy (Chapter 12), the health service (Chapter 13) and employment issues (Chapter 14).

19.18 A declaration such as that cited in Box 19.3 would have several advantages. First, it would have great symbolic significance, for it would recognise the inescapable reality of cultural diversity and the country's collective commitment to cherish it. Second, it would send out an appropriate message to public and private organisations and would encourage them to devise policies that promote diversity as well as equality. Third, it would help to stress that the country is both a community of citizens and a community of communities, both a liberal and a plural society. The new Human Rights Act recognises and reinforces the UK's liberal character and nurtures a culture conducive to the rights of individuals. A declaration on cultural diversity would recognise the country's multicultural character and emphasise the value of communities. Fourth, it would challenge the conventional view of the UK as a broadly homogeneous society, and acknowledge that cultural diversity is not new, simply the consequence of postwar immigration, but a central fact of the country's long history and a continuing source of creativity.

19.19 This chapter has principally been about action by the government – new legislation, a Human Rights Commission and a declaration on cultural diversity. But it has also stressed that organisational change needs to be self-directed as well as enforced. The next chapter, accordingly, is about the processes of self-directed organisational change. It focuses in particular on addressing institutional racism. It is intended to be relevant to all institutions and organisations in the public, private and voluntary sectors.

Chapter 20

Organisational Change

> *Racism is often portrayed as though it is something like a disease which can be cured ...[Racist beliefs] are reinforced in so many ways in white people, from the cradle ... It is not a question of curing me, but of me acknowledging my racism and taking responsibility for operating in an anti-racist way personally and encouraging organisations and institutions in which I have an influence to do the same.*
>
> From a response to the Commission, 1998

20.1 In Chapters 9–17 we made recommendations to government departments and agencies, and in Chapters 18–19 to the administrations at Cardiff, Holyrood and Westminster. It is essentially at city or town level, however, and in the institutions, statutory bodies and voluntary organisations working within cities and towns, that many of the recommendations arising from this report need to be considered and implemented. For it is in local settings that society as a community of overlapping and interdependent communities is most obviously seen, experienced and built upon. It is here that significant decisions about policing, education, health and employment are made; here that institutional racism most urgently needs to be addressed and dismantled; and here that significant interactions take place among people who have diverse backgrounds, cultures and identities, and diverse perceptions and experiences of racism.

20.2 This chapter discusses issues that need to be considered and acted on in every individual authority or organisation – including, incidentally, government departments.[1] It follows on naturally from the previous chapter on legislation, since a recurring emphasis there was that one aim of legislation should be to promote and support self-generated organisational change. It is not necessary to wait for new legislation, however, before considering change at local or institutional levels. Box 20.1 is a mirror image, so to speak, of Box 5.2 at the end of Chapter 5, which listed the interacting components of institutional racism. Between them, they summarise many key organisational issues in the

report as a whole. The questions in Box 20.1 on pages 282–3 can be answered, in any particular setting, on a five-point scale, with each point on
the scale representing a level or stage of development.[2] Alternatively, the
questions can be triggers for discussion. Either way it is important that
whatever responses are offered are backed up by evidence. Further, it is essential to seek feedback from staff at all levels, including of course black,
Asian and Irish staff, and from outsiders – clients, customers, service
users, partners, consultants, and community and pressure groups.

Leadership

20.3   The Commission for Racial Equality's (CRE's) Leadership Challenge[3] is
addressed to the chief executives of organisations in the public and
private sectors. They are expected to use their position to:

• raise the profile of equality and diversity issues by reporting on
achievements in their annual reports, public statements and
speeches; raising issues on boards and committees on which they sit;
and encouraging colleagues, contemporaries and counterparts to
address these issues themselves;

• challenge themselves and others, particularly with regard to personal and institutional racism;

• encourage and support associations and networks of black and
Asian staff;

• ensure that they and their organisations are at the forefront of best
practice in their sector;

• build equality and diversity measures and strategies into their organisations' planning and decision-making processes, with performance goals and milestones;

• provide, in these ways, a framework in which staff at all levels can act
with confidence.

20.4   The 1999 progress report on the scheme quoted an equal opportunities
manager as saying that 'the impact of the chief executive taking a
leading role in sessions with staff, and the clear message that this issue
is a priority at the very top, have provided a marvellous impetus'. The
report acknowledged that different companies and organisations are at
different stages of development, and was keen not to discourage any of
the scheme's participants with premature criticisms. This is under-

standable. However, a close reading of the report clearly shows that there is still much to accomplish, and that there is still considerable thinking to be done. The stringent criticisms made by Her Majesty's Inspectorate of Constabulary (HMIC) about leadership in police forces could also, almost certainly, be made of the vast majority of organisations mentioned in the CRE document. We hope that our report as a whole will be a useful resource in the deliberations in which the participants in the scheme are engaged. We commend in this connection the valuable distinction sometimes drawn between 'transactional leadership' and 'transformational leadership'.[4] *We recommend that evaluative studies be made of leadership styles in relation to race and diversity issues, and that good practice be disseminated.*

20.5 Both kinds of leadership are important in relation to issues of equality and diversity. There must be efficient management ('transactional leadership') concerned with the setting of goals and objectives, and holding staff accountable for achieving them. Such management can be summarised, and indeed needs to be summarised, in terms of abilities that can be assessed with reasonable accuracy. 'Transformational leadership' is concerned with personal qualities rather than abilities. These include empathy, openness to criticism, a degree of judicious risk-taking, enthusiasm, an aptitude for articulating a vision of how the organisation could be different and better, and a readiness to challenge and shape the opinions of others rather than pander to them. In Chapter 16 we discussed the need for political leaders to engage in transformational leadership of this kind, particularly in relation to immigration and asylum. It is relevant for senior staff in all organisations and institutions, and should be a core idea in all management training.

Documentation

20.6 Good-quality documentation is sometimes necessary, often invaluable, but never sufficient in itself. At best it states values and sets out goals and objectives; explains the basis on which resources and contracts are allocated and reallocated; defines the terms of debate; shows staff what is expected of them, and what therefore they need to do to gain commendation and promotion, and what they must not do to avoid sanctions; provides a framework and reference points for staff training; is

Box 20.1 **Ten sets of questions for self-review**

1 Leadership
Do the leaders of our organisation show by their words and actions that they understand and are committed to race equality and cultural diversity issues?

2 Documentation
Does our organisation have intelligible, reader-friendly documentation about race equality and cultural diversity? Is the documentation well known to all staff? Was it produced through processes of consultation? Is it kept under review? Does it include an action plan with short- and medium-term goals, and with deadlines and performance indicators?

3 Quantitative and qualitative checks
Does our organisation check its own progress in relation to race equality and cultural diversity? Do we have the basic quantitative information we need? Do we also collect perceptions and impressions in a systematic way?

4 Mainstreaming
Do we systematically check on the impact of all our policies, including unintended impacts, in relation to equality and diversity issues?

5 Consultation and partnership
Do we consult local communities adequately about issues that concern them? Do we show that we have attended to their views and concerns? Do we work in active partnership with them? Do we accept that we have a responsibility to assist in enhancing capabilities?

6 Rewards and sanctions
Do equality and diversity issues appear in our staff appraisal schemes? Are there rewards and incentives for staff who perform well? Are there sanctions for those whose performance is not satisfactory?

7 Occupational and professional culture
Is our occupational and professional culture positive about equality and diversity issues, or is there sneering about so-called political

correctness, or indifference? Do some staff feel that their cultural identity is marginalised or ignored, and/or that their experiences and perceptions of racism are not recognised? Are our perceptions and
expectations of the public racist, or likely to have racist effects?

8 Recruitment, promotion and retention
Are staff recruited and promoted according to equal opportunities
principles and practices? Are positive action measures used? Is our
staffing structure becoming yearly more inclusive, at all levels of
seniority?

9 Training and staff development
Is there a satisfactory system of developing staff skills in relation to
equality and diversity issues? Has a satisfactory proportion of staff received high-quality training within the last three years?

10 Making a difference
Is our organisation making a discernible and positive difference, in
relation to equality and diversity, in the outside world? Do we have
reliable evidence of this?

---

educative for partners and contractors; establishes standards for others
to follow; and lays out criteria for auditing, assessment, evaluation and
inspection. The processes of creating high-quality documentation, and
of keeping it under review, are frequently valuable spurs to real action.
Furthermore, good documentation is a campaigning instrument for
outsiders, as it is a charter they can use to call an organisation to
account.

20.7 In view of these potential benefits, the content of policy documentation
is of great importance. This is obvious, but needs stressing, because all
too often considerations of policy documents focus more on whether or
not they exist than on whether or not they intelligibly focus on key
issues.[5] Earlier chapters of this report indicate that sound documentation should refer, as appropriate, to rethinking national identity (Chapters 2 and 3), balancing cohesion and difference (Chapter 4),
addressing and dismantling racisms (Chapter 5), reducing inequalities
(Chapter 6) and building a human rights culture (Chapter 7). Ideally,

each organisation needs to develop its own documentation rather than simply adopt another's (from which it can nevertheless valuably learn). We quote in Box 20.2 a statement recently developed in a London borough. Other authorities may be interested to compare and contrast it with their own. It includes an explicit reference to and acknowledgement of institutional racism; an emphasis on sensitivity to the individual employee, citizen or service user; a commitment to representing local communities to other agencies and to including equality and diversity issues in work with partners; and a reference to the responsibilities of individual managers at all levels.[6] *We recommend that a sample of policy documents issued by public bodies be critically evaluated, and that elements of good practice be more widely shared.*

Management and mainstreaming

20.8   It is difficult to take documents such as that quoted in Box 20.2 seriously if staff who are ignorant of or indifferent to equality issues, or even downright hostile towards them, achieve promotion and advancement, and receive performance-related bonuses in addition to their salaries. The director of a racial equality council put the issues to us in these terms:

> There is too much emphasis on training as a solution. Much training reinforces racist stereotypes ... More is achieved by senior managers and politicians demanding that diversity is reflected in their organisations in both employment and service delivery, that regular analysis of this should identify problems, and that people should be sorted out when they are not delivering. I do not think training has changed or will change attitudes, but knowledge that your job or promotion depends on demonstrating diversity is more effective. Training is encouraging people, but we have reached the stage where people must just be told to do it or else.

20.9   Neither fear of sanctions nor desire for material rewards is a sufficient motivation for addressing racism in its various forms. However, sticks and carrots are widely used in all organisations as motivating forces, both formally and informally. If equality and diversity issues are omitted from an organisation's motivational system, the clear message is that they are of low priority, and are a matter of voluntary goodwill rather than of fundamental and non-negotiable professionalism. For

Box 20.2 **A policy statement**

Throughout its work the Council is committed to reflecting the full diversity of the community it serves and promoting equality of opportunity for everyone. We accept that the Council is not free of unintended institutional discrimination and we will work actively to eradicate it.

We aim to ensure equal access to our services by all citizens on the basis of need and to provide services in a manner which is sensitive to the individual, whatever their background. We will represent the needs of our diverse communities to other agencies and make equal opportunities a key guiding principle in all of our work with our partners. We will work to ensure that our workforce reflects the community it serves.

We are committed to eliminating discrimination on the grounds of age, colour, disability, ethnic origin, gender, HIV status, marital status, nationality, national origin, race, religious belief, responsibility for dependants, sexuality, or unrelated criminal conviction. It is the responsibility of every employee of the Council to uphold and implement this policy. It is the responsibility of each individual manager at all levels to plan and provide their services to realise this policy.

Source: Haringey Borough Council, 1999.

this reason all organisations need to do all or most of the following.
- Include equality and diversity issues in staff appraisal schemes, and in schemes relating to performance-related bonuses.
- Include focused reference to equality and diversity issues in all personnel specifications and selection criteria, and in all lists of basic skills and aptitudes, particularly for senior management posts.
- Ensure that there is at least one person present in all shortlisting, selecting and interviewing processes who has expertise in equality and diversity issues, and who can and will ask searching questions.
- Be seen to take disciplinary action when necessary against staff whose performance is unsatisfactory from a race and diversity point of view, and to make the results known.

20.10 The concept of mainstreaming first came to prominence after the

United Nations third world conference on women, held in Nairobi in 1985. It referred principally to measures undertaken by UN agencies in respect of the role and values of women in development work. Definitions of mainstreaming include the following points.

- It is the process of assessing the implications for different individuals or communities of any planned action, including legislation, policies or programmes, in all areas and at all levels.
- It is an integral dimension of the design, implementation, monitoring and evaluation of policies and programmes in all political, economic and societal spheres. The ultimate goal is equality of outcome.
- It involves the integration of equality and diversity issues into all policy development, implementation, evaluation and review processes.
- Equality and diversity issues are an obligation for everyone, including those responsible for the development of strategy, managers of departments, front-line staff, members of boards of directors or trustees, and trade union officials.

20.11 In Northern Ireland and in some local authorities in Britain, mainstreaming has gone well beyond gender and also encompasses religious belief, political opinion, racial group, age, marital status, sexual orientation, disability and dependants. From this experience, and the experience of other countries, it is possible to derive a number of key principles underpinning successful mainstreaming.[7]

- A cornerstone of mainstreaming is the practice of making impact assessments, using a wide range of specialist forecasting methods. The results of such assessments must be available not only to policy-makers and decision-makers but also to the groups in the wider community in danger of being adversely affected.
- It is valuable and often essential that impact assessments should be made by community groups and organisations, not by an organisation's staff alone. Mainstreaming at best is not just one more bureaucratic measure but an approach that encourages more active participation in policy-making by ordinary citizens and marginalised groups.
- There must be a central overall strategy, as outlined above, and centralised responsibility for ensuring that mainstreaming really does happen, and is consistently applied according to common standards.
- Strong commitment and leadership are essential.

- There must be high-quality staff training, of both individuals and teams.

Training

20.12 The Stephen Lawrence Inquiry report was entirely explicit about the need for high-quality racism awareness training. It did not, however, discuss the content of such training, or the profound objections many people would wish to make to the concept of 'awareness' as a way of summarising what is required. Nor did it consider the connections between such training and other aspects of professional development, or issues of practical methodology and organisation. The omissions were reasonable, in view of the report's background and purposes. It is unfortunate, however, that the Home Secretary's action plan and progress report did not pursue the key issues that urgently need clarification.[8] This is not only, and indeed not primarily, a matter for the police. We have argued throughout this report that training on race and diversity issues is required across a wide range of professions and occupations, including the whole criminal justice system, education, arts administration, the health service and faith communities. In all these fields there are people who are specialists in continuing training and adult education, and who also have sound knowledge of race and diversity issues. It would be valuable if they were brought together to reflect collectively on their experiences of what works well and what does not, with a view to formulating shared standards, objectives and methods. *We recommend that a task force be set up to clarify the objectives and content of racism awareness training, and to develop guidelines and standards on practical methodology and organisation.*

20.13 It has been said that training in race and diversity issues involves:[9]

- becoming conscious of unconscious racism, and acknowledging the feelings of guilt and embarrassment that arise;
- recognising that much of this racism was unwittingly imbibed, that racism is not unique to white people, that therefore a white person need not be defensive or feel guilty in acknowledging its presence;
- exploring and understanding the experiences and expectations of people who have suffered directly from racism;
- developing skills in identifying and challenging racism in the institutions in which individuals work, particularly within their own sphere of responsibility, and in practical planning and action to remove it;
- developing cultural literacy – an awareness of problems of misperception and miscommunication in cross-cultural settings, particularly when there is not only cultural difference but also a power differential;
- understanding that the alternative to racism is a community of citizens and communities, and developing therefore concepts of human rights, social cohesion, equality and respect for difference.

20.14 In training in race and diversity issues, as in other kinds of professional training and adult education, attention must be paid to the diverse learning styles of participants, and to the need to design activities accordingly; to the specific professional situations in which new insights and skills are to be applied, and to the value in this respect of case studies and lived experience; to research by practitioners and learning through reflection; and to the need to design and manage educational settings in which participants feel secure enough to question and unlearn current practices and assumptions, and customary notions of professionalism.[10] Box 20.3 on pages 291–2 lists such points in slightly greater detail.

Monitoring

20.15 An audit of the current staffing structure of an organisation, and of its users and clients, is frequently a valuable step in a process of substantial change.[11] However, we have frequently had occasion in preceding chapters to note that record-keeping and monitoring by ethnicity are in many public bodies not of a satisfactory standard. Officials do not have an adequate grasp of fundamental principles; do not use appropriate categories;[12] do not use professional methods of analysis; and do not see monitoring as a high priority, and therefore permit it to be obstructed or delayed by institutional inertia. Even when they do assemble meaningful data, they frequently see its collection as an end in itself rather than as a resource to be analysed and then acted on.[13] Box 20.4 on pages 292–3 summarises points that need urgent consideration. *We recommend that official guidance be issued on monitoring by ethnicity and religion, and on the collection, interpretation and use of statistical data.*

20.16 Institutions and authorities should use not only statistical data but also data derived from questionnaires and group discussions. For example, as already mentioned, the items in Box 20.1 could be used to construct a questionnaire, or as topics for discussion in focus group settings. Further, it is frequently invaluable to involve an outsider – a critical friend or consultant, or someone readily able to identify with an organisation's clients, customers or service users – in qualitative evaluation and assessment.

The listening organisation: openness to pressure and advocacy

20.17 An organisation committed to dismantling institutional racism makes sure that it hears and takes account of views that it may well find uncomfortable. Box 20.5 on page 294 cites the experiences of school governors.[14] It reflects perceptions from a wide range of other situations as well, and shows the challenges that every white-dominated organisation has to face if it genuinely wishes to make itself more inclusive, and more sensitive and responsive to difference.

20.18 In Chapter 18 we stressed that the government must be open to pressure and advocacy from outside, and itemised the features of a satisfactory consultative forum. Box 20.6 on page 295 lists the principles that should underlie specific consultations, regardless of whether or not there is a forum.

20.19 Consultation exercises take place on a wide range of topics and issues. In many settings it may well be appropriate, in late autumn 2000 and throughout 2001 and 2002, to institute consultations on the recommendations made in this report. Some of the recommendations would be best undertaken by the national administrations based at Cardiff, Holyrood and Westminster, either of their own accord or in response to pressure and advocacy from others. Many, however, could be initiated at local levels. A checklist of the recommendations made is provided in the next chapter.

Box 20.3 **Equality and diversity: features of effective training**

Curriculum content
Attention should be paid to theoretical and practical issues relating to cohesion, equality and difference; the nature and history of racism; the components of institutional racism; human rights standards; organisational change.

Materials and methods
Reference should be made as much as possible to real-world situations and critical incidents, explored through role-play and focused discussion of visual and literary material, as well as through talks and lectures. Account should be taken of different learning styles in different individuals.

Reflection and action
Participants should reflect on their own professional practice and the tacit assumptions underlying it. They should be enabled to identify aspects of their practice and theory that need unlearning and changing, and to develop new practical skills and styles of behaviour in their day-to-day work.

Clientele
Participants should frequently be drawn from a range of professional backgrounds. This is particularly valuable at senior management levels.

Community-based trainers
It is essential that some of the trainers, tutors and lecturers be community-based. Resources must be provided to ensure that they are well prepared and appropriately paid, and involved as equals in planning and evaluation as well as delivery.

Evaluation
Quantitative and qualitative approaches to course evaluation should be used – questionnaires for participants, but also observation and interviews, and contacts with participants' seniors and colleagues.

Training the trainers
Trainers, tutors and lecturers must have opportunities to share and reflect on their experience of providing training, and to develop their expertise and insights.

Status
Training in race equality and cultural diversity issues must have high status.

Re-entry
Managers have a duty to help staff who have been away for substantial training to apply their new knowledge when they return to regular work, and to disseminate it to colleagues.

Box 20.4 **Monitoring by ethnicity: some key points**

Clarity of purpose
The overall purpose of monitoring by ethnicity is to collect and collate the information that policy-makers and decision-makers need in order to create and maintain a more equal and inclusive society. If an organisation unequivocally states that this is the purpose, and if the practical methods of collecting, analysing and publishing data clearly serve this purpose, staff are likely to co-operate and assist.

Populations and results
It is crucial to distinguish between the monitoring of populations ('who is here?') and the monitoring of results ('who gets what?'). There are good reasons for doing the first on its own, so that provision can be more sensitive to need. With regard to the second, however, it is not possible to compile statistically valid data unless the first kind of monitoring takes place as well.

Categories
At present too much use is made of unhelpful categories, including 'black other', 'African', 'other Asian' and 'other other'. Institutions need to use more precise and appropriate categories, regardless of

minimum requirements set by the government and by the 2001 census.

Detailed breakdowns
The government itself sets a bad example by frequently using the blanket term 'ethnic minority' in its monitoring and target-setting without acknowledging that the experience of one community may be substantially different from that of another. If detailed breakdowns are not made, substantially false ideas may be held and propagated.

Comparisons by time and place
By definition, monitoring by ethnicity involves making comparisons between different communities. It should also involve making comparisons between places and over time. Each institution or authority needs to be able to chart its progress over time, and needs to know how its own progress compares with that of others.

Gender and class
It is essential to compare like with like. It is always pertinent, therefore, to check whether gender and social class are relevant variables, in addition to ethnicity.

Guidance and assistance
Individual institutions have a right to receive expert guidance and practical assistance from their local or regional authority, and authorities have a right to receive guidance and practical assistance from central government.

Box 20.5 **Voices: Asian and black involvement in school governance**

When I became a governor at a secondary school I found myself in a position where nothing was explained to me and I had to figure it out as I went along. I was not included in the friendship structure, which could have given me information. I learned that these structures were more important than the official ones. I often felt that people had met outside of the meeting and had decided upon things that then became a matter of formality in the meeting.

I was often called in for black exclusions, sometimes for white working-class ones, but not for white middle-class ones. White governors on the panel were often unable to deal with black exclusions effectively because of not having the frame of reference to understand black people and the arrogance not to ask for my views or to take my opinions seriously.

I was pushed on to the pastoral committee before I realised where the power was.

I arrived at my first governors' meeting having gone through a lengthy election process of getting myself nominated, writing a piece for the school weekly newsletter, speaking at a parents' association meeting, and canvassing in the playground. Imagine my astonishment when another parent arrived, asked to be co-opted, was nominated, seconded and on the governing body before I had time to blink. Obviously we have a two-tier system here, one for black people who must jump through hoops to prove our credentials and another where being white and middle-class is enough.

[If] we become more vocal [about racism] we are ... labelled as troublemakers and isolated and marginalised. When we try to enter into a debate, a rational reasonable discussion, the discomfort and anger of our white colleagues in many cases become palpable. The anger is long-lived, leading to all sorts of unhelpful behaviour ... Our point of view is often put to the test as if it were essentially wrong and those of the white constituency inherently correct.

Source: Camden Black and Minority Ethnic Governors Forum, 2000.

Box 20.6 **Principles of effective consultation**

It must be recognised that black, Asian and Irish organisations have built up substantial experience over the years from which public bodies and the wider voluntary sector have much to learn.

The diversity of the Asian and black voluntary sector must be recognised – all too often public bodies seem to see community organisations as all much the same. There are differences not only in terms of ethnicity and culture but also in relation to experiences of racism, demography and patterns of settlement, and gender, age, outlook, perspective and religious affiliation.

Tokenism must be avoided, in both appearance and reality. It is sometimes felt that voluntary organisations are approached just because a public body wants to put a tick in a box saying that it has engaged in consultation.

It is essential to ensure that the voices of women and of young people are heard.

Procedures that have the appearance and effect of divide-and-rule tactics should not be used.

Consultation should start early, and at the early stages should be about the structure and process of the consultation itself.

Following any consultation, feedback should be provided on how views were taken into account, what key points were accepted or rejected, and why.

It is often important to choose venues that are on neutral ground; to include social occasions in consultation processes; to take advantage of informal and chance encounters as well as formal meetings.

It is essential to ensure that there is sufficient time and information for people to respond meaningfully.

It must be recognised that genuine consultation is expensive and must be paid for.

Chapter 21

Checklist of Recommendations

This chapter summarises the recommendations made in Chapters 9–20. In most instances, it is up to a government department or agency at Cardiff, Holyrood or Westminster to take the first initiative. However, it is frequently not necessary or even desirable for other bodies to wait for government action. All individuals and organisations can be involved in advocating and lobbying for the implementation of the recommendations made in this report, and can set up pilot projects and feasibility studies at local and institutional levels. We introduce the recommendations by repeating the seven fundamental principles we proposed earlier.

Three central concepts: cohesion, equality and difference
People must be treated equally but also with regard to real differences of experience, background and perception. These concepts need to be consistently and constantly central in government policy- and decision-making. High-profile statements of ideals by senior politicians and civil servants are important. They remain mere paper commitments or rhetoric, however, if they are not fully incorporated into all mainstream agendas and programmes. See in particular Chapter 4.

Demonstrable change at all levels
The concepts of equality and diversity must be driven through the government machinery at national and regional levels. Responsibility for making them real must be devolved to the local levels at which theory becomes practice, where real change needs to take place. Verbal and financial commitment from the government is essential, but the test of real change is what happens on the ground. See in particular Chapter 20.

Addressing racisms
There must be a sustained and fearless attack on all forms of racial injustice. Such injustice threatens the very basis of citizenship. Street racism and violent racism must be dealt with, but so also must institu-

tional racism. Among other things, the latter is a major factor in the climate in which street racism and violent racism go unchecked. Attention must be paid to racism's different targets: anti-black racism, anti-Muslim racism, anti-Gypsy racism, anti-Irish racism, antisemitism, and so on. See in particular Chapter 5.

Tackling disadvantage
Street racism and violent racism arise and flourish in situations of economic disadvantage and inequality. This is one major reason for addressing social exclusion; another is the fact that it disproportionately affects some (though not all) black, Asian and Irish communities. See in particular Chapter 6.

Colour-blind approaches do not work
There must be a commitment to go beyond the racism- and culture-blind strategies of social inclusion currently under way. Programmes such as the New Deal for Communities are essential. They must, however, have an explicit focus on race equality and cultural diversity. See in particular Chapters 6 and 9–14.

Empowering and enfranchising
There must be vigorous commitment to recognising cultural diversity through, for example, the systematic representation of black, Asian and Irish communities on public bodies. See Chapters 16, 18 and 20.

A pluralistic culture of human rights
Human rights standards provide both an ethical and a legal basis for the changes required.

It is in the light of these seven fundamental principles that the following recommendations are made.

Police and policing

1　A formal declaration about principles of good policing practice in a multi-ethnic society should be drafted and agreed in every town or city.

2　The results of action research on improving the use of stop-and-search should be widely published and considered, and advice sought on what further research is needed.

3   Records categorised by ethnicity should be made of all stops under any legislative provision, not just PACE, and these should include 'voluntary' stops.

4   Police authorities should undertake publicity campaigns to ensure that the public knows the purpose and correct procedure of stops and is aware of its own rights.

5   Evaluation of the use of stop-and-search powers should take the arrest rate into account and focus on the more serious types of crime. Crimes of a minor nature, and especially those that result from an altercation arising from the stop itself, should be weighted lightly.

6   Local commanders should systematically examine how stop-and-search powers are currently used. They should deploy officers on the street to this end, and resulting improvements should be linked to specific objectives within the local crime strategy.

7   Relevant authorities should specify the competencies and core skills required in relation to race and diversity for all practitioners in the criminal justice system, and ensure that these are systematically considered in initial and continuing training, in recruitment and promotion systems, and in all staff appraisals.

8   The Home Office should commission evaluation and action research on the effectiveness of specialist training in issues of race and diversity for practitioners in the criminal justice system, and disseminate the findings to all interested parties and individuals.

9   All candidates for appointment to Association of Chief Police Officers (ACPO) and Association of Chief Police Officers Scotland (ACPOS) status posts should have taken an accredited training module on issues of race equality and cultural diversity.

10   Every death in custody should be independently investigated when it occurs. In cases where it is considered that the actions of officers and

other staff may have contributed to the death, they should be suspended from duty pending and during investigation. Legal aid should be available for families during deaths in custody investigations. There should be full disclosure to families of all evidence and documents in deaths in custody investigations. Information about organisations that provide specialist counselling, advice and moral support to bereaved families should be provided.

11   An independent body to investigate complaints against the police should be established.

12   In association with HMIC, the Home Office should commission an independent audit of progress in implementing the recommendations in the Stephen Lawrence Inquiry report, and ensure that its findings are widely disseminated.

13   HMIC's Winning the Race inspection should be continued annually, with the involvement of local communities in each force area.

The wider criminal justice system

1   Research should be commissioned into the characteristics of persons convicted or cautioned for racially aggravated offences under the Crime and Disorder Act 1998. Such research should identify the strategies most likely (a) to reduce the levels of racist incidents and (b) to be effective in the programmes being developed and applied by the prison and probation services for dealing with offending behaviour.

2   HM Chief Inspector of Prisons should carry out an urgent and thorough thematic inspection of race equality in prisons, similar to the inspection of the probation service completed in 1999/2000 by HM Chief Inspector of Probation.

3   A national committee or forum should be set up on the training of probation officers and prison officers in issues of race and diversity.

4   The government should review all procedures for dealing with complaints about racism in the criminal justice process to ensure that:

- an independent element is included in the investigation;
- investigators have an accredited qualification in dealing with issues of race and diversity.

5   The government should review the disciplinary procedures for public servants working in the criminal justice system to ensure that they cannot evade responsibility for racist conduct by means of technical or procedural devices.

6   A Judicial Appointments Commission should be established to oversee all appointments and promotions within the magistracy and the higher judiciary, and to Queen's Counsel, and it should seek to ensure that the judiciary is more diverse in terms of community background.

7   The government, the courts and the criminal justice services should:
- extend the use of ethnic monitoring to those existing functions of the criminal justice system not already covered, for example sentencing, criminal appeals and the work of the Criminal Cases Review Commission;
- ensure that ethnic monitoring is systematically applied to the new functions and procedures introduced under recent legislation such as the Crime and Disorder Act 1998, the Youth Justice and Criminal Evidence Act 1999, the Access to Justice Act 1999, the Criminal Justice and Court Services Act 2000, the Terrorism Act 2000;
- make the results available for public discussion and for independent inspection, audit and research;
- ensure that monitoring is carried out rigorously and with integrity, and that staff in central government and throughout the system have the expertise to draw the correct conclusions, and apply them to the formation of policy and the development of professional practice;
- prepare and publish appraisals of the effects of its policies and measures.

8   The government should review and improve the quality of the data included each year in *Statistics on Race and the Criminal Justice System*.

9   Qualitative research on perceptions of fairness in the criminal justice system should be undertaken, with particular regard to race and diversity issues.

10 The criteria for appointment to all public bodies, especially those set up under recent legislation, should include a requirement that candidates demonstrate their ability to understand and act in the best interests of all sections of the communities for which they have responsibility.

11 Organisations set up under recent legislation should be required to specify in their reports the action they have taken to promote race equality.

Education

1 National authorities should require local authorities and individual schools to maintain substantially more detailed and helpful statistics on ethnicity than hitherto, and ensure that there is high-quality training available on how such statistics are to be analysed and used.

2 Inspectors should provide detailed guidance to schools on how they should collect, analyse and use statistical information broken down by ethnicity.

3 All institutions of higher education should review and improve their arrangements for ensuring that potential students from Asian and black communities apply for a wide range of courses. This is particularly important in the case of the older and most prestigious institutions and applies to both young and mature students.

4 Courses and syllabi in higher education should be reviewed with a view to making them culturally more inclusive wherever appropriate.

5 All institutions of higher education should review and improve their arrangements for the recruitment and retention of academic staff, particularly at the most senior levels.

6 A voluntary organisation, in co-operation with other organisations, should produce a handbook for schools on issues of race equality and cultural diversity.

7 Education for citizenship should include human rights principles; stress

on skills of deliberation, advocacy and campaigning; understanding of equality legislation; and opposition to racist beliefs and behaviour.

8   Work financed under the auspices of the EMAG grant should be independently evaluated. Particular attention should be paid to the grant's impact on raising the achievement of African-Caribbean, Bangladeshi and Pakistani pupils and reducing their experience of exclusion.

9   There should be a substantial programme of certificated training for specialists in teaching English as an Additional Language.

10   In England a specific Standards Fund grant should be created and used for in-service training in race equality and cultural diversity.

11   Issues of race equality and cultural diversity should be properly covered in initial teacher training, and should be mandatory in all major programmes of management development for head teachers and deputy heads.

12   Funding should be provided for a systematic programme of Training the Trainers courses.

13   The government should set targets for reducing nationally the numbers of exclusions experienced by pupils of particular community backgrounds. The targets should refer to fixed-term exclusions as well as to permanent exclusions. Further, pilot schemes should be established in certain schools to investigate the implications of moving towards a no-exclusions policy. Appropriate funding should be provided, and research should identify the lessons to be learned.

14   Training on inclusion for all members of governors' disciplinary committees and appeal panels should be provided; in-service training in non-confrontational approaches to discipline and conflict resolution should be organised for staff; a member of the governing body should serve as an advocate for any student facing permanent exclusion, or a student should be represented by an advocate of their choice; and procedures should require head teachers to explain and justify how and why necessary support has not been provided.

15   The national authorities should fund independent bodies of trained advocates to support students facing exclusion.

16   Schools and local authorities should develop closer working relationships with local supplementary schools, parents' groups and community organisations.

17   All inspection reports should include the heading 'Race Equality and Cultural Diversity', and high-quality training should be provided for all inspectors.

18   In each education system a national working party should be set up to examine and evaluate the impact of the inspection system on issues of race equality and cultural diversity in schools and local authorities.

19   The Qualifications and Curriculum Authority should require that all exam boards offer only syllabuses in which it is possible to gain at least a C grade at each tier and that all schools monitor tier entry by ethnicity.

20   Independent research should be commissioned to assess the impact on issues of race equality and cultural diversity of recent government initiatives intended to benefit all pupils, but which may have failed to benefit, or have actually disadvantaged, pupils from certain communities.

21   In each education system a forum should be set up in which government officials, academics, practitioners and representatives of non-governmental organisations can jointly review developments in education, including higher education, that have an impact on issues of race equality and cultural diversity.

Arts, media and sport

1   A national cultural policy should be developed through widespread participation and consultation. It should pay particular attention to issues of cultural inclusion and identity.

2   Organisations funded by public bodies should lose some of their funding if they do not make changes in their staff and governance,

and do not demonstrably make their programmes and activities more inclusive.

3   Every major arts organisation should commission an independent audit of its programmes, output, employment profile, representation of wider society and financial investment.

4   Broadcasters and franchise-holders should be required to provide statistics broken down by ethnicity and gender in relation to grades and categories such as producer, editor and camera operator, and by management level.

5   Contracts and franchises should depend on the production of plans (a) to increase black and Asian staff at all levels and grades; (b) to commission more work from black and Asian producers; and (c) to ensure that a proportion of programmes tackle issues of race equality and cultural diversity.

6   The BBC should make the employment and contracting of black and Asian staff and producers an integral part of its latest reviews.

7   Broadcasters should seek to encourage the promotion of black and Asian people to commissioning editor and management posts.

8   Broadcasters and other bodies should find and develop ways of improving networking opportunities for black and Asian people in the industry.

9   Broadcasters should use their websites to provide open-tender documents.

10 Programming targets in relation to race and diversity issues should be set similar to those that exist for countries and regions.

11 Large established production companies should on occasion be required to work in partnership with smaller companies that have developed distinctive expertise in creating programmes about race and cultural diversity.

12   Voluntary-sector organisations should seek funds to set up media monitoring projects, so that they may complain regularly about coverage they find offensive. Newspapers and television companies should be named and shamed in high-profile ways.

13   Every newspaper should publish, both in its pages and on its website, a breakdown of its staff by gender, ethnicity and seniority. The breakdowns should be regularly updated and should be accompanied by statements of the paper's plans to increase the employment of black and Asian staff.

14   The regulatory framework for digital TV should include, at least in the short term, protection for programme suppliers which offer channels targeted at particular cultural interests.

15   The implications and workings of the new digital universe should be closely monitored.

16   There should be further pooling of experience from the range of anti-racist projects that have been implemented in football clubs, and lessons for other major sports should be learned.

17   All sports organisations should be required to draw up and publish equal opportunity policies to show how they intend to increase the numbers of black and Asian people involved as managers, administrators, coaches and officials.

18   All sports organisations should be required to publish anti-racist statements and monitor their effectiveness.

19   The administrations at Cardiff, Holyrood and Westminster should issue policy statements on the interconnections between the arts, media and sport in the development of Britain as a multi-ethnic society.

Health and welfare

1   There should be substantial black, Asian and Irish representation, both professional and lay, on the Service Delivery and Organisation Research and Delivery programme.

2   Research into the impact of racism on health should be given a high priority within the health research programme.

3   Targets should be applied to the provision of interpreting services throughout the health service and culturally specific food in hospitals and residential care homes. Targets should not be colour-blind. For example, waiting lists should not just be monitored, but monitored by ethnicity and religion as well.

4   Record-keeping and monitoring by ethnicity, use of the data to set targets and race equality audits using appropriate categories should be established, as they are an essential part of any efficient management system, in both health and social services. Specific results must be sought, which must be qualitative as well as quantitative.

5   More interpreters should be trained and appointed. All NHS primary care trusts should be required to have a contract with a telephone interpreting service.

6   Child benefit, linked to each individual child, should be increased significantly, to give every child living in poverty, from whatever background, a better chance in life.

7   The Department of Health (DoH) should require social services departments to record information about the ethnicity, religion and home language(s) of all children receiving direct services of any kind.

8   One-stop shops for health issues, including parenting education, should be more widely established. All parenting advice should be available to both mothers and fathers, and men should be encouraged to participate.

9   All those employed in the health and social welfare services should be trained in cultural awareness and sensitivity.

10   Greater priority should be given in housing allocation to helping members of families to live with or near to each other because of the benefits of mutual support.

> **Please note**
>
> As well as Chapter 14, several other chapters in the report contain rec-
> ommendations relating to employment. See, for example, the refer-
> ences to recruitment, retention and promotion processes in the police
> service (Chapter 9), the wider criminal justice system (10), schools
> and universities (11), the arts and media (12) and the health service
> (13).

11 Targets should be set for co-ordinated inter-agency action to cut the
   numbers of young black and Asian men held in state institutions.

12 There should be monitoring by ethnicity of short-term NHS contracts;
   external as well as internal advertisement of all DoH posts; medical recruitment advertising in the black and Asian press; training in equalities issues in recruitment and selection for all medical recruitment
   panel members; and acceptance of the recommendations of the 'Recruitment of Doctors' guidelines produced by the BMA in January
   2000. The DoH should undertake a thorough review and overhaul of
   the consultant distinction award system to ensure that issues of equity
   and diversity are central to its operation, and targets should be set for
   black and Asian membership of the councils of all Royal Colleges.

13 Targets should be set for black and Asian representation on education
   and training consortia and Healthwork UK, and urgent action should
   be taken to achieve these.

14 The DoH should provide guidance for medical school candidates to encourage those coming from family backgrounds other than medicine.
   The DoH should use its sponsorship of student doctors to support the
   anti-racist drive of the Council of Heads of Medical Schools action programme against discrimination in admissions.

Employment

1 As a matter of priority the government should place a statutory duty on
  all employers to create and implement employment equity plans.

2   Achievement of Investors in People status should in future be conditional on the formulation and implementation of an employment equity plan, and equity issues should be explicitly and comprehensively covered in the Business Excellence Model's guidance materials.

3   Guidance on public procurement and the award of subsidies for investment, such as Regional Selective Assistance, should be revised to stress the importance of employment equity.

4   All organisations delivering New Deal programmes should be required to demonstrate that they are contributing positively to employment equity. If they cannot do this, their responsibilities should be transferred to others.

5   Organisations providing personal adviser services in relation to employment should be required to ensure that persons from black and Asian backgrounds are equitably involved in their programmes, as both managers and advisers.

6   Research should be commissioned on the contributions of Asian and black firms to UK gross national product and UK trade balances.

7   The DTI and the Small Business Service (SBS) should commission research into Asian and black business start-up and survival patterns, with a view to formulating local targets and contributing to SBS national strategies.

8   Targets should be set at SBS national council and local council levels for increasing the take-up of support by Asian and black small businesses.

9   The Banking Code and the Mortgage Code should include undertakings on non-discrimination.

10   All providers of financial services should monitor and improve their procedures and ensure that key staff receive race and diversity training.

11   There should be monitoring by ethnicity of lending decisions by financial institutions.

12 British Trade International and Business Links partnerships should set targets for working more closely with the Asian and black business sector, and for highlighting the possibility of international trade as a mechanism for encouraging growth.

13 Business support agencies should develop their expertise in advising and assisting the independent retail sector, and all agencies involved in urban regeneration and business development should recognise the value of independent retailers.

Immigration and asylum

1 The UK government should take action to bring British nationality law into line with international human rights standards, and to deal with the statelessness and racial and ethnic divisions that have been created by its present policies.

2 The UK should sign up to the EU directive extending and protecting family reunion rights.

3 The public funds requirement should be removed for the spouses and children of British citizens and permanent residents, and time-limited for all other family members.

4 Appeal rights relating to deportation should be fully restored.

5 The government should carry out and publicise research into the economic impact, and the potential economic benefits, of immigration.

6 Urgent action should be taken to remedy defects in the systems for determining asylum claims and supporting asylum-seekers, and to provide better settlement services for those granted asylum. This should involve:
- improving the initial decision-making process to ensure that asylum-seekers have the opportunity properly to present their cases, with appropriate legal advice, to decision-makers who are properly trained and well informed, and providing sufficient resources to improve quality and minimise delays;

- government support for asylum-seekers so that those whose claims are accepted have the best chance of successful settlement; this could best be achieved through cash support (at not less than the basic income support level) and a choice of available housing, and must include English language and skills training and social orientation;
- a co-ordinated approach to the settlement needs of those granted asylum, so that the Social Exclusion Unit, or a similar body, with the help of refugee community organisations, can identify needs and develop a national strategy for meeting them.

7   The exemption in the Race Relations (Amendment) Act permitting discrimination on grounds of ethnic or national origin should be removed.

8   In relation to nationality, immigration and asylum issues, independent experts should examine all existing legislation, rules, procedures, guidelines and decision-making criteria for their compliance with the Human Rights Act.

9   The government should accept responsibility for encouraging and leading a positive debate on asylum and immigration through its own publicity mechanisms, and by commissioning research and providing information.

10   The UK should use its best efforts to promote an EU immigration and asylum policy that is aligned with the principles and recommendations of this report and with international human rights standards, and should welcome EU initiatives, such as the enhancement of family reunion and third country nationals' rights, which move towards these goals.

11   An independent commission on all aspects of immigration, nationality and asylum should be established.

Politics and representation

1   Each political party should draw up and publish a statement showing how it will avoid playing, or appearing to play, the race card in local and national elections. The statement should be quoted in the party mani-

festo, and brought to the attention of all candidates and party workers.

2   Each party should conduct an audit by ethnicity of its own membership, and should draw up and publish plans on how it proposes to ensure that more Asian and black candidates are selected for safe and winnable seats.

3   The Appointments Commission should have a statutory duty to ensure that the second chamber (the present House of Lords) is more representative of the country in terms of ethnicity. In any one year, during at least the next 5–10 years, at least one-sixth of new members should be from Asian and black community backgrounds.

4   At least one-third of newly appointed black and Asian peers in any one year should be women.

Religion and belief

1   In all faith communities there should be closer connections between anti-racism and work to improve inter-faith relations.

2   Legislation should be introduced prohibiting direct and indirect discrimination on grounds of religion or belief.

3   A statement of general principles should be drawn up on reasonable accommodation in relation to religious and cultural diversity in the workplace and in schools, and case-study examples of good practice should be provided.

4   A study should be made of police responses to hate crimes containing a religious component.

5   A commission on the role of religion in the public life of a multi-faith society should be set up to make recommendations on legal and constitutional matters.

Government leadership

1   The government should:
    • create further co-ordinating structures;
    • require the various inspection regimes to work more closely together on issues of race equality and cultural diversity, with a view to improving their practices;
    • arrange a programme of equality and diversity inspections of its own departments;
    • commission impact assessments of all new policies that have the potential to exert a detrimental influence on race equality and recognition of cultural diversity;
    • commission independent research on the impact of recent government measures that may have had a detrimental effect on race equality and recognition of cultural diversity;
    • consult widely with interested and experienced persons and organisations on the race equality performance management framework currently being developed;
    • set up for each department and also for the government as a whole an advisory forum on race equality and cultural diversity issues.

Legislation and enforcement

1   There should be a single Equality Act in Britain. It should be supplemented by regulations and regularly updated codes of practice on specific subjects. Both the Act and its supporting documentation should be written in plain language.

2   A new Equality Act should lead towards the creation of a single Equality Commission, covering all grounds of unlawful discrimination.

3   Existing auditing bodies should have formal responsibility for inspection and audit of public-sector equality schemes, and they should require progress towards fair participation and fair access over a defined period of time. The Commission for Racial Equality, or proposed Equality Commission, should have power to issue compliance notices, and in the event of non-compliance to apply to a court or tribunal for an order requiring the public body to comply.

4   In addition to an Equality Commission responsible for enforcing equality legislation, there should be a Human Rights Commission for Britain, the functions of which would include the review of legislation, scrutiny of draft legislation, the provision of advice and assistance to individuals and guidance to public authorities, the conduct of investigations and inquiries, and the general promotion of a human rights culture.

5   The government should allow individuals access to the UN complaints system if they believe that their rights under the Convention on the Elimination of Racial Discrimination have been infringed. The government should give greater priority to fulfilling its obligations under international human rights agreements, and to making the public aware of the commitments that have been made.

6   Officials in central, devolved and local administrations should ensure that the procedures they are operating on human rights issues are harmonised with procedures on equality issues.

7   The Parliamentary Human Rights Committee should ensure that it has a strong focus on race equality issues.

8   The government should formally declare that the United Kingdom is a multicultural society, and should issue a draft declaration for consultation.

Organisational change

1   Evaluative studies should be made of leadership styles in relation to race and diversity issues, and good practice should be disseminated.

2   A sample of policy documents issued by public bodies should be critically evaluated, and elements of good practice should be more widely shared.

3   A task force should be set up to clarify the objectives and content of racism awareness training, and to develop guidelines and standards on practical methodology and organisation.

4   Official guidance should be issued on monitoring by ethnicity and religion, and on the collection, interpretation and use of statistical data.

Non-governmental organisations

1   All non-governmental organisations should consider this report, particularly in relation to their advocacy, lobbying, campaigning and partnership activities with public bodies.

The Runnymede Trust

The Commission on the Future of Multi-Ethnic Britain was set up by the Runnymede Trust. We recommend that the Trust should:

- Ensure that a summary of this report is sent to all public bodies shortly after its publication and that follow-up enquiries are made to all recipients, approximately one year after publication, to ascertain how the report has been discussed and acted on;
- Organise conferences and seminars at which particular parts of this report are considered and debated;
- In collaboration and partnership with other non-governmental organisations, adopt a watchdog role in relation to the implementation of the recommendations in this report, and publish and disseminate reviews and evaluations of progress. Such reviews and evaluations should be available on a website as well as in print.

Notes and References

1 The Turning Point

1 Marina Warner, *Managing Monsters*, 1995, p. 84.
2 Andrew Gamble and Tony Wright, 'The End of Britain?', *Political Quarterly*, January-March 2000, p. 1.
3 Bill Bryson, *Notes from a Small Island*, 1996, pp. 351–2. By summer 2000 over 1.3 million copies of the paperback edition had been sold.
4 Mike Phillips and Trevor Phillips, *Windrush: the irresistible rise of multiracial Britain*, 1998.
5 Throughout this report there are references to the Stephen Lawrence Inquiry report. Stephen Lawrence was murdered in a racist attack in south London in 1993. An inquiry into the police investigation of the murder was set up by the Home Secretary in 1997. It was conducted by Sir William Macpherson of Cluny and its report was published in February 1999. See Chapter 5 for discussion of the report's description of institutional racism and Chapter 9 for reference to media coverage about it and its impact on the police service.

2 Rethinking the National Story

1 Mike Phillips and Trevor Phillips, *Windrush: the irresistible rise of multiracial Britain*, 1998.
2 See Norman Davies, *The Isles*, 1999, p. xli.
3 Cf. Eric Hobsbawm and Terence Ranger (eds), *The Invention of Tradition*, 1983.
4 Norman Davies, *Guardian*, 13 November 1999.
5 Cf. the *Oxford English Dictionary* (1999): 'The distinctiveness and uniqueness of the British as a people has long been taken for granted'.
6 Polly Toynbee, 'We can be English without falling into the racist trap', *Guardian*, 12 January 2000.
7 Davies, *The Isles*, pp. 438–9.

8   See Malcolm Rifkind, 'British Champion', *Prospect*, January 2000, p. 26.
9   Linda Colley, *Britons: forging the nation 1707–1837*, 1992.
10   See Michael Ignatieff, *Blood and Belonging: journeys into the new nationalism*, 1993.
11   See, for example, Roy Foster, *Paddy and Mr Punch*, 1995.
12   Barbara Ellen, 'The land of such dear souls', *Observer*, 16 January 2000.
13   See, for example, Vron Ware, *Beyond the Pale*, 1991, and Catherine Hall, *White, Male and Middle Class*, 1992.
14   Recent discussions of Englishness and Britishness, from a range of political outlooks, include Simon Heffer, *Nor Shall My Sword: the reinvention of England*, 1999; Mark Leonard, *Britain TM: renewing our identity*, 1997; John Redwood, *The Death of Britain? The UK's constitutional crisis*, 1999; Jeremy Paxman, *The English*, 1999; Andrew Marr, *The Day Britain Died*, 2000; and Kevin Davey, *English Imaginaries*, 1999. The first main chapter in Davey's book is entitled 'England: an imaginary country'.
15   For a balanced assessment, see David Held et al., *Global Transformations*, 1999. There is a useful summary in Anthony Giddens's 1999 Reith lectures, *Runaway World*.

3 Identities in Transition

1   Elinor Kelly, 'Stands Scotland where it did? – an essay in ethnicity and internationalism', *Scottish Affairs*, 1998.
2   Tariq Modood, Richard Berthoud et al., *Ethnic Minorities in Britain: diversity and disadvantage*, 1997.
3   See, for example, Stuart Hall, 'Attitude and Aspiration: reflections on Black Britain in the nineties', *New Formations*, 1998.
4   See, for example, Avtar Brah, *Cartographies of Diaspora*, 1996, Floya Anthias and Nira Yuval-Davis, *Racialised Boundaries*, 1992, and Ann Phoenix, *Ethnicized Identities*, 1998.
5   Publications on these themes include Stuart Hall, *New Ethnicities*, 1996, Paul Gilroy, *Small Acts*, 1993, and S. Sharma, J. Hutnyk and A. Sharma, *Disorienting Rhythms*, 1996.
6   For discussion of this idea see Kevin Robbins, 'Tradition and Translation: national culture in a global context' in J. Corner and S. Harvey (eds), *Enterprise and Heritage*, 1993.

7   See, for example, Philip Lewis, *Islamic Britain*, 1997, and Ron Geaves, *Sectarian Influences within Islam in Britain*, 1996.

8   Runnymede Trust, *Islamophobia: a challenge for us all*, 1997.

9   Tariq Modood, '"Difference", Cultural Racism and Anti-Racism', in P. Werbner and T. Modood (eds), *Debating Cultural Hybridity*, 1997.

10 Sharma et al., op. cit.

11 The key authoritative text on the Irish in Britain is Mary Hickman and Bronwen Walter, *Discrimination and the Irish Community in Britain*, published by the Commission for Racial Equality in 1997. See also Mary Hickman, 'Binary Opposites or Unique Neighbours? – the Irish in multi-ethnic Britain', *Political Quarterly*, January-March 2000. The basis for estimating the size of the Irish community in Britain is explained in Appendix D.

12 Israel Finestein, 'A Community of Paradox: Office, Authority and Ideas in the Changing Governance of Anglo-Jewry', in Ilan Troen (ed.), *Jewish Centers and Peripheries: Europe between America and Israel Fifty Years after World War II*, 1998, p. 268.

13 For an authoritative review of issues affecting Gypsies and Travellers see Rachel Morris and Luke Clements (eds), *Gaining Ground*, 1999.

14 Estimates published by the Office for National Statistics, June 2000, based on the *Labour Force Survey*, 1998. See Appendix D for further information.

15 The phrase 'in between' is Homi Bhabha's. See *The Location of Culture*, 1997. Ali Rattansi writes of hybridity in terms of 'being at home with not being at home' – see 'On Being and Not Being Black/Brown British', *Interventions: The International Journal of Postcolonial Studies*, 2000.

16 A key text here is Charles Taylor, 'The Politics of Recognition', in Amy Gutmann and Charles Taylor (eds), *Multiculturalism and the Politics of Recognition*, 1994.

17 Jürgen Habermas defends this position in *The Invasion of the Other*, 1998.

18 For example, Norman Davies in *The Isles*, 1999, and Andrew Marr in *The Day Britain Died*, 2000.

19 Paul Gilroy, *There Ain't No Black in the Union Jack: the cultural politics of race and nation*, 1987.

20 Paul Gilroy in his 1999 lecture at the Institute of Contemporary Arts, *Joined-up Politics and Postcolonial Melancholia*, 1999.

4 Cohesion, Equality and Difference

1   *Race Equality in Public Services*, Home Office, March 2000, p. 1.
2   For references to commitments by earlier governments, see Note 9.
3   For fuller discussion see Bhikhu Parekh, *Rethinking Multiculturalism*,
     2000. For a similar but not identical typology see Tariq Modood in
     Modood and Werbner (eds), *The Politics of Multiculturalism in the New
     Europe: racism, identity and community*, 1997, pp. 20–4. See also the
     discussion in Yasmin Alibhai-Brown, *After Multiculturalism*, 2000.
4   Jürgen Habermas. See, for example, 'Citizenship and national identity:
     some reflections on the future of Europe', in R. Beiner (ed.), *Theorising
     Citizenship*, 1995.
5   Charles Taylor, 'The Politics of Recognition', in Amy Gutmann and
     Charles Taylor (eds), *Multiculturalism and the Politics of Recognition*,
     1994. See also Iris Young, *Justice and the Politics of Difference*, 1990, and
     Anne Phillips, *The Politics of Presence*, 1995.
6   Advocates include Will Kymlicka, for example, in *Multicultural
     Citizenship*, 1995, and Amy Gutmann and Charles Taylor (see Note 5).
7   'Millets' were units within the Ottoman Empire granted substantial
     autonomy in the running of their own affairs. The three largest millets
     were the Greek Orthodox community, the Armenian Orthodox
     community and the Jewish community.
8   'Equal opportunity accompanied by cultural diversity in an
     atmosphere of mutual tolerance': speech by Roy Jenkins to the
     National Committee for Commonwealth Immigrants, 23 May 1966.
9   UK report to the United Nations, 1995, quoted in Runnymede Trust,
     Islamophobia: a challenge for us all, 1997, p. 31. For fuller discussion of
     UK policy debate over the years see Sebastian Poulter, *Ethnicity, Law
     and Human Rights*, 1998.
10   Most obviously Enoch Powell and Margaret Thatcher. Other
     influential opinion-formers opposed to liberalism from a conservative
     position include John Casey, Maurice Cowling, Roger Scruton and
     Peregrine Worsthorne.
11   For a recent critique of liberalism in these and other respects see
     Davina Cooper, *Governing out of Order: space, law and the politics of
     belonging*, 1998.
12   *The Bradford Commission Report*, The Stationery Office, 1996, p. 92.
13   See the distinctions drawn in Chapter 17 between 'open' and 'closed'
     views of the Other. The distinctions apply to all cultural and

intellectual disputes, not to religious disagreements only.

5 Dealing with Racisms

1   Tariq Modood, Richard Berthoud et al., *Ethnic Minorities in Britain: diversity and disadvantage*, 1997. See in particular Table 8.3 on p. 266.

2   The first quotation is from a report by Reading Council for Racial Equality, 1999; the second from Tricia Hamm, *Racial Harassment: just a part of life?*, 1997; the third and fourth from Kusminder Chahal and Louis Julienne, *'We Can't All Be White!' – racist victimisation in the UK*, 1999; the fifth from focus group research by the Commission on the Future of Multi-Ethnic Britain, autumn 1999.

3   See Paul Henderson and Ranjit Kaur (eds), *Rural Racism in the UK: examples of community-based responses*, 1999. The book contains case studies from south-west England, Lincolnshire and the Scottish Highlands. On street and violent racism generally see Benjamin Bowling, *Violent Racism: victimisation, policing and social context*, 1998.

4   With regard to Englishness see Roger Hewitt, *Routes of Racism*, 1996, and Billy Bragg, 'Time to Move On, Boys', *Guardian*, 24 June 2000. The wider European context is discussed by Andreas Wimmer in 'Explaining Xenophobia and Racism', *Ethnic and Racial Studies*, January 1997.

5   Stokely Carmichael and Charles Hamilton, *Black Power: the politics of liberation in America*, 1967.

6   The equivalent in French for the term 'racism and xenophobia' is *'phénomènes racistes et xénophobes'* – racism is understood to consist of a range of phenomena as distinct from, as is implied by the English word, a set of views inside people's heads. The German equivalent is *'Russismus und Fremdenfeindlichkeit'*. The latter word would be best translated into English as hostility or enmity towards strangers or foreigners rather than xenophobia. It is closer to the English words hatred or aversion than to notions of fear or anxiety.

7   Edward Said (1978) defines orientalism as 'making statements about it, authorizing views of it, describing it, teaching it, settling it, ruling over it: in short ... a western style for dominating, restructuring and having authority over the Orient'. The *Oxford Dictionary* records that the term Islamophobia was first used in print in 1991. The phenomena to which it refers are described at length in Runnymede Trust, *Islamophobia: a challenge for us all*, 1997.

8   For discussions of forms of racism see Martin Barker, *The New Racism*,
      1981; Michel Wieviorka, *The Arena of Racism*, 1995; Alistair Bonnett,
      Antiracism, 1999; Tariq Modood, *Racial Equality: colour, culture and
      citizenship*, 1994.

9   See David Cesarani, 'Antisemitism in the 1990s: a symposium', *Patterns
      of Prejudice*, winter 1991; Tony Kushner, 'The fascist as "other": racism
      and neo-nazism in contemporary Britain', *Patterns of Prejudice*, January
      1994; and Antony Lerman, *Antisemitism World Report 1998*.

10   *Q News*, March 1999, and *Muslim News*, 26 March 1999.

11   Perry Curtis, *Apes and Angels: the Irishman in Victorian caricature*, 1997.

12   See, for example, Peter Fryer, *Staying Power: the history of black people in
      Britain*, 1984; Robert Miles, *Racism*, 1989, and *Racism after Race
      Relations*, 1993; and Michael Banton, *The Idea of Race*, 1977.

13   In a study of stop-and-search practices, a female police officer is quoted
      as saying that the style of some male officers 'reeks of testosterone': see
      Marian Fitzgerald, *Searches in London*, 1999, p. 64. For a fuller
      discussion see Ali Rattansi, 'On Being and Not Being Black/Brown
      British', *Interventions: The International Journal of Postcolonial Studies*,
      2000.

14   See, for example, Heidi Safia Mirza, *Black British Feminism: a reader*,
      1997, and 'Redefining citizenship: black women educators and the
      third space', in M. Arnot (ed.), *Challenging Democracy: feminist
      perspectives on the education of citizens*, 2000.

15   Cabinet Papers, CAB 124/1191: *Report of the Working Party on Coloured
      People Seeking Employment in the United Kingdom*, December 1953,
      5364–53.

16   Sir William Macpherson, *The Stephen Lawrence Inquiry*, paragraph 6.17,
      pp. 22–3.

17   Despite the clarity with which Macpherson wrote on this point,
      however, he was misunderstood by various opinion leaders when the
      report was published. Several senior figures in teachers' unions, for
      example, issued statements vehemently denying things that
      Macpherson had not in fact asserted.

18   Tony Sewell, *Black Masculinities and Schooling: how black boys survive
      modern schooling*, 1997, and Simon Holdaway, 'Constructing and
      Sustaining "Race" within the Police Force', *British Journal of Sociology*,
      1997.

19   Eric Williams, writing in 1944. The UK edition of his book, *Capitalism
      and Slavery*, was first published in 1964.

20   In part as a result of radical criticisms of it. Significant in this respect was A. Sivanandan, 'Racism Awareness Training and the Degradation of Black Struggle', *Race and Class*, spring 1985.

6 Reducing Inequalities

1   Annual reports about developments in Europe are issued by the European Observatory on Policies to Combat Social Exclusion. For fuller information see Michael Parkinson, *Combating Social Exclusion: lessons from area-based programmes in Europe*, 1998, and Ali Madanipoor et al. (eds), *Social Exclusion in European Cities: processes, experiences and responses*, 1998.

2   Ralf Dahrendorf et al., *Report on Wealth Creation and Social Cohesion in a Free Society*, 1995.

3   For an overview of progress see *Review of the Social Exclusion Unit*, Cabinet Office, December 1999.

4   Catherine Howarth, Peter Kenway, Guy Palmer and Romina Miorelli, *Monitoring Poverty and Social Exclusion*, 1999.

5   See, for example, Rae Sibbitt, *Perpetrators of Racial Harassment and Racial Violence*, 1997, Benjamin Bowling, *Violent Racism: victimisation, policing and social context*, 1998, and Roger Hewitt, *Routes of Racism*, 1996. For a pan-European survey of the research on this point see Andreas Wimmer, 'Explaining Xenophobia and Racism', *Ethnic and Racial Studies*, 1997.

6   Operation Athena, 1999 onwards.

7   *Review of the Social Exclusion Unit*, op. cit.

8   For a discussion of differences between British and French use of the concept of social exclusion see Stuart Cameron and Simon Davoudi, 'Combating social exclusion: looking in or looking out?', in Madanipoor et al., op. cit., 1998.

9   See, for example, Richard Wilkinson, *Unhealthy Societies: The Afflictions of Inequality*, 1996.

10   *Review of the Social Exclusion Unit*, op. cit.

11   See, for example, *Advancing Together towards a World Class Economy*, Yorkshire Forward, 1999.

12   *Opportunity for All: tackling poverty and social exclusion*, Department of Social Security, September 1999.

13   The points in Box 6.1 are derived from Kusminder Chahal, *Ethnic*

Diversity, Neighbourhoods and Housing, February 2000. In its turn, this is based on a range of studies supported by the Joseph Rowntree Foundation, including in particular Sharon Beishon, Tariq Modood and Satnam Virdee, *Ethnic Minority Families*, 1998, Lucinda Platt and Michael Noble, *Race, Place and Poverty: ethnic groups and low income distribution*, 1999, Richard Berthoud, *Incomes of Ethnic Minorities*, 1998, R. Dorsett, *Ethnic Minorities in the Inner City*, 1998, and Alison Bowes, *'Too White, Too Rough and Too Many Problems': a study of Pakistani housing in Britain*, 1998.

14   Department for Education and Employment, *Jobs for All*, 1999; Department of the Environment, Transport and the Regions, *Race Equality Guidance for New Deal for Communities Partnerships*, February 2000; and Cabinet Office, *Minority Ethnic Issues in Social Exclusion and Neighbourhood Renewal: a guide to the work of the Social Exclusion Unit and the Policy Action Teams so far*, June 2000.

15   Alison Bowes, Naira Dar and Duncan Sim, *Pakistani Housing Strategies in Britain*, 1998.

16   See Gerard Lemos and Michael Young, *The Communities We Have Lost and Can Regain*, 1997, and two publications by Gerard Lemos: *A New Spirit of Community* and *Urban Village, Global City*, 1998.

17   For comprehensive guidance on tackling racist harassment on housing estates see *National Directory of Action Against Racial Harassment*, first published in 1996 and revised in autumn 2000 on www.raceactionnet. co.uk. Also *Facing Reality: evolving responses by London boroughs to racial harassment*, by Katie Argent, Sylvia Carter and Patricia Durr, July 2000.

18   Parkinson, op. cit.

19   Quoted in Sue Brownhill and Jane Darke, *Rich Mix: inclusive strategies for urban regeneration*, 1998, p. 20.

20   Sibbitt, op. cit.

7 Building a Pluralistic Human Rights Culture

1   'Building on a Human Rights Culture', address to the Civil Service College Seminar on 9 December 1999.

2   In Scotland and Wales the ECHR became binding in July 1999, and within less than a year led to substantially greater awareness of human rights principles. Similarly, in Northern Ireland the new Human Rights Commission quickly made its presence felt.

3   For a comprehensive account see Johannes Morsink, *The Universal Declaration of Human Rights: origins, drafting and intent*, 1999.
4   For further references to CERD in this report see the opening and closing paragraphs of Chapter 11, and paragraph 18.16 in Chapter 18.
5   Drawn from W. Wallace, *International Human Rights Texts and Materials*, 1997.
6   'Building on a Human Rights Culture', op. cit.
7   Lord Williams of Mostyn, Second Reading, Human Rights Bill, House of Lords, 3 November 1997, Col. 1308.
8   The interacting components of institutional racism are listed in Box 5.2 at the end of Chapter 5.
9   'Building on a Human Rights Culture', op. cit.
10 *Equal Opportunities Review* No. 87, September/October 1999. See also Sarah Spencer and Ian Bynoe, *A Human Rights Commission: the options for Britain and Northern Ireland*, 1998, and the same authors' *Mainstreaming Human Rights in Whitehall and Westminster*, 1999.

8 Summary of the Vision

1   Ben Okri, *Birds of Heaven*, Phoenix, 1996.

9 Police and Policing

1   For fuller reference to the differences between Britain's two separate legal systems see paragraph 10.5 in Chapter 10.
2   *Guardian*, 24 February 2000.
3   Dianna Yach, quoted in the *Guardian*, 24 February 2000.
4   Editorial in the *Sun*, 19 January 2000.
5   Simon Heffer, *Daily Mail*, 19 February 2000.
6   Tom Uttley, *Daily Telegraph*, 19 January 2000.
7   Leo Mckinstry, *Daily Mail*, 18 March 2000.
8   For further discussion of the media coverage of the Lawrence report see Arun Kundnani, 'Stumbling on: race, class and England', *Race and Class*, April/June 2000.
9   That there should be a ministerial priority to this effect was the first recommendation of the Stephen Lawrence Inquiry. The priority was set in June 1999, and in November 1999 the Home Secretary

announced that it would be one of just two ministerial priorities for 2000/01.

10   David Blakey and Dan Crompton, HMIC, *Policing London – Winning Consent*, Home Office, 2000, p. 45.

11   Marian Fitzgerald, *Searches in London under Section 1 of the Police and Criminal Evidence Act 1984*, for the Metropolitan Police Service, December 1999, pp. 64–5.

12   *Winning the Race Revisited*, HMIC, 1999, p 22.

13   Quoted by Marian Fitzgerald, op. cit., p. 51.

14   *The Rotterdam Charter*, available from RADAR, PO Box 1812, 3000 BV Rotterdam, Netherlands.

15   Organisations involved in these include Charnwood Racial Equality Council, Leicestershire Constabulary, Nottinghamshire Police, Reading Council for Racial Equality, Reading Borough Council, and Thames Valley Police.

16   The powers are exercised under Section 1 of the Police and Criminal Evidence Act 1984. The Act does not apply to Scotland.

17   Jayne Mooney and Jock Young, *Social Exclusion and Criminal Justice: ethnic communities and stop and search in North London*, 1999.

18   Vikram Dodd, 'All hype and no action', *Guardian*, 24 August 1999.

19   Mooney and Young, op. cit.

20   Home Office, *Stephen Lawrence Inquiry: Home Secretary's Action Plan, first Annual Report on Progress*, February 2000, p. 33.

21   For fuller background see the study by Mooney and Young, op. cit.

22   This is one of the principal conclusions of Marian Fitzgerald's study, op. cit.

23   *Winning the Race: policing plural communities*, HMIC, 1997, p. 65.

24   The observations of HMIC. See also Robin Oakley, 'Institutional racism and the police service', and Rajinder Sohpal, 'Community-based trainers and race related training', both in the *Police Journal*, October/December 1999.

25   Police Complaints Authority annual report, 1998/99.

26   See A. Leigh et al., *Deaths in Police Custody: learning the lessons*, 1998, and the valuable summary by Randeep Kular in *The Runnymede Bulletin*, September 1999.

27   See *Deaths in Custody: the risks reduced*, Police Complaints Authority, summer 2000.

28   Quoted by Randeep Kular in a continuation of her September article, *The Runnymede Bulletin*, December 1999. It is also from this source that

the following information is taken.

29   See the report by KPMG for the Home Office, *The Feasibility of an Independent System for Investigating Complaints against the Police*, May 2000.

30   The Home Secretary, quoted in Leicestershire Constabulary's *Community and Race Relations Strategy*, 1998.

31   Accounts of Project Athena include the transcript of a talk by John Grieve, QPM, in a conference report published by Grampian Police in partnership with Grampian Racial Equality Council, *Leading the Way Forward*, 1999.

32   See *Winning the Race* and *Winning the Race Revisited*, ops cit.

10 The Wider Criminal Justice System

1   *Scotland on Sunday*, 18 October 1998, quoted in Elinor Kelly, 'Racism, Police and the Courts in Scotland', *Scottish Affairs*, 30, Winter 2000.

2   See, for example, the detailed commentary on the Scottish Executive's action plan published by the Commission for Racial Equality for Scotland, 1999.

3   Lord Hardie, QC, keynote address at the Leading the Way Forward conference, Aberdeen, June 1999.

4   Official terminology was until recently 'racial', not 'racist'. It has changed as a result of a recommendation in the Lawrence Inquiry report and valuably ensures that the concept of racism is part of legal discourse. Reported racist incidents for all police forces in England and Wales are shown for each year since 1993/94 in *Race Equality in Public Services*, Home Office, March 2000, Annex E.

5   See *British Crime Survey* statistics and, for example, Tricia Hamm, *Racial Harassment: just a part of life*, 1997.

6   Reports by HM Inspectorate of Constabulary in recent years have been strongly critical of police insensitivity and ignorance when reports about racist incidents are made to them – see *Winning the Race: policing plural communities*, 1997, *Winning the Race Revisited*, 1999, *Policing London – Winning Consent*, 2000. The new Home Office guidance is entitled *Code of Practice on Reporting and Recording Racist Incidents* and was formulated as part of the government's response to the Stephen Lawrence Inquiry report.

7   Much official discussion, however, refers to 'racially motivated crime'

as if the distinguishing feature were essentially to do with motivation. See, for example, the autumn 1997 consultation paper issued by the Home Office.

8   See Maleiha Malik, '"Racist crime": racially aggravated offences in the Crime and Disorder Act 1998', *Modern Law Review*, May 1999, and Bhikhu Parekh, *Racial Violence – A Separate Offence?*, 1994.

9   *Report on the Reporting and Recording of Racist Incidents*, July 1999, giving clear and detailed guidance on the recording of both crimes and non-crimes.

10   See, for example, Kusminder Chahal and Louis Julienne, *'We Can't All Be White!' – racist victimisation in the UK*, 1999. There are quotations from this report in Box 5.1.

11   This point is illustrated at length in *The Perpetrators of Racial Harassment and Racial Violence*, Research Study 176, Home Office, 1997.

12   Chapter 5, paragraphs 5.5–5.16.

13   Home Office, *Correctional Policy Framework*, 2000.

14   The Frankfurt project, funded by the European Commission's Cities Against Racism Project in 1996–8, led to a publication in English, *Talk to them? No way!*, published by the Frankfurt Peace Research Institute, 1998.

15   Home Office, *Report of Policy Action Team 6: Neighbourhood Wardens*, 2000, quoted in Cabinet Office, *Minority Ethnic Issues in Social Exclusion and Neighbourhood Renewal*, 2000.

16   For example, the work in Greenwich described in Roger Hewitt, *Routes of Racism*, 1996, and the projects described in Rae Sibbitt, *The Perpetrators of Racial Harassment and Racial Violence*, 1997.

17   The principal sources are the annual Home Office publication *Statistics on Race and the Criminal Justice System*; Roger Hood, *Race and Sentencing*, 1992; Home Office Statistical Bulletin 6/98, *Ethnicity and Victimisation*; Home Office Research Study No. 185, *A Survey of Police Arrests and Their Outcomes*; the Home Office bulletin by Gordon Barclay and Bonny Mhlanga, *Ethnic Differences in Decisions on Young Defendants Dealt with by the Crown Prosecution Service*, published as Section 95 Findings No. 1 in 1999; *Prison Statistics England and Wales 1998*, Home Office, 1999. Statistics for Irish people are for those born in Ireland – they do not include the second and subsequent generations. For fuller discussion see Mary Hickman and Bronwen Walter, *Discrimination and the Irish Community in Britain*, 1997, pp. 124–8.

18   See, for example, John Graham and Ben Bowling, *Young People and*

Crime, Home Office, 1996, and David Farrington, 'Human development and criminal careers', in M. Maguire, R. Morgan and R. Reiner (eds), *The Oxford Handbook of Criminology*, 1994. For anecdotal accounts of young black men's life-experiences see *This Is Where I Live: problems and pressures in Brixton*, Runnymede Trust, 1996.

19   The research is conveniently summarised in NACRO's publication *Let's Get It Right: race and justice*, 2000. This includes references to several other sources, of which the most comprehensive is Marian Fitzgerald, *Ethnic Minorities and the Criminal Justice System*, prepared for the Royal Commission on Criminal Justice in 1993.

20   Barbara Hudson, 'Punishment, blame and ethnicity: understanding discrimination in criminal justice', prepared for the Commission on the Future of Multi-Ethnic Britain.

21   Acquittal rates in contested cases are higher for black and Asian defendants than for white both at magistrates' courts and at the crown court – see Barclay and Mhlanga, op. cit. The data are from 1996 and are for persons aged under 22. The higher acquittal rates for black defendants show that their reluctance or refusal to plead guilty is well founded. But if someone pleads not guilty yet is found guilty, the sentence is likely to be heavier.

22   For full discussions see Lord Windlesham, *Responses to Crime Volume 3: legislating with the tide*, 1996, and *Politics, Punishment and Populism*, 1998.

23   For example, Charles Murray, *The Emerging Underclass*, 1990, and *The Underclass: the crisis deepens*, 1994, both published by the Institute for Economic Affairs (IEA). *Charles Murray and the Underclass* was published by the IEA in 1996. The *Sunday Times* published high-profile articles by Murray on 5, 12 and 19 January 1997. Murray's best-selling book *The Bell Curve*, 1996, co-authored with Richard Herrnstein, claimed that people of African descent have lower intelligence than those of other backgrounds.

24   At the most recent count (autumn 1998) the number of prisoners per 100,000 population in England and Wales was 126 and in Scotland 117. Within Europe only Portugal (144) had a higher number. The figure for the United States was 668. France had 89, Italy 87, The Netherlands 75 and Sweden 60. Source: Philip White, *The Prison Population in 1998, a statistical review*, Home Office Research Findings No. 94, 1999.

25   These statistics are all quoted in Loic Wacquant, 'From welfare state to prison state: imprisoning the American poor', April 2000, and are

taken from publications of the Bureau of Justice Statistics of the Federal Department of Justice. The estimate of unemployment is from 'How unregulated is the US labor market? – the penal system as a labor market institution', presentation to the annual congress of the American Sociological Association, 1997. See also Jerome G. Miller, *Search and Destroy: African-American males in the criminal justice system*, 1997. Other key texts include Mark Mauer, *Young Black Americans and the Criminal Justice System: a growing national problem*, 1995, and a follow-up study five years later, both published by the Sentencing Project, Washington, DC.

26   The story as told here is from CRE press release 714, 19 April 2000.

27   See Box 5.2 in Chapter 5.

28   Notoriously, swift responses to grievance are not common. The Lawrence family had to wait almost five years for the Macpherson Inquiry to be set up. Others have had to wait much longer; cf, for example, the Guildford Four, the Marchioness sinking and Bloody Sunday.

29   Reprinted in the appendices of *Race Equality in Public Services*, Home Office, March 2000.

30   See *Equal Treatment Bench Book: race and the courts*, Judicial Studies Board, with a foreword by the Lord Chief Justice, September 1999. A summary version is available entitled *Race and the Courts: a short practical guide for judges*, with an introduction by Mr Justice Keene.

31   National Association for the Care and Resettlement of Offenders, *Let's Get It Right: race and justice*, 2000.

32   RESPOND is a programme entitled Racial Equality for Staff and Prisoners. It was adopted in December 1998 and launched at the Prison Service conference in 1999.

33   Sylvia Denman, *Race Discrimination in the Crown Prosecution Service*, April 2000.

34   For a valuable discussion of legitimacy in the prison service see Richard Sparks, Anthony Bottoms and Will Hay, *Prisons and the Problem of Order*, 1996.

35   Information about the Imran Khan case is taken from reporting in the *Herald* between 26 September and 15 October 1998, as quoted in Elinor Kelly, 'Racism, Police and the Courts in Scotland', *Scottish Affairs*, 30, Winter 2000.

11 **Education**

1 The 12th periodic report of the UK Government to the United Nations in relation to the Convention on the Elimination of all forms of Racial Discrimination (CERD), paragraph 153, 1991.

2 The story was told in detail in a chapter by Sally Tomlinson in Anna King and Michael Reiss (eds), *The Multicultural Dimension of the National Curriculum*, 1993.

3 With regard to Scotland, see, for example, *Improving Our Schools: a consultation paper on national priorities for schools education in Scotland*, summer 2000. There is a section entitled 'An inclusive system', but no reference in this to issues of race and cultural diversity. However, in Scotland the Race Equality Advisory Forum was in June 2000 compiling an action plan on issues of race equality in education.

4 The first unions in England to provide guidance for their members were the Assistant Masters and Mistresses Association (now the ATL) and the National Union of Teachers. AMMA published *Multi-Cultural and Anti-Racist Education Today* in 1987. The NUT's Antiracist Curriculum Guidelines were widely influential in the early 1990s, as were the racism awareness training courses it organised through most of the 1980s.

5 For example, *Equality in Education: planning for change*, Slough Borough Council, 1999.

6 The students quoted in Box 11.1 refer to the impact of black staff. For further material on this and also on the need not only to recruit but also to retain, support and promote black staff, see Audrey Osler, *The Education and Careers of Black Teachers: Changing Identities, Changing Lives*, 1997.

7 The Rampton Report, *West Indian Children in our Schools*, 1981, p. 83.

8 Cited in *Education and Race*, a sound summary of research findings issued in 1999 by NAS/UWT. The research basis for the estimate was contained in the survey for Ofsted reported by Gillborn and Gipps, 1996. There is, of course, a wealth of qualitative data, from both communities themselves and practitioners. Examples relating to refugee education include Michael Marland, 'Refugee Pupils; A Headteacher's Perspective', *Multicultural Teaching*, autumn 1998, Jeanette Redding (ed.), *The Refugee Education Handbook*, 1999, and Meron Abebaw and colleagues, *Let's Spell It Out*, Save the Children, 1998.

9   Ofsted, *Raising the Attainment of Minority Ethnic Pupils – School and LEA Responses*, 1999.

10 In February 2000 the DfEE published *Removing the Barriers*. Three of its 26 pages were devoted to monitoring. These stressed the importance of monitoring, but did not give the kind of detailed guidance that schools need and did not warn against the pitfalls to avoid.

11 For example, when the Ethnic Minority Achievement Grant (EMAG) started in 1999, local authorities were required to provide data on achievement by ethnicity but not by gender.

12 Research has been valuably summarised in David Gillborn and Deborah Youdell, *Rationing Education: policy, practice, reform and equity*, 2000. See also the study in Robin Richardson and Angela Wood, *Inclusive Schools, Inclusive Society*, 1999. The research it reports was sponsored by the London-based organisation Race On The Agenda (ROTA). See further Shalini Pathak, *Race Research for the Future: Ethnicity in Education, Training and the Labour Market*, 2000, and Zubaida Haque, 'The Ethnic Minority "Underachieving" Group? – investigating the claims of "underachievement" among Bangladeshi pupils in British secondary schools', *Race, Ethnicity and Education*, June 2000.

13 DfEE press release dated 10 March 1999, leading to headlines such as 'Schools Failing Black Pupils'. The figure of 29 per cent A*–Cs was given for 'black' pupils, that is, both African-Caribbean and African clustered together with no differentiation. The figure was repeated in the Home Office's publication of March 2000, *Race Equality in Public Services*, and again there was no acknowledgement that both African-Caribbean and African pupils were included.

14 Arthur Ivatts, HMI, in his Afterword to Jean-Pierre Liegeois, *School Provision for Ethnic Minorities: The Gypsy Paradigm*, 1998, Centre de recherches tsiganes, Hatfield, University of Hertfordshire Press, quoted in Rachel Morris and Luke Clements (eds), *Gaining Ground: Law Reform for Gypsies and Travellers*, 1999.

15 Royce Turner, 'Gypsies and Politics in Britain', in *The Political Quarterly*, 2000.

16 The UCAS figures were analysed for us by Dr Roger Ballard, University of Manchester.

17 The 12 most favoured universities, according to a survey carried out in 1996, were said to be Birmingham, Bristol, Cambridge, Durham,

Edinburgh, Leeds, Loughborough, Manchester, Nottingham, Oxford, UMIST and Warwick. Only one new university – Glasgow Caledonian – featured in the top 25. (*The Times*, 20 August 1996.) On 8 April 2000 the *Financial Times* published a league table of universities which contained not a single former polytechnic in the top 50. The Robert Gordon University, Aberdeen, was the highest-ranking new university at 55.

18   For fuller discussion see T. Modood and T. Acland (eds), *Race and Higher Education: opportunities, experiences and challenges*, 1998.

19   Following the government's failure to issue such guidance, recalled in the first paragraph of this chapter, the Runnymede Trust consulted widely with teachers and lecturers and published *Equality Assurance in Schools* in 1993. This now needs updating, and as far as possible needs to be relevant UK-wide, not just in England. In Scotland CERES (Centre for Education for Racial Equality in Scotland) has published *Bilingualism, Community Languages and Scottish Education: a challenge for policy makers and practitioners in a devolved Scotland*, 1999.

20   Long out of print, but still one of the most important analyses of anti-racist education in Britain. For discussion of the Burnage Inquiry see also David Gillborn, *Racism and Antiracism in Real Schools*, 1995, A. Sivanandan, *Communities of Resistance*, 1990, and Barry Troyna and Richard Hatcher, *Racism in Children's Lives*, 1992.

21   Laurie Fellows, in Lord Swann, *Education for All*, 1985, p. 281.

22   Ofsted, *Raising the Attainment of Minority Ethnic Pupils*, 1999, p. 21, paragraph 81. The DfEE does not include an evaluation of EMTAG (see below) in the list of research projects for 2000 for which it has invited expressions of interest.

23   The scheme is now known as EMTAG, the additional letter referring to traveller pupils. A press release from the DfEE (247/00) in June 2000 reveals that from 2001 all Standard Funds grants will be collapsed into just 12 headings. It seems likely that EMTAG will come under the broad rubric of Social Exclusion.

24   Maud Blair, Jill Bourne et al., *Making the Difference: teaching and learning strategies in successful multi-ethnic schools*, 1998. For the importance of schools respecting learners and parents, and developing structures for their participation in schools, see also, for example, Audrey Osler, *Exclusion from School and Racial Equality*, 1997.

25   See, for example, the case studies in *Newsletter: Exclusions Update*, the bi-monthly bulletin of the Working Group Against Racism in

Children's Resources.

26 See M. Abdelrazack and M. Kemadoo (eds), *Directory of Supplementary and Mother-tongue Classes*, 1999. For an account of African-Caribbean schools, and the key role played in them by women, see Heidi Safia Mirza and Diane Reay, 'Redefining citizenship: black women educators and the third space', in M. Arnot (ed.), *Challenging Democracy: feminist perspectives on the education of citizens*, 2000.

27 The conference was organised by the Centre for Education for Racial Equality in Scotland (CERES). A report was forwarded to the Scottish Race Equality Advisory Forum (REAF).

28 Audit Unit and South Ayrshire Council, *A Route to Equality and Fairness: self-evaluation using performance indicators*, 1999.

29 In early 2000 Ofsted issued *Educational Inclusion and School Inspection*, a brief summary of its approach. Race equality issues appear to be a subset of a subset – race equality is a subset of equal opportunities, and this in turn is a subset of addressing social exclusion. See also Audrey Osler and Marlene Morrison, *Inspecting Schools for Race Equality: OFSTED's Strengths and Weaknesses*, 2000.

30 The research in Britain is well described in Chapter 2 of Gillborn and Youdell, op. cit. See also Sharon Gewirtz, *Markets, Choice and Equity in Education*, 1995. In a study of 1,560 schools in 1994, *Thirty Years On*, 1996, Caroline Benn and Clive Chitty found there were distinct social class differences between schools with black and Asian students and those without.

31 Gillborn and Youdell, op. cit., p. 197.

32 Ibid, passim.

33 Sally Tomlinson, 'Sociological Perspectives on Failing Schools', *International Studies in Sociology of Education*, 1997.

12 **Arts, Media and Sport**

1 Exceptions to this generalisation of course include Celtic and Everton football clubs, founded by and for Irish communities in Britain, and widespread support for cricket teams from India, Pakistan and the West Indies.

2 Our discussion in the following paragraphs draws partly on Stuart Hall, 'Unsettling the Heritage: re-imagining the post-nation', in *Whose Heritage?*, Department of Culture, Media and Sport, November 1999.

3   John Ezard, 'Empire show arouses pride and prejudice', *Guardian*, 23 August 1999.

4   For detailed discussions of the themes in this paragraph see, among many others, Edward Said, *Culture and Imperialism*, 1993, and Marina Warner's 1995 Reith lectures, *Managing Monsters*.

5   For a wide-ranging review of contemporary Asian and black writers see Maya Jaggi, 'From Writing Back to Rewriting Britain', in *Whose Heritage?*, op. cit. There are many valuable discussions of African and African-Caribbean art, literature and culture in modern Britain in Kwesi Owusu (ed.), *Black British Culture and Society: a text reader*, 2000.

6   Marcia Hutchinson, *The Journey*, 1999. The project involved photography as well as oral history and was funded largely by the Joseph Rowntree Charitable Trust. It was also supported by Yorkshire Arts and had a strong local focus in Kirklees.

7   For a fine, vivid summary of contemporary history in Britain, set within an international context, see *Homebeats*, a CD-ROM produced by the Institute of Race Relations in 1996 and reissued with updatings in 1999.

8   Richard Norton-Taylor, *The Colour of Justice*, 1999.

9   There is a useful summary of research findings in Annabelle Sreberny's report *Include Me In*, published by the Broadcasting Standards Commission in conjunction with the Independent Television Commission, December 1999.

10   The link between specific news items and contextualising large narratives has been well documented over the years by the Dutch scholar Teun van Dijk, for example in *Racism and the Press*, 1991.

11   Reported to the Commission by the Muslim Council of Britain.

12   *Guardian*, 1 March 1999.

13   Robert Henderson, 'Is It in the Blood?', *Wisden Cricket Monthly*, July 1995, pp. 9–10.

14   See Ian McDonald and Sharda Ugra, 'It's Just Not Cricket: ethnicity, division and imagining the other in English cricket', in Phil Cohen (ed.), *New Ethnicities, Old Racisms*, 1999.

15   Jas Bains and Sanjiv Johal, *Corner Flags and Corner Shops: the Asian football experience*, 1999.

13 Health and Welfare

1 The episode referred to here is narrated and discussed in detail in *An Investigation into Conditional Organ Donation*, the report of a panel chaired by Chris Kelly, published by the Department of Health (DoH), February 2000.

2 *Guardian*, 24 February 2000.

3 See Box 5.2 in Chapter 5 for a summary of the interacting components of institutional racism. All these components were seen in this episode.

4 We received documentation from health authorities throughout England, Scotland and Wales showing that race equality issues are being taken seriously by the NHS, both as an employer and as a service provider. The then Secretary of State for Health, Frank Dobson, condemned the behaviour of health professionals in relation to the conditional organ donation referred to in the opening paragraphs of this chapter, and set up the investigation whose report is quoted.

5 Ziggi Alexander, *Study of Black, Asian and Ethnic Minority Issues*, DoH, 1999, and *Recruitment and Selection of Doctors*, BMA Career Progress of Doctors Committee, 2000.

6 Will Hutton, Commission on the National Health Service, *New Life for Health*, Vintage, 2000. One principle reads: 'The governance, service delivery and employment practices of the NHS should recognise the diverse, multi-ethnic and multi-cultural nature of British society and should aim both to promote equality and to monitor equality outcomes.'

7 *Bringing Britain Together: a national strategy for neighbourhood renewal*, Social Exclusion Unit, September 1999.

8 See, for example, S. Harding and R. Balarajan, 'Patterns of mortality in second generation Irish living in England and Wales: longitudinal study', *British Medical Journal (BMJ)*, No. 312, June 1996; also John Haskey, 'Mortality among second generation Irish in England and Wales' in the same issue.

9 Their report was discussed in an article in the *Guardian*, March 2000.

10 *The Health of Refugee Children – Guidelines for Paediatricians*, Royal College of Paediatricians and Child Health, November 1999, and *The Health of Refugees – A Guide for GPs*, King's Fund, 1999.

11 Richard Berthoud, *Social Security and Race: an agenda*, Policy Studies Institute, 1987.

12 R. Balarajan and Soni V. Raleigh, *Ethnicity and Health in England*, 1995.

13 Ibid.

14 Tariq Modood, Richard Berthoud et al., *Ethnic Minorities in Britain: diversity and disadvantage*, 1997.

15 Balarajan and Raleigh, op. cit.

16 Ibid.

17 K. Rudat, *Health and lifestyle: black and minority ethnic groups in England*, London Health Education Authority, 1994; J. Naish, J. Brown, B. Denton, 'Intercultural consultations: investigation of factors that deter non-English speaking women from attending their general practitioners for cervical screening', *BMJ*, 1994, pp. 1126–8.

18 J. Atri et al., 'Improving uptake of breast screening in multi-ethnic populations: a randomised controlled trial using practice reception staff to contact non-attendees', *BMJ*, November 1997.

19 James Nazroo, *The Health of Britain's Ethnic Minorities: findings from a national survey*, Policy Studies Institute, 1997.

20 *The New NHS – Modern and Dependable: A National Framework for Assessing Performance*, DoH, January 1998.

21 *Modernising Health and Social Services: Priority Guidance 2000/01–2002/03*, DoH, 1999.

22 *The Race Equality Agenda of the Department of Health*, DoH, January 2000.

23 *National Service Framework for Mental Health*, DoH, September 1999.

24 'Policy Appraisal for Equal Treatment', Cabinet Office, 1998.

25 Alexander, op. cit.

26 Mark Johnson, 'Involvement of black and ethnic minority consumers in health research', Mary Seacole Research Centre, De Montfort University, September 1998.

27 From April 2002 primary care groups will be known as primary care trusts.

28 'Ethnic Inequalities in Health in Birmingham: main findings', Birmingham Health Authority, 1999, cited in Alexander, op. cit.

29 Kamlesh Patel, director, Ethnicity and Health Unit, Central Lancashire University, cited in the *Guardian*, March 2000.

30 *Milan Committee Review of the Mental Health Act (Scotland)*, Second Consultation, Scottish Executive, May 2000.

31 *Sick of Being Excluded*, Health and Social Exclusion Report of the Association of London Government, April 2000.

32 *Protecting Children from Racism and Racial Abuse*, NSPCC, 1999.

33 Ravinder Barn et al., *Acting on Principle*, British Agencies for Adoption and Fostering, 1997.

34 Ibid.

35 Naina Patel, 'Ageing with Care'. A paper written for the Commission.

36 James Nazroo, 'Rethinking the Relationship Between Ethnicity and Mental Health', *Social Psychiatry and Psychiatric Epidemiology*, April 1998.

37 S. P. Singh et al., 'Perceived Ethnicity and the Risk of Compulsory Admission', *Social Psychiatry and Psychiatric Epidemiology*, January 1998, quoted in Alexander, op. cit.

38 'The Stephen Lawrence Inquiry: what now for social services?', *Community Care*, March 1999. Cited in Alexander, op. cit.

39 J. Gluckman, in Dinesh Bhugra (ed.), *Ethnicity: an Agenda for Mental Health*, 1999, cited in Alexander, op. cit.

40 Alexander, op. cit.

41 'Nursing: have you got what it takes?', in *Supporting Diversity*, DoH (undated).

42 White Paper, 'Making a Difference', DoH, 1999, quoted in Alexander, op. cit.

43 I. C. McManus, A. Esmail and M. Demetriou, 'Factors affecting the likelihood of applicants being offered a place in medical schools in the United Kingdom in 1996 and 1997: a retrospective study', *BMJ*, October 1998.

44 Celia Roberts et al., 'Oral examinations – equal opportunities, ethnicity and fairness in the MRCGP', *BMJ*, February 2000.

45 Correspondence, *BMJ*, 31 May 1997.

46 Nicole Veash and J. Carlowe, 'Ethnic doctors "disciplined more harshly"', *Observer*, April 1999.

47 Aneez Esmail, Sam Everington and Helen Doyle, 'Racial discrimination in the allocation of distinction awards?', *BMJ*, January 1998.

48 Ibid.

49 Alexander, op. cit.

50 Ibid.

51 Ibid.

52 Ibid.

53 Ibid.

54 *The Race Equality Agenda of the Department of Health*, DoH, January 2000.

14 **Employment**

1   The most convenient and comprehensive source of data on
    employment is provided by Tariq Modood, Richard Berthoud et al.,
    Ethnic Minorities in Britain: diversity and disadvantage, 1997. For a
    recent authoritative restatement of the problems, see *Jobs for All*,
    published in November 1999 by the Department for Education and
    Employment. Among other things this contains the most up-to-date
    data yet available on employment and unemployment in African,
    African-Caribbean, Bangladeshi, Indian and Pakistani communities.
    However, it does not contain data on Irish people, and it does not
    disaggregate Scotland and Wales.
2   A. Heath and D. McMahon, 'Educational and Occupational
    Attainments: the impact of ethnic origins', in Valerie Karn (ed.),
    Education, Employment and Housing among Ethnic Minorities in Britain,
    1997.
3   Richard Berthoud, *Incomes of Ethnic Minorities*, 1998.
4   *Applications to Universities and Colleges in the UK*, UCAS, 1998. Fifty-six
    per cent of Indian women in the cohort and 49 per cent of Indian men
    were studying A levels. This compared with 34 per cent of white
    women and 27 per cent of white men.
5   Mary Hickman and Bronwen Walter, *Discrimination and the Irish
    Community in Britain*, 1997.
6   *Labour Force Survey*, spring 1998 to winter 1998/99. The data for black
    and Asian people is based on low samples and may therefore be
    unreliable, but is consistent with Modood et al., 1997.
7   The research is summarised in greater detail in John Wrench and Tariq
    Modood, *The Effectiveness of Employment Equity Policies in Relation to
    Immigrants and Ethnic Minorities in the UK*, International Labour
    Office, Geneva, 2000.
8   For example, the research by Esmail and Everington on appointments
    in the health service, referred to in Chapter 13, Notes 43 and 47. For a
    discussion of ethical issues in such research see Michael Banton, 'The
    Ethics of Practice-Testing', *New Community*, 1997.
9   '*We Regret to Inform You ...*', Commission for Racial Equality, 1996.
10 The use of gatekeepers has been strongly criticised by the Commission
    for Racial Equality and is now generally accepted to be a potential form
    of indirect discrimination. Nevertheless, it is still widespread, as
    confirmed by the government's policy action team on jobs, autumn

1999. The principal research on gatekeepers was undertaken in the 1980s.

11   *'We Regret to Inform You ...'*, op. cit.

12   See John Wrench, Edgar Hassan and David Owen, *Ambition and Marginalisation*, 1996, and John Wrench, Tarek Qureshi and David Owen, *Higher Horizons*, 1996. Also Modood et al., op. cit., showing that about 20 per cent of black and Asian people believe discrimination in the labour market to be widespread.

13   House of Commons Northern Ireland Affairs Committee Fourth Report (1998/99 session), paragraphs 37–55; see too Bob Hepple, Mary Coussey and Tufyal Choudhury, *Equality: a new framework*, summer 2000, Appendix 1.

14   Better Regulation Task Force, *Review of Anti-Discrimination Legislation*, 1999.

15   *Jobs for All*, op. cit., p. 69.

16   In saying this we are endorsing the first and most essential recommendation of *Jobs for All*, op. cit.

17   Amendments in 2000 to the Race Relations Act place statutory duties on employers in the public sector only, and do not specify the production of equity plans.

18   These features of an employment equity plan are derived in part from the Policy Action Team on Jobs, recommendation 28.

19   For fuller discussion see Chapter 19 and Hepple et al., op. cit.

20   The data are summarised by Wrench and Modood, op. cit.

21   Cited in Bank of England, *The Financing of Ethnic Minority Firms in the United Kingdom*, 1999. See also London TEC Council, *Strength through Diversity: ethnic minorities in London's economy*, 1999. The term 'small business' refers to firms with fewer than 50 employees. The term 'Asian and black businesses' refers to firms whose owners are Asian or black.

22   Bank of England, op. cit. A small-scale survey of South Asian newsagents in London, published in 1999, found that no one had sought advice from a business advice agency.

23   These recommendations are derived from HM Treasury, *Report of Policy Action Team 3: Enterprise and Social Exclusion*, 1999.

24   Bank of England, op. cit.

25   The London TEC Council found in 1999 that 8 per cent of Asian and black businesses in London operate in EU or international markets compared with 5 per cent of white businesses.

26   See Asian Business Initiative, *Newsagents Mean Business*, 1999.

27 The research is summarised in Monder Ram and Trevor Jones, *Ethnic Minorities in Business*, 1998.

28 Asian Business Initiative, op. cit.

15 **Immigration and Asylum**

1 British citizens, British Overseas citizens, British Dependent Territories citizens, British subjects and British Protected Persons. In 1987, a sixth category, British Nationals (Overseas), was added for British nationals in Hong Kong without rights of entry.

2 Report by the Joint Council for the Welfare of Immigrants, 1985.

3 Note on immigration policy and administration, 19 July 1983: brief for incoming ministers prepared by the Immigration and Nationality Division and endorsed by the Home Secretary (quoted in the *Guardian*, 21 March 1985).

4 See, for example, SOPEMI, *Trends in International Migration*, 1998. For further discussion about these issues see Jeremy Harding, *The Uninvited*, 2000, and Nigel Harris, *The New Untouchables: Immigration and the New World Worker*, 1995.

5 See *Providing protection*, 1997, produced jointly by JUSTICE, the Immigration Law Practitioners Association and the Asylum Rights Campaign.

6 See, for example, The Refugee Council, *Response to 'Fairer, Faster and Firmer – A Modern Approach to Immigration and Asylum'*, October 1998.

7 Heaven Crowley, *Breaking Down the Barriers. A report on the conduct of asylum interviews at ports*, Immigration Law Practitioners Association, 1999.

8 Audit Commission, *Another Country: implementing dispersal under the Immigration and Asylum Act 1999*, June 2000.

9 *A consultation paper on the integration of recognised refugees in the UK*, October 1999.

10 Quoted by Edie Friedman in 'Asylum Madness', *Jewish Chronicle*, 4 June 1999.

11 Audit Commission, op. cit.

16 **Politics and Representation**

1   The project was organised by Operation Black Vote, in partnership
      with the 1990 Trust and the Commission for Racial Equality. Papers
      about it include Simon Woolley, 'Ignore us at your peril', *Guardian*, 19
      August 1999.

2   For discussions of deliberative democracy see Anne Phillips, *The
      Politics of Presence*, 1995, and the same author's *Which Equalities
      Matter?*, 1999; also Iris Marion Young, *Justice and the Politics of
      Difference*, 1990, and Amy Gutmann and Dennis Thompson,
      Democracy and Disagreement, 1996.

3   For a discussion of this as a pan-European trend see Immanuel
      Wallerstein, 'The Albatross of Racism', *London Review of Books*, May
      2000.

4   Infamously, 'If you want a nigger for a neighbour, vote Labour'.

5   On the use of law and order issues for electoral purposes see Lord
      Windlesham, *Politics, Punishment and Populism*, 1998.

6   He received 2 per cent of the votes in the first preference round and 3.2
      per cent (but of a smaller total) in the second. If it is assumed that no
      Asian and black people voted for the BNP, and if the turnout rate was
      much the same across all communities, about 6 per cent of all white
      voters included the BNP as their first or second choice.

7   Published by the Commission for Racial Equality, drawing in part on
      ideas in *Political Speech and Race Relations in a Liberal Democracy*,
      published by the Liberal Democrats in 1993. A key passage is quoted,
      but with modifications to show its relevance to the media, in Chapter 12.

8   Quoted in an article by Andrew Lansley, *Observer*, 10 December 1995.

9   Andrew Lansley, 'Accentuate the negative to win again', *Observer*, 3
      September 1995.

10   The Maples Memorandum, as it came to be known, was quoted at
      length in an article by Roger Preston in the *Financial Times*, 21
      November 1994.

11   In April 2000, in the run-up to local elections in parts of England,
      there were denunciations of 'politically correct' policing and racism
      awareness training. Also, opposition to political correctness was used
      to dismiss objections to the term 'bogus asylum seekers'.

12   *Racism and Xenophobia in Europe*, European Commission, 1997.

13   Reported in Yasmin Alibhai-Brown, *True Colours*, 1999.

14   Apart from the first, these strategies correspond to the options

available to youth workers and teachers trying to change the attitudes and behaviour of individuals and groups, as discussed in Rae Sibbitt, *The Perpetrators of Racial Harassment and Racial Violence*, 1997, pp. 104–6. Her report provides case studies of the fourth approach and a substantial rationale for it.

15   For fuller discussion of such measures see Sarah Spencer, 'The Impact of Immigration Policy on Race Relations', in T. Blackstone et al. (eds), *Race Relations in Britain: a developing agenda*, 1998, and Alibhai-Brown, op. cit.

16   There is comprehensive information in Muhammad Anwar, *Race and Elections*, 1994.

17   For a detailed analysis of the 1997 election see Shamit Saggar, *The General Election 1997: ethnic minorities and electoral politics*, 1998: 93 per cent of the black vote was for Labour, 86 per cent of the Pakistani vote, 84 per cent of the Bangladeshi and 80 per cent of the Indian. But a study in Bradford West found that the majority of Pakistanis (61 per cent) voted for the Conservative candidate compared with the Labour Party candidate's 35 per cent. For the Indians the pattern was just the opposite: 74 per cent voted for the Labour Party candidate and 23 per cent for the Conservative. This was almost certainly connected with the ethnicity of the candidates, for the Labour Party fielded someone of Indian background and the Conservative Party someone of Pakistani background. See Muhammad Anwar, *Ethnic Minorities and the British Electoral System*, 1998.

18   Gutmann and Thompson, op. cit., p. 83.

19   The Shadow Home Secretary was quoted in May 2000 as saying that the emergence of black and Asian MPs should be left to 'time and tide': see Gary Young, 'A Shadow without a Doubt', *Connections*, Commission for Racial Equality, May 2000.

20   The research cited here is reported in Jessica Adolino, 'Integration within the British Political Parties: perceptions of ethnic minority councillors', in S. Saggar (ed.), *Race and British Electoral Politics*, 1998. Research in Birmingham in the 1990s revealed extremely hostile attitudes towards Asian politicians among white Labour Party members and officials. It was reported in John Solomos and Les Back, *Race, Politics and Social Change*, 1995.

21   Adolino, op. cit.

22   *Local Leadership, Local Choice*, Department of the Environment, Transport and the Regions, March 1999.

23 These points are derived from the results of a consultation undertaken by the Home Office in 1999, as summarised in the report *Strengthening the Black and Minority Ethnic Voluntary Sector Infrastructure*. There is further discussion of consultation and partnership in Chapter 20.

24 Gutmann and Thompson, op. cit., p. 83.

17 **Religion and Belief**

1 Department of the Environment, Transport and the Regions, *Involving Communities in Urban and Rural Regeneration: a guide for practitioners*, 1997.

2 The report has been commissioned from the University of Derby and is due in autumn 2000. An interim report, published in January 2000, indicates that the research has great potential to take theoretical debate further and to clarify practical options for new legislative and non-legislative action.

3 The full list in the Article is sex, racial or ethnic origin, religion or belief, disability, age or sexual orientation.

4 The Scotland Act 1998 refers to 'the prevention of ... discrimination between persons on grounds of ... beliefs or opinions, such as religious beliefs or political persuasions'. (Schedule 5, Part II L2.) The Greater London Authority Act places a duty on the Authority, the Metropolitan Police Authority and the London Fire and Emergency Planning Authority 'to promote equality of opportunity for all persons irrespective of their ... religion', and to 'promote good relations between persons of different ... religious beliefs'.

5 All estimates of active and community membership are from Peter Brierley (ed.), 'Religious Trends No. 2', *UK Christian Handbook*, 1999. The estimates are disputed, however, by other organisations. See Appendix A of the Runnymede Trust report on Islamophobia (1997) for estimates of the size of Muslim communities.

6 Tariq Modood and Richard Berthoud et al., *Ethnic Minorities in Britain*, 1997. See, for example, Table 9.7 on Importance of Religion and Table 9.8 on Attendance at Religious Service.

7 Quoted in the Runnymede report, op. cit., p. 39.

8 Paragraph 229 in the UK government's 15th periodic report to the UN Committee on the Elimination of all forms of Racial Discrimination (CERD), summer 1999.

9   House of Lords Select Committee on the European Union, *EU Proposals to Combat Discrimination*, 16 May 2000, paragraph 75. Several speakers in the debate stressed that religious organisations must be allowed to discriminate on religious grounds; that this freedom needs, however, to be limited; and that drawing the line in this respect will often be extremely complex.

10   Lord Ahmed proposed the following definition: 'a system of beliefs and activities centred around the worship of God which is derived in whole or in part from a book revealed by God to one of His messengers'. House of Lords, 28 October 1999, Hansard, Column 457. This definition would not, of course, be acceptable to non-theists, for example Buddhists and Jains, or indeed to any religion which does not share Islamic beliefs about divine messengers and revealed texts.

11   *Preliminary Conclusions: seminar on religion and the integration of immigrants*, Council of Europe, 1999. For a substantial discussion of legal approaches in various countries to the issue of defining religion see Tufyal Choudhury, *Discrimination on Grounds of Religious Belief*, Centre for Public Law, University of Cambridge, January 2000.

12   This was one of the findings of a survey conducted in autumn 1999 by the Commission on British Muslims and Islamophobia.

13   The Policy Studies Institute research found that 40 per cent of South Asians of all religions who had experienced discrimination believed that hostility to their religion had played a part.

14   The Commission on British Muslims and Islamophobia report, op. cit., cites several examples, pp. 47–9.

15   This point is argued in, for example, Yasmin Alibhai-Brown, *After Multiculturalism*, 2000.

16   James Macmillan, 'Scotland's Shame', in Tim Devine (ed.), *Scotland's Shame? – bigotry and sectarianism in modern Scotland*, 2000, p. 15.

17   The Wakeham Report, Royal Commission on the Reform of the House of Lords, *A House for the Future*. See also the reference to this report in Chapter 16.

18   James Beckford and Sophie Gilliat, *Religion in Prison: 'equal rites' in a multi-faith society*, 1998.

19   See, for example, Sebastian Poulter, *Ethnicity, Law and Human Rights*, 1998, pp. 205–8.

20   James Beckford and Sophie Gilliat, *The Church of England and Other Faiths in a Multi-Faith Society*, 1996.

21   Colin Buchanan, Bishop of Woolwich, *Guardian*, 15 April 2000. See

also the same author's *Cut the Connection: disestablishment and the Church of England*, 1994.

22   See Jonathan Sacks, *The Persistence of Faith*, 1991, and Tariq Modood, *Church, State and Religious Minorities*, 1997.

23   The Chadwick Commission, 1970. The chair, Professor Owen Chadwick, was a distinguished Church historian.

24   See, for example, an account of inter-faith co-operation in Bradford hospitals by Christopher Lewis, 'Religion and Spiritual Care', *Theology*, October 1999. In London, the An-Nisa Society has pioneered a course on Islamic Counselling in partnership with Brent Adult Education Services, Brent and Harrow Health Authority, and North West London Mental Health Trust.

25   Patrick Reilly, 'Kicking with the Left Foot: being Catholic in Scotland', in Devine, op. cit.

26   James Macmillan, 'I Had Not Thought about It Like That Before', in Devine, op. cit., pp. 269–70.

27   For fuller discussion of this point see Maleiha Malik, 'Faith and the state of jurisprudence', in Oliver et al. (eds), *Faith and Law*, 2000.

28   Amy Gutmann in her introduction to Charles Taylor, *Multiculturalism and the Politics of Recognition*, 1994. In Britain the guidelines on inter-faith dialogue developed by the Inter-Faith Network have been invaluable in supporting a wide range of projects and activities over the years.

29   Peregrine Worsthorne, *Sunday Telegraph*, 3 February 1991.

30   *Daily Telegraph*, 1 March 1997.

18 Government Leadership

1   *New Britain: my vision for a young country*, 1996. There is little or no reference in books that have influenced New Labour, for example Will Hutton, *The State We're In*, 1996, Anthony Giddens, *The Third Way*, 1998, and the report of the Commission on Social Justice. Philip Gould's account of New Labour's policies and election victory, *The Unfinished Revolution*, 1998, is similarly wholly silent about issues of race equality and cultural diversity in modern Britain.

2   *Modernising Government*, Cabinet Office, March 1999.

3   *Modernising Local Government, in Touch with the People*, Cabinet Office, 1999.

4   *Race Equality in Public Services*, Home Office, March 2000.

5 When this report was completed, in July 2000, the exact proposals, in the form of amendments to the Race Relations Act (Amendments) Bill, had not been published.

6 For the Home Office and the services for which it is responsible, these targets are set out in the March 2000 paper, details in Note 4.

7 See, for example, Sarah Spencer, 'Making race equality count', *New Economy*, March 2000.

8 Sir Richard Wilson, *Report to the Prime Minister on Civil Service Reform*, Cabinet Office, December 1999.

9 The Home Secretary's response was published in May 1999, and a follow-up report on progress was published in February 2000. The priority is also referred to in Chapter 9, passim.

10 The guidance was published by the Department of the Environment, Transport and the Regions in February 2000.

11 *Minority Ethnic Issues in Social Exclusion and Neighbourhood Renewal*, Cabinet Office, June 2000.

12 There was a wide-ranging consultation about the new programme, and also about a code of practice in relations between public bodies and the black and Asian voluntary sector, in summer 1999. It was reported in a Home Office publication of late autumn 1999, *Strengthening the Black and Minority Ethnic Voluntary Sector Infrastructure*.

13 For discussion of the plan see documents issued by the Commission for Racial Equality in Scotland, 1999 and 2000, fuller details in the bibliography in Appendix E.

14 Standing Committee on Equality of Opportunity, *Equality Audit: equal opportunity baseline survey*, National Assembly for Wales, April 2000.

15 For example, in the very title of its June 2000 document. (See Note 11.)

16 For example, in the creation of an 'ethnic minority pupils website' and the Ethnic Minority Achievement Grant.

17 Sir Richard Wilson's report to the Prime Minister (see Note 8) uses the term 'diversity' rather than 'equality'. It is not clear whether the two terms are seen as synonymous, or whether the civil service has consciously chosen to stress diversity rather than equality.

18 See Note 10.

19 *The Government's Equality Statement*, Cabinet Office, November 1999.

20 *Race Equality in Public Services*, op. cit.

21 It is merely stated, and not at all prominently, that 'if anyone would like to discuss the race equality performance management framework set out in this document further, then they should contact ...' Two

names are then given, with telephone numbers and e-mail addresses, plus a postal address. The approach is friendly and pleasantly informal, but does not imply serious consultation.

22   See, for example, the questions being used in surveys of perceptions, as set out in Annex C of the March 2000 document.

23   See paragraphs 9.20–9.21 in Chapter 9.

24   See paragraphs 11.24–11.25 in Chapter 11.

25   *Reshaping Scotland? – let the people speak*, 1999. Details available from Scottish Human Services, 1a Washington Court, Washington Lane, Edinburgh EH11 2HA. There are quotations from this project in Chapter 1, Box 1.1.

26   Andy Pollak (ed.), *A Citizens' Inquiry: the Upsahl Report on Northern Ireland*, 1993.

19 Legislation and Enforcement

1   For an account of the political and conceptual context of the RRA see, for example, Anthony Lester, 'The Politics of the Race Relations Act 1976', in M. Anwar, P. Roach and R. Sondhi (eds), *From Legislation to Integration? – race relations in Britain (migration, minorities and citizenship)*, 2000, and Tessa Blackstone, Bhikhu Parekh and Peter Sanders, *Race Relations in Britain: a developing agenda*, 1998.

2   The one exception, as discussed in Chapter 15, is the immigration service, which is still permitted to discriminate on grounds of ethnic or national origin as well as nationality.

3   Bob Hepple, Mary Coussey and Tufyal Choudhury, *Equality: a new framework*, summer 2000. Generally, the first part of this chapter benefits considerably from access to the study by Hepple and his colleagues.

4   This was written before the precise nature of the new positive duty had been finalised. The proposals made do not seem to go as far as the requirements of the Northern Ireland Act 1998, particularly with regard to transparency and consultation.

5   When this report was completed (June 2000) the amendments had not been fully agreed.

6   Protocol 12 was agreed by the Committee of Ministers of the Council of Europe in June 2000. It will be open for signature in November 2000 and will then need ratification.

7   See House of Commons Northern Ireland Affairs Committee, Fourth Report (1999), paragraph 48; and Hepple et al., op. cit., Appendix 1, paragraphs 10.1–10.6.

8   Lester, op. cit.

9   The inconsistencies are tabulated in Appendix 3 of Hepple et al., op. cit.

10   Ibid, Appendix 2.

11   Ibid, paragraphs 2.13–2.20.

12   Better Regulation Task Force, 1999, p. 4. In its response, dated 14 July 1999, the government indicated approval.

13   Hepple et al., op. cit., paragraphs 3.4–3.7. The notion of an 'enforcement pyramid' was developed with regard to environmental policies, and is explained at length in N. Gunningham et al. (eds), *Smart regulation: designing environmental policy*, 1998. See in particular Gunningham's introduction and the chapter by Gunningham and Sinclair.

14   These matters are considered in detail by Hepple et al., Chapter 3.

15   Adapted from Hepple et al., Recommendation 28.

16   Ibid.

17   This list is derived from the functions of the Human Rights Commission in Northern Ireland. See also Sarah Spencer and Ian Bynoe, *A Human Rights Commission: the options for Britain and Northern Ireland*, 1998.

20 **Organisational Change**

1   The discussions in this chapter are drawn in part from documents developed and issued in 1999 by the Improvement and Development Agency (IDEA) and the Local Authorities Race Relations Information Exchange (LARRIE), with particular reference to responses by public bodies to the Stephen Lawrence Inquiry report.

2   The concept of 'stage of development' is arguably preferable to that of 'level'. The latter is well known, however, through the work on levels of organisational development promoted in recent years by the Commission for Racial Equality. See *Racial Equality Means Quality*, 1995, and *Auditing for Equality*, 1999.

3   *The Leadership Challenge: progress report 1999*, Commission for Racial Equality, July 1999.

4   Beverly Alimo-Metcalfe, *Effective Leadership*, Local Government
     Management Board, 1998.

5   For example, reports of Ofsted inspections of schools indicate whether
     or not a school has an equal opportunities statement, but seldom
     evaluate the statement's content. The CRE standard for local
     authorities implies that the mere existence of documentation,
     regardless of what it actually says and does, is sufficient to reach
     'level 1'.

6   Further, it is noteworthy that this statement refers to a wide range of
     grounds on which discrimination may take place, and that the range
     includes religious belief. On this latter point, see Chapter 17 for fuller
     discussion.

7   See Christopher McCrudden, 'Mainstreaming Equality in the
     Governance of Northern Ireland', *Fordham International Law Journal*,
     April 1999; the documentation developed in the London Borough of
     Haringey under the generic title *From the Margins to the Mainstream*;
     and Julian Clarke and Stuart Speeden, 'Raising the Standard:
     institutional racism and citizenship', Centre for Local Policy Studies,
     Edge Hill College.

8   However, following consultation with the Race Relations Forum, an
     invitation to tender for research on racism awareness training was
     issued on 2 February 2000. As of late June 2000 there was still no
     information about this project on the Home Office website.

9   This list is derived in part from a paper developed by Jozimba Panthera
     for the Camden Black and Minority Ethnic Governors' Forum, May 2000.

10   Key texts in learning style theory include Howard Gardner, *Frames of
     Mind*, 1983, and *Intelligences Reframed*, 1999, and David Kolb,
     Experiential Learning: experience the source of learning and development,
     1983. One of the principal theorists whose work is relevant to racism
     awareness is Paulo Freire. See, for example, essays in Peter McLaren
     and Peter Leonard (eds), *Paulo Freire: a critical encounter*, 1993. Freire
     was famously concerned with a pedagogy of the oppressed, not of the
     oppressor. Nevertheless, his theoretical approach and practical
     methodologies are relevant to the training of managers and leaders
     and should complement the approaches to management development
     derived from Total Quality Management (TQM) and the Business
     Excellence Model (BEM). On the importance of TQM and BEM for
     race equality, see Clarke and Speeden, op. cit.

11   For example, such audits are reported to have been very influential in

Northern Ireland and are frequently mentioned in the 1999 progress report on the CRE's Leadership Challenge. See also Bob Hepple et al., *Equality: a new framework*, 2000.

12 For example, government data on the civil service and public appointments often give no indication of which communities are primarily affected. Or if there is a breakdown into 'black' and 'Asian' there is no reference to whether the black staff are of African or African-Caribbean background, or whether the Asians are Bangladeshi, Chinese, Indian (itself a wide category) or Pakistani. Also, for example, the influential documentation by the CRE on its Leadership Challenge uses the blanket term 'ethnic minority' throughout without providing any indication of which particular communities are being referred to. Minimally, it could have alerted readers and users to the dangers that such aggregating may entail.

13 See, for example, criticisms of the police and criminal justice system in Chapters 9 and 10, education systems in Chapter 11 and the health service in Chapter 13.

14 The quotations are from a report compiled by Jozimba Panthera. See also Note 9.

Acknowledgements

The Commission on the Future of Multi-Ethnic Britain was set up by the Runnymede Trust in 1997 and was officially launched in early 1998 by the Home Secretary, Jack Straw. Funding was provided jointly by the Joseph Rowntree Charitable Trust, the Nuffield Foundation and the Paul Hamlyn Foundation.

The Commission is grateful to the many people who assisted its deliberations by making written submissions, taking part in meetings, answering enquiries, contributing papers and reports, organising and hosting visits, giving interviews, and being involved in specialist task forces and seminars. There are full lists in Appendix B.

The Commission's academic adviser was Tariq Modood, professor of sociology at the University of Bristol, and formerly principal researcher for the Fourth National Survey of Ethnic Minorities, based at the Policy Studies Institute.

The Commission was assisted by the 1990 Trust in its contacts with community organisations. The Trust also provided substantial documentation in relation to the topics considered in the Commission's report, particularly criminal justice, human rights, policing and politics, and valuable advice through its chair, Rita Patel, and its director, Lee Jasper.

The Commission benefited from the findings of focus group research on young people's perceptions of current social issues, and their own personal hopes, aspirations and goals for the future. The research was conducted in autumn 1999 by Philip Gould Associates. There is fuller information in Appendix B.

Parts of the report were read and commented on by Rowena Arshad, Gautam Bodiwala, Paul Gilbert, David Gillborn, Mary Hickman, Peter Jones, Elinor Kelly, Michael Marland, Berenice Miles, Rachel Morris, Audrey Osler, Susie Parsons, Ashok Pathak, Levi Pay, Ceri Peach, Abduljalil Sajid, John Stone, Gilane Tawadros, Veena Vasista, Dinesh Verma, Parminder Vir, David Watson and Silvaine Wiles. Special thanks are due to Elinor Kelly, who acted as consultant for the Commission's visit to Scotland in 1998 and for several aspects of the final report.

Interviews were given by Veena Bahl, David Gillborn, Gus John, Anthony Lester, Julie Mellor, Geoff Mulgan, Fuad Nahdi, Robin Oakley and Peter Ward, and by a group from the Muslim Council of Britain led by Iqbal Sacranie.

The Commission is grateful to organisations that generously provided free accommodation for meetings, including three residential meetings and many one-day meetings. They include Granada and the Posthouse Hotel, Regent's Park; the Nuffield Foundation; the Paul Hamlyn Foundation; the Regency Hotel, Kensington; and United News and Media.

Special thanks are due to Andrew Franklin (Profile Books), Patricia Lankester (Paul Hamlyn Foundation), Stephen Pittam (Joseph Rowntree Charitable Trust) and Anthony Tomei (Nuffield Foundation), and to the trustees and staff of the Runnymede Trust.

The Commission was set up by its first chair, John Burgh, previously president of Trinity College, Oxford. In its introductory phase the members of the Commission were Zaki Badawi, Colin Bailey, Michael Chan, Kate Gavron, Rose Hudson-Wilkin, Nighat Mirza, Rita Patel, Trevor Phillips, Herman Ouseley, Sylvie Pierce, Pushpinder Saini, David Sieff, Seamus Taylor, Geoff Thompson and Sue Woodford-Hollick. Several of these continued to act as advisers to the Commission, and were joined in this capacity by Kumar Murshid, Brian Pearce and David Smith.

The Commission drew not only on the hundreds of submissions and letters it received, and on the meetings and seminars it organised, but also on a wide range of published documents. These are referred to in the report's endnotes. A composite list of all works cited, with full bibliographical references, is provided as Appendix E.

Staff during the Commission's lifetime were Halima Begum, Dee Bunbury, Teresa Clark, Helen Francis, Zubaida Haque, Gail Hopkins, Jessica Penn, Robin Richardson and Helen Seaford. Assistance with consultation processes and bibliographical matters was provided by Kaushika Amin. Jessica Penn steered the Commission's work throughout the academic year 1998/99 and organised the research seminars listed in Appendix B. Zubaida Haque prepared substantial papers on education, and on arts, media and sport. Halima Begum prepared research papers and helped manage specialist taskforces. Dee Bunbury provided secretarial and administrative support for meetings,

1999–2000, and for the report in its successive drafts. Teresa Clark undertook a range of additional studies and investigations for the report's final version and helped to complete the final text. The manuscript was prepared for publication by Ian Paten. The editor was Robin Richardson.

Responsibility for judgements in the report, and for any errors, lies with the Commission, not with any of those whom it consulted.

The Consultation Process

Visits

Tower Hamlets, 10 February 1998
A meeting was held with councillors, officers and Bangladeshi community representatives, and a further meeting was held at the Bangladeshi Cultural Forum. Visits were made to the Headstart Programme and the Youth Parliament.

Bradford, 12 March 1998
An open forum was held at City Hall and visits were made to the Interfaith Education Centre and Feversham College.

Haringey, 21 April 1998
An open forum was held. Visits were made to the Cypriot Community Centre, the Irish Community Care Centre, the Asian Action Group, the Turkish Youth Association and the Broadwater Farm Community Centre. Meetings were held with the Haringey Community and Police Consultative Committee and the Community Safety Executive Board.

Liverpool, 19 May 1998
An open forum was held and visits were made to the Pagoda Centre, Wirral Multicultural Centre, Liverpool Black Sisters and the Yemeni Community Association.

Edinburgh, Glasgow and Stirling, 15/16 June 1998
Submissions were made by eight convenors, who brought in another 42 people, mostly young, from different communities across Scotland. They were organised around the Black Community Development Project, the Chinese Youth Development Project, and the themes of education, law, people and parliament, religion, work opportunities and Scottish identity. The Commissioners were briefed about Scottish education and law, key principles in Scottish history and culture, and the struggle to withstand the hegemony of English rule.

Organisations and institutions

The Commission received assistance and advice on behalf of, or from staff based at, the following organisations and institutions:

Action Group for Irish Youth
Alcohol Recovery Project
Al-Hasaniya Moroccan
  Women's Centre
Arts Council
Assembly of Masorti
  Synagogues
Association of Chief Police
  Officers
Association of Christian
  Teachers
Association of Community
  Trusts and Foundations
Association of First Division
  Civil Servants
Association of Teachers and
  Lecturers

Belgrave Baheno Women's
  Association, Leicester
Belle Vue Girls School,
  Bradford
Bilston Community College
Birmingham City Council
Black Community
  Development Project,
  Edinburgh
Black Community Forum
Black Environment
  Network
Black Training and Enterprise
  Group
Blackburn with Darwen
  Borough Council

Board of Deputies of British
  Jews
Bolton Metropolitan Council
Bolton Racial Equality Council
Bradford Breakthrough
Bradford Metropolitan Council
Bradford National Union of
  Teachers
Brahma Kumaris World
  University
Brent Education Department
Brighton Islamic Mission
Bristol and Avon Chinese
  Women's Group
British Association of Social
  Workers
British Broadcasting
  Corporation

Camden Race Equality Council
Cara Irish Housing
  Association
Cardiff Law School
Carlton Television
Catholic Bishops' Conference
  of England and Wales
Central Council for Jewish
  Community Services
Centre for Black and White
  Christian Partnership
Centre for Education for Racial
  Equality in Scotland
Centre for Equality Issues in
  Education

Centre for European Migration
and Ethnic Studies
Centre for Global Education
Centre for Human Ecology
Centre for Islamic Studies
Centre for Law and Society
Centre for Sport Development
Research
Charnwood Racial Equality
Council
Charter 88
Chinese in Britain Forum
Chinese Community
Development Project,
Glasgow
Chinese Mental Health
Association
Christian Action for Justice in
Immigration Law
Christian Socialist Movement
Columban Fathers
Commission for Racial Equality
Commission for Racial
Equality Scotland
Commission for Racial
Equality Wales
Committee on the
Administration of Justice,
Belfast
Commonwealth Institute
Confederation of British
Industry
Council for Education in World
Citizenship

Department of Trade and
Industry
Derby Asian Christian
Ministry Partnership

Development Education
Centre, Birmingham
Diocese of Coventry

Ealing Education Department
Ealing Travellers Project
Early Years Trainers Anti-
Racist Network
Eastleigh College
East Midlands Regional Local
Government Association
Edinburgh and Lothian Racial
Equality Council
Edinburgh City Council
Educational Institute of
Scotland
Equal Opportunities
Commission
Ethnic Minorities
Representative Council,
Brighton

Falkirk Council
Federation of Irish Societies
Fife Constabulary

General Synod of the Church
of England
Glasgow Chamber of Commerce
Glasgow Race Working Group
Goan Welfare Association
Goldsmiths' College, London
Grampian Police
Grampian Racial Equality
Council

Haringey Borough Council
Haringey Committee on
Community Languages

Haringey Cypriot Community
Centre
Hillingdon Hospital
Home Office
Hull and East Riding Racial
Equality Council
Hull and East Yorkshire
Hospitals NHS Trust
Humane Slaughter Association

Immigration Advisory Service
Immigration Law Practitioners
Association
Inner Cities Religious Council
Institute for Citizenship
Studies
Institute for Public Policy
Research
Institute of Commonwealth
Studies
Institute of International
Visual Arts
Institute of Jewish Policy
Research
Institute of Linguistics
Inter-Faith Network
Interlink Foundation
Irish Housing Forum
Irish Studies Centre
Irish Welfare and Information
Centre
Islamic Foundation
Islamic Party of Britain
Islamic Rights Commission
Islington Borough Council
Israel Diaspora Trust

Jewish Care
John Lewis Partnership plc

Joint Committee for Ethnic
Minorities in Wales
Joint Council for the Welfare of
Immigrants
Joseph Rowntree Foundation
Judicial Studies Board
Juniper Productions

Karibu Refugee Day Centre
Kensington and Chelsea
Borough Council
Kent European Youth
Association
King's College, London

Lancashire Council of Mosques
Leicester City Council
Leicestershire Constabulary
Liberty
Liverpool City Council
Liverpool Health Authority
Liverpool Jewish Resource
Centre
Liverpool Law Centre
Living Heritage Centre
Local Authorities Race
Relations Information
Exchange
London Irish Women's Centre
London Research Centre
London Voluntary Service
Council

Merseyside Racial Equality
Council
Merseyside Police
Methodist Church
Metropolitan Police
Midland Bank plc

Mind
Moray House Institute,
    Edinburgh
Multicultural Resource Centre,
    Bedford
Multiracial Families Support
    Group
Muslim Council of Britain
Muslim Cultural Heritage
    Centre
Muslim World League

National Anti-Racist
    Movement in Education
National Association of
    Probation Officers
National Association of
    Schoolmasters and Union
    of Women Teachers
National Black Police
    Association
National Foundation for
    Educational Research
National Union of Teachers
Nch San Jai Chinese Project
Newham Borough Council
1990 Trust
North West Lancashire Health
    Authority
North West Leicestershire
    District Council
Northern Refugee Centre
Nottinghamshire Police

Odysseus Trust
Office for National
    Statistics
Ofsted
Operation Black Vote

Peterborough Racial Equality
    Council
Plymouth City Council
Project Fullemploy
Public and Commercial
    Services Union

Q News
QED, Bradford
Queen Mary and Westfield
    College

Race On The Agenda
Reading Borough Council
Reading Racial Equality Council
Redbridge Racial Equality
    Council
Refugee Council
Roehampton Institute
Royal College of Nursing
Royal School for the Deaf
Rural Race Equality Project,
    Devon

SAI Consulting
Save the Children
Scottish Churches Agency for
    Racial Justice
Scottish Council for Voluntary
    Organisations
Scottish Refugee Council
Scottish Trades Union
    Congress
Searchlight
Society of Afghans
Somali Community
    Information Centre
South Harringay Infants
    School

Sport England
Staffordshire Education
Surrey Youth Strategy
Swansea City Council

Talawa Theatre Company
Tamarind Books
Thames Valley Police
Three Faiths Forum
Thurrock Council for
    Voluntary Service
Trades Union Congress
Transport and General
    Workers Union
Traveller Law Research Unit
Travellers Education Project
Turkish Youth Association,
    Haringey
Tyne and Wear Racial Equality
    Council

Uhuru Families Support Group
Union of Muslim
    Organisations
Universities of Birmingham,
    Bradford, Bristol,
    Cambridge, City,
    De Montfort, Edinburgh,
    Essex, Glasgow, Glasgow
    Caledonian, Greenwich,
    Hertfordshire, Hull,
    Leicester, Lincolnshire and
    Humberside, Lincoln,
    Liverpool, London,
    Loughborough,
    Manchester, Manchester
    Metropolitan, Middlesex,
    North London,

Open University, Oxford,
    Reading, Sheffield Hallam,
    South Bank, Southampton,
    Warwick
University Colleges of
    Northampton and
    Worcester
Urban Theology Unit, Sheffield

VECTOR (Values, Education,
    Consultancy, Training,
    Organisational Research),
    Scotland

Waltham Forest Racial Equality
    Council
Watford Council
Wellingborough District Racial
    Equality Council
West Midlands Health
    Research Unit
Westminster College
Wiltshire Health Authority
Worcester Racial Equality
    Council
Working Group on Racism in
    Children's Resources
The Write Thing
Wycombe Race Equality
    Council
Wyndham Place Trust

Yemeni Community
    Association
Young Muslims, Glasgow
Youth Charter for Sport,
    Culture and Arts

Research seminars

The following joined members of the Commission for seminars on specific topics:

Economics and Family Welfare –
   17 November 1998
Donatus Anwanyu
Ravinder Barn
Fiona Bartells-Ellis
Richard Berthoud
Gary Craig
Alison Jervis
Gerard Lemos
Mark Johnson
Peter Nokes
Sheila Philogen
David Piachaud

Education – 20 November 1998
Ghazala Bhatti
John Bird
Philip Cohen
Brian Cox
Peter Cunningham
Manjula Datta
Paul Ghuman
David Gillborn
Eve Gregory
Richard Hatcher
Brian Hudson
Martin Mac an Ghaill
Pat Mahoney
Ian Menter
Heidi Mirza
Peter Mortimore
Dianne Reay
John Rex
Tony Sewell

Debbie Weeks
Deborah Youdell

National Identity – 22 March
   1999
Avtar Brah
Diana Brittan
Matthew Festenstein
Jonathon Freedland
Andrew Gamble
Paul Gilroy
Peter Jones
Sunder Katwal
Simon Lee
David Miller
Tariq Modood
Chris Myant
William Outhwaite
Ann Phoenix
Ali Rattansi
Jim Rose
Steven Vertovec
Marina Warner
Malcolm Weisman
Enid Wistrich

Health, Social Welfare and
   Family – 19 April 1999
Donatus Anwanyu
Ravinder Barn
Fiona Bartells-Ellis
Admasu Haile-Selassi
David Kelleher
Randeep Kular

Delena Lawson
Karen McHugh
Meena Patel

Common Values – 28 April 1999
Brenda Almond
Kevin Boyle
Tufyal Choudhury
Karin Eyben
Sandra Freedman
James Griffin
Mark Halstead
Denise Hill
Francesca Klug
Preston King
Heidi Mirza
Nick Pearce
Joseph Raz
Abduljalil Sajid
Vasant Shendge
Mohammed Ali Taghavi
Malcolm Weisman

Criminal Justice – 5 May 1999
Rob Allen
Nicholas Brooke
Ian Byrne
Ruth Chigwada-Bailey
David Coleman
Cressida Dick
Linda Dobbs QC
Harry Fletcher
Cedric Fullwood
Barry Goldson
Paddy Hillyard
Baroness Howells
Matthew McFarlane
Robin Oakley
Daphne Priestly

Fran Russell

Arts, Media and Sport – 6/7 May 1999
Sue Ball
Floella Benjamin
Yvonne Brewster
Margaret Busby
Guy Cumberbatch
Caroline Diehl
Tony Fairweather
Conchesta Fernandez
Jennifer Hargreaves
Munni Kabir
Horace Lashley
Ian McDonald
Sarah Morgan
Novlette Rennie
Samir Shah
Ajay Sharma
Gilane Tawadros
Parminder Vir
Lola Young

Racism and Exclusion – 28 June 1999
Floya Anthias
Les Beck
Sandra Freedman
Mary Hickman
Simon Holdaway
Gail Lewis
Chris McCrudden
Kate Murray
Kumar Murshid
Chris Myant
Syed Pasha
Pravin Patel
Ceri Peach

Ann Phoenix
Anne Phillips
Oonagh Reitman

John Solomos
Steven Vertovec
Fiona Waye

Individuals

As well as those who attended specialist seminars, the following provided evidence to the Commission, or assisted by responding to specific enquiries:

Joe Aldred
Titus Alexander
Peter Aley
Rushanara Ali
Mashuk Ally
Kaushika Amin
Vijay Amin
Linda Appiah
Ilona Aronovsky
Rowena Arshad

Veena Bahl
Nick Baker
Roger Ballard
Chris Banks
Simon Banks
Maggie Beirne
Paul Bellingham
Floella Benjamin
Beverley Berwick
Maud Blair
Bill Bolloten
Yvonne Brewster
Diana Brittan
Elaine Brittan
Margot Brown
Pauline Brown
Irma Burke-Richards

Patrick Castens
Farkhanda Chaudhry
Rita Choudhury
Tufyal Choudhury
Ruth Chigwada-Bailey
Alastair Christie
Teresa Clark
Barbara Cohen
David Coleman
Gary Craig
Barney Crockett
Paul Crofts
Malcolm Cross
Guy Cumberbatch

Anne Darby
Nicholas Deakin
Elaine Delay
Amu Devani
Ranjit Dheer
Fernando Diniz
Ali Dizaei
Ruth Djang
Kapil Dudakia
Ann Dummett

Tony Fairweather
Alison Fenny

Alasdair Ferry
Peter Figueroa
Nadine Finch
Harry Fletcher
Don Flynn
Charles Forgan
Marina Foster
Eileen Francis

Tessfu Gessesse
Paul Gilbert
David Gillborn
Jonathan Glennie
Barry Goldson
Olwyn Gunn

Alan Hall
Jo Hall
Jennifer Hargreaves
Alison Hewitt
Mary Hickman
Simon Holdaway
Ray Honeyford
Barbara Hudson
Gar-Ming Hui

Michael Ignatieff
Michael Ipgrave
Arthur Ivatts

Paul Jackson
Lee Jasper
Gus John
Mark Johnson
Ummanga Jolly
Peter Jones

Ramesh Kapadia
Chitra Karve

Fiaz Khan
Sameah Khawaja
Gillian Klein
Randeep Kular

Amu Lagotse
Harmesh Lakhanpaul
Jane Lane
Horace Lashley
Charmaine Lawrence
Don Lee
Simon Lee
Kenneth Leech
Gerard Lemos
Namasiku Liandu

Ian McDonald
Alistair McIntosh
Matt McIver
Roger McKenzie
Norah McWilliam
Shona Mahon
Maleiha Malik
Michael Marland
Rabinder Martins
Zubia Masood
Berenice Miles
Julian Misell
Raj Mistry
Praful Modi
Sarah Morgan
Rachel Morris
Geoff Mulgan

Neville Nagler

Robin Oakley
Angela O'Hagan
Daniel Onifade

Audrey Osler

Alison Paget
Sarah Palmer
Marie Parker-Jenkins
Susie Parsons
Naina Patel
Rita Patel
Ashok Pathak
Levi Pay
Ceri Peach
Brian Pearce
Richard Penn
Albert Persaud
Andrew Pilkington
Garrick Prayogg
John Prosser

Ghulamur Rahman
Ali Rattansi
Jeannette Redding
Nicky Road
Liz Royle

Haroon Saad
Iqbal Sacranie
Amir Saeed
Imam Dr Abduljalil Sajid
Claude Scott
Muriel Scott
Samir Shah
Ajay Sharma

Carolyn Simpson
John Simpson
Scott Sinclair
Liz Singleton
Rajinder Sohpal
John Stone
Sukhvinder Kaur Stubbs
Susie Symes

Pauline Tambling
Gilane Tawadros

Heather Valentine
Rudy van Kemenade
Veena Vasista
Dinesh Verma
Parminder Vir

Talha Wadee
Sam Walker
Bronwen Walter
Yan Wang
David Watson
Janet Whitaker
Quincy Whitaker
Silvaine Wiles
Paul Winstone
Enid Wistrich
Simon Woolley
John Wrench

Lola Young

Specialist papers

The following were commissioned to provide substantial papers on specific topics.
Muhammad Anwar, The participation of ethnic minorities in politics.

Roger Ballard, Demographic and social characteristics of Britain.

Roger Ballard, The demography of polyethnic Britain.

Michael Chan, Ethnic minorities and the NHS: the user perspective.

Ruth Chigwada-Bailey, Race and the prison population.

Guy Cumberbatch, Ethnic minorities: television programming and advertising.

Ann Dummett, Multi-ethnic Britain in the context of Europe.

David Faulkner, Ethnicity, culture and criminal justice.

David Faulkner, Judith Hunt, Sarah Spencer and Seamus Taylor, Policy-making and service delivery in government and the public sector.

Nadine Finch, Immigration aspects of multi-ethnic Britain.

Barry Goldson, Youth justice and ethnic minorities.

Jennifer Hargreaves and Dr Ian McDonald, A discussion paper on sport.

Mary Hickman, Writing race, invisibilising the Irish in Britain.

Simon Holdaway, Police race relations.

Barbara Hudson, Punishment, blame and ethnicity: understanding discrimination in criminal justice.

Mark Johnson, Ethnicity and health.

Horace Lashley, Sport and leisure for multiracial Britain.

Don Lee, Trends and issues in race and education, 1970–1998.

Antony Lerman, The Jewish community in Britain.

Tariq Modood, Multiculturalism in Britain, some rival versions and thoughts on ways forward.

Robin Oakley, Tackling racism and ethnic diversity in community safety and criminal justice.

Anne Owers, Asylum and immigration.

Naina Patel, Ageing with care.

Charles Reed, Colour and citizenship: a historical review of British race relations.

Sarah Spencer, The implications of the debate on a UK human rights commission for race equality.

Gilane Tawadros, Visual arts.

Veena Vasista and Chitra Karve, UK compliance with international standards on race equality.

Bronwen Walter, The Irish community: diversity, disadvantage and discrimination.

John Wrench, Race and employment issues in Britain, 1970–1999.

Lola Young, Cultural identity.

The Commission also benefited from papers sent by correspondents; presentations by some of those who took part in the specialist seminars; a paper about the Commission's work and related issues by Dr Elinor Kelly of the University of Glasgow, 'Stands Scotland where it did? – an essay in ethnicity and internationalism', published in *Scottish Affairs*, 1998; and two substantial reviews by Dr Zubaida Haque, on education and cultural policy respectively. Many people from outside the Commission sent or drew our attention to books, articles or research reports. In all instances where these were used they are acknowledged in the report's endnotes and listed in Appendix E.

Focus group research

Focus group research was undertaken for the Commission in autumn 1999 by Philip Gould Associates in Cardiff, Glasgow, Birmingham, Manchester and London. There were separate groups for black, Asian, Irish, dual-heritage and white contributors. Some were for those aged 16–24, others for those aged 25–35. There were nine groups altogether, all of mixed gender. Each session began with group members telling their personal stories. They then completed questionnaires showing their agreement or disagreement with a range of statements including:
* I am optimistic about my future
* Britain is a divided and racist society
* I feel I can trust the police

Completion of questionnaires was followed by broad-ranging discussions on themes of identities, racism, education, policing, employment and health. As part of the group discussions participants were invited to respond in writing to questions which included:
* What do you think of as typically British?
* Write down the first three words that come into your head when you read 'Schools and education'
* If you could send one message to the Commission on the Future of Multi-Ethnic Britain, what would that be?

Substantial extracts from the transcripts were provided, summarising reports were written about each group and a presentation was made to the whole Commission at one of its residential meetings.

The Commission's Membership

Bhikhu Parekh (chair)
Emeritus professor of political theory, University of Hull. Deputy chair of the Commission for Racial Equality, 1985–90, and vice-chancellor of the University of Baroda, 1981–4. Trustee of the Runnymede Trust. Raised to the peerage as Baron Parekh of Kingston-upon-Hull in 2000. Publications include *Marx's Theory of Ideology* (1982), *Gandhi's Political Philosophy* (1989), *Critical Assessments of Jeremy Bentham* (1993, 4 vols) and *Rethinking Multiculturalism: cultural diversity and political theory* (2000).

Yasmin Alibhai-Brown
Writer and journalist. Currently a regular columnist on the *Independent*. Frequent radio and television broadcaster. Senior research fellow at the Foreign Policy Centre and recently a research fellow at the Institute for Public Policy Research. Member of the Home Office Race Relations Forum, the Forced Marriage Working Party and the Fourth PSI Survey Advisory Committee. Publications include *True Colours* (1999), *Who Do We Think We Are?* (2000) and *After Multiculturalism* (2000).

Muhammad Anwar
Research professor at the Centre for Research in Ethnic Relations (CRER), University of Warwick, and previously director of CRER, 1989–94. Head of research at the Commission for Racial Equality, 1981–9. Member of the BBC General Advisory Council, 1983–9. Publications include *The Myth of Return* (1979), *Race and Politics* (1986), *Race and Elections* (1994) and *From Legislation to Integration?* (co-editor, 2000).

Colin Bailey
Chief constable of Nottinghamshire Police, 1995–2000. Previously deputy chief constable, 1990–5, assistant chief constable of West Yorkshire Police, 1986–90, and member of Lincolnshire Police, 1962–86. In Association of Chief Police Officers (ACPO) has been chair of the Race

Relations Sub-Committee and the Crime Prevention Sub-Committee.

Amina Begum
Social worker, London Borough of Tower Hamlets. Youth and community worker and trainer in community development. Member of the government's Forced Marriage Working Party. Co-founder of Women United Against Racism in Tower Hamlets.

Michael Chan
Professor of ethnic health, University of Liverpool. Director of the NHS Ethnic Health Unit, 1994–7, and commissioner at the Commission for Racial Equality, 1990–5. Chair, Chinese in Britain Forum. Non-executive director, Wirral and West Cheshire Community NHS Trust. Member of the Sentencing Advisory Panel. Recent publications include articles on the Chinese community in Britain (1999) and quality and race in the NHS (1996, 1998).

Navnit Dholakia
Chair, National Association for the Care and Resettlement of Offenders (NACRO). Formerly member of the Police Complaints Authority, and before that on the staff of the Commission for Racial Equality. Member of the Home Office Race Relations Forum and of the editorial advisory group, Howard Journal of Criminal Justice. Raised to the peerage as Baron Dholakia of Waltham Brooks in 1997.

David Faulkner
Senior research associate, University of Oxford Centre for Criminological Research. Fellow of St John's College, Oxford, 1992–9, and deputy secretary at the Home Office, 1982–92. Chair of the Howard League for Penal Reform. Publications include *Darkness and Light* (1996) and chapters in *Relational Justice* (1994) and *Public Services and Citizenship in European Law* (1998).

Kate Gavron (vice-chair of the Commission)
Trustee of the Runnymede Trust. Trustee and Research Fellow, Institute of Community Studies, with particular interest in the Bangladeshi community in East London. Trustee of Mutual Aid Centre, Bethnal Green. Chair, Carcanet Press. Member of the Commission on British Muslims and Islamophobia.

Stuart Hall
Emeritus professor of sociology, Open University, and visiting professor, Goldsmiths' College, University of London. Professor of sociology at the Open University, 1979–9, and director of the Centre for Cultural Studies, University of Birmingham, 1968–79. Chair of the board of the Institute of the International Visual Arts (INIVA) and of Autograph, the Association of Black Photographers. Recent publications include *Questions of Cultural Identity* (co-author, 1996), and chapters in *Critical Dialogues in Cultural Studies* (1996) and *Revising Multiculturalisms* (2000).

Bob Hepple QC
Master of Clare College and professor of law, University of Cambridge. Former commissioner at the Commission for Racial Equality and former chairman of industrial tribunals. Publications include *Race, Jobs and the Law in Britain* (second edition, 1970), *Discrimination: the limits of law* (co-editor, 1992) and *Equality: a new framework, the report of the Independent Review of Enforcement of UK Anti-discrimination Legislation* (co-author, 2000).

Judith Hunt
Chair of Camden and Islington Health Authority. Formerly chief executive of the Local Government Management Board, 1993–9, and of the London Borough of Ealing, 1986–93. Has served as a Civil Service Commissioner and as a member of the Economic and Social Research Council Priorities Board. Trustee of Common Purpose. Publications include *Fairness or Failure: equal opportunities recruitment* (co-author, 1998) and guidance for local authorities on responding to the Stephen Lawrence Inquiry and the Home Secretary's action plan (co-author, 1999).

Antony Lerman
Formerly executive director, Institute for Jewish Policy Research, 1991–9. Editor of *Patterns of Prejudice*, 1983–99. Member of the Runnymede Trust Commission on Antisemitism, 1991–3, and of the Imperial War Museum advisory committee on a permanent Holocaust exhibition. Editor, *The Jewish Communities of the World* (1989) and *Antisemitism World Report* (1992–8).

Matthew McFarlane
Chief inspector, Nottinghamshire Police. Responsible for strategy and policy on race and community relations issues. Previously staff officer to the chair of the Race and Community Relations Sub-Committee of the Association of Chief Police Officers (ACPO). Attended hearings during Part Two of the Lawrence Inquiry on behalf of ACPO.

Andrew Marr
(Until April 2000.) Chief political editor for BBC Television, from summer 2000. Previously columnist on the *Express* and the *Observer* and editor of the *Independent*. Publications include *The Battle for Scotland* (1996), *Ruling Britannia* (1998) and *The Day Britain Died* (2000).

Tariq Modood (adviser)
Professor of sociology at the University of Bristol and director of the Centre for the Study of Ethnicity and Citizenship. Previously a programme director at the Policy Studies Institute, principal researcher on the Fourth National Survey of Ethnic Minorities, 1993–7, and principal employment officer at the Commission for Racial Equality, 1989–91. Member of the DfEE Race, Education and Employment Forum. Publications include *Not Easy Being British* (1992), *Ethnic Minorities in Britain* (co-author, 1997), *Ethnicity, Employment and Higher Education* (co-author, 1999).

Sir Peter Newsam
Chief Adjudicator of School Organisation and Administrations. Formerly director of the Institute of Education, University of London, 1985–92, chairman of the Commission for Racial Equality, 1981–5, and chief education officer for the Inner London Education Authority, 1975–81.

Sir Herman Ouseley
Director of Different Realities Partnership and Focus Consultancy Ltd. Consultant adviser to Metropolitan Police Service. Chair of Caribbean Advisory Group, Foreign and Commonwealth Office. Formerly chair of the Commission for Racial Equality, chief executive of Lambeth Borough Council and the Inner London Education Authority. Council member of the Institute of Race Relations. Chair of Kick It Out Ltd. Publications include *The System* (1981).

Anne Owers
Director of JUSTICE and previously general secretary of the Joint Council for the Welfare of Immigrants, 1986–92. Member of the Home Office Task Force on implementation of the Human Rights Act, the Crown Office Review Team and the Legal Services Consultative Panel. Previously member of the Lord Chancellor's Advisory Committee on Legal Education and Conduct, 1997–9, and chair of trustees, Refugee Legal Centre, 1993. Publications include *Providing Protection: asylum determination systems* (1997), *Legislating for Human Rights* (1998) and *Economic, Social and Cultural Rights: their implementation in UK law* (co-editor, 1999).

Trevor Phillips
Broadcaster and journalist. Chair of the Greater London Assembly, 2000. Head of current affairs and executive producer of factual programmes for London Weekend Television, 1990–6. Chair of the Runnymede Trust, 1993–8. Member of the Home Office Race Relations Forum and formerly chair of the London Arts Board. Publications include *Windrush: the irresistible rise of multiracial Britain* (co-author, 1998).

Sarah Spencer
Director of the citizenship and governance programme, Institute for Public Policy Research. Formerly general secretary, National Council for Civil Liberties, and director, Cobden Trust. Member of the Home Office task force on implementation of the Human Rights Act and of the British Council Law Advisory Committee. Publications include *Strangers and Citizens* (editor, 1994), *Migrants, Refugees and the Boundaries of Citizenship* (1995) and *Mainstreaming Human Rights in Whitehall and Westminster* (co-author, 1999).

Seamus Taylor
Head of policy: equality and diversity, Haringey Borough Council, and chair, Action Group for Irish Youth. Previously held a range of posts in the voluntary sector and local government, mainly concerned with corporate planning and race equality. Adviser to the Commission for Racial Equality on research study on discrimination and the Irish community. Drafting author of *From the Margins to the Mainstream* series of documents (1991–4).

Sally Tomlinson
Emeritus professor of educational policy, Goldsmiths' College, University of London, and research associate, University of Oxford Department of Educational Studies. Member of the African Education Trust. Publications include *Multicultural Education in White Areas* (1990), *Ethnic Relations and Schooling* (1995) and *Hackney Downs: the school that dared to fight* (co-author, 1999).

Sue Woodford-Hollick
Chair of Index on Censorship, 1993–2000, and founding commissioning editor of multicultural programmes, Channel 4 Television. Vice-chair of the Caribbean Advisory Group, Foreign and Commonwealth Office. Member of the general council of the Royal Commonwealth Society and of Broadcast Diversity Network. Co-founder in 2000 of EQ, a project to increase black and Asian representation in politics.

The Population of Britain: Demographic Tables

At the time of writing (summer 2000) the most up-to-date estimates of the population by ethnicity are provided by the *Labour Force Survey* for the four quarters of 1998. The figures are Crown Copyright and are reproduced here in Table A with permission of the Office for National Statistics (ONS). However, the categories in Table A are not in all respects the same as those used by ONS. The differences are as follows.

- The term 'African-Caribbean' is used to aggregate the ONS categories 'Black Caribbean' and 'Black Other'.
- The term 'African' is used instead of 'Black African'.
- Estimates are included for the Irish community. They are derived by multiplying the Irish-born figures in the 1991 census by a factor of 2.5 in order to produce an estimate of the first and second generations combined. The rationale for this calculation is explained in *Discrimination and the Irish Community in Britain* by Mary Hickman and Bronwen Walter, 1997.
- The inclusion of the Irish as a separate community means that the ONS figures for white people are reduced accordingly.
- The ONS categories 'Other Asian' and 'Other Other' are aggregated as 'Various'. Both categories embrace a wide variety of cultures, countries and communities and are of little value for purposes of analysis.

The main points of interest in Table A are as follows.

- Just over 10 per cent of the population (5.75 million people) have community backgrounds outside Britain.
- Almost 5.7 per cent of the population (3.25 million people) have community backgrounds in Africa, the Caribbean or Asia.
- In Greater London, about 35 per cent of the population have community backgrounds outside Britain, and 22 per cent have backgrounds in Africa, the Caribbean or Asia.
- 57 per cent of all African-Caribbean people in Britain live in Greater London, as do 82 per cent of all Africans, 49 per cent of

Bangladeshis, 42 per cent of Indians, 30 per cent of Irish and 19 per cent of Pakistanis.

- 22 per cent of all Pakistanis live in the West Midlands, 20 per cent in Yorkshire and Humberside, 19 per cent in London and 18 per cent in the North-West.
- 42 per cent of all Indians live in London and 20 per cent in the West Midlands.
- Just under 50 per cent of all Bangladeshis live in Greater London and 13 per cent in the West Midlands.
- 30 per cent of Irish people in Britain live in London and 18 per cent in other parts of the South-East.
- Just over one-third of Chinese people in Britain live in London.

Notes on Table A
- All figures are Crown Copyright. Most are derived from the *Labour Force Survey* 1998, issued by the Office for National Statistics (ONS) in summer 2000. The estimates for the Irish community are extrapolations from the 1991 Census made in *Discrimination and the Irish Community in Britain* by Mary Hickman and Bronwen Walter, 1997.
- All figures are estimates. Because of the small size of many of the samples, several of the figures are unreliable for purposes of analysis. This is particularly the case for African, Bangladeshi and Chinese communities outside London, and for all communities in the North-East and the South-West.
- The ONS categories 'Black Caribbean' and 'Black Other' have been aggregated as 'African-Caribbean', and 'Other Asian' and 'Other Other' as 'Various'.
- The last column is derived from the ONS figures by subtracting the estimates by Hickman and Walter for the Irish community.
- All figures are to the nearest thousand, and have been rounded up or down accordingly. Therefore the totals in the bottom line do not necessarily correspond exactly to the figures in the columns above them.
- Of all black and South Asian people in Britain, 97.6 per cent live in England. About 1.6 per cent live in Scotland and 0.8 per cent in Wales.

Table A

The population of Great Britain by region or country and ethnicity, 1998 estimates (thousands)

Area of residence	African	African-Caribbean	Bangla-deshi	Chinese	Indian	Irish	Pakistani	Various	White (other than Irish)
East	6	40	13	14	54	46	22	35	5,058
East Midlands	7	33	1	6	86	106	22	17	3874
Greater London	289	455	114	58	399	641	107	336	4,583
North-East	4	3	13	5	4	41	12	8	2,492
North-West	14	38	20	21	64	245	105	27	6,322
South-East (not London)	9	46	13	18	64	391	33	69	7,143
South-West	2	13	7	3	10	118	2	19	4,648
West Midlands	9	113	31	17	196	228	125	34	4,530
Yorkshire & Humberside	7	41	14	6	53	101	112	24	4,654
Total England	347	782	226	148	930	1,917	540	569	43,304
Scotland	4	6	1	13	12	123	24	18	4,870
Wales	3	9	5	6	3	52	3	14	2,812
Total Great Britain	354	797	232	167	945	2,092	567	601	50,986

Future projections

Most communities with backgrounds outside Britain have proportionately more young people, and proportionately fewer older people, than those from within Britain. For example, 43 per cent of Bangladeshis, 35 per cent of Pakistanis and 32 per cent of Africans are under 16, but only 20 per cent of white people are. Sixteen per cent of white people are over 65, but no more than 3 per cent of Africans, Bangladeshis and Pakistanis. (Source: *Social Trends 30*, based on *Labour Force Survey* data, 2000. Note that the *Labour Force Survey* counts Irish people within the overall 'white' category.) For these demographic reasons, African, Bangladeshi and Pakistani communities will grow substantially, both absolutely and relatively, over the next 20 years. African-Caribbean and Indian communities will also grow, but not to the same extent. Table B shows broad estimates extrapolated from the 1991 Census and the 1998 LFS figures. Substantially more accurate estimates will in due course become available from analysis of the 2001 Census.

Table B
The changing population of Britain by ethnicity, 1998–2020 (thousands)

Community	Estimates for 1998	Estimates for 2020
African	354	700
African-Caribbean	797	1,000
Bangladeshi	232	460
Chinese	167	250
Indian	945	1,200
Irish	2,092	3,000
Pakistani	567	1,250
Various	601	1,000
White other than Irish	50,986	49,000
Total	56,741	57,860

Notes on Table B
- The estimates for 1998 are taken from Table A.
- The estimates for 2020 are very approximate, and most could differ by at least 15 per cent. Apart from those for Irish and white other

than Irish, they are updated from calculations originally made by Roger Ballard and Virinder Singh Kalra in *The Ethnic Dimension of the 1991 Census*, University of Manchester, 1994.

- In autumn 1999 the ONS set up a specialist working party to advise on projections from the 2001 Census. In due course the ONS will be able to publish substantially more reliable estimates than those shown here.

Growth of religions other than Christianity

Table C, reprinted with acknowledgement to the *UK Christian Handbook*, shows estimates for the period 1960–2000. The estimates are necessarily imprecise, as they involve complex distinctions between 'active membership' and 'community membership' (also sometimes known as nominal membership); the term 'group' refers to a wide range of organisations and congregations; and each faith community has its own body of religious officials or leaders.

Table C
Growth of religions other than Christianity, 1960–2000 estimates

Year	Active members	Groups	Leaders
1960	259,000	548	814
1965	336,000	663	1,122
1970	456,000	855	1,795
1975	573,000	1,091	2,213
1980	739,500	1,233	3,188
1985	899,000	1,563	4,024
1990	1,073,000	1,858	4,786
1995	1,292,000	2,347	5,560
2000	1,460,000	2,650	6,385

Source: UK Christian Handbook, Religious Trends 2000/2001 No. 2, Christian Research, 1999.

Students in British universities

Table D shows that all communities other than white are over-represented in entry to universities. Other figures published by the Higher Education Statistics Agency show marked differences within certain communities in relation to gender; whether study is full-time or part-time; whether the course is for a degree or another qualification; and whether the course is a first or advanced degree. Points of interest include the following.

- African-Caribbean women enter higher education at all levels in greater numbers than do African-Caribbean men. On part-time courses they outnumber men by more than two to one.
- In the case of Asian communities, there are generally more men than women in all kinds of higher education.
- Bangladeshi students are far more likely to be studying full-time than part-time.
- The ratio of African and of Chinese postgraduate to undergraduate students is high.
- Proportionately few Bangladeshi students are studying at postgraduate level.
- African-Caribbean students are concentrated in non-degree higher education courses. Bangladeshi students are unlikely to enter such courses.

Table D
First-year students in British universities by ethnicity, 1997–98, %

Community background	Total in higher education	18–24s in Great Britain
African	2.2	0.4
African-Caribbean	2.0	0.9
Bangladeshi	0.7	0.65
Chinese	1.0	0.4
Indian	4.5	2.0
Pakistani	2.4	1.7
White	84.2	93.0

Source: Higher Education Statistics Agency and 1991 Census.

List of Works Cited

This includes all publications mentioned in the report's notes and references. All were published in the United Kingdom unless otherwise stated.

A

Abdelrazack, M. and Kempadoo, M. (eds), *Directory of Supplementary and Mother-Tongue Classes*, Department for Education and Employment, 1999.

Alexander, Clare, *The Art of Being Black*, Oxford University Press, 1996.

Alexander, Ziggi, *Study of Black, Asian and Ethnic Minority Issues*, Department of Health, 1999.

Alibhai-Brown, Yasmin, *After Multiculturalism*, Foreign Policy Centre, 2000.

Alibhai-Brown, Yasmin, *Who Do We Think We Are?*, Penguin Press, 2000.

Alibhai-Brown, Yasmin, *True Colours: public attitudes to multiculturalism and the role of government*, Institute for Public Policy Research, 1999.

Alimo-Metcalfe, Beverly, *Effective Leadership*, Local Government Management Board, 1998.

AMMA (Assistant Masters and Mistresses Association), *Multi-Cultural and Anti-Racist Education Today*, 1987

Anderson, Benedict, *Imagined Communities*, Verso, revised ed., 1993.

Anthias, Floya and Yuval-Davis, Nira, *Racialised Boundaries*, Routledge, 1992.

Anwar, Muhammad, Roach, Patrick and Sondhi, Ranjit (eds), *From Legislation to Integration? – race relations in Britain (migration, minorities and citizenship)*, Macmillan, 2000.

Anwar, Muhammad, *Ethnic Minorities and the British Electoral System*, Operation Black Vote, 1998.

Anwar, Muhammad, *Race and Elections*, Centre for Research in Ethnic Relations, 1994.

Anwar, Muhammad, *Ethnic Minorities and the 1983 General Election*, Commission for Racial Equality, 1984.

Argent, Katie, Carter, Sylvia and Durr, Patricia, *Facing Reality: evolving responses by London boroughs to racial harassment*, Association of London Government, 2000.

Arnot, Madeleine and Dillabough, Jo-Anne (eds), *Challenging Democracy: feminist perspectives on the education of citizens*, Falmer, 2000.

Asian Business Initiative, *Newsagents Mean Business: the future of Asian-owned cornershops in the new millennium*, 1999.

Association of London Government, *Sick of Being Excluded*, April 2000.

Atri, J. et al., 'Improving uptake of breast screening in multi-ethnic populations: a randomised controlled trial using practice reception staff to contact non-attendees', *British Medical Journal*, November 1997.

Audit Commission, *Another Country: implementing dispersal under the Immigration and Asylum Act 1999*, June 2000.

Audit Unit, *A Route to Equality and Fairness: self-evaluation using performance indicators*, The Scottish Office Education and Industry Department, 1999.

B

Bains, Jas and Johal, Sanjiv, *Corner Flags and Corner Shops: the Asian football experience*, Phoenix Press, 1999.

Balarajan, R. and Raleigh, Soni V., *Ethnicity and Health in England*, Stationery Office, 1995.

Ballard, Roger, 'Negotiating Race and Ethnicity: exploring the implications of the 1991 census', *Patterns of Prejudice*, Vol. 30, No. 3, 1996.

Bank of England, *The Financing of Ethnic Minority Firms in the United Kingdom*, 1999.

Banton, Michael, 'Judicial Training in Ethnic Minority Issues in England and Wales', *Journal of Ethnic and Migration Studies*, Vol. 24, No. 3, 1998.

Banton, Michael, 'The Ethics of Practice-Testing', *New Community*, Vol. 23, No. 3, 1997.

Banton, Michael, *The Idea of Race*, Tavistock Publications, 1977.

Barclay, Gordon and Mhlanga, Bonny, *Ethnic Differences in Decisions on Young Defendants Dealt with by the Crown Prosecution Service*, Section 95, Findings No. 1, Stationery Office, 1999.

Barker, Martin, *The New Racism*, Junction Books, 1981.

Barn, Ravinder, et al., *Acting on Principle*, British Association of Adoption and Fostering, 1997.

Barnes, John, *Federal Britain: no longer unthinkable?*, Centre for Policy Studies, 1998.

Baumann, Gerd, *Contesting Culture: discourses of identity in multi-ethnic London*, Cambridge University Press, 1998.

Beckford, James and Gilliat, Sophie, *Religion in Prison: 'equal rites' in a multi-faith society*, Cambridge University Press, 1998.

Beckford, James and Gilliat, Sophie, *The Church of England and Other Faiths in a Multi-Faith Society*, University of Warwick, 1996.

Beiner, R. (ed.), *Theorising Citizenship*, State University of New York, US, 1995.

Beishon, Sharon, Modood, Tariq and Virdee, Satnam, *Ethnic Minority Families*, Joseph Rowntree Foundation, 1998.

Benn, Caroline and Chitty, Clive, *Thirty Years On*, David Fulton, 1996.

Berthoud, Richard, *Young Caribbean Men and the Labour Market: a comparison with other ethnic groups*, Work and Opportunity Series No. 16, Joseph Rowntree Foundation, 1999.

Berthoud, Richard, *Incomes of Ethnic Minorities*, Institute for Social and Economic Research, 1998.

Berthoud, Richard, *Social Security and Race: an agenda*, Policy Studies Institute, 1997.

Bhabha, Homi, *The Location of Culture*, Routledge, 1997.

Bhabha, Homi, 'Minority Manoeuvres and Unsettled Negotiations', *Critical Inquiry*, 23, spring 1997.

Bhabha, Homi (ed.), *Narrating the Nation*, Routledge, 1990.

Bhugra, Dinesh (ed.), *Ethnicity: an Agenda for Mental Health*, Gaskell (Royal College of Psychiatrists), 1999.

Blackstone, Tessa, Parekh, Bhikhu and Sanders, Peter (eds), *Race Relations in Britain: a developing agenda*, Routledge, 1998.

Blair, Maud and Bourne, Jill et al., *Making the Difference: teaching and learning strategies in successful multi-ethnic schools*, Department for

Education and Employment, 1998.

Blair, Tony, *New Britain: my vision for a young country*, Fourth Estate, 1996.

Bonnett, Alastair, *Antiracism*, Routledge, 1999.

Bowes, Alison, *'Too White, Too Rough and Too Many Problems': a study of Pakistani housing in Britain*, University of Stirling, 1998.

Bowes, Alison, Dar, Naira and Sim, Duncan, *Pakistani Housing Strategies in Britain*, 1998.

Bowling, Benjamin, *Violent Racism: victimisation, policing and social context*, Clarendon Press, 1998.

Bradford Commission, *The Bradford Commission Report*, Stationery Office, 1996.

Bragg, Billy, 'Time to Move On, Boys', *Guardian*, 24 June 2000.

Brah, Avtar, *Cartographies of Diaspora: contesting identities*, Routledge, 1996.

Brannen, J. and Bernstein, B. (eds), *Children, Research and Policy*, Taylor and Francis, 1996.

Brierley, Peter (ed.), 'Religious Trends 2000/2001 No. 2', *UK Christian Handbook*, 1999.

British Medical Association Career Progress of Doctors Committee, *Recruitment and Selection of Doctors*, BMA, 2000.

Brownhill, Sue and Darke, Jane, *'Rich Mix': inclusive strategies for urban regeneration*, Polity Press, 1998.

Bryson, Bill, *Notes from a Small Island*, Black Swan, 1996.

Buchanan, Colin, *Cut the Connection: disestablishment and the Church of England*, Darton, Longman and Todd, 1994.

Bucke, T., 'Ethnicity and Contacts with the Police: latest findings from the British Crime Survey', *Research Findings* No. 59, Home Office, 1997.

Butt, Sajid, *Closing the Gap between Black and White: an assessment of TEC equal opportunities strategies*, Black Training and Enterprise Group, 1998.

C

Cabinet Office, *Minority Ethnic Issues in Social Exclusion and Neighbourhood Renewal*, Social Exclusion Unit, 2000.

Cabinet Office, *Modernising Local Government, in Touch with the People*, 1999.

Cabinet Office, *Modernising Government*, March 1999.

Cabinet Office, *The Government's Equality Statement*, November 1999.

Cabinet Office, *Public Services for the Future: modernisation, reform, accountability* (Cmd 4181), December 1999.

Cabinet Office, *Review of the Social Exclusion Unit*, December 1999.

Cabinet Office, *Policy Appraisal for Equal Treatment*, November 1998.

Cabinet Papers, *Report of the Working Party on Coloured People Seeking Employment in the United Kingdom*, CAB 124/1191, 5364–53, December 1953.

Carmichael, Stokely and Hamilton, Charles, *Black Power: the politics of liberation in America*, Penguin, 1967.

Centre for Education for Racial Equality in Scotland, *Bilingualism, Community Languages and Scottish Education: a challenge for policy makers and practitioners in a devolved Scotland*, University of Edinburgh, 1999.

Cesarani, David, 'Antisemitism in the 1990s: a symposium', *Patterns of Prejudice*, Vol. 25, No. 2, winter 1991.

Chahal, Kusminder, *Ethnic Diversity, Neighbourhoods and Housing*, Joseph Rowntree Foundation, February 2000.

Chahal, Kusminder and Julienne, Louis, *'We Can't All Be White!' – racist victimisation in the UK*, York Publishing Services and Joseph Rowntree Foundation, 1999.

Choudhury, Tufyal, *Discrimination on Grounds of Religious Belief*, Centre for Public Law, University of Cambridge, January 2000.

Clarke, Julian and Speeden, Stuart, *Raising the Standard: institutional racism and citizenship*, Centre for Local Policy Studies, Edge Hill College.

Cohen, Phil (ed.), *New Ethnicities*, Zed Books, 1999.

Colley, Linda, *Britons: forging the nation, 1707–1837*, Yale University Press, New Haven, 1992.

Commission on Representation of the Interests of the British Jewish Community, *A Community of Communities*, Institute for Jewish Policy Research, 2000.

Commission on the National Health Service, *New Life for Health*, Vintage, 2000.

Commission for Racial Equality, *Auditing for Equality*, 1999.

Commission for Racial Equality, *The Leadership Challenge: progress report 1999*, July 1999.

Commission for Racial Equality, *Compact on Free Speech and Race Relations in a Democratic Society*, 1997.

Commission for Race Equality, '*We Regret to Inform You ...*', 1996.

Commission for Race Equality, *Racial Equality Means Quality*, 1995.

Consiglio Italiano per le Scienze Sociali & Centre for European Migration and Ethnic Studies, *Ethnic Conflict and Migration in Europe*, 1999.

Cooper, Davina, *Governing out of Order: space, law and the politics of belonging*, Rivers Oram Press, 1998.

Corner, J. and Harvey, S. (eds), *Enterprise and Heritage*, Routledge, 1991.

Council of Europe, *Preliminary Conclusions: seminar on religion and the integration of immigrants*, 1999.

Cowling, K. (ed.), *Industrial Policy in Europe*, Routledge, 1999.

Criminal Justice Consultative Council, *Race and the Criminal Justice System*, 1994.

Crowley, Heaven, *Breaking Down the Barriers: a report on the conduct of asylum interviews at ports*, Immigration Law Practitioners Association, 1999.

Curtis, L. Perry, *Apes and Angels: the Irishman in Victorian caricature*, Smithsonian Institute Press, 1997.

D

Dahrendorf, Ralf et al., *Report on Wealth Creation and Social Cohesion in a Free Society*, Commission on Wealth Creation and Social Cohesion, 1995.

Davey, Kevin, *English Imaginaries*, Lawrence and Wishart, 1999.

Davies, Norman, *The Isles: a history*, Macmillan, 1999.

Denman, Sylvia, *Race Discrimination in the Crown Prosecution Service*, April 2000.

Department for Culture, Media and Sport, *Whose Heritage?*, November 1999.

Department for Education and Employment, *Jobs for All*, November 1999.

Department of the Environment, Transport and the Regions, *Local Leadership, Local Choice*, March 1999.

Department of the Environment, Transport and the Regions, *Involving Communities in Urban and Rural Regeneration: a guide for practitioners*, 1997.

Department of Health, *The Race Equality Agenda of the Department of Health*, January 2000.

Department of Health, *Modernising Health and Social Services: Priority Guidance 2000/01-2002/03*, 1999.

Department of Health, *National Service Framework for Mental Health*, September 1999.

Department of Health, *Working Together*, September 1998.

Department of Health, *The New NHS – Modern and Dependable: a national framework for assessing performance*, January 1998.

Department of Health, 'Nursing: have you got what it takes?', *Supporting Diversity*, (undated).

Department of Social Security, *Opportunity for All: tackling poverty and social exclusion*, Stationery Office, 1999.

Devine, Tim (ed.), *Scotland's Shame: bigotry and sectarianism in modern Scotland*, Mainstream Publishing, 2000.

Devine, Tim, *The Scottish Nation 1700–2000*, Penguin Press, 2000.

Dorsett, R., *Ethnic Minorities in the Inner City*, Joseph Rowntree Foundation, 1998.

E

Educational Institute of Scotland, *Anti-Racism and Education: breaking down the barriers*, 1999.

Engel, Matthew, *Wisden Cricketer's Almanack*, John Wisden and Co., 1995.

Esmail, Aneez, Everington, Sam and Doyle, Helen, 'Racial Discrimination in the Allocation of Distinction Awards?', *British Medical Journal*, January 1998.

Esmail, Aneez and Everington, Sam, 'Racial Discrimination against Doctors from Ethnic Minorities', *British Medical Journal*, 306, March 1993.

European Commission, *Racism and Xenophobia in Europe*, 1997.

F

Fitzgerald, Marian, *Searches in London under Section 1 of the Police and Criminal Evidence Act 1984*, Metropolitan Police Service, 1999.

Fitzgerald, Marian, *Ethnic Minorities and the Criminal Justice System*, Home Office, 1993.

Forster, E. M., *A Passage to India*, 1924.

Foster, Roy, *Paddy and Mr Punch*, Penguin Books, 1995.

Frankfurt Peace Research Institute, *Talk to them? No Way!*, 1998.

Friedman, Edie, 'Asylum Madness', *Jewish Chronicle*, 4 June 1999.

Fryer, Peter, *Staying Power: the history of black people in Britain*, Pluto Press, 1984.

G

Gamble, Andrew and Wright, Tony, 'The End of Britain?', *Political Quarterly*, Vol. 71, No. 1, January-March 2000.

Gardner, Howard, *Intelligence Reframed: multiple intelligences for the 21st century*, Basic Books, 1999.

Gardner, Howard, *Frames of Mind*, 1983 and Fontana, 1993.

Geaves, Ron, *Sectarian Influences within Islam in Britain*, University of Leeds, 1996.

Geddes, Andrew, *The Politics of Immigration and Race*, Baseline Books, 1996.

Gewirtz, Sharon, *Markets, Choice and Equity in Education*, Oxford University Press, 1995.

Giddens, Anthony, *Runaway World*, Profile Books, 1999.

Giddens, Anthony, *The Third Way*, Polity Press, 1998.

Gillborn, David, *Racism and Antiracism in Real Schools*, Open University Press, 1995.

Gillborn, David and Gipps, Caroline, *Recent Research on the Achievements of Ethnic Minority Pupils*, Stationery Office, 1996.

Gillborn, David and Youdell, Deborah, *Rationing Education: policy, reform and equity*, Open University Books, 2000.

Gilroy, Paul, *Joined-up Politics and Post-Colonial Melancholia*, Institute for Contemporary Arts, 1999.

Gilroy, Paul, *Small Acts: thoughts on the politics of black cultures*, Serpent's Tail, 1993.

Gilroy, Paul, *There Ain't No Black in the Union Jack: the cultural politics of race and nation*, Hutchinson, 1987.

Gould, Philip, *The Unfinished Revolution: how the modernisers saved the Labour Party*, Abacus, 1998.

Graham, John and Bowling, Ben, *Young People and Crime*, Home Office, 1996.

Greenfield, Steve and Osborn, Guy, 'Oh to be in England? – mythology and identity in English cricket', *Social Identities*, Vol. 2, No. 2, June 1996.

Gunningham, Neil, Grabowsky, Peter and Sinclair, Darren (eds), *Smart regulation: designing environmental policy*, Clarendon Press, 1998.

Gutmann, Amy and Taylor, Charles (eds), *Multiculturalism and the Politics of Recognition*, Princeton University Press, US, 1994.

Gutmann, Amy and Thompson, Dennis, *Democracy and Disagreement*, Belknap Press, 1996.

H

Habermas, Jürgen, *The Inclusion of the Other*, MIT Press, United States, 1998.

Hall, Catherine, *White, Male and Middle Class: explorations in British identity*, Polity Press, 1992.

Hall, Stuart, 'From Scarman to Stephen Lawrence', *History Workshop Journal*, No. 48, autumn 1999.

Hall, Stuart, 'Attitude and Aspiration: reflections on Black Britain in the nineties', *New Formations*, No. 33, spring 1998.

Hall, Stuart, Held, David and McGrew, Tony (eds), *Modernity and Its Futures*, Polity Press and the Open University, 1992.

Halliday, Fred, *Islam and the Myth of Confrontation*, I. B. Tauris, 1996.

Hamm, Tricia, *Racial Harassment: just a part of life?*, Sheffield Hallam University, 1997.

Haque, Zubaida, 'The Ethnic Minority "Underachieving" Group? – investigating the claims of "underachievement" among Bangladeshi pupils in British secondary schools', *Race, Ethnicity and Education*, Vol. 3, No. 2, June 2000.

Harding, Jeremy, *The Uninvited*, Profile Books, 2000.

Harding, S. and Balarajan, R., 'Patterns of Mortality in Second Generation Irish Living in England and Wales: longitudinal study', *British Medical Journal*, No. 312, June 1996.

Harper, Peter et al., *Islington Street Crime Survey*, Islington Council, 1995.

Harris, Nigel, *The New Untouchables: Immigration and the New World Worker*, I. B. Tauris, 1995.

Haskey, John, 'Mortality among Second Generation Irish in England and Wales', *British Medical Journal*, No. 312, June 1996.

Heffer, Simon, *Nor Shall My Sword: the reinvention of England*, Weidenfeld and Nicolson, 1999.

Held, David, McGrew, Tony, Goldblatt, David and Perraton, Jonathan, *Global Transformations*, Polity Press, 1999.

Henderson, Paul and Kaur, Ranjit, *Rural Racism in the UK*, Community Development Foundation, 1999.

Henderson, Robert, 'Is it in the Blood?' *Wisden Cricket Monthly*, July 1995.

Hepple, Bob, Coussey, Mary and Choudhury, Tufyal, *Equality: a new framework*, Hart, 2000.

Her Majesty's Inspectorate of Constabulary, *Policing London – winning consent*, Home Office, 2000.

Her Majesty's Inspectorate of Constabulary, *Winning the Race: Policing Plural Communities – a follow-up to the thematic inspection on police and community relations 1998/9*, 1999.

Her Majesty's Inspectorate of Constabulary, *Winning the Race: Policing Plural Communities – report on police community and race relations 1996/7*, 1997.

Her Majesty's Inspectorate of Constabulary, *Developing Diversity in the Police Service: equal opportunities thematic inspection report 1995*, Home Office, 1996.

HM Treasury, *Report of Policy Action Team 3: Enterprise and Social Exclusion*, 1999.

Hewitt, Roger, *Routes of Racism: the social basis of racist action*, Trentham Books, 1996.

Hickman, Mary, 'Binary Opposites or Unique Neighbours? – the Irish in multi-ethnic Britain', *Political Quarterly*, Vol. 71, No. 1, January-March 2000.

Hickman, Mary, *Religion, Class and Identity*, Ashgate, 1995.

Hickman, Mary and Walter, Bronwen, *Discrimination and the Irish Community in Britain*, Commission for Racial Equality, 1997.

Hillyard, Paddy, *Suspect Community: people's experience of the Prevention of Terrorism Acts in Britain*, Pluto Press, 1993.

Hobsbawm, Eric and Ranger, Terence (eds), *The Invention of Tradition*, Cambridge University Press, 1993.

Holdaway, Simon, 'Constructing and Sustaining "Race" within the Police Force', *British Journal of Sociology*, Vol. 48, No. 1, 1997.

Home Office, *Race Equality in Public Services: driving up standards and accounting for progress*, March 2000.

Home Office, *Stephen Lawrence Inquiry: Home Secretary's action plan, first annual report on progress*, February 2000.

Home Office, *Correctional Policy Framework*, 2000.

Home Office, *Report of Police Action Team 6: Neighbourhood Wardens*, 2000.

Home Office, *Strengthening the Black and Minority Ethnic Voluntary Sector Infrastructure*, autumn 1999.

Home Office, *UK Government's 15th periodic report to the UN Committee on the Elimination of all forms of Racial Discrimination (CERD)*, summer 1999.

Home Office, *Prison Statistics England and Wales 1998*, 1999.

Home Office, *Statistics on Race and the Criminal Justice System: Home Office publications Under Section 95 of the Criminal Justice Act 1991*, 1999.

Home Office, *Stephen Lawrence Inquiry: Home Secretary's action plan*, 1999.

Home Office, *Deaths in Police Custody: statistics for England and Wales, April 1997 to March 1998*, 1998.

Home Office, *The Prison Population in 1996*, Statistical Bulletin 18/97, 1997.

Home Office, *UK Government's 12th periodic report to the UN Committee on the Elimination of all forms of Racial Discrimination (CERD)*, 1991.

Home Secretary, 'Building a Human Rights Culture', address to the Civil Service College Seminar, 9 December 1999.

Hood, Roger, *Race and Sentencing: a study in the Crown Court*, Clarendon Press, 1992.

Horton, J. and Mendes, S. (eds), *Toleration, Identity and Difference*, Macmillan, 1999.

Howarth, Catherine, Kenway, Peter, Palmer, Guy and Miorelli, Romina, *Monitoring Poverty and Social Exclusion*, New Policy Institute, December 1999.

Hudson, Barbara, *Penal Policy and Social Justice*, Macmillan, 1993.

Hunt, Judith and Palmer, Sarah, *The Stephen Lawrence Inquiry and the Home Secretary's Action Plan: initial guidance for local authorities, June 1999* and *Further guidance for local authorities, November 1999*, Local Authorities Race Relations Exchange and Information (LARRIE), 1999.

Hutchinson, Marcia, *The Journey*, Primary Colours, 1999.
Hutnick, Nimmi, *Ethnic Minority Identity*, Clarendon Press, 1996.
Hutton, Will, *The State We're In*, Vintage, 1996.

I

Iganski, P. and Payne, G., 'Socio-Economic Restructuring and Employment: the case of minority ethnic groups', *British Journal of Sociology*, Vol. 50, No. 2, 1999.
Ignatieff, Michael, *Blood and Belonging: journeys into the new nationalism*, BBC Books and Chatto and Windus, 1993.
Information on Ireland, *The Same Old Story: the roots of anti-Irish racism*, 1984.
Institute of Employment Studies, *The Organisational and Managerial Implications of Devolved Personnel Assessment Processes*, Greater London Employers Association, 2000.

J

Johnson, Mark, *Involvement of Black and Ethnic Minority Consumers in Health Research*, Mary Seacole Research Centre, De Montfort University, September 1998.
Judicial Studies Board, *Equal Treatment Bench Book: race and the courts*, 1999.

K

Karn, Valerie (ed.), *Education, Employment and Housing among Ethnic Minorities in Britain*, Stationery Office, 1997.
Kelly, Chris, *An Investigation into Conditional Organ Donation*, Department of Health, February 2000.
Kelly, Elinor, 'Stands Scotland Where It Did? – an essay in ethnicity and internationalism', *Scottish Affairs*, 1998 and 'Racism, Police and the Courts in Scotland', *Scottish Affairs*, 30, Winter 2000.
King, Anna and Reiss, Michael (eds), *The Multicultural Dimension of the National Curriculum*, Falmer, 1993.

King's Fund, *The Health of Refugees – a guide for GPs*, 1999.

Kolb, David, *Experiential Learning: experience the source of learning development*, Prentice Hall, US, 1983.

KPMG, *The Feasibility of an Independent System for Investigating Complaints against the Police*, Home Office, May 2000.

Kular, Randeep, 'Black Deaths in Police Custody', *The Runnymede Bulletin*, Nos 319 and 320, September and December 1999.

Kundnani, Arun, 'Stumbling on: race, class and England', *Race and Class*, Vol. 41, No. 4, April-June 2000.

Kushner, Tony, 'The fascist as "other": racism and neo-Nazism in contemporary Britain', *Patterns of Prejudice*, Vol. 28, No. 1, January 1994.

Kymlicka, Will, *Multicultural Citizenship: A Liberal Theory of Minority Rights*, Clarendon Press, 1995.

L

Lansley, Andrew, 'Accentuate the Negative to Win Again', *Observer*, 3 September 1995.

Lee, Simon, *The Frontiers of English Nationalism*, paper at the Nationalism, Identity and Minority Rights Conference, University of Bristol, September 1999.

Leicestershire Constabulary, *Community and Race Relations Strategy*, 1998.

Leigh, A., Johnson, G., and Ingram, A., *Deaths in Police Custody: learning the lessons*, Police Research Series Paper 26, Home Office, 1998.

Lemos, Gerard, *A New Spirit of Community*, Lemos and Crane, 1998.

Lemos, Gerard, *Urban Village, Global City*, Lemos and Crane, 1998.

Lemos, Gerard and Young, Michael, *The Communities We Have Lost and Can Regain*, Lemos and Crane, 1997.

Leonard, Mark, *Britain TM: renewing our identity*, Demos and the Design Council, 1997.

Lerman, Antony (ed.), *Antisemitism World Report 1998*, Institute for Jewish Policy Research and American Jewish Committee, London and New York, 1998.

Lewis, Christopher, 'Religion and Spiritual Care', *Theology*, October 1999.

Lewis, Gail (ed.), *Race, Gender and Nation*, Polity Press, 2000.

Lewis, Philip, *Islamic Britain*, I. B. Tauris, 1997.

Liberal Democrats, *Political Speech and Race Relations in a Liberal Democracy*, 1993.

Local Government Management Board, *Flexible Working: working patterns in local authorities and the wider economy*, 1997.

London TEC Council, *Strength through Diversity: ethnic minorities in London's economy*, 1999.

M

McCrudden, Christopher, 'Mainstreaming Equality in the Governance of Northern Ireland', *Fordham International Law Journal*, Vol. 22, No. 4, 1999.

Mckinstry, Leo, 'Rise of the New McCarthyism', *Daily Mail*, 18 March 2000.

McLaren, Peter and Leonard, Peter (eds), *Paulo Freire: a critical encounter*, Routledge, 1993

McManus, I. C., Esmail, A. and Demetriou, M., 'Factors Affecting Likelihood of Applicants Being Offered a Place in Medical Schools in the United Kingdom in 1996 and 1997: a retrospective study', *British Medical Journal*, 1998.

Mackie, Liz, *New Challenges: regeneration and black communities*, Black Training and Enterprise Group, 1998.

Macpherson, William, *The Stephen Lawrence Inquiry: report of an inquiry by Sir William Macpherson of Cluny*, Stationery Office, 1999.

Madanipoor, Ali et al. (eds), *Social Exclusion in European Cities: processes, experiences and responses*, Regional Studies Association, 1998.

Maguire, M., Morgan, R. and Reiner, R. (eds), *The Oxford Handbook of Criminology*, Clarendon Press, 1994.

Malik, Maleiha, '"Racist crime": racially aggravated offences in the Crime and Disorder Act 1998', *Modern Law Review*, Vol. 62, No. 3, May 1999.

Marland, Michael, 'Refugee Pupils; A Headteacher's Perspective', *Multicultural Teaching*, Vol. 17, No. 1, autumn 1998.

Marr, Andrew, *The Day Britain Died*, Profile Books, 2000.

Mauer, Mark, *Young Black Americans and the Criminal Justice System: a growing national problem*, Sentencing Project, Washington, DC, 1995.

Mercer, Kobena, *Welcome to the Jungle*, Routledge, 1994.

Merkel, Udo and Tokarski, Walter (eds), *Racism and Xenophobia in European Football*, Meyer & Meyer Verlag, 1996.

Metcalf, H., Modood, Tariq and Virdee, Satnam, *Asian Self-Employment: the interaction of culture and economics in England*, Policy Studies Institute, 1996.

Miles, Robert, *Racism after 'Race Relations'*, Routledge, 1993.

Miles, Robert, *Racism*, Routledge, 1989.

Miller, Jerome G., *Search and Destroy: African-American males in the criminal justice system*, Cambridge University Press, 1997.

Mirza, Heidi, *Black British Feminism: a reader*, Routledge, 1997.

Modood, Tariq, 'Anti-essentialism, Multiculturalism and the Recognition of Religious Groups', *The Journal of Political Philosophy*, Vol. 6, No. 4, December 1998.

Modood, Tariq, *Church, State and Religious Minorities*, Policy Studies Institute, 1997.

Modood, Tariq, *Racial Equality: colour, culture and justice*, Institute for Public Policy Research, 1994.

Modood, Tariq, *Not Easy Being British: colour, culture and citizenship*, Runnymede Trust and Trentham Books, 1992.

Modood, Tariq and Acland, T. (eds), *Race and Higher Education: opportunities, experiences and challenges*, Policy Studies Institute, 1998.

Modood, Tariq, Beishon, Sharon and Virdee, Satnam, *Changing Ethnic Identities*, Policy Studies Institute, 1994.

Modood, Tariq and Berthoud, Richard et al., *Ethnic Minorities in Britain: diversity and disadvantage*, Policy Studies Institute, 1997.

Modood, Tariq and Werbner, Pnina (eds), *Debating Cultural Hybridity: multicultural identities and the politics of antiracism*, Zed Books, 1997.

Modood, Tariq and Werbner, Pnina (eds), *The Politics of Multiculturalism in the New Europe: racism, identity and community*, Zed Books, 1997.

Mooney, Jayne and Young, Jock, *Social Exclusion and Criminal Justice: ethnic communities and stop and search in North London*, Middlesex University, 1999.

Morley, C. and Chen, K.-H. (eds), *Critical Dialogues in Cultural Studies*, Routledge, 1996.

Morris, Rachel and Clements, Luke (eds), *Gaining Ground: law reform for Gypsies and travellers*, University of Hertfordshire Press, 1999.

Morsink, Johannes, *The Universal Declaration of Human Rights: origins, drafting and intent*, University of Pennsylvania Press, 1999.

Murray, Charles, *The Underclass: the crisis deepens*, Institute for Economic Affairs, 1994.

Murray, Charles, *The Emerging Underclass*, Institute for Economic Affairs, 1990.

Murray, Charles and Herrnstein, Richard, *The Bell Curve*, Simon and Schuster, 1996

N

Naish, J., Brown, J. and Denton, B., 'Intercultural Consultations: investigation of factors that deter non-English speaking women from attending their general practitioners for cervical screening', *British Medical Journal*, No. 309, 1994, pp. 1126–8.

National Association for the Care and Resettlement of Offenders, *Let's Get It Right: race and justice*, 2000.

National Association of Schoolmasters and Women Teachers, *Education and Race*, NAS/UWT, 1999.

National Directory of Action against Racial Harassment, Lemos and Crane, 1996 and published on www.raceactionnet.co.uk in 2000.

National Society for the Protection of Children from Cruelty, *Protecting Children from Racism and Racial Abuse*, 1999.

Nazroo, James, 'Rethinking the Relationship Between Ethnicity and Mental Health', *Social Psychiatry and Psychiatric Epidemiology*, April 1998.

Nazroo, James, *The Health of Britain's Ethnic Minorities*, Policy Studies Institute, 1997.

Norton-Taylor, Richard, *The Colour of Justice*, Oberon Books, 1999.

Norwich and Norfolk Race Equality Council, *Not in Norfolk: a study of racial harassment in local areas*, 1994.

O

Oakley, Robin, 'Institutional Racism and the Police Service', *The Police Journal*, Vol. 72, No. 4, October/December 1999.

Office for Standards in Education, *Raising the Attainment of Minority*

Ethnic Pupils, 1999.

Okri, Ben, *Birds of Heaven*, Phoenix, 1996.

Oliver, Peter, Douglas Scott, Sionaidh, and Tadros, Victor, *Faith and Law*, Hart, 2000.

Osler, Audrey, 'Citizenship, Democracy and Political Literacy', *Multicultural Teaching*, Vol. 18, No. 1, autumn 1999.

Osler, Audrey, *The Education and Careers of Black Teachers: Changing Identities, Changing Lives*, Oxford University Press, 1997.

Osler, Audrey, *Exclusion from School and Racial Equality*, Commission for Race Equality, 1997.

Osler, Audrey and Morrison, Marlene, *Inspecting Schools for Race Equality: OFSTED's Strengths and Weaknesses*, CRE with Trentham Books, 2000.

Owusu, Kwesi (ed.), *Black British Culture and Society: a text reader*, Routledge, 2000.

P

Parekh, Bhikhu, 'Defining British Identity', *Political Quarterly*, Vol. 71, No. 1, January-March 2000.

Parekh, Bhikhu, *Rethinking Multiculturalism*, Macmillan and Harvard University Press, 2000.

Parekh, Bhikhu, *Racial Violence – A Separate Offence?*, All-Party Parliamentary Group on Race and Community, 1994.

Parkinson, Michael, *Combating Social Exclusion: lessons from area-based programmes in Europe*, The Policy Press, 1998.

Paxman, Jeremy, *The English*, Penguin Books, 1999.

Percy, A., *Ethnicity and Victimisation: findings from the 1996 British Crime Survey*, Statistical Bulletin 6/98, Home Office, 1998.

Phillips, Anne, *Which Equalities Matter?*, Polity Press, 1999.

Phillips, Anne, *The Politics of Presence*, Clarendon Press, 1995.

Phillips, Mike and Phillips, Trevor, *Windrush: the irresistible rise of multiracial Britain*, HarperCollins, 1998.

Phoenix, Ann, *(Re)constructing Gendered and Ethnicized Identities: are we all marginal now?*, University for Humanist Studies, 1998.

Platt, Lucinda and Noble, Michael, *Race, Place and Poverty: ethnic groups and low income distributions*, York Publishing Services/Joseph Rowntree Foundation, 1999.

Police Complaints Authority, *Deaths in Custody: the risks reduced*, Home Office, summer 2000.

Police Complaints Authority, *Annual Report for 1998/99*, 1999.

Pollak, Andy (ed.), *A Citizens' Inquiry: the Upsahl Report on Northern Ireland*, Lilliput Press, 1993.

Poulter, Sebastian, *Ethnicity, Law and Human Rights*, Clarendon Press, 1998.

Pratt, Mary Louise, *Imperial Eyes*, Routledge, 1992.

R

Ram, Mander and Jones, Trevor, *Ethnic Minorities in Business*, Open University Business School, 1998.

Rampton, Anthony, *West Indian Children in Our Schools*, Stationery Office, 1981.

Rattansi, Ali, 'On Being and Not Being Black/Brown British', *Interventions: The International Journal of Postcolonial Studies*, Vol. 2, No. 1, 2000.

Rattansi, Ali and Westwood, S. (eds), *Racism, Modernity and Identity: on the western front*, Polity Press, 1994.

Redding, Jeanette (ed.), *The Refugee Education Handbook*, London Borough of Enfield, 1999.

Redwood, John, *The Death of Britain? The UK's constitutional crisis*, Macmillan, 1999.

Refugee Council, *Response to 'Fairer, Faster and Firmer – A Modern Approach to Immigration and Asylum'*, Refugee Council, October 1998.

Richardson, Robin and Wood, Angela, *Inclusive Schools, Inclusive Society*, Trentham Books, 1999.

Rifkind, Malcolm, 'British Champion', *Prospect*, January 2000.

Robbins, Kevin, *Great Britain: identities, institutions and ideas of Britishness*, Longman, 1997

Roberts, Celia et al., 'Oral Examinations – equal opportunities, ethnicity and fairness in the MRCGP', *British Medical Journal*, February 2000.

Rose, E. J. B. and Deakin, Nicholas et al., *Colour and Citizenship*, Oxford University Press, 1969.

Royal College of Paediatricians and Child Health, *The Health of Refugee Children – Guidelines for Paediatricians*, November 1999.

Royal Commission on the Reform of the House of Lords, *A House for the Future*, Stationery Office, January 2000.

Rudat, K., *Health and Lifestyle: black and minority ethnic groups in England*, London Health Education Authority, 1994.

Runnymede Trust, *Islamophobia: a challenge for us all*, 1997.

Runnymede Trust, *This Is Where I Live: problems and pressures in Brixton*, 1996.

Runnymede Trust, *A Very Light Sleeper: the persistence and dangers of antisemitism*, 1994.

Runnymede Trust, *Equality Assurance in Schools: quality, identity, society*, 1993.

S

Sacks, Jonathan, *The Persistence of Faith*, Weidenfeld and Nicholson, 1991.

Saggar, Shamit (ed.), *Race and British Electoral Politics*, UCL Press, 1998.

Said, Edward, *Culture and Imperialism*, Chatto and Windus, 1993.

Scarman, L., *The Scarman Report: the Brixton disorders*, Stationery Office, 1981.

Scottish Executive, *Milan Committee Review of the Mental Health Act (Scotland)*, Second Consultation, May 2000.

Scottish Executive, *Towards an Equality Strategy*, February 2000.

Sewell, Tony, *Black Masculinities and Schooling: how black boys survive modern schooling*, Trentham Books, 1997.

Sharma, Sanjay, Hutnyk, John and Sharma, Ashwani, *Disorienting Rhythms: the politics of new Asian dance music*, Zed Press, 1996.

Sibbitt, Rae, *The Perpetrators of Racial Harassment and Racial Violence*, Research Study 176, Home Office, 1997.

Sibbitt, Rae and Fitzgerald, Marian, *The Police Recording of Racist Incidents*, Home Office, 1999.

Sivanandan, A., *Communities of Resistance*, Verso, 1990.

Sivanandan, A., 'Racism Awareness Training and the Degradation of Black Struggle', *Race and Class*, Vol. XXVI, No. 4, spring 1985.

Social Exclusion Unit, *Bringing Britain Together: a national strategy for neighbourhood renewal*, September 1999.

Sohpal, Rajinder, 'Community-Based Trainers and Race Related Training', *The Police Journal*, Vol. 72, No. 4, October/December 1999.

Solomos, John and Back, Les, *Race, Politics and Social Change*, Routledge, 1995.

SOPEMI, *Trends in International Migration*, OECD, Paris, 1998.

Sparks, Richard, Bottoms, Anthony and Hay, Will, *Prisons and the Problem of Order*, Clarendon Press, 1996.

Spencer, Sarah, 'Making Race Equality Count', *New Economy*, Vol. 7, No. 1, March 2000.

Spencer, Sarah and Bynoe, Ian, *Mainstreaming Human Rights in Whitehall and Westminster*, 1999.

Spencer, Sarah and Bynoe, Ian, *A Human Rights Commission: the options for Britain and Northern Ireland*, IPPR, 1998.

Sreberny, Annabelle, *Include Me In*, Broadcasting Standards Commission and the Independent Television Commission, December 1999.

Standing Committee on Equality of Opportunity, *Equality Audit: equal opportunity baseline survey*, National Assembly for Wales, April 2000.

Swann, Lord, *Education for All*, Stationery Office, 1985.

T

Taylor, P., Powell, D. and Wrench, John, *The Evaluation of Anti-Discrimination Training Activities in the United Kingdom*, International Labour Office, Geneva, 1997.

Tomlinson, Sally, 'New Inequalities? – educational markets and ethnic minorities', *Race Ethnicity and Education*, Vol. 1, No. 2, 1998.

Tomlinson, Sally, 'Sociological Perspectives on Failing Schools', *International Studies in Sociology of Education*, 1997.

Toynbee, Polly, 'We Can Be English without Falling into the Racist Trap', *Guardian*, 12 January 2000.

Troen, Ilan (ed.), *Jewish Centers and Peripheries: Europe between America and Israel Fifty Years after World War II*, Transaction, 1998.

Troyna, Barry and Hatcher, Richard, *Racism in Children's Lives: a study of 10 and 11 year olds in mainly white primary schools*, Routledge, 1992.

Turner, Royce, 'Gypsies and Politics in Britain', *The Political Quarterly*, Vol. 71, No. 1, 2000.

U

University of Derby, *Religious Discrimination in England and Wales: interim report*, Home Office, January 2000.

V

Van Dijk, Teun A., *Elite Discourse and Racism*, Sage Publications, 1993.
Van Dijk, Teun A., *Racism and the Press*, Routledge, 1991.

W

Wallace, W., *International Human Rights Texts and Material*, Sweet and Maxwell, 1997.
Wallerstein, Immanuel, 'The Albatross of Racism', *London Review of Books*, Vol. 22, No. 10, 18 May 2000.
Ware, Vron, *Beyond the Pale*, Verso, 1991.
Warner, Marina, *Managing Monsters*, Vintage, 1995.
White, Philip, *The Prison Population in 1998, a statistical review*, Research Findings No. 94, Home Office, 1999.
Wieviorka, Michel, *The Arena Of Racism*, Sage, 1995.
Wilkinson, Richard, *Unhealthy Societies: The Afflictions of Inequality*, Routledge, 1997.
Williams, Eric, *Capitalism and Slavery*, André Deutsch, 1944, 1964.
Williams, R., 'Regional Mortality and the Irish in Britain: findings from the ONS longitudinal study', *Sociology of Health and Illness*, 1999, pp. 21–3.
Wilson, Richard, *Report to the Prime Minister on Civil Service Reform*, Cabinet Office, December 1999.
Wimmer, Andreas, 'Explaining Xenophobia and Racism: a critical review of current research approaches', *Ethnic and Racial Studies*, January 1997.
Windlesham, Lord, *Politics, Punishment and Populism*, Oxford University Press, 1998.
Windlesham, Lord, *Responses to Crime Volume 3: legislating with the tide*, Clarendon Press, 1996.
Woolley, Simon, 'Ignore Us at Your Peril', *Guardian*, 19 August 1999.

Worsthorne, Peregrine, 'I Believe in Islamophobia', *Daily Telegraph*, 1 March 1997.

Wrench, John, *Preventing Racism at the Workplace: a report on 16 European countries*, Office for Official Publications of the European Communities, 1998.

Wrench, John and Modood, Tariq, *The Effectiveness of Integration Policies towards Immigrants and Ethnic Minorities in the UK*, International Labour Office, 2000.

Wrench, John, Hassan, Edgar and Owen, David, *Ambition and Marginalisation*, Stationery Office, 1996.

Wrench, John, Qureshi, Tarek and Owen, David, *Higher Horizons*, Stationery Office, 1996.

Y

Young, Gary, 'A Shadow Without a Doubt', *Connections*, Commission for Racial Equality, May 2000.

Young, Hugo, 'Little More than an Extension of France', *London Review of Books*, 6 January 2000.

Young, Iris Marion, *Justice and the Politics of Difference*, Princeton University Press, 1990

Yuval-Davis, Nira, *Gender and Nation*, Sage, 1997.

Index